BENJAMIN FRANKLIN IN LONDON

Also by George Goodwin

Fatal Colours: Towton, 1461 – England's Most Brutal Battle
Fatal Rivalry: Flodden, 1513 – Henry VIII, James IV and the Battle
for Renaissance Britain

BENJAMIN FRANKLIN
IN LONDON

THE BRITISH LIFE OF AMERICA'S
FOUNDING FATHER

George Goodwin

Weidenfeld & Nicolson

LONDON

First published in Great Britain in 2016
by Weidenfeld & Nicolson

1 3 5 7 9 10 8 6 4 2

Text © George Goodwin 2016

A CIP catalogue record for this book
is available from the British Library.

HB ISBN 978 0 297 87153 8

Typeset at The Spartan Press Ltd,
Lymington, Hants

Printed and bound by CPI Group (UK) Ltd,
Croydon, CRO 4YY

Weidenfeld & Nicolson

The Orion Publishing Group Ltd
Carmelite House, 50 Victoria Embankment
London EC4Y 0DZ
An Hachette UK Company

The Orion Publishing Group's policy is to use papers
that are natural, renewable and recyclable products and made
from wood grown in sustainable forests. The logging and
manufacturing processes are expected to conform to the
environmental regulations of the country of origin.

For Cecily, Arthur and Frances

CONTENTS

LIST OF ILLUSTRATIONS

Section One

William Strahan. Oil painting by Sir Joshua Reynolds, 1780. © National Portrait Gallery, London.

Sir John Pringle. Oil painting by Sir Joshua Reynolds, 1774. © The Royal Society, London.

David Hume. Oil painting by Allan Ramsay, 1766. Scottish National Portrait Gallery, Edinburgh/Bridgeman Images.

John Stuart, 3rd Earl of Bute. Oil painting by Sir Joshua Reynolds, 1773. © National Portrait Gallery, London.

William Franklin. Portrait medallion, jasperware, 1787. The Wedgwood Museum, Stoke-on-Trent. Photo © Wedgwood Museum/WWRD.

George Grenville. Oil painting by William Hoare, 1764. By permission of of the Governing Body of Christ Church, University of Oxford.

William Pitt, 1st Earl of Chatham. Oil painting (detail) by Richard Brompton, 1772. Philadelphia Museum of Art, PA, Gift of Caroline Scott Koblenzer, MD, in memory of her father, James Robertson Adamson, FRIBA, 1997/Bridgeman Images.

Charles Watson-Wentworth, 2nd Marquess of Rockingham. Oil painting after Sir Joshua Reynolds, c.1768. © National Portrait Gallery, London.

Charles Townshend. Oil painting by Sir Joshua Reynolds and studio, c.1765. Baddesley Clinton, Warwickshire/© The National Trust.

Francis Dashwood, 11th Baron Le Despencer. Oil painting by Nathaniel Dance, c.1776. © National Portrait Gallery, London.

The Gout. Hand-coloured soft-ground etching by James Gillray, 1799. © Courtesy of the Warden and Scholars of New College, University of Oxford/Bridgeman Images.

Section Two

Benjamin Franklin. Oil painting by David Martin, 1767. Robert Knudsen, White House Photographs, John F. Kennedy Presidential Library and Museum, Boston, MA.

Augustus Henry Fitzroy, 3rd Duke of Grafton. Oil painting by Pompeo Batoni, 1762. © National Portrait Gallery, London.

Frederick, Lord North. Oil painting by Nathaniel Dance, 1773–4. © National Portrait Gallery, London.

George III. Oil painting by Johann Zoffany, 1771. Royal Collection Trust © Her Majesty Queen Elizabeth II, 2016/Bridgeman Images.

John Canton. Oil painting by an unknown artist. 1740s. © National Portrait Gallery, London.

Dr Richard Price. Oil painting by Benjamin West, 1784. National Library of Wales/photo © Christies Images/Bridgeman Images.

Joseph Priestley. Pastel by Ellen Sharples, probably after James Sharples, c.1797. © National Portrait Gallery, London.

The Death of the Earl of Chatham. Oil painting by John Singleton Copley, 1779–81.Tate Gallery, London, on loan to the National Portrait Gallery, London.

Key to the Death of the Earl of Chatham. Engraving by Francesco Bartolozzi, after John Singleton Copley, late-18th century. Harvard Art Museums/Fogg Museum, Gray Collection of Engravings Fund, G4271. © President and Fellows of Harvard College, Cambridge, MA.

John Montagu, 4th Earl of Sandwich. Oil painting after Johann Zoffany, c.1764. © National Portrait Gallery, London.

Josiah Quincy, Jr. Posthumous oil painting by Gilbert Stuart, c.1825. Museum of Fine Arts, Boston, Mr Edmund Quincy, L-R 37.1981. Photo © 2016 Museum of Fine Arts, Boston, MA.

John Dunning, 1st Baron Ashburton; Isaac Barré; William Petty, 1st Marquess of Lansdowne (formerly 2nd Earl of Shelburne). Mezzo-tint by James Ward, after Sir Joshua Reynolds, 1807. © National Portrait Gallery, London.

Benjamin Franklin. Oil painting attributed to Jean Valade, after an original by Joseph-Silfrede Duplessis, c.1786. © Thomas Jefferson Foundation at Monticello, Charlottesville, VA.

Benjamin Franklin. Line engraving by Augustin de Saint-Aubin, after Charles Nicolas Cochin, 1777. © National Portrait Gallery, London.

Caleb Whitefoord. Oil painting by Gilbert Stuart, 1782. Montclair
  Art Museum, NJ. Museum Purchase; Clayton E. Freeman Fund.
David Hartley. Oil painting by George Romney, 1783–4. Art Proper-
  ties, Avery Architectural and Fine Arts Library, Columbia Uni-
  versity in the City of New York, Gift of the Estate of Geraldine
  R. Dodge.

NOTE ON SPELLING AND PUNCTUATION

It was common for eighteenth-century writers to capitalize their nouns, use italics for emphasis and to replace the final 'e' with an inverted comma in words such as 'replac'd'. For ease of twenty-first-century reading, the author has modernized spelling and punctuation when he has quoted Benjamin Franklin. For the same reason he has, in a very limited number of exceptional cases, slightly adapted quotations where the eighteenth-century usage serves to obscure rather than elucidate meaning for the modern eye.* He has attempted to give full references in every case, so that readers may find the original should they wish to do so, in particular should they themselves wish to consider quotation.

However, one has to bear in mind what Benjamin Franklin said in a letter to his son William dated 6 October 1773 about the reproduction of his satirical piece 'An Edict by the King of Prussia': 'It is reprinted in the Chronicle, where you will see it, but stripped of all the capitalling and italicking, that intimate the allusions and mark the emphasis of written discourses, to bring them as near as possible to those spoken: printing such a piece all in one even small character, seems to me like repeating one of Whit{e}field's Sermons in the monotony of a school-boy.'[1] Therefore, in deference to him, Dr Franklin's own capitalization and italics for emphasis have been retained.

---

* Where the editors of the *Papers of Benjamin Franklin* have inserted words in quotations, they are surrounded by square brackets [ ]. Where the author has done so, he has used braces { }.

Prologue

On 1 February 1775 Benjamin Franklin travelled the short distance from his London home to the House of Lords, there to hear a pivotally important debate in an impassioned Parliamentary session. His friend Lord Stanhope had brought his own carriage to Franklin's comfortable lodgings in Craven Street, just off the Strand, and the journey, in spite of the huge crowds, was accomplished with time to spare. The sixty-nine-year-old Franklin was thus able to secure a prime position, resting against the railing known as the Bar of the House, the barrier that separated the Lords from their guests.

Like all its major forerunners since the beginning of the session, the debate would address events in America. The tone had been set by the King's Speech at the Opening of Parliament three months before, which, echoing government sentiment, had decried 'the spirit of resistance and disobedience to the law' and 'the fresh violences of a very criminal nature' in Boston and the Massachusetts Bay colony.[1] The point at issue on 1 February, as in the previous months, was straightforward: should Parliament support the British administration's policy of continued coercion, or – with attitudes hardening in the American colonies – should they attempt a reconciliation?

The Lords' public area had only sufficient space for a mere fifty people.[2] Thousands more would have joined them had they been able, but instead they had to be content with the impressively full Parliamentary reports. The interest was huge, because the question of America was the dominant subject of current conversation. As Horace Walpole wrote to a friend: 'You must prepare, madam, to talk America; there is no other topic to be heard, and in truth it grows a very strange one. You must lay aside your botany from the hyssop to the cedar of Libanus, and study imports and exports, and charters and geography, and religion and government, and {other} such light reading.'[3]

Parliament had naturally been at the heart of the national discussion. The colonists were far from friendless and there had been many brilliant, passionate speeches in their support. Among those in the Commons were orations from Edmund Burke and the young Charles James Fox, not to mention exhortations from the former radical yet unreformed libertine John Wilkes (now Lord Mayor of London). And in the Lords there were contributions from prime ministers past and future, the vastly patrician Marquess of Rockingham and an angry Earl of Shelburne respectively.[4] What had continuing relevance, however, was not the quality of the opposition oratory but the ability of the ministry to win the vote, which they had done easily and repeatedly, on an average basis of three votes to one. However, on 1 February Franklin had the hope, if not the expectation, that a speech from William Pitt, Earl of Chatham, might change the political weather.

There were many who might have invited Franklin to watch the debate. For instance Shelburne was the patron of Joseph Priestley, one of Franklin's greatest friends. Burke was Rockingham's secretary and, like Franklin, a colonial agent, though on a smaller scale. Whereas Burke just represented the interests of the Assembly of New York, Franklin, having arrived in London in 1757 as a representative of the Assembly of Pennsylvania, had also acted for New Jersey, Georgia and, most tellingly, from 1770, the Massachusetts House of Representatives. Franklin could have gained admittance to the Lords' debate through a number of the leading opponents of government policy.

In contrast, his relations with the ministers of Lord North's administration were markedly different, despite his having held the government office of Deputy Postmaster General for North America from 1753 to just the previous year. Franklin had maintained communication through a range of intermediaries, but there had been no formal contact with the ministry since his appearance before the Privy Council at the former royal cockpit in Whitehall on 29 January 1774. The Cockpit proved well named, as Franklin had been denounced in the most vitriolic terms by Sir Alexander Wedderburn, the government's Solicitor General. Two days later he had been dismissed from the Postmastership. The invitation for 1 February had most certainly not come from the administration, but from the Earl of Chatham himself and in person.

Just a dozen years previously, William Pitt (as Chatham was then) had been the most revered man in the entire British empire. Lauded as the architect of Britain's triumph in the Seven Years' War, with victories against the French, in India, at sea and on the continent of North America, he was honoured as the inspirational leader who had made his country the world's greatest power. However, he had suddenly resigned from office in 1761. When he returned as Prime Minister in 1766, 'the Great Commoner' had accepted an earldom and moved to the Lords. Weakened by illness, both physical and mental, he had been more absent than active during his two-year term of office and had then undermined his successor, the Duke of Grafton. This had brought the Duke's resignation and the elevation, in 1770, of Lord North.

Yet, though diminished, Chatham was not finished with politics. He had regained at least something of his old vigour and retained an aura due to his past glories. In that latter regard his closest modern equivalent would be Sir Winston Churchill in his later years.

Chatham had one last great cause to fight, that of America. He sought to repair the divide between King George III's government in London and his no less British subjects in the American colonies. To that end he was preparing a major, perhaps decisive, contribution, which he expected to be treated with the utmost respect.

Chatham and Franklin's personal acquaintance only went back to the previous summer. Franklin had been invited to Chatham's house at Hayes in Kent, been treated with 'an abundance of Civility'[5] and asked to give the fullest possible briefing on American affairs. After that there had been a number of follow-up meetings until, on 19 January 1775, Chatham sent urgent word via their mutual friend

Lord Stanhope. He stressed that it was important for Franklin to meet him the following day in the House of Lords Lobby, when he would personally ensure that Dr Franklin would be able to hear an announcement he intended to make in the Chamber.

This type of consideration was in contrast to the treatment Franklin had received from Chatham following the American's arrival in London in 1757. Franklin had tried to make contact to discuss Pennsylvanian business, but found that Chatham was 'then too great a Man, or too much occupied in Affairs of greater Moment', to deal with him directly.[6] Instead he had to content himself 'with a kind of non-apparent and unacknowledged Communication' via important yet lesser men such as Robert Wood, Pitt's Under-Secretary of State,[7] and with later compliments passed on by Shelburne and Stanhope, aristocrats whom Chatham treated as functionaries. Yet, with Stanhope acting as a facilitator, Chatham was now consulting Franklin as a colleague. From Chatham that was a sign of exceptional respect.

Chatham's special regard was not for Franklin the scientist. In that attitude he differed from many of his contemporaries, because Dr Franklin was something more than just a political representative. Franklin also enjoyed a rather different status from that of the young man he had been during his first stay in London (1724–6). On that earlier occasion he had arrived as a lowly teenage printer; three decades later he was famous.

Franklin was one of the greatest of what were then called 'Natural Philosophers' and now scientists. His *Experiments and Observations on Electricity* (1751) had won him widespread recognition, first in France after a practical demonstration by the Comte de Buffon in front of Louis XV, then in London with the award of the prestigious Copley Medal by the Royal Society, followed by his election to a Fellowship. The Society for the Encouragement of Arts, Manufactures and Commerce (now the Royal Society of Arts) elected him a Corresponding Member with the accompanying declaration that 'Their Desire is to make Great Britain and her Colonies mutually dear and serviceable to each other: {As} They know their Interests are the same.'[8]

Franklin had an international prestige among natural philosophers, with Immanuel Kant hailing him in 1755 as 'the Prometheus of modern times,[9] but he had also achieved a wider celebrity through the reading public's learned interest in the natural world, supported, of course, by a sensationalist fascination for 'magic shows' that sizzled with special effects. Franklin's knowledge and fame had won him access to the tables of the aristocratic, influential and powerful. These were people who would value him, though some purely on account of his scientific reputation.

When Franklin arrived in the Lords' Lobby on 20 January, Chatham welcomed him personally and greeted him warmly. Then he took him by the arm and, though limping badly, led him personally towards the door to the Chamber nearest the throne. The exceptional nature of this courtesy by Chatham was highlighted when they were stopped by a doorkeeper who needed to explain to the Earl that the entrance was reserved for just the brothers and eldest sons of peers. Thus the greatest living Englishman and the renowned Dr Franklin were forced to turn about in the Lobby and to shuffle down passageways to the far end of the Chamber and the entrance door closest to the Bar of the House. There due reverence was restored and, at Chatham's request, Franklin was immediately ushered inside.

The unexpected appearance of the two men together caused a kerfuffle. As Franklin later wrote: 'As it had not been publicly known that there was any Communication between his Lordship and me, this I found occasioned some Speculation. His Appearance in the House I observed caused a kind of Bustle among the Officers, who were hurried in sending Messengers for Members, I suppose those in Connection with the Ministry, something of Importance being expected when that great Man Appears, it being but seldom that his Infirmities permit his Attendance.'[10]

Their alarm was justified, because Chatham formally proposed a motion that British troops be removed from Boston. Then, and even more significantly, he announced that he would shortly present a plan to put an end to the entire quarrel: this is the one he would propose on 1 February.

In succeeding days, Franklin and Chatham met again. Chatham even condescended to have a two-hour meeting at Franklin's lodgings in Craven Street. Returning churchgoers were much surprised to see the grand carriage waiting in the street outside, being instantly recognizable from its coat of arms and coronet. Franklin could not help glowing at that. As he wrote to his son William: 'it was much taken notice and talked of, as at that time was every little Circumstance that Men thought might possibly any way affect American Affairs. Such a Visit from so great a Man, on so important a Business, flattered not a little my Vanity; and the Honour of it gave me the more Pleasure, as it happened on the very Day 12 month that the Ministry had taken so much pains to disgrace me before the Privy Council.' In haste Franklin worked with Chatham in preparation for the 1 February debate.

The continuing choice before both Commons and Lords was straightforward: compulsion or compromise. Strangely, bearing in mind Britain's strength in the world, the underlying emotion for most Members was concern for the future. This was an apprehension quite unlike the flickering fear of a foreign-supported Jacobite invasion which had lingered during the first half of the eighteenth century: that, though alarming, had been more quantifiable.[11] The American question was both very different and more difficult to estimate, though some considered it a problem as large as the area that the ever-expanding population of British Americans could eventually colonize. For Franklin himself, just as for some of his enemies including the Penn Proprietors of Pennsylvania, the potential size of British colonial America was actually a real part of the opportunity it offered. But for many British Members of Parliament, that same vast area was viewed as a threat, because they feared losing control of the administrative process and thus the power to administer at all. They were adamant that the British government must remain supreme and, with that, maintain the right to pass legislation for the American colonies and to tax them. Some, including Lord North himself, felt that the right could be exercised with a light touch, but he, along with the great majority, believed it should be retained. So in truth, did many of the defeated former office holders of the 1760s. This could have remained a sticking point even if the opposition Whigs had defeated the ministry – but throughout the winter there had seemed little chance of that, with the bulk of Members backing coercion. The majority were for snuffing out the insubordination in Boston, as a safeguard against 'the contagion' spreading to the other American colonies, to the sugar-rich West Indies and to Ireland, not forgetting of course the streets of London itself.

It was against this background that on 1 February Chatham rose to present his plan for settling the troubles in America. Franklin himself takes up the story:

> Lord Chatham, in a most excellent Speech, introduced, explained and supported his Plan. When he sat down, Lord Dartmouth rose, and very properly said it contained Matter of such Weight and Magnitude as to require much Consideration, and he therefore hoped the noble Earl did not expect their Lordships to decide upon it by an immediate Vote, but would be willing it should lie upon the Table for Consideration. Lord Chatham answered readily that he expected nothing more. But Lord Sandwich rose, and in a petulant vehement Speech opposed its being received at all, and gave his Opinion that it ought to be immediately REJECTED with the Contempt it deserved. That he could never believe it the Production of any British Peer. That it appeared to him rather the Work of some American; and turning his Face towards me, who was leaning on the Bar, said, he fancied he had in his Eye the Person who drew it up, one of the bitterest and most mischievous Enemies this Country had ever known.[12]

Franklin, as he was wont to do in such circumstances, 'kept my Countenance as immoveable as if my Features had been made of Wood'. But he was appalled. Sandwich, as First Lord of the Admiralty, was enforcing martial law in Boston. He had treated Chatham with total disregard. He had denied Franklin the respect due a gentleman or even a fellow Briton. Worse, he had insulted him as an 'enemy'.

When it was Chatham's turn to speak again, he staunchly defended Franklin, saying that:

> ... he made no Scruple to declare, that if he were the first Minister of this Country, and had the Care of Settling this momentous Business, he should not be ashamed of publicly calling to his Assistance

a Person so perfectly acquainted with the whole of American Affairs as the Gentleman alluded to and injuriously reflected on, one, he was pleased to say, whom all Europe held in high Estimation for his Knowledge and Wisdom, and ranked with our Boyles and Newtons; who was an Honour not to the English Nation only but to Human Nature.[13]

Franklin found 'it harder to stand this extravagant Compliment than the preceding equally extravagant Abuse'.[14]

Chatham had, in Walpole's words, 'recalled the memory of his ancient lustre'[15] and he ended his speech with these sentences savaging the ministry:

The whole of your political conduct has been one continued series of weakness, temerity, despotism, ignorance, futility, negligence, blundering and the most notorious servility, incapacity and corruption. On reconsideration I must allow you one merit, a strict attention to your own interests: in that view, you appear sound statesmen and able politicians. You well know, if the present measure {the Chatham Plan} should prevail, that you must instantly relinquish your places. I doubt much, whether you will be able to keep them on any terms: but sure I am, that such is your well-known characters and abilities, any plan of reconciliation, however moderate, wise and feasible, must fail in your hands. Such then being your precarious situations, who can wonder that you should put a negative on any measure which must annihilate your power, deprive you of your emoluments, and at once reduce you to that state of insignificance, for which God and nature designed you.[16]

Sandwich's categorization of Franklin as a foreigner was totally inaccurate when uttered; only later would it ring true. The opposition had warned of the danger of the dispute between Great Britain and the colonies escalating into a civil war. In fact the American War of Independence would culminate as a war between nations.

The very day after Chatham's plan was thrown out, Lord North rose in the Commons[17] to declare that Massachusetts was in a state of rebellion, supported by 'unlawful combinations and engagements' in other colonies.[18] North's 'Address to the King' calling for stronger military action was supported by the Commons and then, five days later, by the Lords.

As for Franklin himself, on 20 March he took ship for Philadelphia. In the interim he had not stopped attending Parliamentary debates, though he did so with increasing bitterness, being 'much disgusted' at comments from the government side and seeing his fellow Americans 'treated with the utmost Contempt, as the lowest of Mankind, and almost of a different Species from the English of Britain.'[19]

Franklin's last day in London was spent at his long-time home in Craven Street. With his friend Joseph Priestley he read the American newspapers. Priestley later reported that Franklin's 'tears trickled down his cheeks'[20] as he read of the support for Boston, his birthplace, from neighbouring towns.

Franklin was on board ship to America before a warrant could be issued for his arrest, something that he knew his enemies in high places had been seeking for months.[21] As with previous transatlantic crossings, he was using the voyage to observe and theorize about the natural world and he was planning his future conduct on the basis of a thorough analysis of past events. For such a purpose, Dr Franklin, who had identified and invented so many things, had evolved a mathematical basis for weighing the pluses and minuses in decision-making, which he called 'Moral or Prudential Algebra.'[22] As a man, indeed a gentleman, who had long been of both independent means and independent judgement, he was accustomed to spending days of deliberation on the pros and cons of a question. He was quite prepared to change a former position if he considered it to be no longer consistent with what he decided were his unchanging principles. He would then be ready to oppose – and vigorously – any former allies and associates who had not moved with him. That was what he decided now.

There was one new factor that he would have to add to that equation on his arrival in America, because it was during his weeks at sea that the first shots were fired at Lexington and Concord.

Those who, fed by mischievous rumour, expected Franklin to be over-conciliatory to Britain were soon to be disabused. Though Franklin's own view was now hardening, he joined the others in signing the 'Olive Branch Petition' sent directly to George III. The King was being asked to act as a final arbiter who could take the dispute away from what Franklin had called 'the mangling Hands of the present Set of Blundering Ministers'.[23] In 1760 King George had in his first speech to Parliament proudly declared, 'I glory in the name of Briton',[24] but did he consider his American subjects to be the equal of those at home and thus echo Franklin's words of 1754 when he said, 'I look on the Colonies as so many Counties gained to Great Britain'?[25]

Franklin had all his life considered himself to be British. His early reading had been mainly that of British writers. He had imbibed British philosophy and transplanted British ideas, practices and institutions to colonial America and, when he spied an advantage, he had adapted and improved them for local conditions. More recently he had spent nearly fifteen and a half of the last eighteen years based in London. Franklin had fought hard for a solution to the dispute, harder than he might have done had he not been so blinkered by a belief that his logical arguments would win the day. It was because of his British influences, not through a rejection of them, that he was so willing to put the British government to the test of his 'Prudential Algebra', but he was then prepared to become what Sandwich had already believed him to be: 'one of the bitterest and most mischievous Enemies {Britain} had ever known', and at great personal cost.

1

1706–1724

Life Before London

Benjamin Franklin was born an Englishman in Boston, the major town of the Massachusetts Bay colony. His father, Josiah, was born an Englishman in England, at Ecton, Northamptonshire, in 1657. In 1683 Josiah crossed the Atlantic with his first wife Ann to start a new life in Boston. As a surviving account from Josiah's older brother, another Benjamin, makes clear, Josiah left England for economic reasons, seeing a better chance for himself and his children in the New World. In England he had been a silk dyer, but in his new home, with its less ostentatious, more puritanical dress, he changed his trade to that of a tallow chandler and soap maker.

In 1689 Ann Franklin died, shortly after giving birth to their seventh child. Just five months later Josiah married a Nantucket girl, Abiah Folger, and with her he was to have ten more.[1] Though Josiah was now living thousands of miles from his birthplace, he was still very much a Briton, as was his and Abiah's own ninth child and youngest son, Benjamin Franklin, born on 6 January 1706[2] and baptized the same day.

As Daniel Defoe phrased it in 1707: 'Sending our People to the Colonies is no more, nor ought to be esteemed otherwise, than sending people out of Middlesex into Yorkshire, where they are still in the same Government, employed to the Benefit of the same Public Stock, and in the Strength and Defence of the same United Body.'[3] Though there were actual differences in 'Government' both between the colonies themselves and with the British Isles, the former had been united in their loyalty to the 1689 Protestant settlement of

William and Mary. The colonists were, as Defoe went on to say, 'every way a Part of ourselves'.[4] It was a sentiment that Benjamin Franklin echoed almost fifty years later, with his 'I look on the Colonies as so many Counties gained to Great Britain' and when advocating 'uniting the Colonies more intimately with Great Britain, by allowing them Representatives in Parliament'.[5]

Boston, at the time of Franklin's birth, was the largest town in the American colonies. But its population of less than 8,000 was dwarfed by that of London. By the 1720s Boston had grown to 11,000, but New York and Philadelphia, the next-nearest in size, still housed just 6,000 and 4,900 respectively. Importantly for Boston, it was New England's major port, the hub for the colonies' transatlantic trade and busy with shipping.

Benjamin Franklin's life has sometimes been portrayed as a rise from the very bottom of society. However, although his father may have had difficulty in making ends meet and struggled to feed his army of children – with Ben, making twelve living and two more, both girls, to follow – Josiah had an independent position, with his own business and a record of voluntary service to the community.[6]

The home in Boston's Milk Street was the centre of great activity as it also served as Josiah's place of work and manufacture. The dual purpose brought tragic consequences in 1703 when the child who would have been Ben's elder brother Ebenezer, aged sixteen months, was unsupervised for a few minutes and 'drowned in a Tub of Suds'.[7] Another brother, two-year-old Thomas, was to die just seven months after Ben was born.

We do not know whether it was through these sad events, because of some particular qualities shown by the young boy, or his family position as the tenth-born son and thus being seen as a sort of tithe, but Ben seemed destined for the church. Josiah, proud of his own literacy, paid for Ben to go to grammar school. However, he removed him in just under a year, having decided that it would be impossible to fund the future school years and then Harvard. But he did provide his 'little library' of books to which Ben added his own small purchases, including an edition of Bunyan's *The Pilgrim's Progress*.

Josiah's plan to make Ben a church minister remained, but the young boy firmly and continually rejected it. Impressed by the bustle of maritime Boston, he dreamed of going to sea.

Finally, an acceptable alternative was found. At the age of twelve Ben was apprenticed to his printer brother James, who was nearly nine years older. James had recently visited London, where he had bought his own printing press with various loans, including it seems one that his father borrowed on his behalf.[8] It is most likely that Ben's career, with his rejection of the ministry and his love of reading, was chosen at the same time. His workplace certainly gave him 'Access to better Books', which he supplemented through overnight loans from the apprentices of booksellers and the use of a kind customer's library. He thus introduced himself to John Locke's *Essay Concerning Human Understanding*, which he later 'esteemed the best Book of Logic in the World'.[9]

There was also one collection which proved extremely important for his writing as well as his thinking. As he wrote in his *Autobiography*:

> About this time I met with an odd Volume of the Spectator. It was the third. I had never before seen any of them. I bought it, read it over and over, and was much delighted with it. I thought the Writing excellent, and wished if possible to imitate it. With that View, I took some of the Papers, and making short Hints of the Sentiment in each Sentence, laid them by a few Days, and then, without looking at the Book, tried to complete the Papers again, by expressing each hinted Sentiment at length and as fully as it had been expressed before, in any suitable Words, that should come to hand.
>
> Then I compared my Spectator with the Original, discovered some of my Faults and corrected them.[10]

These essays were to serve as a model for the style and content of the 'Silence Dogood' letters, the humorous wisdom of a worldly widow, which the sixteen-year-old Franklin began submitting to his brother anonymously in 1722. They were well received. This was not just because the essay style of James Franklin's *New England Courant* was based on that of the *Spectator*; more than that, they were brilliantly written and a tremendous mixture of spoof and mockery combined with practical plans for improvement.[11]

The admiration of the younger Franklin for the writings of Joseph Addison and Richard Steele was to continue to the very end of his life. Janette Seaton Lewis, in comparing Franklin's *Autobiography* to the *Spectator*, shows how strikingly both 'reflect their authors' shared interest in religion, education, the cultivation of practical virtues and man's use of reason'.[12] It was a debt Franklin was happy to acknowledge in 1748, almost thirty years after Addison's death, describing him as a man 'whose writings have contributed more to the improvement of the minds of the British nation, and polishing their manners, than those of any other English pen whatever'.[13] Writing in the persona of 'Poor Richard' (of whom more anon), Franklin had allowed himself some hyperbole, as Addison himself seemingly did with 'I shall be ambitious to have it said of me, that I have brought Philosophy out of Closets and Libraries, Schools and Colleges, to dwell in Clubs and Assemblies, at Tea-tables, and in Coffee-houses.'[14] Except that it was an ambition both achieved and sustained.

Franklin was delighted to hear the compliments and speculations of his brother's friends and contributors as each new 'Silence Dogood' letter arrived. James was pleased with the pieces themselves and the favourable reaction they received. From the very second letter they appeared as the lead column on the paper's front page.[15] The *Courant* was the second paper that James printed but the first that he edited, with a first issue dated 7 August 1721.[16] Like many a newcomer after it, the *Courant* sought circulation by an assault on the evils of 'the establishment'. It saw an excellent target in the inoculation campaign of Dr Cotton Mather. Mather was a man of prodigious learning and civic importance. He combined being a censorious leading church minister with having an intense and informed interest in natural science and medicine, the latter leading him to champion the earliest form of germ theory and to sponsor a campaign for inoculation against smallpox at a time when the practice was generally regarded as highly experimental.[17] Mather was an authority figure with forceful opinions and a lecturing manner. James Franklin's attack on his campaign was straightforwardly populist, claiming that inoculation spread smallpox rather than prevented it. Young Ben added to a more general attack on the good Doctor; after all, the name 'Dogood' echoed Mather's own *Bonifacius, or Essays to Do Good* and the 'Silence' was heavily ironic, as it was something not normally associated with the verbose Cotton Mather.

A chance street encounter, when the hectoring and prolix Dr Mather gave James a good dressing-down, did nothing to weaken the latter's resolve.[18] In fact it led to his attack becoming increasingly personal. Circulation, however, failed to pick up.

James became even more daring, with the *Courant* of 11 June 1722 alleging that the local authorities were colluding with pirates off the coast. That certainly got him noticed. The next day he was arrested and imprisoned for nearly a month, leaving his younger brother in nominal charge.[19] It was something that Ben relished and James appreciated, but three months later the mood darkened.

On 8 October the fourteenth and last 'Silence Dogood' appeared. Still no one had guessed the author. But then, Ben, feeling that he was running out of steam, revealed himself. The friends were greatly impressed; brother James was not. As Ben later wrote: 'he thought, probably with reason, that it tended to make me too vain. And perhaps this might be one Occasion of the Differences that we frequently had about this Time.'[20]

It was just one of several. Even from Ben's own account one can sympathize with James's irritation with his precocious brother's special pleading to their father, if not with the beatings James exacted in revenge. But, just three months later, James was forced to rely on Ben once more. In January 1723 the *Courant* again overstepped the mark once more, by portraying Boston's civil government, together with its prominent merchants and church ministers, as hypocrites.[21] James fled into hiding to escape arrest and Ben took the reins for some weeks, but this time, as the revealed 'Silence Dogood' author, with a much stronger editorial role. When the case came to court James was forbidden from producing the paper, so he released Ben from his formal indenture and the *Courant* was published under the name of Benjamin Franklin. It was of course still very much James's paper, but he no longer had control over his younger brother.

In September, after a final quarrel, Ben left. There was no chance of other printing work in Boston; James had seen to that. So after a brief stay in New York, young Benjamin Franklin decided to try his luck in Philadelphia.

What he learned in his five years with James never left him. In a note in the *Autobiography*, written so long after the event, Ben added the lines: 'I fancy his harsh and tyrannical Treatment of me might be a means of impressing me with that Aversion to arbitrary Power that has stuck to me through my whole life.' It is highly relevant, if only because it shows the rancour lasted, just as it clearly did with James, who was further embittered when his young brother, all suited and booted and flashing his money around, made a return trip to Boston at the end of the following year. It was hardly surprising that when Ben showed up and showed off at the *Courant* offices, the still-struggling James felt, as Ben reported, that 'I had insulted him in such a Manner before his People that he could never forget or forgive.'[22]

Although the two brothers were personally reconciled shortly before James's death in 1735, Ben did not pause in his future writings to give full credit to him or his fellow *Couranters* such as Nathaniel Gardner. Possibly if he had lived even longer he would have done so; after all, it was during the final years of his life that he amended the *Autobiography* to add Cotton Mather's *Essays to Do Good* to a list of the highlights of his childhood reading that included *The Pilgrim's Progress*, Plutarch's *Lives* and Defoe's *Essay upon Projects*. Franklin wrote that Mather's book '*perhaps*** gave me a Turn of Thinking that had an Influence on some of the principal future Events of my Life.'[23] A lot of ink has been spent on the meaning of that use of the word 'perhaps,'[24] but the mention may partially be due to an elderly Benjamin Franklin having been reminded of his visiting Mather on that same Boston trip and being admonished to 'Stoop! Stoop!' an instant before he cracked his head on a low beam, with the old divine continuing his lecture to the staggering youth with 'Let this be a Caution to you not always to hold your Head so high; Stoop, young

---

* Author's italics

Man, stoop – as you go through the World – and you'll miss many hard Thumps.'[25]

Franklin may not himself have given brother James and Gardner full credit, but the late J. A. Leo Lemay certainly does in the first volume of his pre-eminent twenty-first-century biography of Franklin's first half-century. He believed their influences to be clearly evident in 'Silence Dogood'. This is a matter of great importance as, to follow Lemay in quoting Walter Isaacson: 'One reason the Silence Dogood essays are so historically notable is that they were among the first examples of what would become a quintessential American genre of humour: the wry homespun mix of folksy tales and pointed observations that was perfected by such Franklin descendants as Mark Twain and Will Rogers.'[26]

As Lemay observes, there are also other strong influences there. As well as Mather (used positively as well as negatively) and something of the Puritan sermon balanced by the more earthy Massachusetts clergyman John Wise, there is a host of British and Irish writers who heavily influenced the other *Courant* journalists as well as Benjamin Franklin himself. To Defoe, Lemay adds Jonathan Swift, the 3rd Earl of Shaftesbury, Anthony Collins and the 'Cato' writers John Trenchard and Thomas Gordon. However, he concludes that 'to make a recipe for the writings of Franklin, we may begin with the periodical essays of Addison and Steele in the *Spectator*, *Tatler* and *Guardian*'.[27]

The works of Addison and Steele would also prove crucial to the young Franklin on his first visit to London. They provided him with the 'polite conversation' that would help him gain a quite extraordinary acceptance in the section of London coffee-house society that would acknowledge his breadth and depth of reading, value him for his views and intelligence and ignore both his youth and status.[28]

∽

In his *Autobiography*, Franklin beautifully describes his arrival in Philadelphia. We see him, filthy from his journey, looking like a ragamuffin and indecorously eating in the street, all being observed with disgust by Deborah Read, to whom later he was to get engaged. However, as with much else in the *Autobiography*, his seeming 'warts and all' approach is there for a reason: to offer himself as an example to others, holding the attention with entertaining anecdote and homespun advice, in what is arguably the first in a genre of inspirational autobiographies by American celebrities. Franklin did not even conceive it as an autobiography; it only took that name when published after his death. It is certainly not a 'life', as it only goes as far as the beginnings of his long stay in London from 1757. The memoir was notionally begun in 1771 for the benefit of his son William, but its words of wisdom have an audience of Everyman. With that in mind, readers need to be careful, even when Franklin seems to be at his most open about the most humbling of experiences. For though it is, of course, an extremely valuable document for an understanding of Benjamin Franklin, it would, if taken alone, be just a partial one, with even its seeming openness a clever piece of self-protection.

A full range of other sources is needed. Franklin recounted his tale from long retrospect, with just over a third written in 1771 and the rest, including heavy revisions of the whole, between 1785 and almost the end of Franklin's days. The latter part, in particular, was written with a sense of moral purpose, as Franklin himself explained in a 1788 letter to Benjamin Vaughan: 'If a writer can judge properly of his own work, I fancy, on reading over what is already done, that the book will be found entertaining, interesting and useful, more so than when I began it.'[29]

It certainly is readable, but it lacks completeness. Extraordinarily, it skips over the scientific work that gave Dr Franklin the exceptional international reputation that made him fêted in London and provided him with the gravitas for his political role and his later Founding Fatherhood. Franklin's *Autobiography* is as one with his 1743 aphorism, 'Let all Men know thee, but no man know thee thoroughly.'[30] In that he succeeded too well with the posthumous bestseller. His brilliance as a memoirist has eclipsed his monumental contemporary fame as a scientist. Joyce Chaplin gives a superb modern equivalent in her Introduction to the *Autobiography*'s new standard version: 'It is as if Albert Einstein were now remembered for the charming stories of his childhood and youth, without any clear memory of what he had done to become so famous in the first place.'[31]

Franklin's account of a less than triumphal entry into Philadelphia is at one with the whole when he says: 'I have been the more particular in this Description of my Journey, and shall be so of my first Entry into that City, that you may in your Mind compare such unlikely Beginning{s} with the Figure I have since made there.'[32] In the passages about his first days in the 'City of Brotherly Love', he highlights the kindness of Quakers, both in groups and individually. However, his position was in reality far from desperate, because as he himself says a few pages earlier, he had a trade and was a good workman. For he did soon pick up work and, once given the opportunity to show his skills, he gained a permanent position with Samuel Keimer. However, it rapidly became apparent to Franklin that he was rather better at the mechanics of printing than either the shabby and slipshod Keimer or Philadelphia's more established printer, Andrew Bradford.

Franklin did not lack confidence and, though greatly surprised, he was undaunted when Sir William Keith, the Lieutenant Governor of Pennsylvania, no less, sought him out. Governor Keith invited Franklin to accompany him and Colonel French, of New Castle, Delaware, to the local tavern to taste some excellent madeira. There Sir William, in strictest confidence, outlined his plan. It was nothing less than to set up Franklin in his own business and to give him the official printing for the province of Pennsylvania including Delaware. At subsequent meetings it was decided that Ben should follow in his brother James's footsteps and go to London to buy the equipment, but more immediately he should take that trip to Boston to discuss matters with his father, who, in any case, might like to invest something himself.

Josiah was surprised, thinking Ben too young to take on the responsibility of his own business. He was impressed with the contacts Ben had made in Philadelphia, but thought he should wait a few more years before starting up on his own; by which time he believed that his son, through hard work and prudent parsimony, should have saved almost enough. If so, he would help him with the rest. But Ben was not prepared to wait, particularly when Governor Keith, dismissing Josiah's caution, offered to take on the entire funding himself.

2

1724–1726

A Young Man in London

At the beginning of November 1724, Franklin travelled from Philadelphia to New Castle, further down the Delaware River, where the
well-named *London Hope* waited to take its passengers to the imperial
capital. However, he had one major concern: Governor Keith's letters
of introduction and credit had still not arrived, in spite of repeated
promises. At last Colonel French came on board with the Governor's
dispatches and showed Franklin 'great Respect'. That not only settled
Franklin's mind, but French's appearance was to gain him an upgrade.
Space had become available because a distinguished lawyer named
Andrew Hamilton had suddenly left the ship, together with his son,
to take up a highly remunerative case back in Philadelphia and earn
legal fees that dwarfed the cost of the transatlantic passage, even
considering the special stores of food and drink he had ordered in.[1]
One of the three remaining cabin passengers, a Quaker merchant
called Thomas Denham, was a friend of Hamilton's and, on observing
Franklin's cordiality with the Colonel, he offered a promotion from
steerage for both Franklin and his friend and travelling companion
James Ralph, together with an invitation to share the supplies. As a
result, wrote Franklin, 'we had a sociable Company in the Cabin, and
lived uncommonly well'.[2] Though the weather was appalling, he was
not too inconvenienced by it, as neither seasickness nor a fear of sea
travel was a problem, at least not for him.

Franklin had still not set eyes on his intended letters. However,
when the *London Hope* entered the English Channel, the ship's
captain obliged him by opening the bag containing the Governor's

mail. Taking the fact that none was specifically addressed to him as an oversight, Franklin picked out the half-dozen most likely addressees, such as the King's Printer and a stationer. But his visit to the latter completely disillusioned him. It immediately became clear that the letter was nothing to do with him and wasn't even from Keith. It was from a man called Riddlesden, whom Franklin knew to be a crooked attorney and whom the stationer instantly declared a rascal and handed the worthless piece of paper back to him. For some unfathomable reason, Keith had sent Franklin on a wild goose chase. Cast adrift in what Daniel Defoe described as the 'Great and Monstrous Thing'[3] of eighteenth-century London, this was a devastating experience for the young putative master printer.

Franklin's shock at being so deceived by such a seemingly respectable figure is strongly conveyed in the pages of the *Autobiography*, but then so is his affection for Thomas Denham, for the young man had sense enough to visit the older and more worldly-wise merchant. Here, in his confusion, Franklin found a figure he could trust. It is obvious that he had scrupulously obeyed Keith's instructions to keep their plans secret, otherwise Denham would have enlightened him earlier that the very idea of Keith providing letters of credit was preposterous, as Keith was a man with no credit to give. Denham advised him to make the best of a bad job and to gain experience in London as a printer, because, he said, 'you will improve yourself; and when you return to America, you will set up to greater Advantage'.[4] Wise words, as was his advice to visit Hamilton, who had concluded his business in Philadelphia within a couple of weeks and whose crossing had taken four weeks to Franklin's seven, so that he had already arrived in London. The importance of that meeting was immense, because Riddlesden's letter contained a secret scheme against Hamilton that involved Keith. This information was of great value to Hamilton and certainly well worth the cost of Franklin and friend tucking into his stores. It gave Franklin a small revenge and was also, in the future, to provide him, in Hamilton, with an extremely important friend and contact. More immediately, though, he had to get the measure of his new life in London.

To supplement Franklin's own later reflections on conditions in London during those years, we have the contemporary descriptions of somebody he much admired, Daniel Defoe.[5] Franklin first featured Defoe's views in one of his 'Silence Dogood' letters,[6] but he was to return to him again and again, including in the *Autobiography*, where he rattled off a full list of Defoe titles with enthusiasm. During his first visit to London, Franklin was to see for himself the truth of Defoe's contemporaneous description in *The Complete English Tradesman* (1726) that:

> Frugality is not the national virtue of *England*, so the people that get much spend much; and as they work hard, so they live well, clothe warm and lodge soft; in a word, the working manufacturing people of *England* eat the fat, and drink the sweet, live better, and fare better, than the working poor of any other nation in *Europe*; they make better wages of their work and spend more of the money upon their backs and bellies than in any other country.[7]

Of course the most important words there are 'work' and 'working', because employment was precarious and those who did not put money aside in the good times could find themselves in desperate straits during the bad.

Later in life, Franklin was to achieve both wealth and status. For that reason he seems happy to castigate himself in his *Autobiography*, particularly when it comes to early errors of judgement, which, with his printing background, he calls his errata – though, it has to be said, he usually finds some extenuating circumstances to excuse himself.

However, one real weakness seems to have been exposed in a couple of early friendships with highly intelligent but flawed individuals. One such was with an old Boston friend called Collins, whose fondness for brandy turned him into a soak and then a sponge on Franklin. Another was with James Ralph. Leaving a wife and child behind in Philadelphia, Ralph claimed that he was interested in selling goods on commission. But it was obvious that he had no real interest in becoming a merchant or, as soon became apparent, in returning home. However, Ralph was possessed of the dual advantage of being both entertaining and eloquent. Franklin was certainly also the first of these, but never claimed to be the second. He did, though, enjoy that quality in Ralph, later writing that 'I never knew a prettier Talker.'[8] They took lodgings together in London.

These were in Little Britain, south of Smithfield and near St Bartholomew's Hospital.[9] For a century and a half this had been a street of printers and booksellers, including one Samuel Buckley, whose name Franklin would have known very well from the imprint lines in his copies of the *Spectator*: 'London, Printed for Sam. Buckley, at the Dolphin in Little Britain'. Buckley was also the printer of London's first daily newspaper, the *Daily Courant*, 'Courant' being the then common term for a paper with news.[10]

Franklin soon found himself employment with one of the seventy-five master printers in London:[11] 'I immediately got into Work at Palmer's, then a famous Printing House in Bartholomew Close; and here I continued near a Year. I was pretty diligent; but spent with Ralph a great deal of my Earnings in going to Plays and other Places of Amusement.' On Franklin's earnings, theirs had to be the cheap seats up in 'the Gods', the galleries housing the rowdiest parts of the rowdy audience. We get no more detail from Franklin, but Ralph was to give a description from his own pen a few years later. Writing in the persona of 'a Person of some Taste and some Quality', Ralph entertains his readers by humbly proposing 'that our *Playhouses* may be enlarged after the Manner of the *Grecian* and *Roman* THEATRES, and separate Lodges contrived for those who go there only to chat, intrigue, or eat and drink; that impertinent Mirth, public Amours, or ill-timed Gluttony, may not break in upon the Amusements of those, who go there purely for the sake of the Entertainment.'[12]

As to the galleries, Ralph describes 'their frequent Disorders', considers 'their Delight is to be noisy' and finally explodes with: 'Who can judge sedately of POETRY or MUSIC in *Bedlam* or a *Brothel*? Or what is worse, in THEATRES, with Galleries set aside for Livery Servants to Bully and Swear in.'[13] Of course Ralph was joking, but his comments are merely an amplified version of many others on the noise and misrule of the eighteenth-century gallery, who were not slow in hurling orange peel, whole fruit or quart bottles to signal their displeasure at events on stage and off.[14]

Undoubtedly Ralph's later comments were given extra ire by one of his many failures to find employment in 1724. Franklin takes up his story:

> He first endeavoured to get into the Playhouse, believing himself qualified for an Actor; but Wilks, to whom he applied, advised him candidly not to think of that Employment, as it was impossible he should succeed in it. Then he proposed to Roberts, a Publisher in Paternoster Row, to write for him a Weekly Paper like the *Spectator*, on certain Conditions, which Roberts did not approve. Then he endeavoured to get Employment as a Hackney Writer to copy for the Stationers and Lawyers about the Temple {Inns of Court}, but could find no Vacancy.[15]

Ralph may have been down on his luck, but he was not downhearted. He took up with a young widowed milliner who, with her child, lived in their lodgings. When she moved out, so did Ralph, who battened on her for money, until their joint monetary problems forced him to move away to take up low-paid temporary work as a country schoolmaster. This was not at all what Ralph had in mind for his future: 'He deemed {it} a Business below him, and, confident of future better Fortune when he should be unwilling to have it known that he once was so meanly employed, he changed his Name.'[16]

The name he chose was Benjamin Franklin. He was not at all abashed about it, writing to Franklin to tell him what he had done, asking his friend to look after the milliner and to write back soon and often, but to be sure to address any letters to the school to Mr Franklin, Schoolmaster. For his own part, Ralph continued to write frequently. He sent Franklin large chunks of an epic poem and, in spite of Franklin giving the heavy hint of sending Ralph a newly published satire by Edward Young in the hope of highlighting 'the

Folly of pursuing the Muses with any Hope of Advancement', 'Sheets of the Poem continued to come by every Post'. Franklin did look after the milliner, who was now in greater distress, due to Ralph having alienated her friends and interrupted her business. Franklin began lending her money to keep her head above water and they started spending more time together. Franklin then, in his own words, 'attempted Familiarities' which 'she repulsed with a proper Resentment'. This was a real 'Erratum', and an extremely costly one. The milliner wrote to Ralph; and Ralph, upon his London return, told Franklin that this reprehensible behaviour had cancelled all obligations. Their friendship was at an end.

In one way, Franklin made light of it all, believing Ralph's repudiation of his debt was 'not then of much Consequence as he was totally unable [to repay it]. And in the Loss of his Friendship I found myself relieved of a Burden.' Franklin is also keen to tell us that he bore no residual enmity and that 'I loved him notwithstanding, for he had many amiable Qualities.'[17] One might almost think that Franklin was grateful to Ralph for having made him knuckle down to working hard, economizing and using his wits. But all this was written many years later, after Franklin had returned to London and the two had met again in different circumstances. Yet Franklin doesn't neglect to tell us that the amount Ralph owed him was £27. This was then a staggering sum. It would have taken Franklin six months to earn it.[18]

Franklin changed jobs, moving from Palmer's to the much larger firm of Watts's with its near-fifty workmen in Wild Court just off Lincoln's Inn Fields. On the face of it, this was a gamble because at Palmer's he had been a compositor, whereas at Watts's he now started at the lower grade of pressman. But he was no doubt confident of making the step up and was a hard, honest and sober worker. He was highly productive and energetic. In the press room, for 'Bodily Exercise', he carried around double the large 'Forms of Type' of his colleagues. This was noticed by his fellow workmen who were surprised by the strength of the 'Water-American', as they believed that water made you weak, whereas strong beer naturally gave you strength. Had they been right, then some of them would have been Herculean. They had another reason for being startled by his drinking habits, bearing in mind the role of ale and beer in purifying water so that it could be drunk. Water was supplied from the Thames through leaking pipework, and though there were wells, from which the likes of Clerkenwell and Sadler's Wells got their names, these were used by a number of unhygienic trades and were, like the river itself, polluted – though in no way as heavily as the nineteenth-century Thames.[19] One can only assume that either Franklin's constitution could cope or he found a cleaner source of supply.

As for beer, it was common at the time for a pot-boy from a local alehouse to bring beer direct to a worker at his bench,[20] and Franklin's closest workmate took full advantage on a daily basis. He had a pint in the early morning, a second to wash down his breakfast bread and cheese, a third between breakfast and dinner, a fourth at dinner, a fifth in the afternoon at about six o'clock and then a sixth when he finished work. All of which would lose him four or five shillings from his weekly wage for that 'muddling Liquor'.[21] Franklin does not say, but one can assume that if this man was typical of the time, he would then spend his evenings in the alehouse. Initiation in the workplace and drink went hand in hand. When Franklin was quickly promoted to the composing room, his fellow compositors asked for an initiation fee or 'Sum for Drink' of five shillings. This was resented by Franklin, as he had already paid one such in the press room. Supported by Watts, he held out. Yet even the Master's will was not stronger than that of the 'Chapel Ghost', who for two to three weeks mixed up Franklin's type, transposed his pages and broke up his settings. Strangely, after Franklin paid up, the 'Ghost' went away.[22]

Franklin began to win over his colleagues. At least some of them gave up their breakfast of beer and joined Franklin in eating the far more wholesome porridge, sprinkled with pepper and breadcrumbs and with a bit of butter added. For those who continued with beer and who ran out of credit at the alehouse, Franklin lent them money at a decent rate of interest. This time he made sure that his debts were paid, collecting them direct from the pay table on Saturday nights.[23] He had learned his lesson from his experiences with Ralph.

Franklin found another way of raising money and of gaining himself an important introduction at the same time. On 2 June 1725 he wrote to Sir Hans Sloane, a friend of Sir Isaac Newton, his successor as President of the Royal Society and a great collector. The letter, in *The Papers of Benjamin Franklin*,* reads as follows:

> Sir
>
> Having lately been in the Northern Parts of America, I have brought from thence a Purse made of the Stone Asbestos, a Piece of the Stone and a Piece of Wood, the Pithy Part of which is of the same Nature, and called by the Inhabitants Salamander Cotton. As you are noted to be a Lover of Curiosities, I have informed you of these; and if you have any Inclination to purchase them, or see them, let me know your Pleasure by a Line directed for me at the Golden Fan in Little Britain, and I will wait upon you with them. I am, Sir, Your most humble Servant.
>
> Benjamin Franklin
>
> P.S. I expect to be out of Town in 2 or 3 Days, and therefore beg an immediate Answer.[24]

In his *Autobiography*, Franklin wrote that Sloane heard about the purse and 'came to see me', which is what we might call one of the 'slight adjustments' Franklin made to the account of his earlier life. We do not need that extra detail to realize that, with the postscript in particular, the nineteen-year-old printer was being extremely presumptuous. But his self-confidence worked. Sir Hans 'invited me to his House in Bloomsbury Square; where he showed me all his Curiosities' and 'paid me handsomely' for the purse.[25] And it is

---

* Henceforward 'Franklin Papers'.

good for us that Franklin was persuasive, for Sloane's magnificent collection was to provide a major part of the British Museum at its foundation in 1753; and the purse was one of the natural history objects, including mineralogical artefacts, which were later given their own home in the Natural History Museum. It remains there today, though not on permanent display – it is made of asbestos, after all.

We are not told whether Sloane offered an introduction to Franklin's great hero, Sir Isaac Newton – the bust of whom is shown on Franklin's desk in the David Martin portrait of 1767. Possibly Franklin held back, because we know that he was relying on another friend of Newton for that.

Franklin was already showing an ability to gain personal access to people who shared his interests and enthusiasms but who came from a more socially privileged background. Crucially, once having gained their attention he was able to hold it, not through his oratory, but through being an engaged and attentive listener.

Franklin found time to read a great number of books and he came up with a novel scheme that enabled him to be able to afford to do so, as well as generating an important connection. As he himself explains: 'While I lodged in Little Britain I made an Acquaintance with one Wilcox a Bookseller, whose Shop was at the next Door. He had an immense Collection of second-hand Books. Circulating Libraries were not then in Use; but we agreed that on certain reasonable Terms which I have now forgotten, I might take, read and return any of his Books. This I esteemed a great Advantage, and I made as much Use of it as I could.'[26]

Although Franklin's London work concentrated on printing, he wrote one pamphlet of note. When staying after hours at Palmer's and probably paying the printer through unpaid overtime, Franklin printed 100 copies of a work that he entitled *A Dissertation on Liberty and Necessity, Pleasure and Pain*.[27] It may have been the cause of Franklin leaving Palmer's, because, as he later wrote, 'It occasioned my being more considered by Mr Palmer as a young Man of some Ingenuity, though he seriously expostulated with me upon the Principles of my Pamphlet which to him appeared abominable.'[28] This was completely understandable, because Franklin had read the sceptical works of Shaftesbury and Collins and taken the logic of John Locke's *Essay Concerning Human Understanding* a step further to produce a deistic conclusion.[29] Palmer's concerns were not merely philosophical but also professional. The *Dissertation's* title page did not display the name of its author, publisher or bookseller. Justifiably so, because had the pamphlet come to the attention of a magistrate and their identities been known, then its sentiments could have led to prosecution.[30] But it was exactly these that attracted the attention of one of Wilcox's authors, the surgeon J. Lyons, who had written *The Infallibility of Human Judgment*. Lyons met Wilcox's young next-door neighbour and took him to meet Dr Bernard Mandeville, who 'had a club' at the Horns pale-ale house in Cheapside. Mandeville was the notorious author of *The Fable of the Bees; or, Private Vices, Public Benefits*, which had argued that humans were solely motivated by self-interest.[31] At the time this argument was considered shocking, as was his assertion that some good might derive from a bad event, such as the Great Fire of London.[32] Mandeville was denounced from pulpits and in print and this, naturally, increased his fame. In comparison to Ralph and particularly in contrast to Collins, Mandeville was a disreputable friend of some consequence and young Franklin found him 'a most facetious entertaining {i.e. urbane} Companion'.[33]

Lyons also took Franklin to meet Dr Henry Pemberton at Batson's Coffee House at number 17 Cornhill.[34] Pemberton, a mathematician of about thirty, was working with England's most celebrated intellect, Sir Isaac Newton, on the third edition of Newton's *Principia*. Newton, though still fractious, was now in his eighties and increasingly frail. Sadly, and much to Franklin's regret, Pemberton's promise of an introduction to the great man was one that he was unable to keep.

This disappointment aside, Franklin was now enjoying the club and coffee-house experience for which the *Spectator* had prepared him. It would set a pattern for his life whereby he would join close-knit groups of free thinkers, some of the members notorious for being so, who met on a regular basis to consider the great matters of the natural world and its related human experience.

It is almost certain that a book Franklin read at this time was Daniel Defoe's *A Tour through the Whole Island of Great Britain*, published between 1724 and 1726. We know that Franklin's later plan for the Pennsylvania Hospital, the first public hospital in America, owed much to Defoe's book, as can be seen in his 'Appeals' in the *Pennsylvania Gazette* in 1751 and in his *Some Account of the Pennsylvania Hospital*.[35] We also know that an enquiring mind, extraordinary powers of observation and, when required, impressive administrative ability were among Franklin's great strengths. But whether Franklin's youthful impressions were guided by Defoe or not, passages in *A Tour* are useful for giving descriptions of London at the time of his first visit, with Defoe capturing the vibrant growth and changing aspect of the cities of London and Westminster, respectively the national centres of commerce and government.

Three-fifths of the medieval City of London had been destroyed by the Great Fire of London in 1666.[36] It had engulfed the mansions on the City waterfront, spread west past Fetter Lane, east to modern Tower Hill and as far north as the most northern point of London Wall. Four hundred and thirty acres were devastated and the City lost many thousands of houses, fifty-two guild halls, St Paul's Cathedral and eighty-seven parish churches. As Defoe describes, the destruction was unsurprising, as the medieval streets

> ... were not only narrow, and the houses all built of timber, lath and plaster, or, as they were very properly called paper work ... The manner of the building in those days, one storey projecting out beyond another, was such that in some narrow streets the houses almost touched one another at the top and it has been known that men, in case of fire, have escaped on the tops of the houses by leaping from one side of a street to another.[37]

After the fire the streets were wider and the buildings 'chiefly of brick', and 'by Act of Parliament, every builder is bound to have a partition wall of brick also, one brick and {a} half thick between every house; it is found to be, indeed, very helpful in case of fire'.[38] It was just as well, because Defoe decried the negligence of Londoners: 'The servants, nay, and the masters too in London are the most careless people in the world about fire, and this, no doubt, is the reason why there are frequently more fires in London and in the out-parts than there are in all the cities of Europe put them together.'[39] But in other ways they had learned. Fire insurance had, in Defoe's words, 'attained such a universal approbation, that I am told there are above 70,000 houses thus ensured in London, and the parts adjacent'.[40] Also, most importantly, 'no city in the world is so well furnished for extinguishing fires when they happen', as parish officers were able to open up the water pipes to flood the streets, to supply 'the great number of admirable engines ... so that no sooner does a fire break out, but the house is surrounded with engines, and a flood of water poured upon it, until the fire is, as it were, not extinguished only, but drowned'. And there were specialists to operate them, as the insurance companies paid men 'to make it their business to be ready at call, all hours, and night or day, to assist in case of fire; and it must be acknowledged they are very dextrous, bold, diligent and successful. These they call firemen, but with an odd kind of contradiction in the title, for they are really most of them watermen.'[41]

Franklin moved around the rebuilt City, not least to his meetings in Cornhill and Cheapside. He had seen Boston expand greatly, but its area of new building was small indeed compared to the City's vast expanse. The City of London of the 1720s had still not lost that sense of newness, with St Paul's finally completed in the decade before and the red brick of the houses being better than stone at resisting the discolouration from sooty fires and grime. When one considers Franklin's later public works and the eye for detail in his writings from 1726 onwards,[42] the practical developments of the new City did not go unnoticed.

But if the post-1666 streets were wider, then there were more of them. There was much infilling, the large houses with their gardens and courtyards being replaced with new streets of smaller dwellings. Thus, according to Defoe, 'there are many more houses built than stood before upon the same ground; so that taking the whole city together, there are more inhabitants in the same compass than there were before'.[43] This was not due to a grand plan, but through population pressure. By the end of the seventeenth century the French-born Huguenot Henri Misson described greater London as the largest city in Europe.[44] It continued to grow and its population would be around 675,000 by the mid-century.[45] In the City, the result was the creation of a maze of alleyways, not only in the newly rebuilt wards of Cripplegate and Candlewick, but in areas beyond the old London wall and Temple Bar. These were potentially fruitful for robbers, whether the violent footpads or the more stealthy pickpockets. César de Saussure, a Swiss visitor in 1726, was shocked by the amount of London crime, estimating that fewer robbers were caught in all of Switzerland during a whole year than were judged at a single six-weekly London assizes. He was a victim himself: 'Quite lately a valuable snuff-box was stolen from me. I had placed it in the pocket of my carefully-buttoned waistcoat; my coat was buttoned likewise, and I was holding both my hands over the pockets of my coat. It is true the theft occurred in a very narrow, crowded street, or more properly called passage.'[46]

In spite of the savage penalties, some of the felons were career criminals. Others were driven by desperation, the victims of economic downturns and their inability to save during the good times. Luxury trades such as tailoring, silk-weaving and cabinetmaking were highly seasonal. Many who served the aristocrats and gentry who spent the winter months in London's burgeoning West End found themselves with little trade in the summertime. Printing was less badly affected. This was due to the growing interest in newspapers, which may have been expensive for individuals but not for their multi-reader audience in the coffee houses. Books had also become part of popular culture.[47] A pressman was a skilled worker, with his eighteen shillings a week far better than the insecure eight to twelve shillings of the unskilled; while a compositor could expect a guinea or more.[48] It was the fault of the individual printer, rather than the printing trade, if he was driven to crime.

Franklin's writings do not mention whether he was physically robbed during this stay in London. He would not have been an obvious target, being sober in dress and behaviour as well as young and muscular. He also did not have far to walk to work, particularly after he moved from Little Britain to what is now Sardinia Street,[49] which cut the distance from a mile to a few hundred yards. He was also very fit: he swam the nearly three miles along the Thames from Chelsea to Blackfriars,[50] which, he tells us, he did 'whilst performing on the Way many Feats of Activity both upon and under Water, that surprised and pleased those to whom they were Novelties'. This was almost turned to spectacular advantage, as Sir William Wyndham, 'a great Man', had heard of Franklin's aquatics and of his ability to teach some friends to swim 'in a few Hours'. Sir William asked to see Franklin and offered to reward him handsomely for teaching his teenage sons. In the event, Franklin could not take this up, because he had already accepted another opportunity; though it is entertaining to ponder these words: 'from this Incident I thought it likely, that if I were to remain in England and open a Swimming School, I might get a good deal of Money'.[51] As with so much else, he would have been good at it, as we can tell from the letters full of swimming instructions that he wrote many years later.[52]

⌯

Franklin was making more money at Watts's and living frugally. He persuaded his elderly landlady near Lincoln's Inn to reduce his rent by being both a good house guest and an appreciative audience for her flood of excellent anecdotes. In spite of these adjustments, Franklin was worried about money. Not only had his own funds been depleted by Collins and exhausted by Ralph, but so had £35 supposedly being kept safe back in Philadelphia for Samuel Vernon, a friend of his brother John.

At Watts's, Franklin had a like-minded friend called Wygate. They planned to travel around Europe, picking up printing work here and there – though in which languages is not made clear. It is likely that this time Franklin's companion would not have been a drain on resources, because Wygate had rich relations. However, the avuncular Mr Denham advised against it. Better than that, he offered Franklin a job helping to prepare and run a new store back in Philadelphia that came with the expectation of Franklin first becoming a mercantile agent and then, in time, Denham's junior partner. As

Franklin put it: 'I immediately agreed, on the Terms of Fifty Pounds a Year, Pennsylvania Money; less indeed than my then Gettings as a Compositor, but affording a better Prospect.'[53] Denham also lent him the fare home. Franklin's youthful sojourn in London was at an end, but was by no means forgotten.

He regretted the state of his financial position at the end of his stay, but not 'the very ingenious Acquaintance whose Conversation was of great Advantage to me,'[54] nor the knowledge he had gained. He may have been leaving London, but London did not leave him.

∽

On 21 July 1726, Franklin and Denham were on board the *Berkshire* and bound for Philadelphia. The influence of his past nineteen months shines out in his writings from the time. Unlike the *Autobiography*, these were not impressions blurred by the passage of decades and then re-polished with the application of hindsight and maturity. There, on the pages of his 'Journal of a Voyage' and his 'Plan of Conduct', are his ideas and attitudes recorded at the very time itself, and set down for his later use.

He had a long time to collect his thoughts because contrary winds turned a journey that might have taken five weeks into one of thirteen. The weather forced unscheduled stops at Gravesend and the Isle of Wight and Franklin's Journal describes these places in the manner of Defoe, with the first condemned and the second appreciated. But there is something even more striking, as Joyce Chaplin pinpoints in *The First Scientific American: Benjamin Franklin and the Pursuit of Genius*, her authoritative biography of Franklin: 'the journal was the progenitor of all Franklin's work in the sciences. It was his first extended inquiry into the natural world – indeed the first sign that he thought he had something to say about it.'[55]

Franklin had been unable to meet Newton, but he had talked with Pemberton, Newton's collaborator. It was irrelevant that he had not read (nor ever did read) Newton's *Principia*, because the work had inspired a more general interest in science and a craze for the scientific. As Joyce Chaplin explains: 'The *Principia* was one of the most talked-about unread books of all time ... {However,} Newton made nature seem regular and rational, more accessible to human comprehension... he set new standards for the sciences; observation (as with telescopes), calculation, and re-examination of old principles. These practices had an amazing impact on the reading public's ideas of nature.'[56]

Natural philosophy, later described as science, had captured the public imagination. It was also socially acceptable. For one could have both a belief in a Christian God and an appreciation of the natural world. It was therefore not necessary to have the deistic principles that Franklin had expressed in his *Dissertation on Liberty and Necessity, Pleasure and Pain* – and later, if only for public consumption, repudiated.[57] Francis Bacon, Robert Boyle and Newton – all of whom were celebrated in the pages of the *Spectator*[58] – had created a philosophical path where observing, analysing and explaining natural phenomena could be a means of celebrating the Christian God who had created them. Alexander Pope captured the mood with his epitaph for Newton:

> Nature, and Nature's Laws lay hid in Night.
> GOD said, *Let Newton be!* And All was *Light*.[59]

At one in this context was Cotton Mather, who was given a Royal Society Fellowship on the basis of his early 'Curiosa Americana' letters and their observations of the natural world; and whose *The Christian Philosopher* (1721) has been credited as the most important initial disseminator of Newtonian science in America.[60]

On the *Berkshire*, Franklin's brilliantly analytical and practical mind focused on the world around him. He took note of the bird and marine life, spending hours watching schools of dolphins and the variances in their behaviour when faced with the lures of sailors keen to catch and cook them to supplement the ship's dwindling rations. He witnessed two eclipses, first of the sun and then of the moon. Regarding the latter, he compared the times of the mid-point of the eclipse as he observed it with that expected for London – 12.30 a.m. and 5 p.m.; from the time difference he estimated their longitude; and from that he judged they were 100 leagues (equivalent to 300 nautical miles or roughly 345 miles) from the American coast. Over the following days he tried to get members of the ship's crew to agree that the nature of the water was changing and thus his judgement was correct. With growing impatience towards this curious young man, they demurred.

Franklin also provides interesting remarks on human behaviour, contrasting the black mood on board when forever tacking into a facing wind or when becalmed with the exhilaration felt when the ship was skimming the surface under full sail. He ponders on the nature of solitude and the pain of social exclusion, which was the fate of a man caught cheating at cards. He even gives us some prototype 'Poor Richard' aphorisms, such as 'that if two persons *equal* in judgement play {a game} for a considerable sum, he that loves money most shall lose; his anxiety for the success of the game confounds him'.

Franklin must have spent time discussing his future with Denham, but the length of the voyage gave plenty of time for introspection and for Franklin to create his 'Plan of Conduct'. It comes with an introduction, but its essence is distilled in four short principles:

1. It is necessary for me to be extremely frugal for some time, till I have paid what I owe.
2. To endeavour to speak truth in every instance; to give nobody expectations that are not likely to be answered, but aim at sincerity in every word and action – the most amiable excellence in a rational being.
3. To apply myself industriously to whatever business I take in hand, and not divert my mind from my business by any foolish project of growing suddenly rich; for industry and patience are the surest means of plenty.
4. I resolve to speak ill of no man whatever, not even in a matter of truth; but rather by some means excuse the faults I hear charged upon others, and upon proper occasions speak all the good I know of everybody.[61]

This voyage, like those in the future, gave Franklin thinking time that was unfettered by the daily demands of ordinary life. Many years later, on reviewing the 'Plan',[62] he acknowledged its importance and was rather impressed with his junior self, commenting that 'it is the more remarkable, as being formed when I was so young, and yet being pretty faithfully adhered to quite through to old Age'. 'Pretty faithfully' is right, because on occasion Franklin found it impossible to adhere to his own high standards. It was, however, the starting point for an extraordinary transformation. On his next transatlantic voyage, just over three decades later, he was to return to Britain as a politician of importance in America and a natural philosopher of international fame. In the meantime he had laid the British foundation stones of some of America's longest-lasting cultural institutions.

3

_____

1726–_c._1748

Foundations

Franklin began working for Denham, and working hard; but after just a few months Denham became ill and totally incapacitated. Then Franklin himself contracted pleurisy and almost died; he was completely out of action during the spring of 1727. His illness might have killed an older man, just as Denham's constitution proved too weak and he eventually died on 4 July 1728.[1]

Franklin had worked industriously enough for Denham, who, in his will, waived the cost of Franklin's passage home and thus did something to lighten the debts. Franklin was not disheartened at going back to work for Keimer, which he did in late 1727. One can tell from his own writings that though he revered Denham, he missed his former work of printing and journalism. Keimer was open to regaining Franklin's expertise and the returnee was happy to provide it, but under the surface their relationship became more of a duel. Keimer took a greater interest in his more profitable stationery business than in printing, but he was sly. He realized that Franklin could teach the inexperienced apprentices and then be fired. However, Franklin was now more worldly-wise and recognized this opportunity to gain additional experience and strengthen his contacts before setting up his own printing business. Once, too early for either of them, Keimer insulted Franklin and the young printer walked out. However there was a rapprochement, reinstatement and a return to more cordial relations.

An opportunity for progress came when one of Keimer's apprentices, Hugh Meredith, suggested to Franklin that they leave Keimer's and set up in partnership. Franklin, however, had learned to be wary.

He realized that young Meredith was unreliable and had a liking
for the bottle, but that he had the financial backing of a father who
believed that Franklin had the technical skills and industrious attitude his son lacked. It was not a partnership that was destined to last
for many years, but it was long enough to establish the business, and
Franklin was able to buy out the Merediths in July 1730 with funding
from William Coleman and Robert Grace, both of whom were to
remain firm friends.[2] He was now set on a course of two decades
of hard work that would result in his producing the most successful American newspaper of the period, the hugely bestselling *Poor
Richard* almanacs, and a highly profitable printing business. During
that time he had settled down domestically with a common-law
wife and led a contented family life. He had also started a sequence
where he established the small beginnings of what would become
great institutions, sometimes the first of their kind on the continent.
These would develop to be strongly American in character, but more
often than not with an initial, if long-buried, foundation stone that
was British in concept, practice or both.

There is one great unknown in Benjamin Franklin's personal life:
the identity of the mother of his illegitimate son William, who
was born between September 1730 and March the following year.[3]
Franklin does not address the matter in his *Autobiography*, whereas
he chooses to tell the reader how he took Deborah Read as his
common-law wife. But here also he disguises rather than discloses
the truth of the matter. It is an important point, because it goes some
way to explaining the nature of their relationship over a cumulative
decade and a half of separation during Franklin's time in London.
Franklin's official version was that he and Deborah, the daughter
of his landlady in Philadelphia, had agreed to marry before he set
off in 1724 for London; he had then neglected to write to her, she
had concluded that he had rejected her and, quite understandably,
she had entered another marriage that quickly failed. This meant
that Franklin, after his return in 1726, had a chance to make amends
and was grateful that she accepted him in a common-law marriage.

Leo Lemay, however, presents an altogether different history based on extensive research of shipping times and postal services. One does not need to go into the minutiae of these to present his conclusion: that Franklin was chivalrous in his *Autobiography*. He judges that, far from Franklin neglecting Deborah, she in fact abandoned him in favour of marrying a potter called John Rogers, who left her and Philadelphia a year after Franklin's return.[4]

Franklin nobly picked up the pieces and, as Deborah was still technically married, took her as his common-law wife in 1730. It perhaps better explains why William was taken into their Philadelphia household and also Deborah's extraordinary forbearance during Franklin's later London years. She did not cross the Atlantic with him due to a professed fear of sea travel, but, considering matters in harsh functional terms, she was of much greater use to him in Philadelphia, where she could protect his interests. She would have been of far less value in London, out of her depth playing the expected role of hostess; and with her absent, Franklin was able to lead a public London life as a bachelor, while retaining all the domestic comforts he required.

That is not to deny that there was affection in the marriage, which produced two children: a son, Francis Folger Franklin, born in 1732, and a daughter, Sarah or 'Sally', over a decade later. For a number of years William was to be the only child in the household, because in 1736 Francis died of smallpox. He had not been inoculated. This did not mean that Franklin had held true to his brother's campaign against it; far from it. In line with his adult belief in the practical application of science, he was firmly in favour. The problem was that little Francis was a sickly child and thought not yet strong enough to fight off the mild form of the disease that inoculation created. The death brought Ben and William, if not Deborah and William, even closer together.

༄

Franklin amended his Last Will and Testament over the years, but one thing did not change: his description of himself as 'printer'. Regardless of all the other honours and titles he won, it is the word 'printer' that continuously follows his name. Rightly so, as printing was the foundation for his later success. He was suited for it by aptitude and attitude. It chimed with an immense practicality that he seems to have inherited from his father Josiah, described by Ben as 'a mechanical genius' and 'very handy in the Use of other Tradesmen's tools'.[5] At Keimer's he had found a lack of duplicate letters and, rather than wait for replacements from England, created the moulds and then the letters himself. He was therefore, in this small way, the first manufacturer of types in North America. During this same period he was able to master the intricacies of printing currency, which enabled Keimer to win the contract from the Assembly of New Jersey, though the relevant Assemblymen were soon in no doubt as to who was the brains behind the operation and whom they should invite to their houses during the three months of the project. As Franklin himself put it: 'My mind having been much more improved by Reading than Keimer's, I suppose it was for that Reason my Conversation seemed to be more valued.' Thus, after the two parted company, it was Franklin who kept the connection: 'These friends were afterwards of great Use to me, as I occasionally was to some of them.'[6] It was to stand Franklin in good stead more than three decades later.

Once in business for himself, Franklin succeeded because he was innovative and reliable. He had one other massive advantage as a printer: he was personally able to supply excellent copy. In the autumn of 1728, while in partnership with Meredith, Franklin stated his intention to start his own newspaper, to be called the *Pennsylvania Gazette*. Unfortunately, young Franklin had still not quite learned whom to trust, as he told the wrong person, who then leaked the information back to Keimer; and the latter had no compunction in stealing both idea and title, bringing out the first issue on Christmas Eve. By now Franklin had the measure of both Keimer and himself. The new paper was a threat to Andrew Bradford's existing *American Weekly Mercury*, so Franklin offered his services to Bradford as a journalist and feature writer. Keimer's limp efforts could not compete and within nine months, facing a cash crisis,[7] he sold the title to Franklin 'for a trifle'[8] and not long after departed for Barbados and further misadventures.[9]

Under Franklin's stewardship, the *Pennsylvania Gazette* was transformed. He was capable of handling everything personally – from copy to print. But more than that, he made the paper better than anything seen before in the colonies. It had more news and features. It was better written, genuinely witty and far more entertaining. Leo Lemay doesn't hold back, describing Franklin as 'the ablest journalist and the greatest innovator of newspaper techniques of his day', and credits him with a number of firsts, including the first American political cartoon and the first important newspaper interview.[10] It was a successful venture, in time bringing Franklin an estimated £750 per year, many times the income of a skilled compositor.[11]

That interview, in 1733, was with Andrew Hamilton, the legal grandee whom he had warned about Governor Keith in 1724. In March 1729 Franklin and Meredith had tried to get the contract to print the proceedings of the Assembly of Pennsylvania. This was a brave move by the young firm and the Assembly decided to retain the more established Andrew Bradford. But then Bradford made a mistake. His poor design and printing of the Assembly's Address to the Governor gave Franklin an opportunity which he cleverly grabbed by printing the Address as it should have looked and distributing a copy to each member free of charge. Bradford, unlike Keimer, was a proper rival for young Franklin and the older man upped his game. Then in October 1729 Hamilton became Speaker of the Assembly and Franklin's firm was appointed the following January. Five years after Sir William Keith's false promises, Franklin had become an official printer for Pennsylvania. Notably, demonstrating the balance in Pennsylvania politics, it was the Assembly Speaker and not the Lieutenant Governor who had the power to bestow that patronage.

It was Franklin's first appointment in public service, to be followed in 1736 by the Clerkship of the Assembly and in 1737 the position of Deputy Postmaster at Philadelphia. In contrast Sir William Keith's career had taken a distinctly downward path.[12]

✑

Franklin was true to his 'Plan of Conduct' 'to apply myself industriously to whatever business I take in hand'. He developed a 'Scheme of Employment' for ordering his day,[13] which, with its 5 a.m. starting time can be best summarized with his own aphorism of 'Early to Bed and early to rise, makes a Man healthy, wealthy and wise.'[14] Importantly, he planned two hours between 12 noon and 2 p.m. 'to read, or overlook my accounts, and dine'. Though, as he later admitted, his ambitions for self-improvement were honoured as much in the breach as in the observance, he operated on the principle that 'the best is the enemy of the good,'[15] and held to the plan when he could. He worked hard because that was his inclination, but also to clear himself of his debts: not just what he owed to Coleman and Grace for buying out Meredith but the more long-standing sum due to his brother's friend Samuel Vernon that had been frittered away on Collins and Ralph. The debt to Vernon gave his conscience 'great trouble.'[16] He was able to clear that in 1730 or soon after and by June 1733 was already repaying Grace. As for Meredith, Franklin's former partner had moved to North Carolina to farm but, failing in that, he returned to Philadelphia in 1739 and Franklin loaned him small sums over the next decade. By 1749, when he finally disappeared, he was in Franklin's debt to the tune of more than £13 and with a stock of books worth £30.[17] What would once have been a crippling debt for Franklin was now comparatively trifling and, remembering the opportunity Meredith had provided, more like charitable giving than the improvident subsidies to the feckless Collins and Ralph.

Franklin himself had another sort of debt to repay and a family breach he was determined to repair. In late 1733, Ben visited his brother James in Rhode Island and it was then that 'former Differences were forgotten' and their 'Meeting was very cordial and affectionate', and touchingly so as James was in failing health.[18] Old times and family news aside, they had much to discuss. They were both printers, publishers and editors, they were also both the producers of almanacs: James's *Almanac by 'Poor Robin'* (taking its exact title from its English precursor, published since 1663) was available in late 1727,[19] whereas Ben's – after various false starts – was first rushed out in December 1733. Ben's persona of 'Poor Richard' or 'Richard Saunders' also had an English origin in the Richard Saunder (*sic*) of the *Apollo Anglicanus* (1684–1736). The almanac contained local information, daylight and tide times, astronomy mixed with astrology and interesting facts blended with humorous articles and aphorisms.[20] There is no indication that the brothers collaborated – the jokes and sayings are different – but their efforts outshine their competitors'. James's personal involvement with *Poor Robin* lasted only a few years, as he died on 4 February 1734, his thirty-eighth birthday. Ben's with *Poor Richard* lasted a full quarter-century. Over those years it was to become extremely successful and highly profitable. The almanac was a popular publication in the colonies and there were many competing versions, but *Poor Richard* outsold all others, firstly in Pennsylvania and then along the entire Atlantic seaboard. So successful was it that even by the 1739 almanac 'Richard' has to explain that he is still 'Poor' because his printer (i.e. Franklin) takes most of the profit.[21]

Its superiority was not so much due to its facts as to its entertaining 'other matter', combined with Franklin's skills at marketing and selling.[22] As with his own journalism and his newspaper editorship, Franklin took initial inspiration from elsewhere, but then enhanced and transmuted the form or format to make it brilliantly different and highly original. With the Prefaces to the first three almanacs, Franklin adopted his satirical approach directly from Jonathan Swift's *The Bickerstaff-Partridge Papers*; he firstly introduced his character Richard Saunders as a stargazer and immediately predicted the death of a competitor – Titan Leeds, the most successful almanac maker of the middle colonies. Leeds played into his hands by publishing outraged counterblasts, which gave Franklin even more fuel for merciless fun and increased sales.[23] But by 1739, the sprite that was the 'Poor Richard' of the first few years was maturing into the character who dispensed moral improvement as part of his homespun wisdom,[24] though the next year he could not resist one final cruelly entertaining hoax about Titan Leeds, after which the much-abused fellow did actually die.[25] To the mixture of influences that had inspired 'Silence Dogood'[26] was added that of William Penn, the late founder and Proprietor of the colony of Pennsylvania, whose *Some Fruits of Solitude* contained 855 serious maxims in its 1702 edition.[27] By the time Franklin's almanac was rebranded as *Poor Richard Improved* for the 1748 edition, the eclipse of the funster Richard by the instructor Richard was complete.[28] And it was a transition that proved highly successful. As Leo Lemay points out, most of the predominantly rural colonial population read little other than the Bible, elementary school books and the annual almanac. Thus, 'The almanacs were important agents in the evolution of early American culture.'[29] But though he says of Franklin that 'as an almanac maker, he had no peer', he adds, 'Characteristically, he viewed that achievement ironically.'[30]

Following James's death, Ben took care of his brother's young son, educating him and then, in 1740, giving him an apprenticeship. Seven years later, young James returned to Rhode Island to help his mother continue the firm and Ben took a stake in return for technical and financial support. Ben also financed start-ups with former apprentices, according to a regular model. He chose the location, financed the premises, printing supplies and machinery – with standard Caslon typefaces, so large jobs could be shared between them – and he took a third of the profits during a six-year contract term, which would roll on for another six years if the partner was unwilling or unable to buy Franklin out.[31] By this means he set up more than two dozen printers,[32] with print shops from South Carolina right up to Rhode Island and across to Antigua in the West Indies.[33] This was something new. There previously had been small infra-colony networks provided by family members, but Franklin did not just rely on his family, wisely so, because his nephew Benjamin Mecom gave him a great deal of trouble, including abandoning their joint venture in Antigua in 1756.[34] Some partnerships prospered and others not, some kept close links with Franklin and others not, but taken altogether it grew to become the largest network in colonial America.[35] It was at its peak in the 1740s and 1750s, taking full competitive advantage of an absence of postal charges, a perquisite of Franklin's position as Deputy Postmaster. By 1755 a majority of the fifteen papers in the North American and West Indian colonies were published either by Franklin himself, his continuing partners or his former protégés.[36]

In 1748 Franklin took a non-executive approach to the management of his own business, creating a partnership with his former journeyman David Hall. He could afford to do so at the age of forty-two, because with his business interests and properties along the Atlantic seaboard he had become a wealthy man. He could now turn his mind more fully to the practical application of science and a more active role in public affairs.

⟡

One can say that Franklin progressed in civil society even before he established himself in business, but the two tended to dance in tandem in 1720s Philadelphia. It may have been, with Boston and New York, one of the three largest urban areas in colonial America, but its population at that point was just 7,500 or so.[37] And, in any case, Franklin, in Michael Zuckerman's words, 'did not set any sharp distinction between private pursuits and a self-conscious consideration of the public welfare.'[38] His first step, in 1727, was to form a club with his cleverer friends. This like many others was called the Junto, after the Spanish *junta* or fraternity.[39] From the very first it was serious in intent, with 'Morals, Politics or Natural Philosophy to be discussed by the company' according to fixed rules.[40] Membership was to wax, with the integration of other clubs, and to wane over the years, but the Junto only finally ceased meeting in 1765, when the surviving founder members were in their sixties and at a time when Franklin himself was in London. It provided the initial spark for an extraordinary range of civic improvements and the creation of institutions that were the first of their kind, not only in Philadelphia but in colonial America.[41] The same childhood and young adult influences that Franklin himself cites in his *Autobiography* and that underlie the 'Silence Dogood' letters can be seen inspiring Franklin and the Junto. So can Franklin's initial time in London, because, as George Boudreau explains, 'The club was the quintessential activity of the intellectual movement sweeping Anglo-America, known as the Enlightenment, and Franklin had imbibed the ideas of "clubbable men" as he frequented the taverns and coffee houses of London during his months there.'[42] This certainly nods towards young Franklin's time with the sociable Bernard Mandeville, but there is also one particular philosopher whose thinking is behind the Junto's four qualifications for membership, as they were standardized in 1732, and that is John Locke. In his *A Collection of Several Pieces* (1720) Locke laid down 'Rules of a Society which met once a week, for their improvement in useful knowledge and for the promotion of truth and Christian charity'. Would-be members had to answer three questions in the affirmative:

1. Whether he loves all men, of what profession or religion soever?
2. Whether he thinks no persons ought to be harmed in his body, name or good, for mere speculative opinions, or his external way of worship?
3. Whether he loves and seeks truth for truth's sake; and will endeavour impartially to find and receive it himself, and to communicate it to others?

As has been pointed out,[43] these are almost word for word the same as the Junto's. The Junto added another for a society dedicated to debate: 'Have you any particular disrespect to any present member?' Franklin tried to take the attitude of the Junto's additional point into his clubs in his later period in London. Sensibly so, as what would be the point of spending many hours in discussion with people whose fundamental principles one could not respect?

Locke's *A Collection of Several Pieces* is one of the oldest books belonging to the Library Company of Philadelphia. In 1731 books were expensive, even for printers; the books Franklin and his fellow Junto members wanted for reading and reference were mainly produced in London. Initially they followed Franklin's practice in London with Wilcox, the bookseller in Little Britain, and borrowed books from each other. Then fifty founder shareholders pooled funds, contributing forty shillings initially and agreeing a further ten shillings annually thereafter. From these small beginnings, as the Library Company itself proudly states, 'America's first successful public lending library and oldest cultural institution was born'.[44] The Library Company's first Secretary was the writer and naturalist Joseph Breintnall, who introduced the London-based Quaker merchant and naturalist Peter Collinson as the company's first book-purchasing agent. When supplying the first order, Collinson also donated *A View of Sir Isaac Newton's Philosophy* by Henry Pemberton (his former collaborator) and, reflective of Collinson's own eminence as a botanist, Philip

Miller's *The Gardeners Dictionary*.[45] As Breintnall's gushing letter of thanks dated 7 November 1732 testifies,[46] the subscribers were absolutely delighted. Franklin, when writing to Collinson's son in 1770, paid full tribute to the father and said that the success of the library was 'greatly owing to his kind Countenance and good Advice', and that Collinson had been the ideal person when they had 'needed a judicious Friend in London to transact the Business for them'.[47] But the greatest beneficiary of this connection would be Benjamin Franklin himself. Some years later the thoughtful Collinson was to send another gift, this time to Franklin personally. It was of practical scientific interest and it was to transform the American's already successful life.

The company gained the support of the owner of Philadelphia's largest personal library, James Logan. Having first crossed the Atlantic with William Penn in 1699, Logan had been the long-time secretary and business manager to Penn and his widow Hannah. He remained the continuing adviser to their sons, the co-Proprietors of Pennsylvania. In the words of the Library Company Committee, Logan was 'a Gentleman of universal Learning, and the best Judge of Books in these Parts'.[48] At their first meeting, Franklin and his friend Thomas Godfrey 'stayed late', hardly surprisingly, as Logan has been described as perennially desperate for intellectually stimulating company with whom he could exchange ideas and information.[49] He very much took to these young men and to their friend John Bartram, a Pennsylvanian botanist and farmer. The admiration was mutual and it was made clear to the new Librarian in November 1732 that Logan was the one non-subscriber allowed to take books out of the library. It seems that Logan and Franklin had a reciprocal arrangement for Franklin to borrow books from Logan's own collection, something of continuing benefit to this great autodidact.[50]

Franklin's relationship with Logan was one that continued to blossom over a long period. In February 1750, Logan wrote fondly to Collinson about their mutual friend: 'Our Benjamin Franklin is certainly an Extraordinary Man ... one of a singular good Judgement, but of Equal Modesty. He is Clerk of our Assembly, and there, for want of other Employment, while he sat idle, he took it into his head to think of Magical Squares, in which he outdid Frénicle himself, who published above eighty pages in folio on that subject alone.'[51]

That is some doodling! Franklin had taken the work of the French mathematician Bernard Frénicle de Bessy, refined it and created what might be regarded as a superior version of Sudoku. Here in Logan's anecdote is a fair summary of Benjamin Franklin's approach to science and of his attitude and aptitude more generally. He was happy to take up the work of others, but, having done so, he did not hesitate to subject it to his own uniquely brilliant blend of intellectual curiosity married to detailed practical application and thus, very often, to offer improvements.

Franklin was not only capable of exceptional organizational thinking when it came to the inanimate and the abstract. By 1750 he was well versed in the strategic management of relationships. A fortnight before Logan's letter to Collinson, Franklin had written to Logan that 'The magical squares, how wonderful soever they may seem, are what I cannot value myself upon, but am rather ashamed to have it known I have spent any part of my time in an employment that cannot possibly be of any use to myself or others.'[52] Thereby Franklin was admired for 'modesty' as well as 'singular judgement', when Logan wrote to Collinson,[53] and the whole exercise was of course to prove extremely useful to Franklin in further demonstrating his extraordinary mental capacity to men who were in a position to help him.

The success of this Library Company subscription initiative led Franklin to advocate a practical American application to the plans and observations he had read in Daniel Defoe.[54] In the 1750s this would lead to his proposal for the Pennsylvania Hospital and to a fire insurance scheme. But Franklin began in the 1730s with firefighting. For though William Penn had taken note of the Great Fire of London and ensured that the buildings in his new city of Philadelphia were widely spaced,[55] conflagrations were still common. Franklin's Union Fire Company (1736) was another 'first'. It used the subscription model to buy firefighting equipment and inspired many imitators.

∽

Franklin's organizational and therefore quasi-executive role in the public affairs of Pennsylvania was bound to create concern among the absentee Proprietors and their adherents on the ground. However, James Logan still looked favourably on him. In 1750 he did not hesitate to send Franklin's *Proposals Relating to the Education of Youth in Pennsylvania* to Thomas Penn, and sought to elicit Penn's support for an academy with the comment that 'The Enclosed is just now sent me from the Press by that most Ingenious Man Benjamin Franklin.'[56] After this encomium, Franklin might have been disappointed that, though this project and his plans for a hospital were of obvious public benefit, the Penns showed initial reluctance to lend their support. But it was also a sign of the decline in Logan's health and of a lack of closeness with William Penn's sons, who were increasingly suspicious of Franklin.

Actually Logan was himself being modest, as Franklin integrated almost verbatim Logan's summary account of his own library into the *Proposals*.[57] Together they propounded what is described by the University of Pennsylvania – itself the final product of the initiative, with the addition of tertiary education – as 'a unique institution' for those times, because 'Franklin's concept of higher education was new in the mid-18th-century western world'.[58]

Franklin set out the project's importance in the first sentence of the *Proposals*: 'The good education of youth has been esteemed by wise men in all ages as the surest foundation of the happiness both of private families and of commonwealths.' What is profoundly striking about the *Proposals* is that Franklin did not suggest an establishment with core principles based on the type of education he might have gained through a full course at grammar school and then Harvard.[59] That would have been the simpler approach, had this 'good work' been merely a vehicle for the social advancement of a man who added 'Esq.' to his name as soon as he was entitled to do so,[60] and who was for ever Dr Franklin from the very moment he received his first honorary doctorate. Yet, as was ever the case with the mature Franklin, he had greater ambitions. He was confident of the usefulness of his own life and of his own rectitude. He had striven to and in some cases succeeded in replicating his firm through his network of partnerships. Now he proposed an academy founded, at least in part, on what he had taught himself and thus to generate a breed of analytical and deeply practical mini-Franklins.

He was certainly keen to back up his argument in the *Proposals* so that, in the published version, his fewer than 2,400 words in the main text are supported by over three times that number in footnotes, and thus on some pages all the space, bar three lines, is taken up by the smaller type. He also has a Foreword on his influences, all British with the exception of the French ancient historian and educationalist Charles Rollin. Locke and his *Some Thoughts Concerning Education* are there, so are John Milton, Francis Hutcheson and Obadiah Walker for his *Of Education, Especially of Young Gentlemen*. Perhaps with a view to Franklin's later political connections in Britain, most striking is his citation of 'Dr George Turnbull, Chaplain to the present Prince of Wales', for his *Observations upon Liberal Education*.[61]

Most importantly, with the understandable exception of his obscuring his deistic beliefs in favour of Christian ones, the 2,359 words of that main text give a pretty clear indication of Franklin's philosophical principles as he began to attain greater prominence in the social and political life of Pennsylvania. As a personal 'credo' it is instructive, with passages on good diet and exercise including swimming. His recommended authors include his old favourites – Addison, and Trenchard and Gordon – as well as Pope and Algernon Sidney.

He recommends that the rector be a man rather like the best version of himself: 'A man of good understanding, good morals, diligent and patient, learned in the languages and sciences and a correct, pure speaker and writer of the English tongue.' And that the Academy: 'Be furnished with a library if in the country (if in the town, the town libraries may serve), with maps of all countries, globes, some mathematical instruments, an apparatus for experiments in natural philosophy, and for mechanics; prints, of all kinds, prospects, buildings and machines.'

Franklin, like his fellow Founding Father Thomas Jefferson, was a brilliant thinker and writer, but no Demosthenes. One's attention is caught when he seems, for once, to be highlighting the importance of a skill in which he was himself deficient, by asserting that 'History will show the wonderful effects of oratory ... they {the students} may be made acquainted with the best models amongst the ancients.' But then he elaborates: 'Modern political oratory being chiefly performed by the pen and the press, its advantages over the ancient in some respects are to be shown; as that its effects are more extensive, and more lasting.'

The *Proposals* is a document worth reading in its entirety,[62] but some of the passages on history are particularly relevant for demonstrating Franklin's educational priorities. Thus he advocates the study of 'the best modern histories, particularly of our mother country; then of these colonies; which should be accompanied with observations on their rise, increase, use to Great Britain ...' 'With the history of men, times, and nations should be read at proper hours or days some of the best *histories of nature*', then perhaps most noteworthy for its practicality: 'The *history of commerce*, of the invention of arts, rise of manufactures, progress of trade, change of its seats, with the reasons and causes, may also be made entertaining to youth, and will ... naturally introduce a desire to be instructed in mechanics, and to be informed of the principles of that art by which weak men perform such wonders, labour is saved and manufacture is expedited.' This last was a clear exposition of how the colonies with their wealth of raw materials and growing labour force could and should become a powerful motor for Britain's economic expansion.

It was a bold plan, but it suffered dilution and then abandonment when his absences on business and a deepening divide with the Proprietary party led to his removal as President of the Trustees in 1756. The other Trustees wanted the Academy, designated a college in 1755, to be more like Harvard, Yale and William & Mary, institutions designed to produce church ministers rather than mechanical engineers.[63] Only much later would Franklin's vision be realized, not only at the University of Pennsylvania but throughout the Western world.[64]

However, Franklin would also provide the organizational ability needed to create the American Philosophical Society (1743). It was modelled on the Royal Society and still 'promotes useful knowledge in the sciences and humanities through excellence in scholarly research'.[65] Based on the idea of John Bartram for forming an organization that linked together 'natural philosophers' from all the American colonies, it was the first cross-colonial learned society. It was important for Franklin, because it established a network that would, with the active support of Peter Collinson, link him into the European scientific communities.

4

---

c.1748–1757

Conductor

In 1681 an area of North America almost the size of England, taken from the Dutch during the wars of the 1660s and 1670s, was granted to the Quaker William Penn by a Royal Charter of Charles II. As the Charter stated, it was hoped that the new colony would serve the Crown by 'reducing the Savage Natives by gentle and just manners to the love of civil Society and Christian Religion.'[1] Most importantly it would be a Proprietary colony owned and run by William Penn on Quaker principles, but as a 'holy experiment' of religious toleration. Its capital was to be Philadelphia, built from scratch on the banks of the Delaware River. At its inception the new colony was very thinly populated, but there were existing inhabitants: as well as the Dutch and Indians these included Swedes and Finns and some, mainly Anglican, English.[2] The numbers, though, were soon to be swollen by a religiously diverse population from throughout the British Isles, together with a large number of mainly Lutheran Germans.[3]

Penn arrived in late 1682 and spent two years settling the administration before urgent business called him back to England. He was unable to return to his colony until 1699, when he did so with his second wife Hannah and a young James Logan in tow. He stayed there for under two years before returning to England in 1701 and for good.[4] He lived for another seventeen years but, increasingly troubled by ill health, he was forced to put the affairs of the colony in other hands. Because of his lack of personal supervision, his intention of a controlled 'holy experiment' became less controllable.

Penn had intended his to be a personal rule and to have final approval over those elected as sheriffs, justices, coroners and to a provincial council designed to serve as the upper house of a bicameral legislature whose lower house would be expected to pass legislation but not to initiate it. Had he been there in person he might have achieved that intention, but a succession of lieutenant governors acting as deputies were unable to do so in his absence. By 1701 Penn had been forced to retreat from his position of expecting to exercise power 'far greater than any kings [sic] governor in America'[5] and to share it with an oligarchy. As George Boudreau describes it: 'The colony's new one-house legislature would have more power than any other elected body in England's North American colonies, including the right to elect their speaker and to draft legislation. The Council was now just an advisory body for the Governor, and the Governor could not dissolve the legislature at his will.'[6]

It was a recipe for deadlock. The consequences might have been avoided had Penn, whose personal finances were in a very bad state by 1712, been able to sell his lands and his administrative rights to Queen Anne and make Pennsylvania a royal colony. It was the obvious solution and one that the Crown advocated. However, in that year Penn had the first of a series of debilitating strokes, and matters were delayed and shelved on Anne's death in 1714.

The Penns remained absentee landlords, ruling through assorted lieutenant governors many of whom were in conflict with the legislative Assembly, and with a hard-pressed James Logan trying to bring order to their financial affairs. William and Hannah's three sons, John, Thomas and Richard, had no interest in their father's 'holy experiment', or in the Quaker religion itself. They had abandoned Quakerism for the Church of England and acceptance within the social elite back in England. Their intention was to squeeze as much profit as possible from the colony so they could finance their social ambitions across the Atlantic in what they considered to be their real home.

In 1732 Thomas Penn was the first Proprietor to set foot in the colony for over thirty years and he received a warm welcome on arrival.[7] His personal rule during that single nine-year stay in the colony did not, however, bring harmony to the relationship between Assembly and Executive. Thomas Penn was rigorous and meticulous.

Bearing in mind what he was trying to achieve, he was also extremely ambitious, particularly in attempting to collect annual 'quit rents' – payable in lieu of quasi-feudal dues – from widely dispersed property owners. He was determined to increase his control of the land register and of the sales it produced from a wider area. To do this he had to ensure clear title, involving negotiating in poor faith with Indian tribes, the worst example of this being the infamous 'Walking Purchase' of 1737 – rightfully described as 'the most egregious land grab in eighteenth-century America'.[8] These activities effectively upset the balance of territory between the Indian tribes and created actual and potential conflict between displaced Indians and the incomers, mainly 'Scotch-Irish' and Germans, who sought to establish themselves in these new areas of 'settlement'.

How Franklin was to fit into the fractious relationship between Assembly and Proprietors during the 1730s, 1740s and early 1750s was to call for some careful management on his part. He needed the support of the Proprietary element for his initiatives in public works, something more easily gained through his relationship with James Logan, and thus did not want to be seen to be acting against Proprietary interests either in person or, as Pennsylvania's leading newspaperman, in print. His position was somewhat protected up to the retirement of his mentor Andrew Hamilton in 1739, as the Speaker of the Assembly showed the way in adjudicating between the interests of the Proprietors and those they sought to govern.[9] It also explains what has been described as Franklin's 'extreme reticence'[10] during a period of great conflict between the Assembly and Thomas Penn, supported by his Council. Instead, Franklin carried on with his business and his Clerkship duties and patiently observed. He was not yet ready for personal political engagement,[11] besides which he was quite able to stay silent when presented with an unresolved problem or with people he did not know. It became a lifelong habit and one he would employ in London, even at his favourite 'Club of Honest Whigs', as he called it, where among trusted friends he was described as 'the life of the club; but when a stranger was introduced was always mute'.[12]

What brought Franklin to the fore was the deadlock between the

Proprietors and the Assembly that threatened to leave Philadelphia defenceless in time of war.

Spain had been fighting Britain in the West Indies and on the southern part of the Atlantic coast since 1740 and in 1744 she was formally joined by France, when Europe's War of the Austrian Succession spread to North America as King George's War. On the whole the actual fighting stayed further south, but by 1747 Philadelphia shipping was under attack and an assault on the city by French forces was a real possibility. With the pacifist Quaker-dominated Assembly refusing to vote money or cede power to the Proprietors and their Lieutenant Governor, it seemed that the city would be undefended. That is, until Franklin used the power of the press to write an article entitled 'Plain Truth' for his *Pennsylvania Gazette* in order to point out the danger. It attacked Quaker Assemblymen and Proprietors alike and was a call to action that led to Franklin being the prime mover in creating a 10,000-man voluntary militia complete with artillery batteries and small arms. This was achieved through financial subscription, including, intriguingly, a lottery. Had Philadelphia remained unprepared, a seaborne invasion up the Delaware River would have been a real possibility. This was recognized within the colony, as was Franklin's role in forestalling it. Lemay succinctly describes what this meant for Franklin personally: 'When peace was proclaimed in August 1748, he was the most popular person in Pennsylvania.'[13]

This brought a qualitative change in Franklin's position: the newly non-executive printer and long-time functionary as Clerk of the Assembly had taken centre stage. He had the support of prominent Church of England men such as the merchant William Allen and clergyman Richard Peters, who aligned themselves with the Proprietors, and he had also won over rich Quaker merchants whose trading business was being devastated by enemy privateers. There were many Quakers in the Assembly who were furious, but not quite enough to get him sacked from the Clerkship. Thomas Penn – although the Militia Association provided the military expenditure he had long advocated, and he even admitted the success of the initiative to an outsider[14] – was incandescent with rage about the means used.

He believed the reaction to a temporary alarm had caused permanent damage to good government, as he wrote to one associate: 'The paper called "Plain Truth" I am afraid has done much mischief, as such a spirit raised in a people cannot be of any service, but under proper and legal regulations.'[15]

He was even more pointed in letters to Richard Peters, writing that he could not believe that James Logan had supported the Association; and, using an allusion to the English Civil War, he described the establishment of 'a military commonwealth' as 'little less than treason'.[16] Warming to his theme, he added, 'This Association is founded on a contempt to Government, and cannot end in anything but anarchy and confusion.'[17]

Penn was in no doubt as to where the chief blame lay, but in a back-handed compliment to Franklin's new importance he described him thus: 'He is a dangerous Man and I should be very Glad he inhabited any other Country, as I believe him of a very uneasy Spirit. However as he is a Sort of Tribune of the People, he must be treated with regard.'[18] By 'regard' Penn certainly did not mean respect. He might have substituted the word 'Plebs' for 'people', in the manner of an ancient Roman patrician. And he had to take note of Franklin as their 'Tribune', because the artisan class were able to vote in elections and thus had political power.

As the author of 'Plain Truth', Franklin had signed himself as 'A Tradesman of Philadelphia'. It was an accurate description of a proud and successful printer and craftsman. He was supported by the 'leather-apron men' of Philadelphia because they saw him as one of their own. They continued to do so, even following his retirement from the day-to-day management of his printing firm the following year.[19]

∽

The next decade was a time of ever-increasing prominence for Franklin.

In 1748, in recognition of his role as an active citizen he was elected to Philadelphia's Common Council, which governed the city under the mayor. In 1751 he was elected to the Pennsylvania Assembly, his son William being elected to replace him as Clerk. He was soon appointed to all the key committees by Speaker Isaac Norris who, incidentally, was James Logan's son-in-law. He continued to advocate the position of the Proprietary element in pressing for continuing military expenditure – and that in the face of the outright hostility of a Quaker party minority under Israel Pemberton and with only the grudging, qualified acceptance of the majority under Norris. However, he did fully support the Quaker party's three major policy initiatives to increase the power of the Assembly and to limit fundamentally that of the Proprietors: by making the Proprietors bear part of the expenses for Indian relations; through the Assembly gaining control of finances; and by giving the Assembly the ability to tax Proprietary lands.[20] More than that, Franklin soon had a leading position as an indispensable behind-the-scenes organizer.

In 1753 he was appointed joint Deputy Postmaster General for North America. This was not a sinecure but a British government position with a financial risk, or, given Franklin's administrative skills, a possible handsome profit. Peter Collinson, who knew the Postmaster, supported Franklin's candidacy along with William Allen, Philadelphia's richest man, who mistakenly believed – as did Thomas Penn – that this patronage would bend Franklin more to the Proprietary interest.[21]

In 1754, Franklin's growing reputation outside Pennsylvania was recognized when he was part of the Pennsylvania delegation to the Albany Congress (along with Isaac Norris, Richard Peters, the Indian expert Conrad Weiser and John Penn, Thomas's twenty-four-year-old nephew and Lieutenant Governor). Weiser's participation was particularly pertinent, as Lord Halifax, President of the Board of Trade in London, had commanded the Governor of New York to bring together representatives of the colonies of Connecticut, Maryland, Massachusetts, New Hampshire, New York, Pennsylvania and Rhode Island to improve relations with the Indians. Halifax's instruction was 'that all the Provinces be (if practicable) comprised in one general Treaty to be made in his Majesty's name, it appearing to us that the practice of each Province making a separate Treaty for itself in its own name is very improper and may be attended with great inconveniency to His Majesty's Service.'[22]

By the time the Congress met on 19 June 1754, the representatives knew of a skirmish at Jumonville Glen, between fewer than three dozen French troops and a slightly larger group of British, with Indian allies, commanded by twenty-two-year-old Major George Washington.[23] No one could have anticipated that this marked the beginning of what, from 1756, was to develop into the Anglo-French struggle for global supremacy of the Seven Years' War, but the British government had been prescient in seeing a need for the colonies to be brought into closer collaboration for frontier defence. However, a far greater ambition for a number of the representatives was to suborn the Indians for the advantage of their own colony.[24]

Franklin was not involved with such sordid backstage dealings. He could see a much bigger opportunity for the British empire and for himself. He fastened on the strategic importance of lands in the Ohio Valley, seeing that two new colonies there would be a bulwark against French expansion from the interior.[25] He also saw the potential there for investment of his own, as he continued to do up to 1775 – and beyond. Working with a number of others, including Thomas Pownall (whose younger brother, John, was Secretary to the Board of Trade) and Thomas Hutchinson (the personal representative of Governor Shirley of Massachusetts), Franklin conceived a plan for a more permanent intercolonial representative assembly. This would be a Grand Council to meet once a year, with representatives drawn in proportion from the then eleven American colonies, with the largest – Massachusetts Bay and Virginia – each having seven representatives, and the smallest – New Hampshire and Rhode Island – just two. The Grand Council was to be served by 'a general government' to co-ordinate policy on defence, trade and Indian affairs. The general government would work with an appointee of the British Crown to be called, intriguingly, the 'President General'. Much to the disappointment of its framers, the Albany Plan was rejected by the colonial Assemblies – some did not even bother to debate it. Intercolonial rivalry would continue and London, as some ministers wished anyway,[26] would need to send a general to co-ordinate defence.

As far as Franklin was concerned, logic had not prevailed – the logic that pointed to an America which was not to consist of separate entities that sent natural resources to Britain and received manufactured goods in return, but was one whole, not just of itself but of an integrated and greater Britain. In his 22 December letter to Governor Shirley he began with sentiments that echoed those of Daniel Defoe,[27] but went on to portray the potential of British America:

> Now I look on the Colonies as so many Counties gained to Great Britain, and more advantageous to it than if they had been gained out of the sea around its coasts, and joined to its land. For being in different climates, they afford greater variety of produce, and materials for more manufactures; and being separated by the ocean, they increase much more its shipping and seamen; and since they are all included in the British Empire, which has only extended itself by their means; and the strength and wealth of the parts is the strength and wealth of the whole; what imports it to the general state, whether a merchant, a smith, or a hatter grow rich in *Old* or *New* England? And if, through increase of people, two smiths are wanted for one employed before, why may not the *new* smith be allowed to live and thrive in the *new Country*, as well as the *old* one in the *Old*? In fine, why should the countenance of a state be *partially* afforded to its people, unless it be most in favour of those who have most merit? and if there be any difference, those who have most contributed to enlarge Britain's empire and commerce, increase her strength, her wealth, and the numbers of her people, at the risk of their own lives and private fortunes in new and strange countries, methinks ought rather to expect some preference.[28]

It was a clear-sighted vision of the future. He saw just how America, with its vast lands, abundant resources and a population doubling every twenty-five years, could contribute both to Britain's future and to that of proud Britons such as himself.

In the short term, however, the future of Pennsylvania itself was anything but clear. Its politics were energized by the urgent need to defend the frontier against the French and those Indians who were their allies. As in 1747, positive action was blocked through political deadlock – not this time by the Assembly, which had successively voted money in 1752, 1753 and 1754, but by the lieutenant governors. They, under instruction from the Proprietors, had vetoed the bills as part of their protection of Proprietorial privilege.[29] By the end of 1755 the position had become so urgent that the Secretary of State in London warned Penn of a potential 'Parliamentary Inquiry'; he, under advice, offered a gift of £5,000 and the Assembly for their part voted a £60,000 supply bill.[30]

There was no doubt now as to which side Franklin was on. He had become, with the possible exception of Norris, the most important man in the Assembly, which greatly benefited from his gifts for strategy and propaganda. His opponent in these arts was the Reverend William Smith, a man Franklin had previously hand-picked for a role very dear to his heart: that of Rector of the Academy. Franklin had misjudged someone who, after meeting Thomas Penn in England in 1753, had become the Proprietors' man. By the winter of 1755–6 he was Franklin's vituperative enemy.

It was the Anglican Smith who co-ordinated an attempted knock-out blow against the Quakers in early 1756. This was the presentation to the Privy Council in London of a petition signed by William Allen and the leaders of the Proprietary faction that Parliament enact a loyalty oath, similar to the one for nonconformists in England, which would naturally debar Quakers from membership of the Assembly. The Privy Council did not send it to Parliament due to the organized opposition by leading Quakers in England such as Collinson and his close friend Dr John Fothergill (Thomas Penn's own physician) who had the support of the President of the Council, Earl Granville (Thomas Penn's own brother-in-law). The petition failed and, by failing, it merely succeeded in driving the Pennsylvanian Quaker party and Franklin closer together.[31]

But its very deployment showed the increased intensity of the struggle, and for Franklin the personal consequence was that Allen, Peters and other Proprietary-supporting Trustees removed him from his cherished position as President of the College (formerly Academy) of Philadelphia. Former friends had become fierce personal as well as political enemies. Added to Smith's intense open hostility, there was a particular bitterness from Allen who had been a generous supporter of Franklin's public projects and who, a quarter-century before, had appointed Franklin to his first office as a Freemason. Allen was now Grand Master of Pennsylvania, with Franklin as his Deputy.[32]

The acrimony at the College was repeated in January 1757, when Franklin was not even consulted on a decision as to who should replace another Trustee who had recently died. Franklin was outraged, as Richard Peters related to Thomas Penn, telling him that a furious Franklin had declared that 'it was a piece of Justice due to him as he was the Father and principal support of the Academy' (sic). Peters added, 'this is true, but for all that it was not thought proper to gratify his Pride which now grows insufferable.'[33]

As for Thomas Penn himself, Franklin, in the words of Lemay, 'thought Penn proud, avaricious and despicable'. Penn, in his turn, 'thought Franklin a rabble-rousing, contemptible leader of the poor and "lower sort" of people.'[34] Both, according to their own lights, were right. By 1756, what had begun with Major Washington's skirmish at Jumonville had developed into the Seven Years' War. Philadelphia again seemed under threat. Franklin once more responded by raising the militia and this time commanding it. He was ostentatiously saluted whilst doing so, a severe breach of etiquette and an open insult to Thomas Penn. Richard Peters, naturally, reported this to Penn, whose fury increased yet further. Franklin tried to dismiss the matter as 'a silly affair',[35] and something he had not initiated. He defended himself in a letter to Peter Collinson, writing: 'I must tell you the Matter as it was. The People happen to love me. Perhaps that's my Fault.'[36]

Penn saw things very differently and complained of this 'piece of state' to the long-serving Lord Chancellor, the Earl of Hardwicke, who was apparently 'much astonished at it'.[37] Penn had been busy, reporting that he had informed the Duke of Cumberland, the Earl Granville and Commons Leader Henry Fox of Franklin's 'real character'.[38]

∽

Franklin – Penn's 'Tribune of the People' – had in less than a decade transformed himself from being the long-time observer and recorder of the Assembly's proceedings to becoming its most important participant. This was, in itself, an exceptional achievement for the non-Quaker outsider. But it was merely the latest stage of an extraordinary social climb from the time when young Ben had arrived in Philadelphia with no money and no connections, though with a skill and a sharp intelligence that would be honed through experience.

By 1757, Franklin had every justification for holding an extremely high opinion of himself, and for an altogether different reason. His success in what had started as a hobby had gained him renown in Europe as one of the leading figures of the eighteenth-century scientific Enlightenment.

It was for his work in the field of physics and specifically in that of electricity that he won an astounding international reputation in middle age, and the reason Immanuel Kant described him in 1755 as 'the Prometheus of modern times'.[39] It was why David Hume in 1762 called him America's 'first philosopher' and 'first Great Man of letters';[40] why Chatham, in the House of Lords in 1775, hailed him as 'an Honour not to the English Nation only but to Human Nature';[41] and why, in France, Turgot would hail him as having 'snatched lightning from the heavens' as well as 'the sceptre from tyrants'[42] and Mirabeau, after Franklin's death, would elegize him as the 'sage whom two worlds claim'.[43]

Over the last 150 years the most celebrated popular image of Franklin the scientist is of his 1752 kite experiment, designed to draw electricity from the clouds and safely take it down to earth. By the 1860s, its re-imagining in pictures had taken years off the age of Ben's son and assistant, transforming the twenty-one-year-old William into a much younger boy. One can even say that this image became common currency, because it was printed on issues of United States banknotes.[44] The picture varies in later reproductions: sometimes William is restored to his proper age but Ben looks more like the man at the time of the Declaration of Independence than his forty-six-year-old self, but these are just added details to a faulty initial premise. In the 1750s and 1760s it was not the kite experiment that was the starting point for Franklin's extraordinary fame. His own kite experiment followed many already undertaken in France, some of which were successful in drawing down atmospheric electricity and, of those, some fatally so to the experimenter involved. And it was merely an additional proof to a theory Franklin had already proved. It is appropriate that Franklin sent a description of the kite flight to Peter Collinson, as Collinson and Fothergill had been crucial in their support for his work,[45] with Collinson adding Franklin and John Bartram to an international correspondence network that included the Swedish taxonomist Carl Linnaeus and his fellow countryman, the botanist Pehr Kalm.[46]

Collinson was himself a man of energy and curiosity: as Fothergill said of him, 'he suffered nothing useful, in either art or science to escape him'.[47] Collinson recognized somebody equally motivated in Franklin. As early as 1745 he had sent Leyden jars and other equipment to Franklin and by 1747 their recipient had sufficient time to make proper use of them. Franklin found this work, which combined theory and practice, totally absorbing. As he wrote to Collinson on 28 March: 'I never was before engaged in any study that so totally engrossed my attention and my time as this has lately done; for what with making experiments when I can be alone, and repeating them to my Friends and Acquaintance, who, from the novelty of the thing, come continually in crowds to see them, I have, during some months past, had little leisure for any thing else.'[48]

Little wonder at the crowds' enjoyment at the new phenomenon of seeing the sparks fly. The experiments would have attracted those with a ghoulish tendency, because this 'playing with fire' could have dire consequences if things went wrong. Franklin was honest enough to tell Collinson, and thus us, of what happened when he was about to kill a turkey by electric shock, because 'Birds killed in this Manner eat uncommonly tender.' Distracted for a moment, he managed to put a shock through himself instead. There was a flash and a crack, neither of which he personally saw or heard, as the numbing was so quick. He reported that 'my Breastbone was sore for a Week after, [as] if it had been bruised. What the Consequence would be, if such a Shock were taken through the Head, I know not.'⁴⁹ He was more careful after that. However, as was his wont, he noted down all the circumstances and effects in detail. As ever, he was interested in the practical applications of his experiments and he later told Dr John Pringle how he had used controlled electrotherapy to strengthen 'paralytic Limbs'.⁵⁰

Less than two months after his letter of March 1747, Franklin was writing to Collinson again to describe how his innovative and successful experiments had produced some startling results. However, in spite of the support of both Collinson and Fothergill – both well-connected Royal Society Fellows – and their efforts to publicize his findings, Franklin only began to gain some proper recognition in 1751. That April, at Collinson's request, Edward Cave of London published Franklin's reports of his experiments in a volume entitled *Experiments and Observations on Electricity made at Philadelphia in America*, edited and with an Introduction by Fothergill. The next year it appeared in France in French. In both editions men of science were invited to try out the experiments for themselves. The French were first to take up the challenge.

The French knew about electrical conduction. The King's official experimenter Abbé Nollet had demonstrated it to Louis XV by linking together 180 members of the Royal Guard and passing a charge through them – the sort of hair-raising entertainment that was popular at both Versailles and Paris.⁵¹ Nollet repeated the experiment and made over 200 Carthusian monks involuntarily leap into the air simultaneously.⁵² But he did not support Franklin's theories. The Comte de Buffon and Thomas-François Dalibard did, though; and in May 1752, with a large, pointed rod driven into the earth, Dalibard drew atmospheric electricity downwards in a way that Franklin was to repeat with his kite experiment. Fortunately in 1752 Britain and France were at peace, so when Dalibard reported his results the achievements of the provincial Briton could be celebrated unreservedly, and the story passed on to the London papers. That initial French connection would have an uncontemplated dividend for Franklin and France a quarter of a century later, but it also provoked a reaction in London. Franklin was awarded the Royal Society's highest award, the Copley Medal, for 1753. It is still awarded annually today and has immense prestige[53] – in the eighteenth century it was pre-eminent. Franklin's two immediate predecessors were his fellow 'electrician' John Canton (who would win it again in 1764) and John Pringle, who would become one of Franklin's greatest friends, as would Joseph Priestley (winner in 1772). Other recipients with a very close connection would be William Watson (1745), William Hewson (1769), Captain Cook (1776) and Benjamin Wilson (1760), a friend who would become an enemy.

Franklin was the first Briton from outside the British Isles to gain the award. As a provincial outsider, Franklin had been treated with scepticism by the scientific establishment, but the support of the French, the championing of Collinson and Fothergill and 'proofs' provided by Canton had won the day.[54] As Joyce Chaplin highlights in *The First Scientific American*: 'In no time at all, admirers attached the terms *philosopher* and *genius* to Franklin. The first word did not even need the modifier *natural* before it: the sciences were the apex of learning, philosophy for the modern age. Poets, clergymen, naturalists, and complete nobodies all agreed.'[55] This was about more than drawing atmospheric electricity down to earth and taming its destructive power through his invention of the lightning conductor. The colonial American had, using his acute analytical powers, made a major breakthrough in theoretical physics with his one-fluid theory that identified the two kinds of electricity as positive and negative and their tendency to seek equilibrium.[56] He had introduced names and concepts still in use, such as battery, charge, conductor, plus, minus and many more. Yet far greater even than that, his theories, themselves based on sound Newtonian principles, provided the starting point for the later industrialization and then domestication of electrical power which would revolutionize everyday life.

Franklin after his death was compared to Leonardo da Vinci.[57]

These two great polymaths have much in common, not least because of the number of their achievements. Among those in science alone, Franklin was the first to identify the workings of the Gulf Stream, and he created a new type of stove and a new musical instrument in the glass armonica. But it was his work in the field of electricity that made him famous, producing a greater self-confidence for his work in other areas, or what Richard Peters termed his 'insufferable pride'. The *Oxford English Dictionary* notes that the first literal use of the word 'electrify' was in 1747, but its first figurative use, as in 'to startle, rouse, excite, as though with an electric shock', dates to 1752, the year when Franklin's scientific eminence was recognized.

It was thus no surprise that in 1757, with the French and their Indian allies on the march in Pennsylvania and the Assembly and the Proprietors once again at an impasse over the provision of money for proper defence, it was Franklin whom the Assembly authorized to travel to London to address their concerns to Penn directly. Though in view of what they thought of each other, it promised to be an interesting meeting.

Franklin's mission was urgent. He knew from his own experience the vulnerability of Pennsylvania. What had surprised him were the limitations of the British forces arriving in North America. More than that, he had been shocked by the mixture of arrogance and ineptitude of the British generals in the early stages of what would be a global war between Britain and France.

5

1757

Return to London

Franklin's return to England in 1757 would be rather different from his maiden voyage of over thirty years before. The fifty-one-year-old Franklin would be travelling in proper style and instead of James Ralph he had William, his son and secretary, for companionship. With them were Benjamin Franklin's personal household slave Peter, and William's, whom they called King. All were booked to travel on the *Halifax*, a packet (or mail boat), which was to sail from New York on 15 March,[1] but the British Commander-in-Chief, John Campbell, Earl of Loudoun, arrived in Philadelphia and demanded that Franklin join him in conference, so the ship was missed. This time it was Franklin's sea stores that were enjoyed by others. Franklin and Loudoun travelled separately to New York, and Franklin boarded the *General Wall*, ready to depart on Friday, 8 April. But the ship did not move, either then or during the next three days. Everyone had to wait for General Loudoun's important dispatches, which consistently failed to appear as each new day ended. As time went by, a second and then a third packet boat were also ready to sail.

For a very casual observer, this delay would have appeared to have nothing to do with Loudoun, for he was always writing whenever he was visited by Franklin or others. But Franklin suspected that indecision was Loudoun's vice, and it was a feeling confirmed on meeting a messenger who had been waiting a fortnight to take urgent dispatches to Philadelphia and who described the Earl's approach as like St George on an inn sign, 'always on horseback, and never rides on'.[2]

Rather than just wait, Franklin risked missing his ship and travelled the few miles to Woodbridge in New Jersey to settle some private business. From there on 21 May he wrote respectfully to Loudoun for information: 'I hear that it is reported, that the second Packet is to accompany the Fleet, and that the third may probably be sooner in England. If this is so, a Hint of it from your Secretary would be esteemed a great Favour.'[3] Towards the end of May there were reports that the French fleet was sailing north from the West Indies, which would threaten the whole expedition, but Franklin hoped he could just dismiss it as 'Town Talk'.[4]

There was at last some movement in early June, when the Franklins with their two slaves boarded the *General Wall* on the 5th and it sailed the short distance south to the spit of land known as Sandy Hook, at the entrance to New York Bay. Many passengers preferred to stay on board ship, expecting the order to depart to be given at any time and fearing they might be left behind. Yet still they waited. In the meantime they consumed their sea stores and had to buy more.

Finally, all three packet boats, now part of a large convoy of more than 100 ships, left 'the Hook' on 20 June. The Earl was with them, as was his army, as he had decided to attack Fort Louisburg on Cape Breton Island. Decision made, he soon changed his mind. All three packets were commanded to stay close to the flagship to await dispatches. Finally, after five days, Franklin's ship was allowed to set sail for Falmouth, England's port for mail ships for a century and a half.[5] Furious as Franklin was at the delay, it could have been worse: Loudoun detained one of the other packets, the *Harriott*, complete with its passengers, until October.[6]

Franklin's view of Loudoun as a commander is hardly surprising: 'I then wondered much how such a Man came to be entrusted with so important a Business as the Conduct of a great Army.'[7] When Franklin had first met the Earl the year before, he had written to his friend William Strahan in London and told him how impressed he had been.[8] He had now most definitely changed his mind. He expected far better from the ministers in London.

⁓

Once more Franklin used the voyage as an opportunity for reflection and a time to prepare for the life he was to lead at his journey's end. On his 1726 voyage he had created his 'Plan of Conduct' for the return to Philadelphia; now in 1757 he prepared for London with a final written contribution from 'Poor Richard', his American provincial persona. It was a tour de force: the most famous of all the 'Poor Richard' writings is 'the Harangue' introduction to *Poor Richard Improved, 1758*. It is dated 7 July 1757, when the *General Wall* was still at sea.

With, as ever, an eye for a healthy profit, Franklin reworked and reused some of the best of the back catalogue of pithy sayings for this final offering. Of course, as with any 'Best of', the individual reader might disagree with the selection. For instance, two from the very first *Poor Richard* of 1735 – 'Necessity never made a good bargain' and 'Three may keep a secret, if two of them are dead' – were not selected. Neither was 'Forewarned, Forearmed' from the next year. All three make it into the current *Oxford Dictionary of American Quotations*.[9] However, *Poor Richard Improved, 1758* includes a number of other well-known adages: the aforementioned 'Early to Bed and early to rise, makes a Man healthy, wealthy and wise';[10] 'God helps them that help themselves'; 'There are no Gains without Pains'; 'Little Strokes fell great Oaks'; 'the used Key is always bright'; and 'a Word to the Wise is enough'. One of his purported aphorisms, 'a penny saved is a penny earned' – actually 'a penny saved is a penny got' – was expressed elsewhere by another of his personae, 'Celia Single'.[11] It is a rare case where his original 'saying' has been improved by posterity; normally he fine-tuned the work of others. Franklin was quite open about it. Those in the 'Harangue' (separately published from 1774 as *The Way to Wealth*) are recited by another created character, 'Father Abraham', who delivers a secular sermon full of the proverbial maxims of 'Poor Richard'. This allows 'Richard Saunders' himself to say:

I found the good man had thoroughly studied my almanacs, and digested all I had dropped on those topics during the course of five-and-twenty years. The frequent mention he made of me must have tired anyone else, but my vanity was wonderfully delighted with it, though I was conscious that not a tenth part of the wisdom was my own which he ascribed to me, but rather the *gleanings* I had made of the sense of all ages and nations.

In his painstaking analysis for his article 'Franklin's *The Way to Wealth*: A Florilegium of Proverbs and Wise Sayings', Stuart Gallacher is not convinced that it was even as much as a 'tenth part' and describes the whole as 'not a creation of expressions, but rather a collection'.[12] So it is entertaining that so many of these maxims are credited to Franklin himself, when what he was doing was adapting other people's sayings and doing so from the humble 'honest-to-goodness' perspective of his created character of Richard Saunders. In that sense, 'Poor Richard' is less Benjamin Franklin than 'Silence Dogood', 'Celia Single' and other Franklin creations such as 'Obadiah Plainman' and 'Polly Baker'. But with 'Poor Richard', 'actor' and 'role' have over time become conflated in the public mind.

The Way to Wealth has been staggeringly successful. There were 145 editions in the years before 1800 alone,[13] and it has seldom, if ever, been out of print since. But its 'be *industrious* and *free*; be *frugal* and *free*'[14] elements have overshadowed the great remainder of 'Poor Richard's' common-sense advice. And there has been an even greater distortion: a re-imagining of Franklin that celebrates him not so much as a highly successful entrepreneur but as a 'greed is good capitalist'. This is a complete misunderstanding of Franklin's approach towards money. He was not interested in his wealth for its own sake, but in the fact that it enabled him to pursue activities of private interest and public benefit: the proper pursuits of someone who could call himself and be called a gentleman. He summed up his attitude, just two years after his retirement from active printing, in a 1750 letter to Strahan:

Your sentiments of the general Foible of Mankind, in the Pursuit of Wealth to no End, are expressed in a Manner that gave me great Pleasure in reading. They are extremely just, at least they are perfectly agreeable to mine. But London Citizens, they say, are ambitious of what they call *dying worth* a great Sum. The very Notion seems to me absurd ... I imagine that what we have above what we can use is not properly *ours*, though we possess it; and that the rich Man who *must die* was no more *worth* what he leaves than the debtor who *must pay*.[15]

The area that interested Franklin for its own sake was scientific discovery and its practical application. He proudly refused to patent any of his many inventions, including the lightning conductor, taking the view 'That as we enjoy great Advantages from the Inventions of Others, we should be glad of an Opportunity to serve others by any Invention of ours, and this we should do freely and generously.'[16] In that sense, if Franklin is representative of a more modern tradition, it is of those of great wealth embracing philanthropy. Franklin was rightfully peeved when others took out patents themselves, even more so when he believed ineffective modifications were made to his inventions. One such case was in 1781 when a London man patented what is otherwise known as the Franklin stove, but not before, as Franklin believed, 'making some changes in the Machine, which rather hurt its Operation'[17] – though, truth be told, Franklin's own design was far from perfect. But Franklin's basic point held good: that the spirit of the age was that scientific research should be collaborative and its benefits available for humanity.

The huge sales of *Poor Richard* – even by the time of the 1739 almanac, 'Richard' was making excuses for the continuing use of the prefix 'Poor'[18] – were a notable part of the business success that enabled Franklin to retire and thus concentrate on the scientific work for which he wished to be remembered. Its importance to him was captured in his very first letter to Collinson about his experiments, when he wrote: 'I never was before engaged in any study that so totally engrossed my attention and my time as this has lately done.'[19]

However, the lasting echo of *Poor Richard* and, in particular, *The Way to Wealth* has skewed the public perception of him, right down to the present. Franklin is quoted daily with the bulk of the examples coming from the *Poor Richard* canon. Of course his most famous quote of all – 'In this world nothing can be said to be certain, except death and taxes', which wonderfully echoes Daniel Defoe's 1726 line of

'Things as certain as Death and Taxes, can be more firmly believed'[20] – did not appear in *Poor Richard*, but in a letter to his French friend Jean Baptiste Le Roy. But it is in the same spirit as *Poor Richard*, because during his years in France he did reprise the role of the provincial American and did so in person. It was a performance, and the greatest of his life, but it was completely at variance with the gentleman he more naturally presented in England.

That said, there was always an element of role-playing with the mature Benjamin Franklin. As he was in his writings, so, when necessary, he was in life. Franklin was not only true to one of his earlier 'Poor Richard' sayings – 'Let all Men know thee, but no man know thee thoroughly'[21] – but he took it to the extreme. His combination of exceptional intelligence and resourceful application had enabled him to wear the mantle of journalist, master printer and businessman, and then leading citizen, famous scientist and colonial representative. But by 1757 he was no longer the open-spirited young man he had been; he was now extremely guarded. Joseph Priestley was to become one of Franklin's greatest English friends; perhaps by 1775 he was closer to Franklin than anyone. As one might expect of one of the founders of chemical science, Dr Priestley was an acute observer. His observation of Franklin was that: 'To strangers he was cold and reserved; but where he was intimate, no man indulged to more pleasantry and good humour.'[22]

The mature Franklin was certainly withdrawn when meeting strangers, happy to use others he knew and trusted to engage them while he took their measure. That was perfectly sensible behaviour for a man of Franklin's analytical skills, kindled through journalism and science, in an age when personal introduction and recommendation was the currency of professional and social interaction. As for the second part of the quote, once you had won Franklin's trust and loyalty he could be amiability itself, but with a thunderously negative and unforgiving reaction if he felt that trust had been betrayed.

In London, as brilliantly captured in the David Martin portrait,[23] Benjamin Franklin most happily would take on the identity of Dr Franklin, gentleman philosopher. In contrast to what would come later in France, this was much less a role, more an ambition realized.

As early as 1748 Franklin had signed off a letter to Strahan with the words, 'By this time twelvemonth, if nothing extraordinary happens to prevent it, I hope to have the Pleasure of seeing you both in London.'[24] In 1750 he had asked Strahan to put William's name down for the gentleman's legal 'finishing school' of London's Inns of Court, leaving it to Strahan to choose 'one of those Inns as you think best'. In the letter, Ben made it clear that he would accompany his son, and he was now doing just that.[25]

∽

As well as writing and planning, Franklin used his Atlantic crossing to observe the natural and physical world, as he had on his westward voyage in 1726. This began when the ship left Sandy Rock in convoy. Walter Lutwidge, the *General Wall*'s skipper, had boasted beforehand that his ship was the quickest but instead it proved the slowest – that is, until all the passengers were temporarily made to stand aft, as far back as possible, and speed immediately picked up. This proved, as suspected, that the forward hold of the vessel was too heavily laden. With the cargo and great casks of drinking water better balanced throughout the ship, speed and pride were soon regained. This was of great interest to Franklin, because of his love of an empirical experiment producing a useful result. And what was of very great benefit in time of war was that it enabled the *General Wall* to outrun enemy shipping. Both Franklins wrote that they were several times chased by French warships in the Atlantic but were able to outsail everything. Yet in spite of that, they nearly came to disaster on the final night of their voyage as they approached their destination. To escape enemy privateers, the *General Wall* raced through the dark under full sail but was blown too close to the rocky shoreline of the Scilly Isles, the scene of over 800 reported shipwrecks since the sixteenth century.[26] At midnight, with the look-out half asleep and the captain in his cabin, suddenly, as the ship yawed, those on deck saw the light of the warning St Agnes lighthouse 'as big as a cartwheel', as Franklin himself described it.[27]

They may have seen the lighthouse late, but they saw it, and that was one of the things that saved them. The other was the decisive action of one Archibald Kennedy, a naval captain and known to the crew as such, who ordered 'hard about', which risked breaking the masts with the ship in full sail. Had that happened they would have been doomed anyway; instead, the manoeuvre brought their salvation.

They docked in Falmouth the next day, Sunday, 17 July, and William celebrated their safe arrival with a hastily written letter within two hours to his sweetheart Elizabeth 'Betsy' Graeme. He said: 'I am so much hurried in getting our things ashore, and enquiring for horses and carriages for transporting us up to London, that I have not the leisure to give you any of the particulars of our voyage.' Though he did have time to tell her how they 'narrowly escaped running ashore on the rocks of Scilly'. As for Ben's reaction, he summed it up – as it summed him up – brilliantly. He wrote to Deborah: 'The bell ringing for church, we went thither immediately, and with hearts full of gratitude, returned sincere thanks to God for the mercies we had received: were I a Roman Catholic, perhaps I should on this occasion vow to build a chapel to some saint; but as I am not, if I were to vow at all, it should be to build a *lighthouse*.'[28]

Writing thirty years later, Franklin recaptures his sense of relief when Falmouth came into view with a touchingly lyrical passage in the *Autobiography*:

> About 9 o'Clock the Fog began to rise, and seemed to be lifted up from the Water like the Curtain at a Playhouse, discovering underneath the Town of Falmouth, the Vessels in its Harbour, and the Fields that surrounded it. A most pleasing Spectacle to those who had been so long without any other Prospects than the uniform View of a vacant Ocean! And it gave us the more Pleasure, as we were now freed from the Anxieties which the State of War occasioned.[29]

∽

On 26 July the Franklin party, having taken a short detour to Stonehenge and nearby Wilton House, finished their journey at Peter Collinson's estate at Mill Hill, just outside London.[30] The Franklins would immediately have felt at home in the grounds because many of the plants and trees were native American species. The sixty-three-year-old Collinson was acknowledged to be one of the country's most distinguished botanists and had been a Fellow of the Royal Society for nigh on three decades. As well as importing plants for his own interest, he had established a subscription scheme with John Bartram to supply great landowners with American seeds and seedlings. Politics and landscape gardening were each part of the eighteenth century's aristocratic competition and Collinson included among his subscribers the Dukes of Bedford, Richmond and Argyll, who were all prominent figures in both arenas. As a Quaker in England, Collinson, like his close friend and first biographer John Fothergill, was excluded from political power by the lasting provisions of Charles II's Test Act. But both he and Fothergill had very strong political connections. Collinson had known Henry Pelham, Robert Walpole's successor as a long-serving Prime Minister. He was also close to John Stuart, 3rd Earl of Bute, whose friendship with Frederick, the late Prince of Wales, and with Frederick's widow Princess Augusta had led to the creation of the Botanical Gardens at Kew.[31] This was an extremely important connection, because in 1757 Bute was the tutor and surrogate father to Frederick's eldest son, nineteen-year-old Prince George, who, with his grandfather now seventy-three, seemed likely soon to inherit the throne.

Other men who had been long-distance friends of Franklin were delighted that he was now among them. To the fore was the printer and publisher William Strahan, who through their mutual acquaintance James Read had in 1743 recommended David Hall to Franklin as an apprentice. Within the year they were doing business together and Franklin judged that Strahan, a man in the same trade as himself, was like-minded enough to keep him in touch with public affairs and to be his window on the wider European world. As Franklin had written to Strahan on 4 July 1744:

I have long wanted a Friend in London whose Judgement I could depend on, to send me from time to time such new Pamphlets as are worth Reading on any Subject (Religious Controversy excepted) for there is no depending on Titles and Advertisements. This Favour

I take the Freedom to beg of you, and shall lodge Money in your Hands for that purpose.

We have seldom any News on our Side the Globe that can be entertaining to you on yours. All our Affairs are *petit*. They have a miniature Resemblance only of the grand Things of Europe.[32]

By 1746 the relationship had warmed to the extent that Franklin was able to write in this jesting vein to Strahan: 'I have had no Line from [you] since that dated June 1745, which, with your equal Silence to our Friends Hall and Read, made me apprehend that Death had deprived me of the Pleasure I promised myself in our growing Friendship. But Lieut. Grung, writing in February last that you and your Family were well, convinces me that some unlucky Accident has happened to your Letters.'[33] By 31 January 1757 Franklin was writing: 'Our Assembly talk of sending me to England speedily. Then look out sharp, and if a fat old Fellow should come to your Printing House ... depend upon it, 'tis Your affectionate Friend and humble Servant.'[34]

Strahan, a proud Scot, would be another conduit to Bute as well as to titans of the Scottish Enlightenment such as David Hume. He was also Dr Johnson's publisher, but that was one introduction Strahan did not contemplate. He took the wise approach of not introducing Johnson to clients and friends whose opinions differed from those of the great lexicographer, as Johnson did not hold back from confrontation. On an exceptional occasion when Strahan let Johnson meet Adam Smith, the evening went so badly that, following Smith's early departure, Strahan had to give Johnson a severe rebuke for his rough treatment of his host's fellow Scot.[35] However, we know that the deist 'Honest Whig' Franklin and the High Anglican Tory Dr Johnson did actually meet on at least one occasion. That was on 1 May 1760.

The idea of such an encounter is the sort of thing to make a playwright's eyes light up. The reality was different. In all likelihood, aside from some opening pleasantries, there was little verbal communication between them. They met, with six others, at a committee meeting and Johnson, satisfied with the work of Franklin and others, never attended again. What the two men had in common on this occasion had nothing to do with them both being brilliant writers – whether of serious pieces or of highly entertaining spoofs – but their common humanitarian interest in the cause that the committee promoted. It was the education of 'Negro children'.[36] Johnson had a personal interest, because Francis Barber, his servant, adopted son and finally his principal beneficiary, was black. As for Franklin, he was instrumental in setting up a number of special schools to further 'Negro education'. He was true to his principles, for when William's absconding slave King was found to be in the good care of a Suffolk lady who was paying for his lessons and personally teaching him the violin and French horn, the Franklins were happy to leave him there.

A few days after Franklin's arrival in London, he visited Dr Fothergill, whom he later described as 'among the best Men I have known'.[37] Fothergill offered to act as an intermediary with Penn and advised Franklin to meet the Proprietor before going to the government with the Pennsylvania Assembly's complaints. In the meantime, however, Collinson told Franklin that the rich Virginia merchant John Hanbury had arranged to take him to meet Earl Granville. This was quite an introduction and one Franklin felt he could in no way refuse. John Carteret, Earl Granville, had been Secretary of State and, with the support of George II, a dominating figure in the government for a short period in the 1740s.[38] Although now sixty-seven and no longer directing policy, Granville was still Lord President of the Council and could offer Franklin the benefit of over four decades' experience of moving in the top circles of British politics.[39]

If Franklin was concerned that Granville's and Thomas Penn's wives were sisters, then he would have been reassured by Granville's support for Fothergill against Penn's scheme for a Pennsylvania loyalty oath the year before. Franklin would have had no doubts about being received with all due courtesy, with Hanbury himself collecting the new agent in his carriage and personally introducing the two men. In any case Granville was well known for possessing impeccable manners.[40]

It was not Granville's behaviour as a host but what he said that shocked Franklin and led him to write down 'his Lordship's

Conversation' the moment he returned to his lodgings.[41] The nub of what Granville said was that: '"The {Privy} Council is *over all* the Colonies; your last Resort is to the Council to decide your Differences, and you must be sensible it is for your Good, for otherwise you often could not obtain Justice. The King in Council is THE LEGISLATOR of the Colonies; and when his Majesty's Instructions come there, they are the LAW OF THE LAND; *they are*", said his Lordship repeating it, "the Law of the Land, and as such *ought to be* OBEYED." '[42]

The statement's reference to '*all* the Colonies' would logically give even the governors of Proprietary colonies and the men who appointed them greater legal authority in their dealings with the Assemblies, but, interestingly, Franklin did not stress that point in his stunned response. He also took a 'pan-colonial' approach, as he sought politely to correct Granville: 'I told his Lordship this was new Doctrine to me. I had always understood from our Charters, that our Laws were to be made by our Assemblies, to be presented indeed to the King for his Royal Assent, but that being once given the King could not repeal or alter them. And as the Assemblies could not make permanent Laws without his Assent, so neither could he make a Law for them without theirs.'[43] This was received with the words: 'He assured me that I was totally mistaken.'

In point of fact the mistake was Granville's, because he was thinking of a clause in a Bill that had been presented in the Parliament of 1744, but which had not been passed before the end of the session.[44] However, Franklin was to find that Granville's attitude towards colonial rights was one generally held. As he highlighted in a 1759 letter to Isaac Norris, 'The Prevailing Opinion, as far as I am able to collect it, among the Ministers and great Men here, is that the Colonies have too many and too great Privileges; and that it is not only the Interest of the Crown but of the Nation to reduce them.'[45]

The meeting with Granville had unsettled Franklin. That it had taken place at all was doubly counterproductive. First, Granville was sure to discuss the conversation with Thomas Penn. Secondly, as Fothergill had warned him, the fact that Franklin had discussed Pennsylvanian business with the President of the Council before he consulted the Proprietors was a gross discourtesy to the latter. It enabled them to besmirch Franklin's name as an uncouth provincial with neither the appropriate social skills nor the innate knowledge of the proper political conduct required in London.

However, the forgiving Dr Fothergill kept his promise to act as intermediary, and a visit to the Penns was arranged for the middle of August. That gave Franklin the opportunity to get to know his fellow agents, the seventy-five-year-old Richard Partridge (a London merchant born in New Hampshire who had been acting for the Assembly since 1740) and Robert Charles (a long-time friend of Isaac Norris and agent from early in the decade). It is unclear to what extent they regarded the famous Benjamin Franklin as a cuckoo in the nest: in one sense he was arriving as the third agent of the Assembly, but in another he had been issuing advice and instructions to them for a number of years. There would be no need for them to introduce him to the New England Coffee House in Threadneedle Street or the Pennsylvania Coffee House in Birchin Lane, both near the Bank of England in the City. These he had long used from afar in his business dealings and he had been directing mail to the latter to await his arrival.[46] The significance of these places for colonial agents was in the names. They were meeting places and postboxes for specific interest groups, where newspapers could be read and political and business intelligence exchanged. Agents were the lobbyists to government and Parliament for the Assemblies they represented and the communities they served. In the words of Michael Kammen:

> As paid lobbyists the agents had various responsibilities: forwarding documents and news, preparing and presenting petitions, securing acceptance of colonial legislation and preventing adverse bills from passing through Parliament, promoting trade, settling land disputes, and handling Indian and military affairs as well as colony finances in London. In short, they were political brokers – extraconstitutional cogs in the machinery of colonial government.[47]

The Franklins had time to settle into the comfortable lodgings of a widow named Margaret Stevenson and her daughter Mary, known as Polly, in Craven Street. Although Craven Street had been recommended by Robert Charles, Franklin's own account book reveals that he thought it wise to take a trial meal there on 30 July. He must have been favourably impressed because the small cost of their hotel bill, indicating just a handful of days, shows that the Franklin foursome of father, son and their two slaves moved into Craven Street immediately afterwards.[48] Craven Street* was to prove ideal for Franklin. He found Mrs Stevenson to be both 'very diligent' and 'very obliging'. She was still his landlady when he left England, finally, in 1775.

Craven Street was in an excellent location, not far from Whitehall and just off the western end of the great thoroughfare of the Strand that links the cities of Westminster and London. Until the seventeenth century this had been a neighbourhood of noble mansions. These, with the exception of Northumberland House (the largest non-royal residence in London), had been replaced by smaller houses and shops. The Franklin abode was not far from Parliament and the houses of the aristocracy in Mayfair; it was also convenient for the elderly King's 'drawing room' appearances at Kensington Palace.

The accommodation, which Ben described to Deborah as 'four Rooms furnished, and every thing about us pretty genteel', suited the Franklins very well. He did, however, complain about London in general, writing that 'Living here is in every respect very expensive,'[49] but then one reason for that was because he felt it necessary to rent his own carriage at the extravagant rate of twelve guineas per month.[50] However, the common vehicles for hire did not provide an option for Franklin, as he found that 'Hackney Coaches at this End of the Town, where most People keep their own, are the worst in the whole City, miserable dirty broken shabby Things, unfit to go into when dressed clean, and such as one would be ashamed to get out of at any Gentleman's Door.'[51] As for walking to appointments, the dirt of the streets – including that in Franklin's own – together with safety considerations made it an extremely unappealing proposition for someone of Franklin's age and eminence.

---

* In Franklin's time it was 7 Craven Street. Renumbered in the nineteenth century, it is now 36 Craven Street.

Craven Street was a home from home. Franklin even had another newspaperman as a neighbour in Caleb Whitefoord, originally from Edinburgh, who doubled most happily as a successful wine merchant.[52]

⚬∕∞

London in 1757 was very different from the city Franklin had left over thirty years before and the 1750s alone were a decade of great change. Hogarth's *Gin Lane* has wrongly been seen as representative of the eighteenth century as a whole in depicting the worst of London street life, but its publication in 1751 came towards the end of the craze for the cheaper version of the spirit, which Dr Johnson's 1755 *Dictionary* described – under 'Geneva' – as 'a distilled spirituous water, made with no better an ingredient than oil of turpentine'.[53] *Gin Lane* came as a pair with *Beer Street*, which celebrated beer as the lower-strength alternative. A Gin Act that actually worked, enforceable licensing and excise duties and, most importantly, a series of poor harvests that greatly increased the price of even the cheapest grain had ended the worst excesses of the gin craze by the time of Franklin's arrival in 1757.

During this decade, changes in London's infrastructure were to prove transformative. The wide east–west/west–east New Road running to the north of the City unblocked the existing routes of their vehicles and livestock and made it easier for City merchants to commute from the countryside of Middlesex and Essex. The unfashionable old houses on top of London Bridge that made it difficult for traffic to pass began to be demolished in 1758 and the replacement of its two central arches by one of a much wider span removed the swirling waters and treacherous six-foot drop from upstream to down.[54] Just as this work opened up the artery of one of the twin cities of London and Westminster, the completion of the impressive stone-built bridge at Westminster itself did the same for the other. It was finally ready in 1750 after a dozen years of construction. Until then, there had been no bridge between the City of London and Putney, with the latter having merely a weak wooden structure that had only been in place since 1729. Westminster Bridge enabled a flow of traffic from north and south that could now cross directly to and from the fashionable areas of Mayfair and St James's and the homes of most of the ruling aristocracy. It was to be followed by a bridge at Blackfriars, named after William Pitt, which was completed in 1769.

There was also a cultural change, a greater celebration of knowledge and scientific invention that helped to accord Franklin the reception he received on his arrival in 1757. The British Museum was founded in 1753, and the Society for the Encouragement of Arts, Manufactures and Commerce during the following year. London was gaining the sort of institutions commensurate with its status as the greatest city in the world.

London had always acted as a magnet for the landed classes. Yet until 1689 there had been some constraint on numbers by Tudor and early Stuart monarchs, who had restricted access to court and issued proclamations ordering less favoured nobles and gentry out of the metropolis. After the 'Glorious Revolution' of 1688/9,[55] the politically active aristocracy were expected to be in London to attend the annual Parliaments, which most often ran from November to June.[56] It was the King who would be away from the capital for extended periods – with William III directing wars against the French and the first two Georges returning to their electorate of Hanover.[57] All who were able to do so continued to escape to their estates in the country during the summer, but otherwise social life cohered with the Parliamentary calendar and thus the 'London season' evolved. Access to the court was still important, because a monarch's disapproval could blight a career,[58] but the demonstration of talent in the cockpit of Parliamentary politics was also a significant weapon for those seeking social advancement for themselves and their families.

A more permanent presence required a more permanent residence, and this changed the face of London. Between 1689 and the middle of the next century, grand squares fanned out north and west between the Restoration developments of St James's Square and Bloomsbury Square to create new boundaries for the spreading metropolis, which were broadly Park Lane to the west and up beyond Oxford Street and towards the New Road in the North.[59]

By the middle of the eighteenth century, London's population of

675,000 far outstripped that of Paris.[60] Its multitude was more than thirteen times greater than that of Bristol,[61] the next-largest English city, and almost twelve times greater than the figure for Edinburgh and its suburbs.[62] For centuries London had attracted workers, both skilled and unskilled, from the rest of the country and it had winnowed down the national population through disease and a mortality rate far greater than the country at large. In the eighteenth century, with or without the aid of gin, deaths still exceeded births. But there were always more people wanting to travel to London and to try their luck there.

6

A London Life

Franklin's first meeting with Thomas Penn amounted to no more than an exchange of surface pleasantries. Thomas Penn explained that his brother Richard was out of town and it would be inappropriate to discuss business without him. This was obviously a tactic. Both men knew who was the decision maker in the Penn family. With the death of John Penn, their elder brother, Thomas now owned three-quarters of the Proprietary interest to Richard's quarter;[1] furthermore he was the dominant personality. Yet it may have been the reasonable cordiality of the meeting that caused Franklin to fall into the simplest of traps that Penn laid for him: he agreed to bring a statement of the Assembly's position to the first business meeting.[2]

The Proprietary supporters in Philadelphia had certainly long been aware of what a Franklin mission to England could mean. At the end of January, Richard Peters had written to Thomas Penn:

> Certain it is that B.F.'s view is to effect a change of Government, and considering the popularity of his character and the reputation gained by his Electrical Discoveries which will introduce him into all sorts of Company he may prove a Dangerous Enemy. Dr Fothergill and Mr Collinson can introduce him to the Men of most influence at Court and he may underhand give impressions to your prejudice. In short Heaven and Earth will be moved against the Proprietors.[3]

Thomas Penn was not so concerned. As he wrote back to Peters in a letter dated 14 May:

I think I wrote you before that Mr Franklin's popularity is nothing here, and that he will be looked very coldly upon by great People. There are very few of any consequence that have heard of his Electrical Experiments, those matters being attended to by a particular Set of People, many of whom of the greatest consequence I know well. But it is quite another sort of People who are to determine the Dispute between us.[4]

Penn, albeit in the short term, may well have been right about that. But he certainly had not been prepared to risk giving Franklin the opportunity to prove him wrong. Thus by the time the Assembly's new representative arrived in London, Penn had spent many months preparing the ground. He was to be given assistance by the normally sure-footed Benjamin Franklin himself.

✑

On 20 August Franklin presented his 'Heads of Complaint' on behalf of the Assembly. There was nothing in it that was new to the Proprietors. Its complaints were threefold: first, the Proprietors' distant control of their lieutenant governors by the threat of personal financial penalties should they stray from their instructions; secondly, the vetoing of the Assembly's money bills even in time of emergency; thirdly, the exemption of the Proprietary estates from tax, even when it came to defence of the province. From the informality of style and the lack of any preamble addressing the Proprietors, it is obvious that Franklin presented the 'Heads of Complaint' as a short discussion paper.[5] But Thomas Penn chose to treat it, after the meeting, as a formal document. He put the matter in the hands of his solicitor, Ferdinand John Paris, with the instruction to seek a future legal opinion from the government's Law Officers, the Attorney General and Solicitor General. Franklin had been trumped on three counts. First, his credibility could be questioned as someone who did not know the proper form. Secondly, because Penn was technically a royal official, the Law Officers were obliged to consider the documented case that the legally brilliant Paris presented to them – whereas Franklin was denied a right of reply as a mere representative of the

Assembly of Pennsylvania.[6] Thirdly, Paris, himself a former agent for the Pennsylvania Assembly,[7] could counter Franklin's thin 'argument' with such conviction that the Law Officers, whatever their political views, could scarcely gainsay him. Of course Franklin could appeal to the Board of Trade and the King in Council, but they would act on the advice of the Law Officers. In any case, there could be no quick appeal because Paris deliberately held back the application. The timetable was in his hands, with delay maintaining the status quo. Unsurprisingly, he dawdled for three months over the work of a day or two. Franklin the master tactician had been completely outwitted.[8]

In the meantime the Penns were able to continue their whispering campaign against Franklin. As Fothergill later wrote to Israel Pemberton: 'Great pains had been taken, and very successfully, to render him odious and his integrity suspected, to those very persons to whom he must first apply.'[9]

One might wonder why Franklin, usually so deft, had been out-manoeuvred so spectacularly. He may have let his guard down in response to the admiration he had received from the gentlemen and aristocrats of the scientific community. However, there was another likely reason: he was suffering the early symptoms of what was to become fully developed malaria.

∽

Franklin was laid low with what he thought initially to be 'a violent cold and something of a fever'. That was how he described it in a letter to Deborah of 2 September, adding that 'it was almost gone'.[10] He was feeling better on 7 September, because at 6 p.m. that evening he attended his first meeting of the Society of Arts.[11] However, by November he was describing something different, an illness of eight weeks, writing that soon after the first bout:

> ...it was not long before I had another severe cold, which continued longer than the first, attended by great pain in my head, the top of which was very hot, and when the pain went off, very sore and tender. These fits of pain continued sometimes longer than at others; seldom less than twelve hours, and once thirty-six hours. I was now

and then a little delirious: they cupped me on the back of the head which seemed to ease me for the present.

Then, crucially, he continued:

> I took a great deal of bark, both in substance and infusion, and, too soon thinking myself well, I ventured out twice, to do a little business and forward the service I am engaged in, and both times got fresh cold and fell down again; my good Doctor {Fothergill} grew very angry with me for acting so contrary to his Cautions and Directions, and obliged me to promise more Observance for the future. He attended me very carefully and affectionately; and the good Lady of the House nursed me kindly; Billy was also of great Service to me, in going from place to place, where I could not go myself, and Peter was very diligent and attentive. I took so much bark in various ways that I began to abhor it; I durst not take a vomit, for fear of my head; but at last I was seized one morning with a vomiting and purging, the latter of which continued the greater part of the day, and I believe was a kind of crisis to the distemper, carrying it clear off; for ever since I feel quite lightsome, and am every day gathering strength; so I hope my seasoning is over, and that I shall enjoy better health during the rest of my stay in England.[12]

Franklin did not know the insect cause of his ailment but, thanks to his clear description of its symptoms and of the final curative treatment, he enables us to do so. It seems that he was suffering from what at the time was called the ague, or what we now know as the *Plasmodium vivax* form of malaria, made all the worse through not being treated before it firmly established itself in his liver. It is extremely likely that he was the victim of one of the *Anopheles atroparvus* mosquitoes which bred in the marshlands of Westminster and Lambeth. *P. vivax* can have a long incubation of up to six or twelve months but, with the normal period being twelve to seventeen days, it is likely that Franklin was bitten in London at some point in early August.[13]

Dr Fothergill, one of London's leading physicians, with many other distinguished patients aside from Thomas Penn and Benjamin Franklin, cannot be blamed for the slowness of administering the magic 'bark'. City-living people, even the well-off who lived in better social conditions, suffered from all kinds of illnesses and ailments for much of the time. Then, as now, there was no cure for the common cold – though Franklin was to develop some highly accurate theories for both its causes and prevention – so Fothergill, when presented with those cold-like symptoms, would not have prescribed cinchona or what was known as 'Jesuit's bark' (from its use by Catholic missionaries in South America), because it was an experimental and highly expensive 'cure-all'. It is possible that Franklin himself suggested cinchona, because as early as 1739 'Poor Richard' was recommending its use for fever and in 1750 he was advising a friend to take it as a preventive against both fever and ague. It may even have been Franklin who gave the following to David Hall, who chose to insert it in the Pennsylvania Gazette of 8 September 1757, as follows:

> We are desired to insert the following Receipt, the good Effects of which have been experienced by many that were afflicted by fever and ague.
>
> Take two Ounces of Jesuits Bark, one Ounce of Snakeroot, one Ounce of Salt of Tartar, and Half an Ounce of Camomile Flowers; put them into a Half Gallon Bottle, filled with Jamaica Spirit, and set it into a Kettle of Water, over a moderate Fire, and let the Ingredients infuse three Days, the Water being kept rather warmer than Blood warm. Dose for a grown Person Half a Jill, three or four times between the Fits; for a Child of a Year old a Tea Spoonful, mixed with Balm Tea; the Quantity to be increased according to the Age of the Person. The Ingredients, by adding more Spirit to them, make a good preventing Bitter.

It was also used in the 1758 Poor Richard Improved almanac – the last to be prepared by Franklin – which was printed in October 1757.[14] We cannot be sure as to when and where Franklin contracted the 'ague'. But we can certainly understand its importance in making Franklin inactive during the autumn months, unable to combat the

Penns in a campaign of briefing and counter-briefing and reliant on William to carry on the fight.

By January 1758, Franklin was well again. He needed to discuss another matter with Thomas Penn, who had no choice but to meet him. Yet once again Franklin would disobey Fothergill's 'doctor's orders' and this time his great supporter would be extremely angry.

✑

Ben's illness proved to be a liberating experience for the younger Franklin, who, after all, was now nearer to thirty than twenty. The two Franklins were certainly close: Strahan cast Ben as William's 'friend, his brother, his intimate and easy companion'. He also thought that William 'seems to me [to] have a solidity of judgement, not very often to be met with in one of his years'.[15] Certainly William was to offer a sage assessment of Thomas Penn's political manoeuvrings, but whether he was wise in the action he took in countering them is open to question.

One cannot tell to what extent Ben was giving instructions from his sickbed, but William was certainly active 'in going from place to place' for his father. He had no difficulty in picking up news of Penn's whispering campaign and responded to what he believed to be a Penn-authorized anti-Assembly and anti-Ben Franklin letter in the newspapers. Ben almost always deployed a pseudonym, but his son was more than happy to put his own name to a mid-September letter in *The Citizen, or General Advertiser* which was reprinted widely in London and in the *Pennsylvania Gazette* of 8 December.[16]

The patient Dr Fothergill worried that the letter to the press only succeeded in making the Proprietors more inflexible.[17] A December letter from William to his fiancée, Betsy Graeme, was one to fan the flames. In it he denigrated the 'Obstinacy and Wickedness of the Proprietors', before continuing in like vein:

You will think me justifiable in speaking thus of the Proprietors when you consider that during the Time they expressed themselves strongly inclined to settle Matters amicably with my Father, they were repeatedly publishing scandalous and malicious Falsehoods against the Assembly and People of Pennsylvania ... They trusted that as my Father was obliged to a friendly Negotiation with them (which they could easily contrive to continue till the Sitting of the Parliament) that he would not take any Notice of nameless Aspersions in a News Paper. In the Advantages they expected from this Piece of poor low Cunning they have, however, been egregiously disappointed (as you will have seen before this reaches you) by a Paper I published in the Citizen. For although it might not be so proper for my Father to take Notice of those Aspersions, while the Negotiation was on foot there could be no Reason why I, as an Inhabitant of Pennsylvania, now on my Travels in England, no ways concerned in conducting the Negotiation, should not vindicate the Honour and Reputation of my Country when I saw it so injuriously attacked. My putting my Name to the Paper, and the Place where I was to be found, was judged necessary, as it would be the most effectual Means of putting a Stop to further anonymous Attacks, and as otherwise the Public could have no Reason for giving greater Credit to one Representation than the other. It has had all the good Effects I could have wished; but I am told the Proprietor is much incensed against me on that Account, though he don't venture to complain as he is sensible that he was the Aggressor.[18]

William was incorrect in his view that Thomas Penn believed himself to be in the wrong or that he was holding back from complaint. Penn may not have fired an answering salvo through the public prints, but he was continuing to blacken the Franklins' name in private. Their actions were being held against them, just as the words in William's December letter to Betsy Graeme would be. Perhaps surprisingly, William had in Philadelphia become close to a girl whose father was an ally of the Proprietors. He had previously failed to write for five months and then, in a letter that was careless rather than intentionally callous, combined his comments on the Penns with descriptions of the magnificent time he was having in London. Whatever William's intention, his 'dear Betsy' took it as his cowardly way of ending the relationship. She wrote back a furious letter which described William's father as 'a Collection of Party Malice' and denounced William himself as having neither morals nor judgement.[19] One can have no doubt that William's sentiments about the Proprietors would have been relayed back to Thomas Penn.

Like his father, William did not just reserve his criticisms for the Penns. He was also shocked by the attitude of the British administration. He complained to Betsy of 'the little Knowledge of (or indeed inclination to know) American Affairs, among most of those concerned in the Administration; {and} their Prejudices against the Colonies in general, and ours in particular'. Comments that would prove useful to Thomas Penn.

Although, like his father, he was at this point a political outsider, he was advancing socially. He was at large in the greatest city in the world and was making the most of it.

✏

William had to pay some attention to his studies at Middle Temple and he was called to the Bar on 10 November 1758,[20] but the law was not uppermost in his thoughts when he arrived in London. He may have been in his mid-twenties in 1757, but he had a youthful exhilaration in coming from the periphery to the centre of the British empire and its capital city, with a population well over thirty times that of Philadelphia.[21]

His letter to Betsy Graeme showed that he was having a tremendous time. Of course he had been busy with 'frequent Engagements amongst Politicians, Philosophers, and Men of Business' and in 'making Acquaintances with such Men as have it in their Power to be of Service in settling our unhappy Provincial Disputes', but he also confessed to 'now and then partaking of the public Diversions and Entertainments of this bewitching Country'. He described the 'infinite Variety of new Objects; the continued Noise and Bustle in the Streets; and the Viewing such Things as were esteemed most curious'. There had been a visit to Windsor and trips to the country, and he provides a lengthy description of Vauxhall Gardens which, like the newer Ranelagh Gardens (1746), was a place for 'the beau monde' to see and be seen:

The enchanting Scenes at Vauxhall, is another Theme on which I could dwell for Hours together. What would I not have given for a

Power of instantaneously transporting you to that delightful Spot! The many agreeable Walks amidst Rows of beauteous Trees lighted with Lamps; the elegant Paintings and Sculpture with which the Boxes, the grand Hall, and Orchestra, are adorned; the curious artificial Fall of Water; the ravishing Music, vocal and instrumental; and the Gaiety and Brilliancy of the Company; would have made you conceive yourself in a Situation beyond even the Elysium of the Ancients.

This is high-flown stuff, but the phrase that stands out is 'the Gaiety and Brilliancy of the Company'. It may have been financially possible for the 'middling sort' to buy tickets to Vauxhall, but not for them to visit on a regular basis or to enjoy the full facilities. Members of fashionable society would pass among the crowd, but not be of them. Their presence and those in their company would be noted – as they intended it should be – and become the subject of conversation and reported in the likes of the *Gentleman's Magazine*. In the same way, someone with no connections and no means of introduction would just be ignored. William, however, as his father had hoped, had been accepted.

Another place to see and be seen was the theatre. Indeed, according to Hannah Greig's analysis of the correspondence of the time, members of fashionable society wrote to each other far more about who was sitting where and with whom, than to review what was happening on stage.[22] William did, in this instance, show himself up as a newcomer to this social milieu by writing about David Garrick rather than commenting on 'who was who' in the boxes, but one can be sure that he would have not been sitting in 'the Gods' like his father in the 1720s.

He was, though, coming to terms with Society in other ways and in the package to Betsy he enclosed 'one of the newest fashioned muffs and tippets worn by the gayest ladies of quality at this end of town, also a basket for counters which is the workmanship of a poor reduced Lady of Family who now has no way of getting her livelihood'. William was on the social circuit, enjoying himself in 'this great metropolis'. Given time he would be invited to Northumberland

House, the vast metropolitan home of the Earl and Countess of Northumberland, just a stone's throw from Craven Street, and be delighted to send some of the Countess's cards to his sister.[23]

Whether it was a conscious decision or not, it seems that he no longer had time for Betsy Graeme.[24]

⁊

Benjamin Franklin was also moving – and more immediately – within important social circles. Thomas Penn may have been right in his belief in 1757 that the people likely to resolve his dispute with the Assembly would be unmoved by Benjamin Franklin's scientific fame. He was, however, completely wrong in asserting that Franklin would 'be looked very coldly upon by great People' and that 'there are very few of any consequence that have heard of his Electrical Experiments'.[25] Penn might have dismissed Franklin as 'the electrician', but others did not.

Franklin had been elected a Fellow of the Royal Society the previous year. Among those who proposed him were fellow Copley Medal winners John Canton and William Watson, both of whom were to become good friends. A club of Royal Society Fellows met fortnightly for dinner at the Mitre Tavern in Fleet Street and Franklin was a guest on Thursday, 11 August 1757, within weeks of his arrival.[26] He was back a fortnight later,[27] when he was one of eleven at a Royal Society Club dinner, which he attended as a guest. Other attendees included the Earl of Macclesfield and a Mr Wilson, almost certainly Benjamin Wilson.[28] At the bottom of the record commemorating the occasion there was a special note regarding another of the diners, a Mr Wray. It said, 'The Company being Entertained with a Haunch of Venison by Mr Wray{,} his health was drank in Claret.'[29]

This reflected venison's great value. It had been regarded as the preserve of the elite since the time of the Normans, with game laws that were enforced. These still held sway. It could be obtained commercially, but at a price, so its presence was a sign of Mr Wray's own quality. Happily for Franklin, venison was his favourite meat. Not that he would have starved if it had not been present. The record spelled out the other food on offer: 'Salmon & Smelts';[30] 'Trout &

flat fish'; 'Fowles & bacon'; 'Roast Beef'; 'Goose Roast'; 'Pidgeon Pye'; 'Pease'; 'Plumb pudding'; 'Codling pye Creamed';[31] 'Currant & Cherry Pye'; 'Butter & Cheese'. The Club dinner was exactly the sort of occasion that Franklin enjoyed during his time in England: one that combined good food and wine with learned conversation. His illness that first autumn meant that he did not attend his first formal Royal Society meeting until 24 November, but he then followed that with its Annual Dinner on the 30th.[32] His regular attendance began from that time onwards.

Far from being 'treated coldly', Franklin was welcomed with open arms by those interested in (natural) philosophy and science, whether they were aristocrats or commoners. This was also true of the Society of Arts, right from his very first attendance on 7 September 1757. These two organizations and the spin-off clubs of their members were to provide most of Franklin's greatest friends during his time in London.

Though he never formally joined the Royal Society Club, Franklin was a guest on more than sixty occasions between that first dinner and his last in January 1775. In some years he was invited more than anyone else and the fact that invitations continued right through the politically volatile year of 1774 underlines Franklin's own assertion in 1769 that the Club, like the Royal Society itself, was non-political. The talk was of science and philosophy, not politics. Most often he was the guest of Dr (later Sir John) Pringle, who in 1757 was already well connected as doctor to the Prince of Wales (from 1760, George III) and his tutor the Earl of Bute. By the end of the year he and Franklin were the firmest of friends and would continue as highly competitive chess-playing companions who holidayed together in Europe, taking the travelling chess set with them. Pringle was an important figure in the Royal Society and would become its President in 1772. Verner Crane goes further: 'Pringle must have ranked as the premier host in London to men of science and learning: in the club at the Mitre, at his private dinners in Pall Mall, and at those Sunday evening "conversations" ... among philosophical friends to which he also invited interesting British and foreign visitors in town.'[33] But Franklin was equal to these occasions. As Pringle rather sweetly wrote to Franklin, then back in Philadelphia, in 1763: 'Our friends continue to meet at my house on the Sunday evenings. I suspect they would not be so punctual if they did not hope for your return; for having that in their view they could not with any face leave me now and come back with you.'[34] A nice compliment, but as Crane goes on to say: 'manifestly, Pringle's "conversations" played a great part in Franklin's initiation into learned society in London'.[35] And those interested in talking about natural philosophy included the socially great as well as the intellectually gifted. Franklin could justly be optimistic that, over time, some of the former would replace Thomas Penn's 'other sort of people' in power.

ℒ

The Royal Society Club was one of a half-dozen philosophical clubs of which Franklin was a regular attender, as either member or guest, during his time in London. They each had in common that the nucleus of their membership came from the Royal Society, the Society of Arts, or both. They were also organized on the same basis: that of small groups who met with their friends in the supper rooms of favoured hostelries. The Royal Society Club was grander than, for instance, the Club of Honest Whigs, which met on alternate Thursdays. Though each may have differed in emphasis or in the level of their formality, they did not in their enthusiastic philosophical conversation.

Franklin was in his element. As a youth he had read of the ideal club in Addison and Steele's *Tatler*; as a very young man in London he had been able to enjoy the club centred round Bernard Mandeville; and back in Philadelphia he had formed a club of his own with his friends in the Junto. But this was something else: here he was with the men he regarded as the greatest minds in the capital of the world's greatest empire. More to the point, he was having fun. Writing of his love of club meetings to his old Junto friend Hugh Roberts, he explained their appeal: 'I find I love Company, Chat, a Laugh, a Glass and even a Song, as well as ever; and at the same Time relish, better than I used to do, the grave Observations and wise Sentences of old Men's Conversation.'[36]

Aside from the events with Dr Pringle, his two favourite clubs were the Monday Club at the George & Vulture in Castle Court, off Birchin Lane, and the Club of Honest Whigs which met at St Paul's Coffee House before moving in 1772 to the London Coffee House.[37] When he was away he missed them. As he explained in 1763 to John Ellicott, an FRS whom Franklin had met at his first Club dinner, who was now clockmaker to George III but also a founder member of the Monday Club: 'The Monday scarce comes round but I think of you and am present with you *in Spirit*; and shall take it kindly if, when you are not crowded, you would order a Chair for me, and only caution one another not to tread upon my Toes.'[38] Among the other Monday Club members was Captain Cook. In 1780 Anthony Merry told Franklin of the death 'of that great & useful man and Our amiable Club-mate',[39] and Franklin agreed with those sentiments, later asking Benjamin Vaughan (the son of his great Honest Whig friend Samuel) to get him a good print of the explorer with the comment: 'I should be glad to have it, being personally acquainted with him.'[40]

As to the atmosphere at the Club of Honest Whigs, no less a source than James Boswell provides a sketch, following his attendance on 21 September 1769:

> I went to a club to which I belong. It meets every other Thursday at St Paul's Coffee-house. It consists of clergymen, physicians and several other professions ... We have wine and punch upon the table. Some of us smoke a pipe, conversation goes on pretty formally, sometimes sensibly and sometimes furiously. At nine there is a sideboard with Welsh rabbits and apple-puffs, porter and beer. Our reckoning is about eighteen pence a head.[41]

Boswell was wrong about the 'physicians' in the Club. The Club was generally one for men who were dissenting clergymen and/or schoolmasters and friends. What linked them all was their interest in natural philosophy and libertarian political thought.[42] Boswell talked to Franklin there. It was the second time he had seen him that week, as the previous Friday he had called at Dr Pringle's to find the two of them playing chess, where he described Franklin, in contrast to Pringle, as being 'all jollity and pleasantry'.[43] At the Club

Boswell and Franklin talked of Pasquale Paoli, the great Corsican anti-French patriot who had fled to London, and Franklin passed on some information he had heard from Robert Wood, the Under-Secretary of State. But the collective talk was of philosophy, inspiring Boswell, on getting home to his lodgings with a Mr Careless, to describe himself as the 'Philosophe de Sans Souci'.[44] He was then himself careless with a maid called Phoebe.[45]

✑

Franklin's interest in science during his time in London was constant. We know that he continued to conduct practical experiments, such as his 1758 demonstration to Lord Charles Cavendish and others of some electrical apparatus he called his Philadelphia Machine, which obliged him by producing a spark nine inches long.[46] Though he produced a damper for chimneys and stoves and, in 1768, the first map to chart the Gulf Stream,[47] on the whole his science in London was philosophical, theoretical and speculative. He did, though, definitely invent two noteworthy physical items. One was a three-wheel clock, the other being the glass armonica.

James Ferguson, the Scottish natural philosopher and instrument maker, described Franklin's clock in great detail in his *Select Mechanical Exercises*, first published in 1773. Perhaps the most interesting aspect of its design was that the larger of its two faces would show only four hours. Thus when the single hand was on the hour I, it would also be on the hours V and IX – the assumption being that the viewer would be sufficiently compos mentis to realize which of the three was appropriate. Each of the clock's four quarters had the individual minutes marked up to sixty with each ten-minute mark enumerated. Above the larger face was a much smaller one which showed the seconds. The whole was a combination of style, simplicity and efficiency. The fact that Ferguson made improvements to the design was certainly not a criticism of a man classed by Franklin as someone 'whom I rejoice to call my friend'.[48] Rather it was reflective of a joyous collaborative spirit of scientific enquiry and practical experimentation that was common to the age. Ferguson summed up Franklin's effort thus: 'Several clocks have been made according to this ingenious plan of the Doctor's, and I can affirm that I have seen one of them, which measures time exceedingly well. The simpler that any machine is, the better it will be allowed to be.'[49]

Franklin also had a general love of music and applied his practical skill to create the new musical instrument that he called the armonica, in honour of *armonia*, the Italian word for harmony, as he believed it to be 'peculiarly adapted to Italian music, especially that of the soft and plaintive kind'.[50] He also thought it suitable for playing 'the softest' of the Scottish folk tunes, which he adored.[51] The armonica consists of twenty-five vertical glass bowls, linked together with a spindle, rotated with a treadle and 'played' with fingertips. He was very proud of his instrument, believing its tones to be 'incomparably sweet beyond those of any other', and in his friend John Stanley, the brilliant blind organist and composer, he had a musician with superb touch to play it.[52] The armonica was more than a curiosity; its potential as an instrument for chamber music was quickly appreciated. A great number of composers, including Mozart and Beethoven, produced pieces for it. It fell out of fashion in the nineteenth century, but its ethereal tones have been recently harnessed by John Williams in his music for the Harry Potter films. As so often with Franklin, his creation came from adapting the work of others. He was happy to pay credit to Edward Delaval, whom in the early 1760s he was pleased to describe as 'a most ingenious member of our Royal Society'. As Franklin noted, Delaval had adapted the work of a luckless Irish adventurer called Pockrich, who had collected a number of glasses of different sizes and filled them with varying amounts of water to attain the appropriate note.[53]

The armonica and Franklin's version of the three-wheeled clock were definitely invented in London. He is also often described as the inventor of bifocals, but, as Lady Reid of Benjamin Franklin House and Neil Handley of the College of Optometrists demonstrate, there is no definitive evidence either way. It is known that he commissioned bifocals when he was in France, but he may already have known about their use by artists including Sir Joshua Reynolds and Benjamin West, Franklin's friend and fellow Philadelphian. However, it can be said that he probably first introduced them into America, popularizing them after his return from France in 1785.[54] By then such was his reputation that it would have been natural for his fellow countrymen to credit yet another accomplishment to his name.

∽

Franklin clearly felt comfortable among London's scientific intelligentsia and in Craven Street he was creating his home from home. He had the run of the place.[55] As well as the house's best floor, its first, for his own rooms, he had the use of Mrs Stevenson's downstairs reception rooms.

There were, though, things missing from his life in Philadelphia that he expected Deborah to send him. This was the cause of his writing to her sharply in January 1758: 'Goodies I now and then get a few; but roasting Apples seldom, I wish you had sent me some; and I wonder how you, that used to think of everything, came to forget it. Newtown Pippins would have been the most acceptable.'[56] That was certainly remedied in later years and there are letters thanking her for sending large quantities of both apples and cranberries. The cranberries are understandable – they were not then grown in England.[57] Apples less so, because with so many English apples to choose from it is surprising that Franklin so favoured those from home that had to travel thousands of miles. However, it was not just a case of 'home comforts', because Newtown Pippins, if well packed, did not suffer from the sea voyage and the flavour actually improved from being given time to mature after picking; he was not the only one to like them, because Dr Fothergill sent some to Joseph Banks, who appreciated them 'in a pye' on board Captain Cook's HMS *Endeavour*.[58]

Franklin enjoyed other special foods from America's abundant larder, such as nuts and dried peaches. In a letter of 1760 he was particularly appreciative of Deborah's efforts: 'The dried Venison was very acceptable, and I thank you for it. We have had it constantly shaved to eat with our Bread and Butter for Breakfast, and this Week saw the last of it. The Bacon still holds out; for we are choice of it. Some Rashers of it yesterday relished a Dish of Green Peas. Mrs Stevenson thinks there was never any in England so good. The smoked Beef was also excellent.'[59]

The type of transatlantic trade between Ben and Deboroah Franklin mirrored the British trading system. From America it was raw materials and from England it was manufactures. Living in London, Franklin was determined to make the most of the opportunity to acquire the best of British goods. He bought some furniture, including a bed, but overall the purchases in England tended to be smaller, high-value, more easily shipped items such as silver, china and fabrics of excellent quality.[60] In the early months of his stay in London he, with Margaret Stevenson as his personal shopper, went on a spree. He bought a great quantity of china, with some in sets and a lot of individual pieces, which he explained to Deborah thus: 'to show the difference of workmanship there is something from all the china works in England'. It seems that he had more of an interest in admiring materials for the novelty and intricacy of their manufacture than in buying matching items, as he shows with his itemization of 'fifty-six yards of cotton printed curiously from copper plates, a new invention, to make bed and window curtains; and seven yards chair bottoms printed in the same way, very neat; these were my fancy'. However, he admits that 'Mrs Stevenson tells me I did wrong not to buy both of the same Colour'! Perhaps Margaret Stevenson was not there when he chose seven yards of blue cotton, having bought it by candlelight and then found it looked rather different by light of day – but he gives himself a get-out of 'if you do not fancy it, send it as a present from me to Sister Jenny'. He is rather more confident with 'a better gown for you of flowered tissue, of sixteen yards, of Mrs Stevenson's fancy', but it wasn't cheap – it cost nine guineas.[61] They just did not make material of that price and quality in America, and mercantilist British policy based on restraining manufacturing competition was intent on keeping it that way.

Franklin was not blind to changes in fashion and customs, so that with 'six coarse Breakfast diaper Cloths' he included instructions for their use, writing that 'they are to spread on the Tea Table, for nobody breakfasts here on the naked Table, but on the Cloth set a large Tea Board with the Cups'.[62]

The mutually beneficial relationships he maintained with the packet-boat captains, such as his friend Nathaniel Falconer and his nephew by marriage Isaac All, proved extremely useful for transporting various large boxes and cases to and from Philadelphia and London.

∽

Franklin was delighted to be shipped American 'goodies' to add to the English standard fare of bread and butter for breakfast. The former might be toasted. Pehr Kalm, the Swedish botanist friend of Peter Collinson who in 1748 stayed in England en route to America, alleged, somewhat fancifully, that toast was a response to the difficulty of spreading bread with hard butter in cold English houses.[63] Breakfast bread could be fruited and there was the option of 'wigs', light yeast-raised bread buns flavoured with ground ginger, cloves, nutmeg and caraway seeds.[64] Wealthier houses had honey and, more rarely, what Boswell called 'that admirable viand, marmalade'.[65] In the modern Continental style, there was also ham and cheese.

Deborah sent over buckwheat meal for buckwheat cakes, popular in Philadelphia as a winter breakfast food, which Pehr Kalm noted after meeting Franklin.[66] She also sent over Indian meal which may have been turned into 'Mush' or 'Mush cakes' or pancakes. At times of stress he certainly enjoyed the American imports, writing to Deborah on 28 January 1772 that 'The Buckwheat and Indian Meal are come safe and good. They will be a great Refreshment to me this Winter. For since I cannot be in America, everything that comes from thence comforts me a little, as being something like Home.'[67]

Benjamin Franklin lived in London as a gentleman, and a gentleman's breakfast was typically served at half past nine or ten. Chocolate, perhaps spiced and flavoured with vanilla, was a popular breakfast drink, but then so was tea.

By the 1750s tea, though extremely expensive, had replaced coffee as the more acceptable beverage, particularly among women. Whereas coffee was associated with the masculine world of the coffee house, tea was the more domestic drink. It was easier than coffee to serve well at home, but not so easy as to deny a hostess the rituals involved in bringing together tea, water and temperature in the right proportion at the right moment. These small performances gave it a cachet and sense of occasion that made it a popular drink to offer social callers throughout the day and Franklin himself enjoyed an afternoon cup of tea.[68] Even by the time of Franklin's first visit to London tea-drinking was becoming fashionable, with satires such as Eliza Haywood's periodical *The Tea-Table*, first published in 1724, authenticating its rituals as it mocked them. The young Ben Franklin almost bowed to fashion himself, because in 1727, soon after his return to America, he hesitated over a wedding present for his sister Jane. First he considered a tea table but, with more thought, the young printer decided that a practical spinning wheel would be more suitable.[69] The commercially powerful East India Company fostered and exploited the fashion for tea and taking tea. Their political muscle, so much greater than that of the West Indian coffee interests, had gained a lowering of the rates of duty between the 1720s and 1740s and driven up demand. Having achieved this, they ensured that taxes and tariffs continued to advantage tea against coffee and rigorously controlled its quality.[70]

Tea had formerly been taken black, but by the mid-century that had changed and 'most people pour a little cream or sweet milk into the teacup, when they are about to drink the tea', as Pehr Kalm observed.[71] It was also customary to add sugar to the strong, bitter Bohea and Congou teas, with the English sweet tooth getting ever sweeter as the century progressed; annual consumption per person increased from four pounds in the first decade to eight in the 1720s and eleven by the 1770s.[72] Taken over the longer term, the power of the West Indian sugar producers and merchants far outstripped their coffee-producing neighbours. Tea and fine sugar were important mass commodities, and escalating demand for them would have major geopolitical repercussions in the 1760s and 1770s.

∽

On 12 January 1758,[73] now totally recovered from his illness, Franklin visited the Penns at Thomas's house in nearby Spring Gardens. Although the Penns and their lawyer Paris had contrived to turn their formal consideration of the 'Heads of Complaint' into one that would take some months, that did not mean they were completely free of Franklin. He still had the need to visit them on urgent Assembly business. When he arrived for his appointment, the veneer of cordiality was wafer-thin. During the meeting it visibly cracked. Afterwards it disappeared completely. Franklin had asked to see the Proprietors because the Penns' Lieutenant Governor had vetoed the Assembly's choice of Commissioners to consider the best means of regulating trade with the Indians.[74] Once again an executive action had become a matter of constitutional significance. In just a few sentences, the discussion between Franklin and Thomas Penn narrowed down to the basis of Pennsylvania's Charter from the Crown and William Penn's own character. A quick series of moves and countermoves began with Franklin saying that the Assembly, like the House of Commons, had the right to appoint Commissioners. Penn replied that it did not, because the rights of the House of Commons did not pertain as the Assembly was merely a corporation acting by Charter from the Crown, and unless a right and privilege was specified in the Charter it was not applicable. Franklin countered with 'Your Father's Charter expressly says that the Assembly of Pennsylvania shall have all the powers and privileges of an assembly according to the rights of the freeborn subjects of England, and is usual in any of the British Plantations in America.' Penn responded that if his father had granted matters that he was not empowered to grant by the Charter then they were invalid. At this, Franklin, with rising incredulity, said that if Penn's father had no right to grant the privileges then those who settled in the province were 'deceived, cheated and betrayed'. Franklin was visibly shocked by Thomas Penn's response that '"they should have themselves looked to that ... that the royal charter was no secret ... {and} ... if they were deceived, it was their own fault"'. Franklin, describing the encounter to Isaac Norris, was thunderstruck: 'Finding myself grow warm made no other answer to this than that the poor people were no lawyers themselves and confiding in his Father did not think it necessary to consult any.'

But the manner as well as the matter of Penn's final words appalled Franklin. As he wrote to Speaker Norris:

That He said with a Kind of triumphing laughing Insolence, such as a low Jockey might do when a Purchaser complained that He had cheated him in a Horse. I was astonished to see him thus meanly give up his Father's Character and conceived that Moment a more cordial and thorough Contempt for him than I ever before felt for any Man living – a Contempt that I cannot express in Words, but I believe my Countenance expressed it strongly. And that his Brother was looking at me, must have observed it.[75]

Richard Penn certainly had done so, afterwards describing Franklin as seeming 'like a malicious villain' but then adding 'like he always does'.[76] However, Thomas Penn had more than his brother's observation to tell him of Franklin's depth of feeling. A Proprietary Assemblyman, probably William Allen, saw the letter to Norris and copied its contents.[77] Richard Peters sent the copy to the Proprietor.[78] None other than Dr Fothergill was able to tell Franklin of Penn's reaction to the letter, because Penn had read it to him. The Proprietor was understandably furious, but he was also calculating. He both denied Franklin's charges and showed the letter to men such as Lord Halifax, still President of the Board of Trade and with a keen interest in American affairs.[79] Fothergill angrily blamed Franklin for the intemperate language towards someone of Penn's social standing. He was right to do so, as Penn was able to use the letter to justify his refusal to deal personally with Franklin in future.[80]

In June 1758 Fothergill wrote to Israel Pemberton that 'Benjamin Franklin has not yet been able to make much progress in his affairs', but he also asked for him to be allowed time. He referred to the Penns' propaganda against Franklin and that they had succeeded in having 'his integrity suspected'. He emphasized that 'These suspicions can only be worn off by time and prudence.'[81]

Franklin's career successes had been built on the rigorous and dispassionate application of logic to practical problems. Yet, faced with what he regarded as deceitful and underhand behaviour, he could be anything but calculating. Overtaken by righteous indignation, he would become what Jonathan Dull has described as 'Franklin Furioso' – capable of both careless hot anger and long-nursed cold fury.[82]

The former was displayed in his missive to Norris, the latter in one to Joseph Galloway written over a year later that discussed the furore caused by the letter. Franklin, having admitted that Fothergill had blamed him 'for writing such harsh Things' and confessing that perhaps he might 'have spared the Comparison of Thomas to a *low Jockey*', could restrain himself no further and wrote 'but Indignation extorted it from me, and I cannot yet say that I much repent of it. It sticks in his Liver, I find; and even let him bear what he so well deserves.'[83]

Despite his anger, Franklin was nobody's fool. His approach to Granville and attempt at direct negotiations with Penn had foundered, but he was quite capable of playing a longer and more prudent game for the benefit of the Assembly of Pennsylvania and for himself.

1758 Onwards

Benjamin Franklin's British Family

In the summer of 1758, when the business with the Penns was in abeyance and 'all the great folks were out of town, and public business at a stand', Franklin took the opportunity to travel.

He and William had already stayed in Cambridge earlier in the year and been 'entertained with great kindness by the principal people, and shown all the curiosities of the place'.[1] He felt that it had been good for both his health and his spirits. Thus when he and William were invited to attend Commencement and the graduation ceremonies at the beginning of July, Franklin did not hesitate to accept. It was another success. As he wrote to Deborah, 'We went accordingly, were present at all the ceremonies, dined every day in their halls, and my vanity was not a little gratified by the particular regard shown me by the chancellor and vice chancellor of the university, and the heads of colleges.'[2] But an opportunity was lost – not by Franklin, but by Cambridge. Franklin had already been awarded honorary degrees by Harvard and Yale and a Masters from William and Mary; it would have been the opportunity for Cambridge to do the same or even to award him a doctorate. The next year St Andrews did just that. From that very moment Ben was very much Dr Franklin and given yet another reason for feeling a keen affinity with Scotland and the Scots.[3]

Franklin certainly nursed a healthy ego and took great pride in the fact that, though he was the youngest son of the family, he was conspicuously the most successful. With notionally the most junior position in the male hierarchy, he had enjoyed taking a dominant role in family affairs. He had brought his nephews James Franklin and Benjamin Mecom into his printing business. And it was he who, shortly before the 1757 voyage to England, composed the epitaph for the stone over his parents' grave, taking credit with the words: 'Their youngest Son, in filial Regard to their Memory, Places this Stone'.[4] Thus it was the most natural thing for the Franklin party, after leaving Cambridge, to take a detour to visit his father's birthplace at Ecton in Northamptonshire.

Franklin had long taken an interest in family history and in 1739 had sent his father some questions about it. Josiah wrote back with a series of entertaining family legends and the fact that Ben's Uncle Benjamin, having 'made inquiry of one skilled in heraldry', had been told that there were two Franklin coats of arms, 'one belonging to the Franklins of the north, and one to the Franklins of the west'. However, Josiah did not know to which, if at all, their branch of the family was related and in any event, as he wrote, 'our circumstances have been such as that it hath hardly been worth while to concern ourselves much about these things, any farther than to tickle the fancy a little'.[5] By 1737 Ben was in a position to go further, writing as 'Philomath' in the *Pennsylvania Gazette* that: 'The first thing requisite in an Almanac-Writer is That he should be descended of a great Family, and bear a Coat of Arms; this gives Lustre and Authority to what a Man writes, and makes the common People to believe that Certainly this is a great man.'[6] So at some point thereafter he adapted and adopted the arms of the Franklins of Badlesmere in Kent – incidentally, of neither the north nor the west – which had been confirmed by a Heralds' visitation in 1592.[7] He had them engraved on a silver tankard, which was one of the artefacts in the exhibition that celebrated the tercentenary of his birth in 2006 and afterwards travelled across the United States.[8] He also had them integrated into his personal seal and they were used on the seal of office of the Deputy Postmaster of North America when he and William Hunter, a Virginian printer, jointly gained that position in 1753.[9]

Josiah also wrote that Ben's grandfather had been born as long ago as 1598 in the village of Ecton and that he (the local smithy and a small freeholder) and Ben's grandmother (the niece of a Colonel

White of Banbury) had produced nine children. Josiah himself was the youngest son and he made special mention of Thomas, his eldest brother, and of Thomas's only child, a daughter who was married to a Mr Fisher at Wellingborough, also in Northamptonshire; though Josiah also gave the detail that the town had 'lately burnt down' and he did not know whether Mary Fisher was alive or dead. He said that her father had bequeathed her £1,500, but could not speak for her current circumstances. Josiah also mentioned that there were children of his brother John and sister Eleanor Morris but that he had lost touch with them.

In his childhood Ben had himself heard stories from his Uncle Benjamin, who had lived with his brother's family for a time, if not always happily.[10] Uncle Benjamin had been an impecunious silk dyer in London, a luxury trade subject to seasonal slumps and long depressions. He had also suffered ill health, as did his family as a whole, with him losing his wife and nine of their ten children before he followed his surviving son to Boston in 1715. But he was also a poet, storyteller and 'an ingenious man, the inventor of a shorthand which he taught his nephew, a collector of books and family anecdotes'.[11] It was partly because of his fond memories of his uncle that in the summer of 1758 Benjamin Franklin (the younger), taking with him William and slave Peter, stopped off at Wellingborough and Ecton on his summer travels. In the manner of a modern family detective he was interested in discovering more. He did find Mary Fisher in Wellingborough, who together with her husband was 'weak with age' but very glad to re-establish contact with the American branch of the Franklin family after a gap of more than thirty years.

From Wellingborough the Franklin party went to Ecton. On reading the parish register, Franklin was delighted to trace his descent through two centuries and to discover that he was actually the youngest son of the youngest son for five generations rather than a mere two. Thus, as he joked, 'had there originally been any Estate in the Family none could have stood a worse Chance for it'.[12]

Barbara Whalley, the vicar's wife, 'a good natured chatty old lady', directed them to the moss-covered gravestones and provided a hard brush and basin of water so Peter could scrub them clean. Not only did she help Franklin to find a quantity of deceased relatives; she helped him to learn more about one of great quality too.[13] Mrs Whalley was both the wife of the incumbent vicar of Ecton and the granddaughter of one of his most distinguished predecessors, John Palmer, who had spotted the nascent talent of Thomas Franklin, Mary Fisher's father, who was born twenty years before his youngest brother Josiah, Ben Franklin's own father. Thomas, of all the Franklin children, had particularly benefited from being 'encouraged in learning' by Mrs Whalley's grandfather and then, 'being ingenious' himself, had qualified as a scrivener and succeeded in becoming 'a very leading man in all county affairs', 'much employed in public business' and 'a chief mover of all public spirited undertakings'. Thomas not only arranged a subscription for church bells for the village but also designed a successful new scheme to protect the village meadows from flooding when 'nobody could conceive how it could be'. Most importantly, Ben tells us that Thomas 'was much taken notice of and patronised by the then Lord Halifax', one of the greatest men in the land. This was the sort of relative Ben was delighted to have – one, in short, who sounded to him exactly like himself. If there is any doubt of that, then a comment in the autobiography substantiates it: on hearing that Thomas had died on Ben's birthday, though four years earlier, William said that, had his death occurred on Ben's actual birth date, 'one might have supposed a transmigration' of his soul. William may have been flattering his father's sometimes considerable vanity, but Ben took it at face value and wrote it down thirteen years later.

If Ben was happy to have found such a suitable long-dead English relative, he was to have decidedly mixed emotions about some living family members as, seemingly inexorably, he gravitated towards becoming the paterfamilias of the Franklin family in England just as he had done in America.

The complexity of his involvement with his English relations began when the Fishers of Wellingborough both died within a fortnight of each other in December 1758. Much of Richard Fisher's money may have come to him from Mary, first through marriage and then through the death of her father, but according to the law it was his to dispose of as he wished. His will was clear: Mary was left £100 per annum for her lifetime but the residue of the estate, thought to be worth £5,000, was to go to his nearest blood relative, the Reverend William Fisher.[14] As £111, including the value of Mary's personal clothing, was taken to be in her estate and she had no surviving children, it was to be shared amongst her seven first cousins, of whom three, including Franklin, were in England, and four in British America. Except it was not £111 but less than £80 as, according to the Reverend Fisher, Mary had requested she be given a funeral as lavish as her husband's and on that basis the £31 cost was deducted.[15] At this point Franklin showed great benevolence to his two English first cousins, Anne Farrow and Eleanor Morris, whom he described as 'ancient Women and poor',[16] by directing that his share of the inheritance, totalling £11 8 shillings and 4 pence, be divided between them.[17]

He would have saved himself some trouble and Mrs Stevenson some expense if he had ended his benevolence there. But he was to take on the role of continuing benefactor and was to provide a lifeline for one desperate woman, Anne Farrow's daughter Hannah.

Curiously, the first letter Anne Farrow sent to her cousin, dated 8 January 1759, made no mention at all of the events at Wellingborough, even though Mrs Fisher's funeral must have taken place before the turn of the year, as is made clear in a letter to Franklin from Richard Quinton, a gentleman, sent from Wellingborough and dated 4 January.[18] Anne Farrow's letter was one of invitation, and though she did stress that she was a poor widow of seventy-four, she assured him that she had 'a good bed to lodge' him, because it would give her 'joy without measure' to see him.

Franklin quickly replied to the widow Farrow with, as one might expect from him, a barrage of questions that related to his English relatives. These she attempted to answer in her reply, dated 19 January, which began, importantly, by thanking him for defraying the cost of the post. It was co-signed by her and her daughter Mrs Hannah Walker.

There are no further letters from Mrs Farrow, but it was the beginning of an intermittent series of nearly a dozen often pathetic, supplicatory, grateful or grovellingly apologetic letters from Mrs

Walker, with the last dated January 1775. Franklin's letters to her do not survive but it is possible to piece together her sad story. In tune with his role as the senior member of the family, Franklin was prepared to help her. She was a lace maker at a time when there was a slump in demand, but it is clear that Hannah's greater problem was her husband, who was a lazy, grasping ne'er-do-well with unsavoury friends. It is also apparent that at one point the husband had used Franklin's or Mrs Stevenson's name to obtain money without their permission and in 1769 the kind benefactor was strongly advised to ensure that any money going to the household went secretly to cousin Hannah without her husband knowing.[19] The advice came from Richard Payne, a surveyor, whom Ben employed to see if he could find the Walkers a better house than the hovel in which they lived. We have an account of their conditions from someone making a detour, when accompanying another Franklin relative to her home. That someone was not the busy Ben Franklin himself, but Margaret Stevenson, whom he sent in his stead. One can tell that she found much to be desired there, though not from the welcome from 'Aunt Morris', who lived with the Walkers, or from Hannah Walker herself. The welcome was far warmer than the house itself at the end of November, though Mrs Walker did her best. Even the husband was on good behaviour and working, as was Hannah Walker at her lace.

Margaret Stevenson noted that food, except butter (and one assumes milk), was dearer than in London. As for the tea, the quality in the Walker household was so poor that Mrs Stevenson could not drink it and had milk instead. Although she metaphorically 'rolled up her sleeves', making bread and pasties for the family, she was all too obviously out of place. The village notables noticed, as she reported that the parson had offered wine and sent a mat to put under her feet to keep out the draught, while the squire's lady had invited her to call.

It was after Mrs Stevenson's report that the offer to move the Walkers was made and Payne did find a suitable house in 1769, though it was some distance away and he advised that the Walkers should move quickly. This they possibly failed to do, as their address in 1775 was still Westbury. In the interim things got worse, with a visit from the bailiffs and a plea for help from Hannah to her wealthy relation. Sadly, not even Benjamin Franklin was able to find a charitable institution to look after one of Hannah's sons who was steadily going blind. But for another he did the best thing he could, which was to get him out of the household by apprenticing him to his great-nephew Josiah Williams, who after a few years took him with him back to America.

Franklin brought another English relative into his care. Like Hannah Walker, Thomas Franklin (the younger) was a grandchild of Ben's long-dead English uncle John.[20] Like Hannah, Tom Franklin, a dyer who lived in Lutterworth, Leicestershire, was not wealthy. Yet after what had been a difficult period, in January 1765 he was, in his own words, 'in my way again of business', as he wrote to Cousin Ben, and said that he would like to come to London to meet him. As a sign of his affection he told him that he was sending a fresh hare, which he knew would be appreciated.[21] The next spring, when Tom Franklin came to London he brought his thirteen-year-old daughter Sally with him. It is likely, as the editors of the Franklin Papers believe,[22] that he had been recently widowed and his head, if not his heart, welcomed Mrs Stevenson's persuasion 'to leave the Child under her Care for a little Schooling and Improvement'. The decision to bring Sally into London's less healthy air almost led to great remorse, as that autumn she was so 'ill of a violent Fever' that Ben thought she would die. However, to the relief of all she recovered, and it was when Mrs Stevenson was taking her home for a visit that they interrupted their journey at the Walkers'. Franklin described Sally as 'a fine Girl' and 'sensible' with 'a sweet obliging Temper'.[23] She was to become a good companion for Mrs Stevenson and stayed with them until 1771. Considering that Ben's grandfather had seven Ecton-born sons who grew to adulthood, it was extraordinary that Sally and her father were, as Ben wrote to Deborah, the only 'two Franklins remaining in England descended from {him}'. After them there were none named Franklin.[24]

In contrast to the Franklins, Deborah's relatives were extremely numerous. Ben and William met great numbers of them for breakfast and dinner during a week in Birmingham, their next stop after Ecton in 1758. Ben described them in a letter to Deborah as 'industrious,

Major British influences on the young Benjamin Franklin

Daniel Defoe

Joseph Addison

John Locke

Sir Isaac Newton

Benjamin Franklin (with lightning strike in the bottom left of the picture) by Benjamin Wilson, Franklin's friend and later bitter foe

Deborah Franklin, Ben's wife and business partner – in Wilson's companion portrait

Franklin's London home in Craven Street, welcoming visitors at Benjamin Franklin House since 2006.

Franklin's own armonica, an instrument he invented.

Polly Stevenson, the clever daughter of Franklin's landlady

Thomas Penn – Proprietor of Pennsylvania and Franklin's first major adversary in London

Dr John Fothergill – a great supporter of Franklin as scientist and man: in the 1750s he was an intermediary between Franklin and Penn; in 1775 between Franklin and the British government.

Franklin had a general affinity with Scotsmen, including:

William Strahan, like Franklin a highly successful printer and a long-time correspondent

Sir John Pringle, President of the Royal Society, travelling companion and chess opponent

David Hume, the great philosopher, was Franklin's host during his month in Edinburgh in 1772.

The Earl of Bute, tutor to the young King George III and then his Prime Minister (1762-3). Through Bute's influence, Franklin's son William became Governor of New Jersey in 1762, much to the fury of Thomas Penn.

This Wedgwood portrait medallion of 1787 honours William Franklin the Loyalist.

George Grenville of the Stamp Tax

William Pitt, Earl of Chatham

Marquess of Rockingham

Charles Townshend of the 'Townshend Duties'

Francis Dashwood, Lord Le Despencer, Franklin's friend of scandalous reputation. In the early 1770s, Franklin spent many happy weeks at Dashwood's country house.

Franklin, like many of his wealthy contemporaries, was a victim of gout, here gruesomely personified by Gillray.

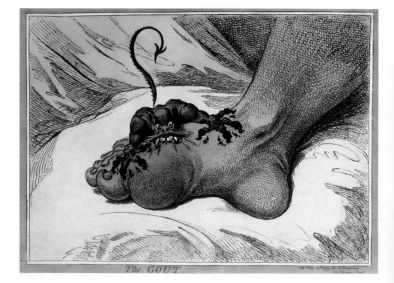

ingenious, working people and think themselves vastly happy that they live in dear old England'.[25]

⚬⚬⚬

There was one English family, the Stevensons, who emotionally meant far more to him than his English blood relations, though young Sally Franklin was also part of that because she was a member of Franklin's household at Craven Street. Others whom Franklin brought into it at this time, of course, included his and William's slaves. Though King left them early, Peter settled much better and soon got to know London through running Franklin's errands. He would not have been at all conspicuous as a black person, because it has been estimated that there were 15,000 people of African origin living in London in the 1760s.[26]

It is right to refer to it as 'Franklin's household', as it had become his own very soon after his arrival. Margaret Stevenson took on the management role that Deborah had fulfilled for him back in Philadelphia. Such is the reputation of the eighteenth century – a time when for form's sake George II felt obliged to take a royal mistress though he did not really want one – that some assume Franklin and Mrs Stevenson must have had a physical relationship.[27] However, there is no evidence that they actually did. Franklin was no prude and he could enjoy a lewd joke. He had sown wild oats in his youth, just as his son and grandson were to do after him. Yet once he had done so, he settled for a matrimonial bliss with Deborah that matured into a mutual reliance – a very deep friendship combined with a partnership in management – though with him at all times seeking to take the leading role. This is what he recreated with Margaret Stevenson.

Much of the speculation about Franklin's relationship with Mrs Stevenson is historiographical backwash from Franklin's later period in France, when flirtatious and louche behaviour in the aristocratic circles in which Franklin moved and sought to influence was not only accepted but expected – though not by a shocked John and Abigail Adams. Thus Abigail Adams's horrified description, both of the dinner party behaviour of Madame Helvétius (Franklin's neighbour and frequent hostess) and of Franklin's benign acceptance of it, should be viewed as a gem of unintentional comedy, and certainly not treated as a deep and damning insight into Franklin's personality.[28] As almost always with Franklin, he was playing a role, even if it was a role he was happy enough to play.

In order to understand Franklin's home life in London, it is best not to guess at what he and Mrs Stevenson may or may not have done, but more useful to consider what they actually did do, which was to form an incredibly close friendship. He was able to treat Craven Street as his home, with Margaret Stevenson managing it for him, and to enjoy a domestic life, just as he would from 1777 at Passy near Paris. There, Madame Helvétius remarked that he 'loved people only as long as he saw them'.[29] That was an overstatement designed to tease him, but there is no doubt that in his personal life he focused on those around him.

Franklin's life at Craven Street was not a sign that he wanted to make himself independent of his wife, but, on the contrary, it demonstrated his previous reliance on her. As Page Talbott points out, they had not only been domestic partners, but long-term business partners:

> From 1730 to 1748, Deborah Franklin worked steadfastly by Franklin's side as they nourished their printing, stationery, and post-office business. Deborah's regular entries in their shop book are testimony both to her daily involvement with sales and inventory – initially ranging from slates to sealing wax to spectacles, later including chocolate, codfish and cheese – and to her propensity toward phonetic spelling.[30]

That last point, as Dr Talbott has made clear,[31] is important. Deborah wrote as she spoke, because she had not been taught otherwise as a child. It was a sign of a lack of education rather than a lack of intelligence for a woman of her age and upbringing; Margaret Stevenson was in the same category. The shop had been an important part of their enterprises, because Franklin had been a serious trader in different commodities, including making himself the largest paper merchant in the colonies.[32] Deborah purchased the rags used in papermaking and Franklin sold the papermakers 166,000 pounds of them between 1739 and 1747, bringing the Franklins the considerable sum of more than £1,000.³³ In that sense it was a 'rags to riches' story.

Acknowledging the importance of his wife, Franklin, in the second part of his *Autobiography* (1785), wrote that 'it was lucky for me that I had one as much disposed to Industry and Frugality as myself', and he had previously emphasized that they 'throve together, and have ever mutually endeavoured to make each other happy'.³⁴ Franklin trusted his wife and respected her business acumen, so that when preparing to take ship for England in 1757, he had felt able to write to her that 'I leave Home, and undertake this long Voyage more cheerfully, as I can rely on your Prudence in the Management of my Affairs'.³⁵ This she was prepared to do until his return.

Franklin's transatlantic relationship with Deborah should be seen in this light. Deborah had not accompanied him to London and he knew that, because of her fear of seagoing, she would never do so. This he clearly understood, as when he wrote to her in January 1758, 'I am sure there is no inducement strong enough to prevail with you to cross the seas'.³⁶ It was not an excuse on her part, but a quite understandable phobia, comparable with those afraid of air travel today and reinforced by the real hazards of eighteenth-century voyages. Thus, bearing in mind her fears, Ben's report to her from Falmouth following his and William's fortunate deliverance from watery disaster was not exactly sensitive.³⁷ Neither, it might appear, was his 1742 song 'I Sing My Plain Country Joan' or his 'Old Mistresses Apologue' of 1745 – both of which, rather ungallantly, paid tribute to the practical advantages and practicalities of an older woman such as his wife, though these pieces were for the benefit of friends and may not have been known to Deborah. Admiration for her practicality was not at the sacrifice of his real affection for her. On the face of it, his words comparing her to 'a large fine jug for beer', when writing to her in February 1758, would not seem particularly complimentary, but actually they demonstrate real and mature fondness: 'I fell in Love with it at first Sight; for I thought it looked like a fat jolly Dame, clean and tidy, with a neat blue and white Calico Gown on, good natured and lovely, and put me in mind of—Somebody'.³⁸

It was because of the very importance of Deborah's managerial role in Philadelphia that Franklin came to rely on Margaret Stevenson in England. In one respect she went further, being for much of the time, and often crucially, Franklin's financier. This was even the case in matters involving his own blood relations: it was she, not he, who was the potential creditor of Franklin's unreliable relatives, Mr and Mrs Walker. At several points Franklin himself owed her prodigious sums of money, and when he left England in 1775 the debt included four years' rent of £100 per annum and just over £470 more in additional loans and expenses.[39] He did ensure she was properly and promptly repaid on his arrival in America; but the vastness of these sums shows a bond of trust between them.

∽

There has also been much speculation about Franklin's relationship with Margaret Stevenson's daughter Mary (Polly), who was eighteen when Franklin arrived in London. There is a 'What the Butler Saw' deliberately indistinct drawing of Franklin with a young woman on his knee, by Charles Willson Peale, who visited Craven Street in 1767. James Srodes in *Franklin: The Essential Founding Father* raises the question that the woman depicted might be Polly Stevenson, only immediately to dismiss it because 'she was very prim and moral'. In fact he concludes that 'it had to have been in jest, for Franklin was no fool to allow such an indiscretion to be captured unless it was innocent'.[40] That seems most likely, bearing in mind that Peale, a brilliant artist, was also a superb illusionist with a boyish sense of humour.[41]

Franklin may have been flirtatious in his relationships with young women, he might have enjoyed having them sit on his knee, but it is fair to say that he would have run a mile had any of them suggested anything more than that. This is not the view of just one historian but of many. Larry Tise brought a distinguished group together at a symposium at the Franklin Institute in Philadelphia to consider the matter and then edited *Benjamin Franklin and Women* with their contributions. In the introduction Tise concluded that, when it came to young women at this stage of Franklin's life, 'his relationship with them was also a complicated affair that always had much less to do with sex than with the fine interplay of minds, with Franklin in the role of mentor'.[42] That was certainly the case with Polly, who might be called his star pupil. Although Polly spent much of her time living with an elderly and wealthy aunt, the delightfully named Mrs Tickell, at Wanstead, which was then around ten miles outside London, Franklin became very fond of her. This matured from something avuncular to fondly paternal. When she was away, she clearly missed Franklin and he missed her.

She was a remarkable young woman, bright and highly literate. Whereas Margaret Stevenson, like Deborah Franklin, wrote phonetically, Polly's command of written English was superb. She was well educated, in a contemporary ladylike fashion, and that may have been because she had been a pupil at Dr and Mrs Hawkesworth's School for Young Ladies in Bromley, Kent. All records have long been lost, but it seems possible, as there is no other obvious connection and she was certainly close to them; and it was she who introduced Franklin to John Hawkesworth, then approaching the peak of his career as an author.[43] But whatever her education, what marks Polly out in particular is her extraordinary thirst for knowledge.

In 1759 she came up with a brilliant scheme for ensuring a regular and entertaining correspondence with her mother's famous house guest. One area where she felt herself to be less than knowledgeable was that of natural philosophy. She suggested that Franklin teach her. If one considers the eminence of Franklin's friends and acquaintances in the world of natural philosophy, this was certainly presumptuous. When he received Polly's letter, in the autumn of 1759, Franklin had just returned from a three-month trip with William and Peter to Scotland, via Derbyshire and the Lancashire towns. Ben had received civic awards in Edinburgh, Glasgow and St Andrews and he and William had travelled west to Inveraray to visit the Duke of Argyll, recently restored to British political influence, helped by his being the Earl of Bute's uncle. In Edinburgh, with Strahan there for part of the time and smoothing the way, the Franklins had breakfasted, dined and supped with the brightest of the Scottish Enlightenment, including David Hume and Adam Smith. Franklin was described after one of these occasions as 'a silent man', in contrast to William who was 'open and communicative';[44] but as he became better acquainted with each individual Franklin relaxed and delighted in the philosophical exchanges. He was soon firm friends with Sir Alexander Dick (President of the Royal College of Physicians of Edinburgh), and the Franklin party stayed with him at Prestonfield, by Holyrood Park. They broke their journey home at the Berwickshire home of another new friend, the judge and philosopher Henry Home, Lord Kames.[45] So impressed was Franklin with his time in Scotland that he was rhapsodic in a letter he wrote to Kames following his return:

> On the whole, I must say, I think the Time we spent there was Six Weeks of the *densest* Happiness I have met with in any Part of my Life. And the agreeable and instructive Society we found there in such Plenty has left so pleasing an Impression on my Memory that, did not strong Connections draw me elsewhere, I believe Scotland would be the Country I should choose to spend the Remainder of my Days in.[46]

As to Franklin's gifted understanding of the more mechanical elements of natural philosophy, it had been further enhanced in Birmingham in 1758, when he and William had made the most of their days in and around the town,[47] 'continually on the foot, from one manufactory to another, and were highly entertained in seeing all the curious machines and expeditious ways of working'.[48] Franklin had spent time with Matthew Boulton and the type designer and printer John Baskerville.[49] In 1760 he would go there again and undertake experiments with Boulton as a prelude to their discussing the transformative potential of industrial steam power with Erasmus Darwin.[50] Add to these great minds those of all the people he met week after week in London – would he really want to discuss science with a young girl?

Certainly with this one. He was delighted to do so. The first line of his reply, started at ten o'clock at night, was 'At length I have found an Hour, in which I think I may chat with my dear good Girl; free from Interruption.' That was followed, after a paragraph of thanks for some garters she had knitted for him, with 'The question you ask me is a very sensible one, and I shall be glad if I can give you a satisfactory Answer.'[51] There then followed a long explanation of the workings of chimneys. It was the beginning of a correspondence where Polly put the great man through his paces. Over the next three years they ranged across the gamut of physical phenomena, mixed in with theology and moral philosophy as well as some comments on the scientific method. Franklin sent book lists, the books themselves and tips on how to study. Polly came up with questions, and he endeavoured to give answers, on subjects such as the following: barometers; the relative importance of insects to mankind; rivers and tides; rainfall and the evaporation of water; church architecture; electricity (not surprisingly); the nature and properties of air, gases and winds; fire and the flammability of different substances in different chemical states; and the nature of absorption and reflection of the sun's rays according to colour. Polly showed a sparkling intelligence, often working out her own answers in a way that delighted him. He greatly enjoyed the correspondence. So much so, that when there was a slacking of tutorial pace, he was the one who in March 1762 wrote plaintively: 'Have you finished your Course of Philosophy? No more Doubts, to be resolved; no more Questions to ask?'[52]

8

1758–1762

Moves and Countermoves

When it came to fulfilling his primary mission on behalf of the Assembly of Pennsylvania, Franklin had time on his hands in 1758 and 1759.

Ferdinand Paris's expert legal comments on Franklin's short 'Heads of Complaint' took two and a half months. He wrote to the Law Officers at the beginning of November and asked for their legal opinion. Charles Yorke, the Solicitor General, responded comparatively quickly, on 13 January 1758, the very day after Franklin's fractious meeting with the Penns. Yorke found totally in favour of the Proprietors. However Yorke alone was not enough; the opinion of the Attorney General, Charles Pratt (later Lord Camden), was also required and he had an unresolved conflict of interest. Robert Charles, Franklin's fellow agent, had earlier in 1757, before Franklin's arrival and before Pratt's appointment, paid the latter a retainer to act for the Assembly. This made Pratt technically a party to the dispute. One can only surmise what the Penns and Franklin knew of the Law Officers' respective positions from their own subsequent actions. There was from this point a near-farcical joint reversal of tactics.

Franklin must have believed that untying Pratt's hands at that point would be fatal to the Assembly's case, because when the Attorney General sought to return the retainer money to Charles, Franklin advised Charles not to accept it. The Proprietors, in their turn, pushed for a decision.[1]

There was further conflict due to Thomas Penn's support for the Reverend William Smith. Smith had recently been imprisoned in

Philadelphia for libel by the long-suffering Assembly and, in his own view, falsely so.[2] In April 1758 Thomas Penn had personally appeared on Smith's behalf at a hearing before the Law Officers in London and did so by 'abetting the abuses thrown on the assembly'. Franklin was appalled at Penn's open defence of this 'ready scribbler ... employed in all the dirty work of abusing and libelling the Assembly',[3] who was also, as he might have added, the author of a cascade of exceptional vituperation against Franklin himself.[4] It was, as Franklin was quick to tell his Assembly allies, 'looked upon by everybody as an open Declaration of War'.[5]

In November 1758, almost a year after receiving Paris's request, Pratt at last felt that sufficient time had elapsed for him to give his advice. Paris was under no obligation to reveal the nature of what he had received in confidence, nor did he do so. On 27 November he issued his 'Answer' to Franklin. It both refuted the matter and repudiated the bearer of the 'Heads of Complaint'. The next day the Penns sent their own letter, not to Franklin but direct to the Assembly. Like Paris, they identified Franklin as a man without candour, attacked the slipshod nature of his paper, deliberately misrepresented him as saying that he lacked the authority to act for the Assembly and added that he had been disrespectful towards them. The intention was clear: they were refusing to have anything further to do with Franklin and they wished him to be recalled in disgrace. That was also made clear to the man himself when he wrote to Paris querying a point in his 'Answer to the Heads of Complaint'. Paris responded with a letter dripping with venom. In a curt note of a few lines, he referred to Franklin's 'very extraordinary Paper ... which you have been pleased to call Proposals', and stressed that Franklin had already been notified that the Proprietors were going to write direct to the Assembly and that therefore he 'cannot conceive it will answer any good purpose, to continue a Correspondence with a Gentleman, who has already acknowledged his Want of Power to conclude proper Measures'.[6] To complete his satisfaction, Paris delivered it to Franklin in person.[7]

It was the end of Franklin's formal contact with the Proprietors, but he was certainly not recalled to Philadelphia. He ensured that

Norris, Galloway and the Assembly majority knew his side of the story and he was helped by reports of Thomas Penn's continuing support for William Smith, who arrived in London on 1 January 1759. On 26 June Smith eventually received a ruling from the Privy Council in his favour, but not before Galloway and his allies had successfully launched further assaults on his reputation back in Philadelphia.[8]

Now that direct communication with the Proprietors was at an end, Franklin would have to approach the British government on the Assembly's behalf. But that was not inappropriate because Franklin had come to the conclusion that Pennsylvania must throw off the Penns and become a Crown colony.[9]

⌘

The matter of the 'Heads of Complaint' had run on for more than fifteen months and Franklin had been active in the meantime. He had been thinking strategically in order to reverse his tactical defeat by Thomas Penn. He knew that he would not win a battle of legal points with someone like Ferdinand John Paris. Not that he was wholly ignorant of the law, having been a Justice of the Peace in Philadelphia, with the rank of Esquire, which he had immediately used. He had given up the role itself in 1754, partly because all his fellow magistrates were adherents of the Proprietors,[10] but also, more pertinently, because he had a much greater interest in understanding the laws of science, mathematics and logic rather than the common law of man.[11] In his autobiography he explained it thus: 'The Office of Justice of the Peace I tried a little, by attending a few Courts, and sitting on the Bench to hear Causes. But finding that more Knowledge of the Common Law than I possessed was necessary to act in that Station with Credit, I gradually withdrew from it.'[12] But this was a man who could master any branch of knowledge that interested him; so one must agree with Leo Lemay's conclusion that Franklin found it boring as well as time-consuming.

Franklin was, however, able to call on someone who found the law anything but dull. This was Richard Jackson, who was generally nicknamed the 'Omniscient', though the admiring Dr Johnson preferred 'all knowing' in deference to God.[13] Jackson had earned his soubriquet through his extraordinary fund of knowledge. More particularly Franklin was able to tell the Assembly that Jackson was 'esteemed the best acquainted with our American Affairs, and Constitutions, as well as with Government Law in general'.[14] With Jackson, as with so many others, Franklin had converted a long-running epistolary relationship into a strong personal acquaintance. As noted earlier, taciturn and cautious with people until he knew and decided he liked them, Franklin nevertheless had a gift for making friends – and useful ones. He had long been able to guide people into fulfilling particularly helpful roles. As his years and his fame advanced, and with mentors being replaced by collaborators, he seemed to become even more accomplished at it, to the extent that though new individuals might replace the old, their roles could remain strikingly the same, with Franklin deftly deploying them as if they were pieces on a chessboard.

Chess fascinated him – hardly surprising for a man who had previously developed his own decision-making system in the form of 'Moral or Prudential Algebra' and had improved Frénicle's Magical Squares. He was obviously not only very good at the game but highly competitive. It was not a mere diversion but a chance to pit his wits against clever people and to win on a regular basis. This explains his chagrin, expressed in a 1752 letter to Strahan from Philadelphia, that 'my principal Antagonist at Chess is dead, and the few remaining Players here are very indifferent'.[15]

Judging from letters to him in London, there was no shortage of men and indeed women keen to take him on. A promise of a decent game of chess, like a delicious piece of venison, was likely to tempt him out to dinner. A Mrs Katherine French, of whom we know little except that she used this tactic, even told him in advance of an opponent she had specially invited.[16]

What is most instructive is that he viewed his approach to chess problems and political problems as being remarkably similar, as he himself explains in an essay entitled 'The Morals of Chess'. Though this was first published in 1779, the editors of the Franklin Papers trace its formulation to as early as 1732.[17] It is certainly worth reading in its entirety,[18] but the following excerpts give more than a flavour:

Life is a kind of chess, in which we have often points to gain, and competitors or adversaries to contend with, and in which there is a vast variety of good and ill events that are, in some degree, the effects of prudence or the want of it. By playing at chess, then, we may learn:

1. *Foresight*, which looks a little into futurity, and considers the consequences that may attend an action ... 2. *Circumspection*, which surveys the whole chess-board, or scene of action, the relations of the several pieces and situations ... 3. *Caution*, not to make our moves too hastily.

He then made an additional point, perhaps the most interesting of all, before writing at length about the importance of etiquette and fair play, the latter being rather amusing if one believes tales – surely apocryphal – of Dr Franklin drumming his fingers in annoyance at slow play or rearranging a piece or two when his opponent left the room.[19]

But to return to that additional point and Franklin's advice:

Lastly, we learn by chess the habit of *not being discouraged* by *present* bad appearances in the state of our affairs, the habit of *hoping for a favourable change,* and that of *persevering in the search of resources.* The game is so full of events, there is such a variety of turns in it, the fortune of it is so subject to sudden vicissitudes, and one so frequently, after long contemplation, discovers the means of extricating oneself from a supposed insurmountable difficulty, that one is encouraged to continue the contest to the last, in hopes of victory by our own skill, or, at least, of giving a *stalemate.*[20]

He hoped for a stalemate, at the very least, with Thomas Penn.

৵

Richard Jackson was one of a startlingly small group of people, aside from those with business interests, who had an informed knowledge of America. In 1760 he would become an agent for Connecticut and in 1763, with Franklin back in America, he would take on the same role for Pennsylvania. Before that, in deepest secrecy so as not to damage his ambition to become an MP, Jackson was more than happy to help the Franklins, both father and son. It is likely that he assisted William with his letter to the press in 1757; it is now certain that *An Historical Review of the Constitution and Government of Pennsylvania* was written by him with information produced by Franklin. Financed by Franklin and published in June 1759 by Strahan, this was no minor undertaking but a 380-page documented political history of Pennsylvania from its 1681 Charter up to 1756, designed to show the arbitrary and illegal actions of the Proprietors and their governors.[21] It came with sixty-four pages of appendices, including remarks on what were described as Thomas Penn's own estimates of Proprietary estates and revenues (vastly inflated and certainly not his own figures)[22] and William's letter of 1757. Franklin denied authorship of *An Historical Review*, but his fingerprints were all over it. Penn was certain of Franklin's involvement. This was a highly professional propaganda exercise, including a press announcement of its publication at the end of May 1759.[23] Franklin was satisfied with its effect on Penn. He reported that 'When I meet him anywhere there appears in his wretched Countenance a strange Mixture of Hatred, Anger, Fear and Vexation.'[24] However, more generally it had a disappointing reception, selling poorly in England and even Pennsylvania.[25]

Franklin was making other moves. One was his attempt to mobilize the enfeebled grandson of William Penn by his first wife to make a legal claim that the Proprietorship had been illegally transferred in 1731. It was a hare-brained scheme involving complicated legal manoeuvres, and, after the sacrifice of much time and ink, it finally died with twenty-six-year-old Springett Penn in 1766.

What put the matter of Thomas Penn and his tax avoidance back into play was not done by the hand of Franklin, but through the un-Quakerlike action of the Assembly leaders in bribing Penn's Governor in Philadelphia, William Denny. In April 1759 Denny agreed a £100,000 supply bill which included the principle of taxing the Penn estates.[26] Thomas Penn was, unsurprisingly, outraged. He began legal proceedings that autumn, but matters were delayed partly due to the illness and death in December of Ferdinand Paris and the need to appoint another solicitor, and partly through other business at the

Board of Trade. The hearing finally began at the end of May 1760 and it included the substantive issues that had led the Assembly to send Franklin to London in 1757. Representing the Penns were the government Law Officers, Pratt and Yorke. For the Assembly was William de Grey (a skilled barrister who, in the 1760s, would successively occupy the Law Officer posts of his opponents), supported by Richard Jackson. This was a battle between legal heavyweights. Of the eleven points at issue, the Board found in favour of the Proprietors by seven points to four. It was a substantial as well as a numerical defeat for the Assembly, but it was not the final judgement, as the solicitor acting for the Assembly's agents Franklin and Robert Charles appealed to the Privy Council. The appeal was heard at the end of August at the Cockpit in Whitehall, so named after a previous incarnation of the site as the arena for royal cockfighting at the time of Henry VIII.[27] This time six of the eleven points went to the Proprietors, but the decision was not clearly in favour of either side, as was shown by each claiming victory and by the division of historians' opinions. However, the editors of the Franklin Papers come to a judgement, after examining the evidence in great and often entertaining detail and by balancing the points against each other in the manner of Franklin's own 'Prudential Algebra'.[28] Though haggling between Lieutenant Governor John Penn and the Assembly continued in the early 1760s and up to 1764,[29] the main point had been decided, as the editors of the Franklin Papers explain:

> The Assembly gained full recognition of the right to tax the proprietary estates, and the Penns won legislative safeguards of the principle that they should not be discriminated against in future taxation. Neither side can be said to have achieved a complete victory on this major point of dispute. The colony as a whole, however, benefited most of all because the matter of taxing the proprietary estates, a barrier to effective government since 1755, was never again a central issue of Pennsylvania politics.[30]

As far as Franklin himself was concerned, he was able to claim that, because it had been decided that the Proprietary estates could be taxed, he had fulfilled the most important part of his mission to England. It was of less concern to him that the Penns had negotiated all kinds of safeguards including the right to be taxed at the lowest possible tax level. And it was now far less important than the conviction he had formed, shared at this point by Speaker Norris, that the final resolution to the dispute between the Assembly and the Proprietors would come only once Pennsylvania had ceased to be a Proprietary colony and become a royal one.

*

As Penn had predicted, Franklin had found it difficult to make headway with the ministers at the top of government. The old Whigs, Granville, Halifax and Lord Hardwicke, formerly a Lord Chancellor of long standing and father to the Solicitor General Charles Yorke, all shared the view that the colonies had claimed too much for themselves. As for the 'Oldest Whig' of them all, the Prime Minister, the Duke of Newcastle, there is no record of business meetings, though it is possible that he and Franklin may have met at the Masonic Grand Lodge of England.[31]

The Americans were far from friendless; for instance the Attorney General, Charles Pratt – legal duties aside – had shown himself to be generally sympathetic and William Pitt, Secretary of State and war leader, was not only a friend of America but, in the 1759 'Year of Victories', triumphantly acclaimed there. But Pitt, high-handed with his ministerial colleagues, was too busy winning the war to be interested in Representative Franklin.

All the same, Franklin was making a start. He had been disappointed by Granville in 1757, but he had learned from it. He had realized that he had to lobby government at a lower level, that of the workhorse under-secretaries who acted both as administrators and political advisers to their aristocratic superiors and could provide or deny access to them.

This was a long game, but Franklin seems to have started with Robert Wood (Under-Secretary to Pitt), Thomas Potter (Paymaster to the Forces before his death in 1759)[32] and John Clevland at the Admiralty.[33] John Pownall, Halifax's loyal Secretary at the Board of Trade and a crucial 'gatekeeper', had not proved obstructive. Unlike his brother Thomas, Pownall was not a particular friend of Franklin's,[34] and Halifax had not favoured the American, but by 1759 Franklin was writing to Norris to tell him that he had free access to the all-important records at the Board of Trade, including the 'manuscript Volumes of old Pennsylvania Laws', which William researched.[35] These had proved useful in their case against the Proprietors and Pownall could have made their life difficult by denying them. Franklin was at last making some progress in cultivating the necessary contacts and connections within the administration.

⟨∞⟩

On 3 December 1760, Franklin was approached by the Society of Arts and asked to become one of the two chairmen of the Committee of Colonies and Trade. This completely suited his scientific interests, because it was the role of the committee to award 'premiums' or financial awards as part of the Society's 'encouragement'. At the first meeting he chaired, on 6 January 1761, the discussion covered persimmon gum, botanic gardens, dyes from logwood trees, myrtle wax for candlemaking, silkworms, American sturgeon, isinglass, hemp, silk grass and opium. It will be noted that the focus was on the development of natural resources rather than on manufacture. In time this emphasis would greatly irritate Franklin, but at this point he was delighted to throw himself into the work.[36]

He was one of two Members of the Society invited to chair the committee, displacing two others. The appointment was, of course, highly flattering to Franklin and it was certainly not the cause of any lasting ill-feeling with one of the replaced chairmen, Israel Wilkes. Israel, the far more respectable brother of John Wilkes, remained a friend; the Franklin Papers show, for instance, that he invited Ben to Christmas lunch in 1766.[37] What is also striking is the identity of the other invited chairman, who had accepted the position a week before Franklin and who would have been consulted as to the choice of his colleague. That other man was the Board of Trade's Secretary, John Pownall.[38]

In spite of Thomas Penn's sneer of 1757,[39] Dr Franklin was very effectively combining science and politics. Franklin, as in his work with John Pownall's brother at the 1754 Albany Conference, was not just focused on Pennsylvania, but had an eye to the interests of British America more generally.

The colonial Assemblies' rejection of the plan for Union did not diminish Franklin's faith in a British America that could be peopled with a hard-working population of what he narrowly defined as Anglo-Saxons.[40] In his 'Observations Concerning the Increase of Mankind', which was published in 1754 and republished in 1760 as an Index to his *The Interest of Great Britain Considered, with Regard to her Colonies*, Franklin estimated that the white population of the American colonies was doubling every twenty-five years[41] – an estimation that is impressively supported by the figures of modern historical statisticians: 265,000 for 1700, rising to just over 2 million for 1770.[42]

In *The Interest of Great Britain Considered* Franklin argued that the retention of Canada in any peace treaty with the French was far more important for the long-term advancement of the Great British economic model than the short-term sweet delights of the sugar-rich island of Guadeloupe. He emphasized that the addition of Canada to the American colonies, the military expulsion of the French and the removal of barriers to settlement would promote the population expansion required to increase the quantity of primary products needed to match the ever-increasing scale of British manufacture. That in turn could be sold to the vastly proliferating population of the colonies. Adopting a Malthusian approach pre-Malthus, Franklin could see the way to accommodate the rise in population of both Britain and the American colonies. The latter, with a much lower death rate, were of course expanding far more quickly – but then they had the land into which to expand. Franklin could see the potential of the American land mass. In his role as Deputy Postmaster for America he travelled vast distances in his quest to determine the shortest postal routes. As ever, he was able to invent a practical aid to help him: a means of measuring the number of turns made by a wheel of his carriage, through which the milometer was born. Franklin also keenly observed the country as he passed. He may not have written down his impressions of America in the manner of Defoe's *Tour through the Whole Island of Great Britain*, but he took in what he saw.

It is difficult to assess the influence on government decision-making of his near-14,000-word essay, written in the guise of an Englishman and with assistance from Richard Jackson.[43] But that holds true for the propaganda on both sides. One can say, though, that Franklin's was a coherent case and the Canada argument won. What is even more important about the pamphlet is that it incorporates Franklin's view of the exceptional potential and hence importance of British America for the future of the empire and for Britain itself.

Franklin was concerned, however, that the quality of the future British Americans should match their expected quantity. As early as 1751 he had written his article 'Felons and Rattlesnakes' for the *Pennsylvania Gazette* under the pen name of Americanus. In it he ridiculed the fact that the government in London had for many years supported the principle of exporting criminals to the Americas for the 'IMPROVEMENT *and* WELL PEOPLING of the Colonies'.[44] In fact, unsurprisingly, those convicts who broke their bonds were a major source of criminal activity. Hence Franklin's entertaining suggestion that, as part of a balance of trade, rattlesnakes should be exported to Britain and in particular they should be 'carefully distributed in St James's Park, in the Spring-Gardens and other Places of Pleasure about London; in the Gardens of all the Nobility and Gentry throughout the Nation; but particularly in the Gardens of the *Prime Ministers, the Lords of Trade* and *Members of Parliament*; for to them we are *most particularly* obliged'.[45] Even then he was not sure that the trade was well balanced. After all, 'the *Rattle-Snake* gives Warning before he attempts his Mischief; which the Convict does not'.[46]

Franklin was a proud Briton, but he was not starry-eyed. Between 1751 and 1760 he gained further experience of how Britons from the British Isles could be far from ideal, including those at a very senior level.

The London government had hoped, like Franklin, that the colonies would unite on defence and security matters following the Albany

Conference. As that failed to materialize, they appointed a British commander, General Edward Braddock, to co-ordinate countermeasures against the French threat. Braddock, however, was not even able to co-ordinate the supply and logistics for his own campaign in 1755 – with one Benjamin Franklin patriotically organizing the necessary renting of transport wagons and, furthermore, providing the finance at no interest in order to do so. But disaster was to follow when Braddock's 2,000 troops were ambushed and routed by an 800-strong French force, of whom three-quarters were native Americans: Braddock died and two-thirds of his men were killed or wounded. It was almost ruinous for Franklin, with Loudoun, Braddock's successor, unwilling to rubber-stamp his request for the money and accusing him of having joined the general ranks of profiteers. Fortunately Braddock had supplied the necessary authorizations and Franklin received almost all he was owed from London. Franklin was to describe the whole campaign, if such it can be called, as 'frivolous, expensive and disgraceful to our nation beyond conception'.[47] But it was still 'our nation' and Franklin retained a belief in the possibility of change. In 1760 one event ushered in a stream of changes that altered the political picture entirely.

☙

On Saturday, 25 October 1760 the seventy-six-year-old King George II, as was his custom, took his morning chocolate and then repaired to his close stool. Shortly afterwards his valet 'heard a deep sigh, immediately followed by the noise like the falling of a billet of wood from the fire'.[48] The King had suffered a massive heart attack and he died shortly afterwards. His twenty-two-year-old grandson succeeded him, as George III, and the new King was very different from his Hanoverian predecessors, being 'English born and Bred' and hopeful of placing government in the hands of his former tutor and continuing favourite, John Stuart, 3rd Earl of Bute. In the long term the accession of the new King George would have lasting consequences for the American colonies; in the shorter term, Bute's influence offered a great opportunity for the Franklins.

The new King had lost his father, Frederick Prince of Wales, in 1751. Frederick had died from the bursting of an abscess in a lung that was probably the result of the unusual accident of being hit very hard by a cricket ball two years before. However, not long afterwards young Prince George gained a surrogate father as well as a tutor in Bute, who during the next decade instilled an emotional dependence as well as a growing sense of duty in his young charge. That sense of dependence was later recalled by the Duchess of Northumberland (in 1760 still Countess) who described the young King as 'naturally of a cheerful even Sociable Disposition and a clear Understanding, yet he lived in the utmost Retirement, owing I believe to the Ascendancy Lord Bute had over him, which certainly was very great. The King had his Picture at whole length in his private Closet.'[49]

The King was not alone in admiring Bute's portrait. Benjamin Franklin had two engravings: one in London and one at his home in Philadelphia, and they were each prominently and publicly displayed. John Adams, who was more than happy to recall the British elements of Franklin's pre-revolutionary life, later remarked on that fact and related that when Franklin was challenged on his proud claim to have had great influence with the British ministry, he 'broke out into a Passion and swore, contrary to his normal reserve.'[50] Adams intended this as a smear, but Franklin was certainly well connected to Lord Bute.

We do not know who first brought Dr Franklin into the Earl of Bute's orbit, but there were many who would have been willing and able to provide the initial introduction. Bute was not only a great botanist in close contact with Peter Collinson, but had a more general scientific interest, with his own fine collection of electrical equipment.[51] Franklin might have been introduced to him by his friend John Pringle, the Earl's personal physician. Pringle like Bute himself was a well-connected Scot, as were Strahan and also Franklin's neighbour Caleb Whitefoord, another man close to Bute.[52]

But it is also possible that Ben, for once, may have been following in his son William's footsteps. The Earl of Northumberland was on close terms with Lord Bute (the son of the former was to marry the latter's daughter in 1764) and William had certainly found a welcome at Northumberland House, which overshadowed its near-neighbours in Craven Street.[53] On one occasion William showed himself, in a very literal sense, to be more of an insider than his father. The two Franklins had rushed back from a tour of the Low Countries to attend the Coronation on 22 September 1761, deliberately designed to be the greatest ceremonial event of the age. William was a member of the Westminster Abbey congregation whereas Ben, in contrast, was part of the lesser ticketed throng outside.[54]

The Coronation was an occasion when the new young King had shown his character. He had seen it as his duty to study all aspects of the ceremony down to the minutest detail and thus, with good humour, he happily corrected the mistakes made in procedure by the heralds and then the wording of the Archbishop of Canterbury.[55] His approach to the event was representative: George was an earnest young man who was determined that the correct forms and procedures should be followed. This did not just concern ceremonial but extended to his entire role. No one could argue that George III was the cleverest of kings, on a par with the likes of Frederick the Great; but he certainly had a profound sense of duty.

By 1760 George had, through Bute's tuition and with dogged determination, already studied the requirements of his constitutional position. George wrote down his conclusions in an essay written earlier that year. Some might be surprised to read that the royal heir feared that a king might exercise unrestrained power through his control of the army and upset the balance between monarch and Parliament through, for example, the indiscriminate creation of peers; but that was so, with his essay advocating royal restraint.[56] What it also demonstrated was a seriousness of purpose, a sense of royal 'honour' and an expectation of ministerial 'virtue'.[57] Thus, on succeeding to the throne, George reasserted the King's right to appoint ministers and he sought a government that was 'a coalition of the best men', rather than a coalescence of self-interested factions.[58] The best man of all he naturally believed to be Bute, an opinion not shared, unsurprisingly, by the incumbent dominant ministers, Newcastle and Pitt. Bute was, however, inserted into the ministry and gradually took on increased responsibilities.

The King would ultimately prove far more resolute than Bute in pursuing their plan to purify politics. However, their good intentions in 1760 helped to create a decade of ministerial instability at the very time that British policy towards the American colonies needed clear direction.

King George did not seek to dictate policy, merely to maintain his right to appoint ministers. He was not a tyrant; but, with a certain inflexibility of mind and a rigid adherence to what he believed to be the correct political form and practice, he was perfectly capable of being a pedant.

✍

Franklin had another possible link to the powerful Earl of Bute through a very old acquaintance: James Ralph. He had neither heard from nor even of him for three decades, until after the arrival in 1756 of Pennsylvania's new Lieutenant Governor, William Denny, who, as Franklin writes in the *Autobiography*, 'gave me the first Information that my old Friend James Ralph was still alive, that he was esteemed one of the best political Writers in England, had been employed in the Dispute between Prince Frederick and the King, and had obtained a Pension of Three Hundred a Year; that his Reputation was indeed small as a Poet, *Pope* having damned his poetry in the *Dunciad*, but his Prose was thought as good as any Man's.'[59]

This succinct summary is spot on. Ralph had firmly ignored Franklin's warning about 'the folly of pursuing the muses' and soon after their breach had begun to establish himself as a writer and a critic. However, his career as a poet was short-lived. Though his first book of poetry was published in 1727, only a year after Franklin's return to America, and his second, *Night* (1728), brought him some success, he ended all chance of further poetic fame by ridiculing the *Dunciad* of Alexander Pope, the dominant literary personality of the time. In response Pope added a new verse to his second edition attacking Ralph and, with the line 'Answer him, ye owls', he called on the owlish critics to descend.[60] They did.

Ralph was forced to turn to the theatre. He may have started as a critic with his *Touch-Stone* (1728), but he soon, in collaboration with Henry Fielding, took to writing and staging plays. This lasted until

1737, when the success of Fielding's satires against both Sir Robert Walpole and his government brought the counter-reaction of the theatrical Licensing Act. That turned Fielding's thinking towards lighter plays, great novels and the legal profession; it sent Ralph to potential penury. However, in 1739 they collaborated again, on an opposition journal called *The Champion*, which enabled Ralph to show his talent for penning political polemics. He also began writing well-researched history books and sparked a fierce controversy by attacking the reputation of the then ancient but no less forceful Sarah, Duchess of Marlborough, finding himself opposed, in this case, by Fielding.[61]

Finally, in the late 1740s, it seemed Ralph's moment had come. He had been personal secretary to the wealthy George Bubb Dodington since 1743 and Dodington, though sometimes treated as a court jester, was in the inner circle of Frederick, Prince of Wales, who in true Hanoverian tradition was not only the heir to the throne but the active leader of the opposition to his father's government. In 1747 Ralph, under Dodington's patronage, began editing *The Remembrancer* on Frederick's behalf. At that point, with George II seriously ill and Frederick, before the cricket ball accident, very healthy, it seemed the Prince was poised to inherit.[62] Frederick had promised Dodington a Secretaryship of State and Dodington had promised Ralph the riches of working for him in government. Perhaps Ralph would have gained even more than that, but when it was Frederick and not his father who died first in 1751, he left Ralph an unpaid debt of £65.[63] This forced Ralph, in the short term, to work for the Duke of Bedford and William Beckford. In the longer term he gained a pension from the then Prime Minister, Henry Pelham, and his brother the Duke of Newcastle. The pension gained Ralph's public silence, but did not stop him writing to the Duke every six months with a private opinion, including the view, in January 1756, that a Stamp Tax on the American colonies would be a good idea.[64]

Ralph's later career had been a clear demonstration of the topsy-turvy world of aristocratic politics. It was a potential object lesson for Franklin to learn when he visited Ralph in 1757. He brought with him a letter from Mrs Mary Garrigues, Ralph's long-lost American daughter, at which Ralph, suffering grievously from gout, was greatly heartened. However, as Franklin reported in a letter to Deborah, Ralph was worried in case his bigamously married English wife 'should know anything of his having any connections in America'.[65]

Though Franklin and Ralph could never retrieve that earlier friendship, Ralph was at the very least a good source of history and information. From the late 1750s he had sensibly been cultivating Bute and he received another pension on George III's succession. He was about to edit a pro-Bute newspaper when he died in January 1762.

That was the reason why, on successive evenings just a couple of months later, Franklin travelled the very short distance to a Covent Garden bookshop. His purpose was to attend a sale of Ralph's books and he was one of two major bidders, spending a not inconsiderable £6 and 5 shillings. His rival was an agent for the Earl of Bute, who spent £25. What is intriguing is that an eyewitness recorded that the agent 'showed a most uncommon eagerness in bidding against his competitor Dr Franklin of Pennsylvania'.[66] Whether the agent's counter-bidding was a compliment to the good taste of Dr Franklin or an exercise in putting the American in his place is not known, but the Franklins were certainly in contact with Bute, because just months later, due to the Earl, William would receive the appointment that would clearly establish his separate identity. Not that following in his father's footsteps was necessarily a problem for William – when Ben received an honorary doctorate from the University of Oxford that same April, William received an honorary MA on account of his apparent learning in municipal law.[67] However, William, a man in his thirties, was now looking to his own future and that of his potential wife.

Following his estrangement from Betsy Graeme, William began at some point after 1758 to court a Miss Elizabeth Downes.[68] The old Betsy may have been well connected in Philadelphia, but the new Betsy had the far greater advantage of being well connected in London.

William was far advanced on the course set for him when his father had asked Strahan to find a place at the Inns of Court.

William now had the status of a gentleman and the charm and the skill to move within elevated social circles. Yet Ben was unhappy. He had hoped for the far less advantageous union of William with Polly Stevenson, one that would bind Polly more closely to himself. Ben was extremely ambitious for his son, but this was a juncture where the elder Franklin put heart before head.

Ben could not deny that Elizabeth Downes was the better bet financially. She was the daughter of a rich Barbados planter, and though her father had died when she was very young, he had put aside enough money for her to be the beneficiary of a 'refined education' and £1,200 a year from the age of eighteen. As well as two siblings she had a large extended family of wealthy uncles and aunts and a home in the highly fashionable St James's Street.[69] Aside from which, Elizabeth was described as 'Sensible and Agreeable' by Ben's old friend Peter Collinson and 'of so amiable a Character' by Ben himself, in a letter to his sister Jane.[70]

Just as William's social future looked promising, so did his professional life when, unexpectedly, the Royal Governorship of New Jersey fell vacant and he was proposed as the replacement. In the words of Sheila Skemp, William's biographer, 'No one knows the exact train of events that led to the rather surprising appointment,'[71] particularly bearing in mind that William's principal qualifications from his time in London were merely a law degree and working for his father. William's confirmation came on 20 August, the whole process moving with such rapidity and so little fanfare that the Penns were unable to mount effective opposition. Thomas Penn was in no doubt that 'it was done by the direction of Lord Bute' and that Sir John Pringle, 'a Friend of Franklins' (sic), had acted as an emissary to the Secretary of State, Charles Wyndham, Lord Egremont.[72] Penn was no longer able to dismiss Franklin, as he had in 1757, as someone who was 'looked very coldly upon by great People'.[73]

It was Ben himself who almost ruined William's chances through the escalation to an even greater pitch of his mutual enmity between himself and William Smith. Yet it all started with a meeting between the two men where the hatchet, if not buried, was at least put to one side. As James Hutson describes, this took place in March 1762 in

London.[74] Franklin was still, even after all the acrimony, a Trustee of the College of Philadelphia and his fellow Trustees had instructed Provost Smith to visit Franklin for advice on how the College might raise funds. The one thing that the two men had in common was that they were great educationalists and Franklin, with admirable magnanimity considering his former treatment, offered to talk to friends and supplied a list of potential donors. He explained that he was unable to do more because he was expecting to return to Philadelphia shortly and in the meantime he would be travelling. One place on his list was Oxford, where he went to receive his honorary doctorate. It was here the trouble began. Franklin discovered that three years earlier Smith had written to the President of St John's College with a letter that was supremely critical of Franklin and was purposely designed to ruin his chances of receiving the doctorate he sought. Any attack on his scientific credentials and his academic entitlements was an assault on Franklin's *amour-propre*. As Hutson explains, this 'threw Franklin into a "great dudgeon"'.[75] He was now neither the calculating chess player nor the wise dispenser of 'Poor Richard' maxims. He was 'Franklin furioso'. As soon as he got back to London he ceased helping Smith's campaign and began sabotaging it. Not surprisingly, the money dried up. Now it was Smith's turn to seek revenge. He had not been able to take it before Franklin had left for America, but then, reading the announcement of William's appointment in the *London Chronicle* of 24–6 August, Smith saw the means. He contacted Thomas Penn.

Surprisingly few in London knew about William's illegitimacy. It was something that Franklin had tried to keep to himself, in the manner of the 'Poor Richard' saying, 'Three can keep a secret if two of them are dead'. Thomas Penn obviously did not know or he would have used it, and Smith, who did, had neglected to deploy the information before.

The attack was stalled by a delay: perhaps Smith had seen the paper a few days after its publication or perhaps Penn, as it was midsummer, was in the country and had to be contacted. Whatever the reason, Penn was too late, making his move three days after the Privy Council had given its formal approval. All the same, William's illegitimacy was a matter that could not be brushed away for a prominent servant of the Crown, not with a rather priggish young King to consider. That would seem to be borne out by a comment of Richard Jackson's brother-in-law that 'I hear there was some difficulty in his being Confirmed in his place, for in our Conscientious Age, many Scruples were raised.'[76] Even though William's commission received the Great Seal on 9 September, he probably still had a rough time of it. Had another Franklin 'skeleton' come to light during William's 'examination' then surely he would have failed, because it would have been considered a step too far. That was another case of sowing wild oats, this time by William himself, who had sired an illegitimate son of his own in London and relied on his father to act discreetly and to place the boy in a good foster home and later to fund his education. Thus even William's new bride did not discover the child's existence until thirteen years later,[77] by which time his grandfather had taken him to his heart.

William's acceptance within Society was marked by his marriage to Elizabeth Downes on 4 September 1762 in the country's most fashionable parish church, St George's, Hanover Square, although the smoothness of his passage was further marred by Smith covertly leaking William's secret more widely. Smith left no obvious traces, but William knew who was responsible, as he demonstrated in letters to Strahan.[78]

However, it is likely that William was the Franklin whom the Countess of Northumberland records as one of her dinner companions on Saturday, 6 November.[79] If so, it may have been something of a send-off, as the new Mr and Mrs Franklin were on board ship just a few days later.

The Countess's dining companion certainly could not have been Ben: he had sailed from Portsmouth in the middle of August. It might seem strange that, having stayed so long in England after the completion of his business with the Penns, he did not delay another month to attend his son's wedding. On the other hand he had urgent business back in Philadelphia.

⌒

Franklin had invested a large sum of money based on his reading of the political landscape within weeks of the accession of the new King. At first his choice of investment seemed inspired, but then things turned sour. He feared his enemies would accuse him of financial impropriety as well as ineptitude, because the money was not his own but Pennsylvania's.

In November 1760 the British Exchequer had made a payment to the colonies to cover their war costs,[80] with Pennsylvania's share coming to a fraction over £26,648.[81] With the war going well and it seeming likely that peace would be gained on favourable terms, Franklin took the decision to invest the entire sum in government annuities, which had soon risen to £30,000. But by October the next year the peace talks had collapsed, Pitt had suddenly resigned and Spain had allied with France. The consequence was that the value of the investments plummeted and a paper profit of almost £3,400 became an actual loss of nearly double that, because, at that very moment, Franklin received instructions from the Assembly to pay outstanding bills. Franklin's broker, John Rice, had to sell at a very bad time. As an embarrassed Franklin sought to explain in a letter to the Assembly's General Loan Office: 'All imaginable care and pains was taken to sell our stocks to the best advantage, but it could only be done by degrees and with difficulty, there being sometimes no buyers to be found.' In all only £21,936 and 10 shillings were raised – this against outstanding bills that totalled £22,500.[82] The result for the financial position, and for Franklin's state of mind, was a change from extreme happiness to one of acute misery.

Worse, because this was a slow process, urgent calls for payment arrived before the required money came in to cover them. As a result, an increasingly desperate Franklin spent months going from bank to bank in search of credit and, increasingly, found it refused. Only in January 1762 did the firm of Sargent Aufrere agree to pay outstanding bills, with just Franklin's 'Character' and 'good Offices with the Colony' as security for their own reimbursement.[83]

For Franklin, this ongoing financial debacle was a cause of great worry, personal humiliation and a long-lasting stick for his enemies

– with the Reverend Smith in 1764 still trumpeting that Franklin had lost the colony £6,000.[84]

In actual fact the situation could have been very much worse. Franklin had appointed John Rice as his broker because the latter was both well respected and highly successful. Yet, very shortly after Franklin had closed the account, Rice faced ruin due to his own rash speculation and the fraud of some of his customers. Rice's desperation led him to forge powers of attorney and begin using his clients' money to bolster his own position. The gamble failed and he fled to France, a safe bet at a time of Anglo-French hostilities – except, he had not been there long when Franklin's hoped-for peace was actually signed. The peace dividend for Rice was arrest, extradition and his being hanged at Tyburn in May 1763.[85]

However, Rice's fall from virtue was probably not known when the matter of the Assembly's money in London, together with Franklin's own, came under serious consideration. That was in February 1763 and with Franklin there in person. In January 1762 Franklin had written to Thomas Leech and Charles Norris that 'I now hope to be with you pretty early in the Summer, when I shall render a particular Account of this Transaction.'[86] Though he did not actually leave London until August, this was unlike some of his less than reliable projections to Deborah. For at last he had an urgent reason to return. Not only was there the question of his honour and reputation in the matter of the investment losses, there was also the issue that the Assembly owed him thousands of pounds for his salary and the expenses he had accumulated in more than four and a half years in London.[87] It was a pressing concern to ensure that these and the investment money did not get wrongly conflated.

⌘

Claude-Anne Lopez, for one, believed that an even greater reason for his departure in August was that he could not bring himself to see William marry someone other than Polly.[88] A letter he wrote from Portsmouth, as he waited for his ship to sail, would seem to support that view:

My dear Polly

This is the best Paper I can get at this wretched Inn, but it will convey what is entrusted to it as faithfully as the finest. It will tell my Polly how much her Friend is afflicted, that he must, perhaps never again, see one for whom he has so sincere an Affection, joined to so perfect an Esteem; whom he once flattered himself might become his own in the tender Relation of a Child; but can now entertain such pleasing hopes no more; Will it tell *how much* he is afflicted? No, it cannot.

Adieu, my dearest Child: I will call you so; Why should I not call you so, since I love you with all the Tenderness, all the Fondness of a Father? Adieu. May the God of all Goodness shower down his choicest Blessings upon you, and make you infinitely Happier than that Event could have made you. Adieu. And wherever I am, believe me to be, with unalterable Affection, my dear Polly,

Your sincere Friend

B Franklin[89]

9

1762–1764

Intermission

Franklin knew that the Proprietary party were preparing poisonous attacks to greet him on his return from Philadelphia. James
Hamilton, the son of Franklin's great benefactor of the 1720s and
1730s, was now not only William Allen's brother-in-law but the
Penns' Lieutenant Governor. He summed up the party's general view
when in July 1762 he wrote a scathing letter to his and Franklin's
mutual friend Jared Ingersoll of Connecticut:

> I cannot find that his five years negotiation at a vast expense to the
> province, hath answered any other purpose with respect to the public,
> than to get every point that was in controversy, determined against
> them. Yet what is this to Mr Franklin? Hath it not afforded him a
> life of pleasure, and an opportunity of displaying his talents among
> the virtuosi of various kingdoms and nations? and lastly hath it not
> procured for himself the Degree of Doctor of Laws, and for the
> modest and beautiful Youth, his son, that of master of Arts, from
> one of our most famous universities? Let me tell you, those are no
> small acquisitions to the public, and therefore well worth paying for.[1]

In spite of the likely attacks on him, Franklin presented incomplete
financial information to the Assembly's Committee of Accounts.
For instance, there was a distinct absence of receipts. Franklin also
explained that there had been a difficulty in separating his own and
William's private expenses from those incurred on behalf of the
Assembly. Furthermore there was the question of separating out the

costs of his travels in Britain and Europe, which were taken for his health and William's 'improvement' as well as for 'Visits to Persons of Influence'. There was the need to repay hospitality in an appropriate manner when he had been 'honoured with Visits from Persons of Quality and Distinction'. And there was also the fact that he 'was obliged (for the Credit of the Province) to live in a Fashion and Expense, suitable to the Public Character {he} sustained'.[2]

All this may have raised suspicions among some, but considering the details of his life during the previous six years – he submitted his expenses in February 1763 – this was not an attempt at an expenses fraud. Indeed, in submitting such receipts as he had, he suggested that anything without a receipt should not be paid and thus he should pay back more than half the £1,500 advance he had already been given.

With William Allen on the committee there must have been some interesting committee-room conversations, but Franklin had paved the way by emphasizing his strong connections in England. Certainly Richard Peters noted that Franklin 'speaks much of Lord Bute',[3] and no one could have failed to notice the portrait of the Earl in its pride of place in Franklin's home. There was also, to many in Philadelphia, the extraordinary news of 'Billy' Franklin's appointment as the Royal Governor of New Jersey.

In the event, Franklin was not only reimbursed for his receipts in full but told that he need not repay any of the advance. In addition he was given a further £3,000 or £500 p.a. for the six years.[4] As for the losses on investments, they were accepted. These were huge sums, giving reason enough for him to return home. Their payment was a sign that the party of Franklin and Isaac Norris had retained control of the Assembly.

Once back in America, Franklin spent a great deal of time travelling to secure greater efficiencies in the postal service, now starting to provide a healthy profit and a return on his investment. But he was in Philadelphia to greet his son William, en route with his new wife to New Jersey. The young Franklins had suffered a stormy sea crossing, one so bad that William told Strahan that 'I would not wish the devil, nay Parson Smith to experience a winter's passage like ours.'[5] He must also have told Deborah about it because he reported that 'my mother is so entirely averse to going to sea, that I believe my father will never be induced to see England again'. William also mentioned Ben's major building project, by adding, 'He is now building a house to live in.'[6]

Franklin was also back physically in the Assembly, where Isaac Norris had retired from the Speakership and Franklin's great ally Joseph Galloway had taken his place. Franklin and Galloway looked to have long-term control of the Assembly, until events on the frontier threatened to break it.

∽

On 14 December 1763, fifty-seven men from Pennsylvanian frontier townships entered an Indian village and brutally massacred three men, two women and a child. The remaining fourteen from the small Indian community were taken into protective custody. But the doors of the workhouse were not strong enough to save them. A fortnight later they were killed in their turn. This had been a small, peaceable tribe, supposedly protected by law. They had been murdered in revenge for some alleged atrocities that they could not possibly have committed. Franklin, like most of his 20,000 fellow citizens in Philadelphia, was absolutely appalled. In a mood of fury he wrote and published *A Narrative of the Late Massacres* at the end of January 1764.[7] In a long and impassioned piece he made an oblique reference to 'freckled, red-haired Men',[8] clearly meaning the Scotch-Irish who were settling the frontiers in great numbers. The Indian-hunting frontiersmen, known as the Paxton Boys, were in no way deterred. One hundred and forty Christian Indians had fled to Philadelphia for protection.[9] At the beginning of February the Paxton Boys began their march from the frontier. Philadelphia was in panic. Once again it was Franklin who ignored the qualms of the Quakers and organized the defence. He knew that his own house might come under attack and fortified it. He must have seemed secure because John Penn, 'with his Counsellors at his heels', deemed it essential to run to Franklin's home at two o'clock in the morning 'for Advice' and 'made it his Headquarters for some time'.[10]

Though Penn had already sent a request to General Gage for British regulars,[11] such was his state of alarm that he offered Franklin the formal command of the militia. The latter declined, preferring to be considered a common soldier, though in the event he was one of those who parlayed with 500 rioters at Germantown,[12] then outside Philadelphia, and persuaded them to disperse. This threat had been countered, but what about future pressing emergencies, when a more formal command structure might be needed and a hastily assembled militia insufficient?

The alarm caused by the Paxton Boys came at a time when the Assembly was objecting to the Penns' interpretation of the Privy Council's rulings of 1760. It seemed a propitious time to press the case for royal government.

Franklin re-emphasized his strong connections in England. These were undamaged, even though Bute had recently resigned, because people in Philadelphia wrongly believed that George Grenville was not only Bute's successor but his protégé.[13] There was also the Assembly's recognition that Richard Jackson, another of their representatives, was Secretary to the Chancellor of the Exchequer and thus to Grenville, who held that post as well as that of First Lord of the Treasury and Prime Minister.[14]

There was no doubt that in the closed meetings of the Assembly, Franklin's assurances of British government co-operation would secure a large majority. Yet there was a realization that a demonstration of overwhelming public support would be needed for such a fundamental change.

Franklin and Galloway faced challenges. Norris, fearing the new regime would bring more restrictions than the Proprietors, backed away into retirement; another staunch critic of the Penns, John Dickinson, had an even greater dislike of the idea of royal government and actively opposed it. In addition, the over-zealous customs searches by British warships in the Delaware Bay were not timely.[15] Even so, with a campaign deploying Galloway's oratory and Franklin's power of the press, the proponents of change were expecting mass support.

In the event, 3,500 signed a petition supporting change, of which half are estimated to have come from Philadelphians.[16] Their opponents were slow to move in response, but when they did they raised 15,000 signatures for a counter-petition that drew its support from the estimated 230,000, or 92 per cent, of the Pennsylvanian population who lived outside Philadelphia.[17]

The whole question rolled into that autumn's Assembly campaign. Franklin faced a coalition whose elements were united by a desire to punish him for past insult. The Pennsylvanian German community were reminded of a decade-old slur in Franklin's pamphlet 'Observations Concerning the Increase of Mankind' when he referred to them as 'Palatine Boors ... herding together' – a phrase that his enemies skilfully adapted to brand him as having also insulted the Dutch as 'a herd of hogs'. Then there was the more recent 'freckled, red-haired' categorization of the Paxton Boys that rallied the Scotch-Irish frontiersmen to support 'the Proprietary or Gentlemen's Party', with the latter soubriquet highlighted to demean Franklin as being nothing of the sort.

Dickinson's and Galloway's speeches in the Assembly, blending logical argument with verbal assault, were separately published, each with special Prefaces that amplified their belligerence. Dickinson's Preface came from the Reverend Smith, who took swipes at Franklin as a financially self-serving man of outrageous ambition.[18] Galloway's was written by Franklin, who explained why so many of the Loyal Addresses to John and Thomas Penn during their time in Pennsylvania had concentrated on the colony's founder: 'First, a vain Hope the Assemblies entertained, that the Father's Example, and the Honours done his Character, might influence the Conduct of the Sons. Secondly, for that in attempting to compliment the Sons on their own Merits, there was always found an extreme Scarcity of Matter.'[19] This was rancorous stuff from Franklin, but then his opponents were throwing everything they could at him in terms of his morals, his upbringing and his social and political ambition. William's bastardy was raised once more, as was the accusation of his father's misappropriation of public funds during his time in England. Franklin was categorized as having come 'from the meanest circumstances' and thus, unsurprisingly, as being of a 'levelling disposition'. In short, as one of Franklin's defenders described, the anti-Franklin forces 'from the tall Knaves of Wealth and Power, to the sneaking Underlings of Corruption, they seem to a Man ... sworn to load him with all the Filth and Virulence that the basest Heads and basest Hearts can suggest'.[20] No surprise that a contemporary called the campaign 'perhaps the warmest that was ever held in this Province'.[21]

English Civil War analogies abounded as the Proprietary party spread fear of what might happen under a royal government. The accusation was made that Franklin's plan for royal government was principally conceived so that he would himself govern, either directly or through his socially elevated son – a charge that was made the stronger because of its plausibility.[22]

The result when it came was close. Franklin and Galloway lost by just nineteen and seven votes respectively out of a total of over 3,900, but they did lose their seats.[23] Franklin took the defeat philosophically. He and Galloway had lost, but their anti-Proprietary party still held a healthy Assembly majority and thus Franklin was reappointed as the Assembly's agent by nineteen votes to eleven and asked to return to London.

Dickinson and Allen took to print in protest and in Andrew Bradford's *Pennsylvania Journal* they listed a number of reasons to debar Franklin, perhaps chief among them that he was 'very unfavourably thought of by several of his Majesty's Ministers' and 'that it will be disrespectful to our most Gracious Sovereign, and disadvantageous to ourselves and our constituents, to employ such a person as our Agent'.[24] This was not one of those times when Franklin was happy to issue satire under pseudonym. His reply was open, direct and personal – it was from 'Franklin furioso'. He rebutted the charges point by point, but not before addressing Allen as 'my Enemy of seven Years Standing'.[25]

Allen had categorized the Quaker party as continuing to follow Franklin, as 'still they appear to be afraid of disobliging him, and as I tell them they worship him as the Indians do the devil, for fear'.[26] But he was himself frightened that Franklin would return to England 'fully freighted with rancour and malice',[27] and he wrote as much to Thomas Penn.

Galloway and Franklin may have lost their seats, but only

temporarily. Galloway was back in the Assembly the following year and he regained the Speakership. Franklin was elected once more, though in absentia, because by then he was back in London.

The procession that escorted Franklin to his ship at Chester on the Delaware River was a loyal throng of around three hundred. A dozen artisan freeholders from the White Oak Company[28] rowed him across to the *King of Prussia*, a ship named after Britain's ally in the victorious war against France.

Franklin had already written his valedictory words, of possibly taking his 'last leave' of the country he loved. He was crossing to his other world.

10

1764–1766
The Stamp Act

Mrs Stevenson was absent when Franklin re-entered his London home in Craven Street, accompanied by John, the servant he had brought with him from Philadelphia.[1] When he wrote to Polly at Mrs Tickell's new house in Kensington, Franklin was able to recount with delight that her mother was a 'good deal surprised to find me in her Parlour'.[2] Soon all was as normal. He was back at his clubs or otherwise spending time with friends keen as ever to invite him out to dinner, with perhaps the promise of estate venison to tempt him.[3] It was dinner and never lunch, as the latter was not to take on its current substance and timing until much later.

'As much food as one's hand can hold'[4] was how 'Lunch' and 'Luncheon' were defined by Dr Johnson in his 1755 *Dictionary*, and, as other dictionaries make clear, lunch did not necessarily fit between breakfast and dinner, but was the equivalent of a modern snack between meals. It was in the 1760s that bread with a filling, that handy solution for the hungry, was called a 'sandwich' after the Earl of that name, though, as his biographer N.A.M. Rodger declares, salt beef between two slices of bread was almost certainly a response to hunger during long hours spent working at the Admiralty, rather than at the gaming tables – as legend has it.[5]

For those with independent means, something was increasingly needed to sustain them between breakfast and dinner, the main meal of the day, because the time of the latter grew increasingly later as the eighteenth century progressed. Earlier in the century dinner had gradually moved from noon to 3 p.m.; by the early 1760s an invitation from the Earl of Morton to Franklin suggested between 3 and 4 p.m.; and in the 1780s London society was to dine at 5.[6] These changes were a matter of fashion, designed to increase the difference between London's leisured classes and those labouring for them. The latter's dinner time remained at 1 p.m. This difference in timing separated Franklin's London life from his previous incarnation as a Philadelphia printer, with its dinner at 1. This did not go unnoticed by his printer friend Strahan: on 19 November 1769, and that a Sunday, Franklin was invited at 2.30 p.m. However, on 27 August 1772 the time had become the more fashionable 4 p.m. There might of course have been variations for the time of year, but the point was made entertainingly by the wording in another invitation: 'Mr and Mrs Strahan present their Compliments to Dr Franklin and the Ladies, and conceiving it may be more agreeable and convenient for them, will not dine till *three* o'Clock today.'[7]

To avoid confusion and embarrassment, the invitation would make clear what kind of occasion the guest could expect; for example, if it was 'to eat a piece of mutton' then it was likely to be relatively informal.[8]

The English were renowned for the quality of their meat and the quantity of their meat-eating; Pehr Kalm wrote that 'I do not believe that any Englishman, who is his own master, has ever eaten a dinner without meat.' This exaggeration might have been read with pleasure by the English. However, Kalm went further with 'Englishmen understand almost better than any other people the art of properly roasting a joint, which is also not be wondered at; because the art of cooking as practised by most Englishmen does not extend much beyond roast beef and plum pudding.'[9] That would not have gone down so well with the professional and leisured classes. The eighteenth century was the first great age of the bestselling cookbook, such as Eliza Smith's *The Compleat Housewife* (1727), Hannah Glasse's *The Art of Cookery Made Plain and Easy* (1747) and Elizabeth Raffald's *The Experienced English Housekeeper* (1769), which are all full of elaborate recipes. The authors take pride in their English cookery and stress that it is the quality of the cooking rather than the nationality of the cook that is important, with Hannah Glasse fulminating that 'if gentlemen will have French cooks, they must pay for French tricks' and 'so much is the folly of this age, that they would rather be imposed on by a French booby, than give encouragement to a good English cook'.[10] Entertainingly, she has it both ways, including many French recipes, a whole chapter of them entitled 'Read this chapter, and you will find how expensive a French cook's sauce is.'[11]

But if perhaps some of the recipes – as with a number of twenty-first-century cookbooks – are for show rather than cooking, very many of them correspond, in general principle, with those in a highly relevant private household book. This belonged to Margaretta Acworth, who lived in Westminster during the time Franklin was in London. It was discovered by chance in the 1980s by Alice and Frank Prochaska and its recipes first published, as *Margaretta Acworth's Georgian Cookery Book*, in 1987. It cannot be an exact indicator of what Benjamin Franklin himself preferred, though he was to give us an indication with some of his later writings. It is, however, a clear guide to the sort of dining available to him in the houses of his well-heeled acquaintances on the basis that Mrs Acworth was a wealthy Westminster gentlewoman and that this was her own aide-memoire for her kitchen staff. By reading this and other personal household books of the time, Franklin's letters and, of course, by looking at his portraits, we can tell that Franklin, like others of his class and stage in life, ate very well indeed. A rich diet heavy in meat and dairy fats filled out his once athletic frame and was at odds with the more ascetic principles expressed in the aphorisms of *Poor Richard*. But why not? Temperance and frugality may have helped him win fame and fortune – and now was the time to enjoy it. Though, of course, there was always the risk of gout – the scourge of the overindulgent.

૭૦૦

While Franklin found his social world practically unchanged during his absence, the political landscape was different. When Franklin left in the summer of 1762, the Earl of Bute was the sole survivor of the uneasy government triumvirate of himself, Pitt and Newcastle. Pitt had been the first to go in October 1761, resigning when his colleagues refused to back his ambition to declare war on Spain, newly, if then passively, allied with France. Newcastle followed in May 1762, the great political tactician having been outmanoeuvred by Bute, who succeeded him as Prime Minister.

Bute had much in his favour as Prime Minister. He had the support of the King and the backing of individuals in Parliament dubbed the 'King's Friends', who, without the coherence of groups such as the Newcastle–Rockingham Whigs or the men led by the Duke of Bedford, could still be relied on for their votes in Parliament. The war continued to go well; Bute's problems did not stem from failure in war but from its victorious conclusion. A provisional peace signed in Paris by the Duke of Bedford in November 1762 was followed by a formal version the following February, supported in both Houses of Parliament by large majorities. Looked at dispassionately, it was a very good peace treaty, giving back some captured territories but firmly securing others such as, to Franklin's satisfaction, Canada. But it was poorly received in the streets, because the atmosphere there was far from dispassionate owing to the unpopularity of the Bute government, the Earl himself and even his master the King. In contrast, Franklin, when writing on 27 June 1763 from New York to John Whitehurst, the scientific instrument maker who would later build his three-wheel clock, celebrated the treaty:

I am ashamed to read here the Clamour of your political scribblers against the Peace. Never did England make a Peace more truly and substantially advantageous to herself, as a few Years will evince to everybody; for here in America she has laid a broad and strong Foundation on which to erect the most beneficial and certain Commerce, with the Greatness and Stability of her Empire. The Glory of Britain was never higher than at present, and I think you never had a better Prince.[12]

Part of the outcry against Bute was his government's attempt to deal with the cost of the war. Exceptional measures were required, but the Cider Tax introduced by Sir Francis Dashwood, his Chancellor of the Exchequer, went down nearly as badly as Sir Robert Walpole's proposed Excise Tax of thirty years before. Though in the end the government forced it through, it was not before 'the scribblers' had whipped up agitation against it, with John Wilkes devoting number 43 of his satirical newspaper *The North Briton* to denouncing it. *The North Briton* was a response to the pro-Bute *The Briton* edited by Tobias Smollett. The reason for Wilkes's choice of title was that Scots or 'North Britons' were not, as a race, popular among the more riot-ready elements in London. Fellow Britons only since the Act of Union of 1707, successful Scots in London were hated by those who regarded them as foreigners, and the more so for their pre-eminence. The Bostonian Josiah Quincy, observing with an outsider's eye on his London visit a decade later, was 'astonished to find [the] extravagant hatred there is prevailing among multitudes of this kingdom for the Scotch nation.'[13]

In 1763, the Scottish Earl of Bute was detested for having seemingly displaced Pitt, the popular hero, for his access to the ear of the King and, so Wilkes dared to suggest, the bed of the King's mother. *The Briton* was not a success but its rival most certainly was, outselling it ten times over. Wilkes's assault on Bute was motivated by cynical opportunism and sheer devilry, as he later made clear to Bute's daughter with the response, 'Hate him? No such thing. I had no dislike to him as a man, and I thought him a good Minister. But 'twas my game to abuse him.'[14] It was a 'game' played out against a background of economic dislocation and social unrest. The mob repeatedly targeted Bute's carriage in the street, pelting it with filth and smashing its windows. He was protected by bodyguards and needed to be. Whether or not Bute was right in believing that these attacks were being co-ordinated by his political opponents, he decided at the beginning of April 1763 that he had had enough. He was vastly wealthy, with gardens to transform, and neither a sense of duty nor the pleas of the King were sufficient to dissuade him. On 9 April he resigned and Dashwood happily joined him.

That event led to an extraordinary exchange of letters between Franklin and Strahan. Strahan wrote to his friend, blaming Bute but also the corruption of politics:

You have seen, in general, by the public papers, what a Cry is raised against the peace, and how unpopular it has rendered Lord Bute. I wish I could say, that making this peace was Lord B's only fault, for I agree with you in thinking it a very good one. But I am sorry to tell you, that my Countryman has shown himself altogether unequal to his high Station. Never did a Ministry, in our Memory, discover so much Weakness. They seem to have neither Spirit, Courage, Sense, nor Activity, and are a Rope of Sand. Of Course the essential Interests of the Nation are neglected. Lord Bute, with even an enthusiastic Desire to promote the Glory and Prosperity of this Country, can never more take the Lead. He continues to see nobody, and seems vastly pleased that he has shaken off that Burden to which his Shoulders was {sic} so unequal ... From all this you may easily conceive, we are in a very unaccountable and untoward Situation. Here is a Young, virtuous, *British* King, who can have no Interest separate from that of his People, and who, though not possessed of any striking Talents, or any great Degree of Sagacity, yet having much Good Nature, and a Disposition to please, rendered, in the beginning of his Reign, singularly unpopular; and a Minister, hating Corruption, abhorring Hypocrisy, and having the Prosperity of his Country really at heart, the Object of universal Disgust ... Of Course, it requires great knowledge of Men in the Minister {sic} of this Country, to balance Parties, and keep things quiet. Of this Knowledge Lord Bute is totally destitute, and was his temper suitable, which it is not, it is too late for him to learn. This Ignorance of the world, with a Timidity altogether inexcusable, has encouraged the Opposition to go {to} lengths hitherto unprecedented.[15]

Franklin, replying from faraway Philadelphia, was altogether more optimistic:

You now fear for our virtuous young King, that the faction forming will overpower him, and render his Reign uncomfortable. On the contrary, I am of Opinion that his Virtue, and the Consciousness of his sincere Intentions to make his People happy, will give him Firmness and Steadiness in his Measures, and in the Support of the honest Friends he has chosen to serve him; and when that Firmness is fully perceived, Faction will dissolve and be dissipated like a Morning Fog before the rising Sun, leaving the rest of the Day clear, with a Sky serene and cloudless. Such, after a few of the first Years, will be the future Course of his Majesty's Reign, which I predict will be happy and truly glorious. Your Fears for the Nation too, appear to me as little founded.[16]

Bute was accused of continuing to exercise a 'secret influence' with the King. Rockingham and Bedford both made that claim in 1767, a year after the King and Bute had quarrelled and had finally ceased communication; Pitt repeated the charge a full three years later.[17] As for the loosely connected 'King's Friends', they had effectively been deserted by their leader in 1763. Men such as Dashwood, the Earls of Northumberland, Hillsborough and Suffolk, the ambitious lawyer Alexander Wedderburn and Lord George Sackville (later Germain) either operated independently or joined other groups.

One man closely connected with Bute, the Earl of Shelburne, joined the incoming ministry of George Grenville as President of the Board of Trade. Bearing this in mind, a badly torn and damaged letter from John Pringle to Franklin is tantalizing. Its date has been established as May 1763,[18] and within it the following has been transcribed:

> Lord Shelburne made no promises, but [torn] hear me with some indulgence.
> This being the state of that affair, I am persuaded that if you were determined before to return to England, you will now see a good reason for hastening your departure; because your being present yourself, may be a considerable weight in the scale, in case matters should come near to a balance.[19]

Unfortunately, on inspection, the tear can be seen to be much less of a rip and more the absence of a key part of the document. Franklin would later work closely with the Earl of Shelburne. He would also seek a role within the British government in London. One can only speculate whether this was a job offer that was removed either by time or by Shelburne's resignation from the government later that year.

∽

Franklin returned to England with clear instructions from the Assembly to secure royal government, but not, it seems, before a final attempt at negotiation with Thomas Penn. It was thought that Penn might be willing to compromise due to the supposed continuing influence in the Grenville government of the Earl of Bute – and Franklin's connection with him – together with the new dual role of Richard Jackson as Assembly agent and Under-Secretary to the Chancellor of the Exchequer. Negotiations between Franklin and Penn were unthinkable. However, Jackson, together with Dr Fothergill, entered into talks which ultimately failed in July 1765. In early November, after hearing from Galloway about his party's and his own success in the Assembly elections and having been given confirming instructions so to do, Franklin formally petitioned the Privy Council for royal government. In spite of warnings from Richard Jackson, he had every confidence of the petition's success when it was heard the same month. It failed, if not totally so. The official record stated 'postponed for the present',[20] which Thomas Penn construed as 'for ever and ever'[21] and Franklin 'as soon as these other Affairs are out of hand'[22] – 'these affairs' being the last knockings of the Stamp Act controversy.

Franklin and Galloway were convinced that, given time, the Proprietors would be displaced and they and their supporters would be entrusted with a royal government which would retain the province's special Charter rights. In the meantime they would show themselves worthy of London's trust by behaving as loyal citizens. It is a clear explanation of why the leadership of the Assembly of Pennsylvania and Franklin himself acted with a great deal of forbearance between the autumn of 1765 and that of 1768.

∽

The French and Indian War in North America was just one part of the global conflict of the Seven Years' War. Britain waged a maritime and colonial war against France, joined, latterly, by Spain. Britain and

Hanover fought in Europe against the French and paid subsidies to Frederick the Great of Prussia to support him in his conflict against France, Russia and the Hapsburg Empire. Britain's success in the Seven Years' War was extraordinary, but so was the financial cost. On the resignation of Bute in April 1763, the incoming government of George Grenville sought to introduce administrative and financial stability.

The French and Indian War is well named, as the great majority of the native Americans who fought did so on the side of the French. As the British moved into captured French territories, the Indians there rebelled in 1763 in what has become known as Pontiac's Rebellion. John Pownall lobbied both his new boss at the Board of Trade, Lord Hillsborough, and his old boss Lord Halifax, now Secretary of State, and pleaded for urgent action. The result was the Royal Proclamation of October 1763, which sought to freeze the frontier broadly at the Appalachians. It was not strictly enforced nor was it enforceable, and frontier atrocities between settlers and Indians, even hitherto friendly ones, such as those killed by the Paxton Boys, continued. The Royal Proclamation was, though, at least an attempt to deal with a near-insuperable problem, but the building, manning and supplying of frontier forts by British troops added to the overall debt.

There was a growing demand in Parliament for the colonists to contribute towards the cost of imperial defence. A start was made with the American Revenue Act of April 1764, popularly known as the Sugar Act, though it also covered other goods. It actually cut the tax on foreign molasses but was far more strongly enforced. It caused a good deal of discontent because molasses meant rum and the fall in smuggled supplies meant much less of it. However, the protest was as nothing in comparison to that against the Stamp Act.

✑

The Stamp Act was not introduced without warning. Grenville gave the American colonial representatives in London a full year to come up with alternative suggestions, though to what extent he intended to take any of them seriously is a different matter.[23] For instance, Franklin, with an understanding of paper currency going all the way back to his Keimer days when working for the Assembly of New Jersey,[24] suggested the issuing of bills of credit to make up for the lack of gold and silver coin in circulation – a scarcity that was holding back trade. The bills of credit would be redeemable at a rate of interest of 6 per cent per annum.[25] This proposal would have helped encourage trade and brought in revenue. Also, as Edmund Morgan concludes, 'It was an ingenious scheme and might have worked in 1765.'[26] But Grenville took no notice, because, as Franklin remarked, 'he was besotted with his Stamp Scheme'[27] – though, bizarrely, Grenville would advocate a paper currency scheme of his own in 1767, when he was in no position to introduce it.[28]

The Stamp Act did not just tax correspondence but all stamped documentation. Its reach extended right across both business and pleasure. It was a tax on living. Among its fifty-five clauses were those covering legal papers, bills of sale, mortgages, warrants for surveying land and bills of lading. College degrees were included, as were liquor licences. Then there were newspapers, advertisements in newspapers, almanacs, calendars, printed pamphlets and playing cards. Its provisions were far from blind and unconsidered; Thomas Whately, Grenville's Under-Secretary, had gone to great lengths to gain information on how the tax might be most equitably applied across the twenty-six American and Caribbean colonies.[29]

Overall the Stamp Tax would be lower in the colonies than its long-standing British equivalent,[30] but it was the fact of the tax rather than its amount that was the cause of colonial objections. It was viewed by the colonial representatives as a charge on the daily round of human activity; as virtually impossible to avoid; and as fundamentally unconstitutional, because it was an internal tax that was levied by Parliament in London, rather than by their own Assemblies.

After Grenville requested it, a four-man colonial delegation called upon him in person on 2 February 1765. The four were Richard Jackson, Benjamin Franklin, Jared Ingersoll and Charles Garth. The point at issue was that Grenville believed that the expenditure of the British government incurred in defending the colonies in the late war legitimized their collective taxation in order partially to defray the cost. He also argued that precedent under George II, let alone Queen

Anne, gave Parliament the right to levy it.[31] Though Jackson had a foot in both camps, being Grenville's own Secretary to the Exchequer as well as an agent for both Pennsylvania and Connecticut, he took the lead in contending that such action would subvert the powers of the colonial Assemblies. He argued that it was a point of principle with seemingly no room for compromise. He did so in vain, with Grenville introducing the Stamp Bill into the Commons a mere four days later.[32] There was a period of over seven months between the Stamp Act becoming law on 22 March and its introduction on 1 November 1765. The time lag was necessary to set up the tax collection, but it also gave the protesters time to organize and they had unstinting support and assistance from the newspapers – hardly surprising, as these identified themselves as major potential victims.

Grenville's chief interest was in financial control and in tackling the unprecedented level of the national debt.[33] He was determined to address matters throughout the empire. This may have been an admirable strategic aim but it was fatally undermined by Grenville's lack of tact as well as tactical sense, not least in his management of the King. George III developed an intense dislike of his Prime Minister. The situation was bound to be difficult initially, because George believed that Bute, his tutor and mentor, had been harried from office. Grenville's approach lacked guile and never more so than when he flatly refused to give the King the necessary £20,000 to buy land adjoining Buckingham House (later Palace).[34] As a result, a speculative developer built a row of houses and happily sold them on the very basis that their new owners could enjoy a gawp at the Royal Family as they walked in the royal gardens. This greatly rankled with the King, who by the summer of 1765 was finding Grenville's prolixity and his lecturing manner insufferable. On 10 July he dismissed him. The King made it clear in the final interview that his objection to Grenville was personal.[35] He had found nothing wrong with his policies and nor had Parliament.

The Stamp Bill had passed through both Houses of Parliament without a vote, after its opponents realized that they were completely outnumbered by those in its favour.[36] There seemed to be no likelihood that the new government under the Marquess of Rockingham would repeal it. In a letter dated 11 July, Franklin reported the change of government to Charles Thomson, once one of Franklin's Academy appointees but now an active politician. Yet he made no suggestion that the Act would be repealed. Rather, knowing the mood of Parliament, Franklin counselled that it should be accepted as a fait accompli:

> Depend upon it my good Neighbour, I took every Step in my Power to prevent the Passing of the Stamp Act; no body could be more concerned in Interest than myself to oppose it, sincerely and Heartily. But the Tide was too strong against us ... We might as well have hindered the Sun's setting. That we could not do. But since 'tis down, my Friend, and it may be long before it rises again, Let us make as good a Night of it as we can. We may still Light Candles. Frugality and Industry will go a great way towards indemnifying us. Idleness and Pride Tax with a heavier Hand then {sic} Kings and Parliaments; If we can get rid of the former we may easily bear the Latter.[37]

This letter shows that Franklin was both out of touch with popular feeling and did not yet understand its strength. On first examination the letter might just seem to be extraordinarily blasé. Yet the clue to Franklin's thinking is in the homily's position towards the end of a letter dominated by plans to remove the Proprietors and containing the hope that this objective would be achieved through the new government, once 'particular friends are put in place'.[38] In short, Franklin saw the Stamp Act as the lesser of two evils and believed that resistance to it would harm their efforts in resolving the greater problem. He was to be disabused, not least by the words and actions of men such as Thomson.

However, it is almost certain that Franklin was one of the North American agents in London who, describing themselves as 'the only representatives of America', entered into a war in print with Christopher D'Oyly, Deputy Secretary at War, over the introduction of what was called the Quartering Bill. The government deemed that a lack of barracks made it a necessity to billet soldiers in private houses. The agents, in an open letter responding to one signed 'C.D.', denied the premise, and questioned the wisdom of the measure and retorted, 'Let Mr C.D. or his master, first try the effects of quartering soldiers on butchers, bakers or other private houses here, and then transport the measure to America.' But most of all they challenged the introduction of an Act in America which was against the law of England, with these words: 'The people of England and America are the same; one King, and one law; and those who endeavour to promote a distinction, are truly enemies to both.'[39]

With the Stamp Act and the Quartering Act, the seeds of all future disputes between the government in London and its American colonists were sown: these were unpopular measures that would promote resistance that was itself liable to provoke countermeasures involving the use of alien and alienated armed troops.

The problem with the Stamp Tax was the nature of the tax, and not the amount of taxation. Certainly the financial assessments newly introduced into the Admiralty courts were higher because of the greater problem of smuggling, but no corporation tax was introduced into America and there was none on indentures, due to the already high cost of labour.[40] But the crucial point was that the British Parliament was usurping the role of the colonial Assemblies and consequently united them in opposition as firmly as they had been against the Albany Plan in 1754.

From the moment that the Stamp Act was passed there was uproar in America. There were votes of non-compliance at Assembly level, beginning with the 'Virginia Resolves' at the end of May. Across the colonies 'Sons of Liberty' groups formed to resist the tax. In October representatives of nine of the thirteen colonial Assemblies gathered at a special congress in New York to declare the Act unconstitutional. Pennsylvania was represented and John Dickinson took a leading role but he, as much as Galloway, had been against the mob action that had erupted along the Atlantic seaboard during the previous months.

The threat of mass violence came to Philadelphia comparatively late, but on 16 September the city heard the news that Grenville was gone and the celebrations took an ugly turn. A mob planned to burn down the house of Franklin's friend John Hughes, who was the appointed Stamp Tax Collector.

As a sensible move, Grenville via Whately had asked the American agents to nominate responsible men as distributors of the stamped paper for collecting the tax. Franklin had put forward Hughes's name. But the appointment of his friend was a mistake, because this led opponents in Philadelphia to spread a rumour that Franklin himself had helped plan the Act. Thus Franklin's own home was threatened, forcing a brave Deborah to fortify it.[41] The situation was saved because the loyal White Oaks craftsmen were mobilized and the cowed mob melted away. However, trouble flared again on 5 October, when the ship was sighted that held both Hughes's commission and the stamped paper; Hughes agreed to delay his duties but did not resign. Nor did he when, in the second week of November, Charles Thomson called a mass meeting to compel him to do so. Though this time Franklin's own property did not come under threat, the orations of Galloway and the muscle of the White Oaks were needed to protect both Hughes and his house.[42]

Though in November Pennsylvania joined other colonies in non-importation of British goods, in comparison to other colonies it had been restrained.

By then Franklin had received a flood of letters that left him in no doubt that he had completely misjudged the public mood in the American colonies. He was appalled at the suggestion that he had in any way supported, let alone instigated, the Act. He realized that he should actively, if somewhat cautiously, take up the cause of repeal with the new British government of the Marquess of Rockingham. Fortunately he was in a position to do so.

&

On 9 November 1765 Franklin wrote the following to his son:

Mr Cooper, Secretary of the Treasury, is our old Acquaintance, and expresses a hearty Friendship for us both. Enclosed I send you his Billet proposing to make me acquainted with Lord Rockingham. I dine with his Lordship To-morrow.

I had a long Audience on Wednesday with Lord Dartmouth. He was highly recommended to me by Lords Grantham and

Bessborough, as a young Man of excellent Understanding and the most amiable Dispositions. They seemed extremely intent on bringing us together. I had been to pay my Respects to his Lordship on his Appointment to preside at the Board of Trade; but during the Summer he has been much out of Town, so that I had not till now the Opportunity of conversing with him. I found him all they said of him. He even exceeded the Expectations they had raised in me. If he continues in that Department, I foresee much Happiness from it to American Affairs. He enquired kindly after you, and spoke of you handsomely.[43]

We do not know whether Franklin was one of a few or one of many who dined with Prime Minister Rockingham, and to what extent Cooper ensured Franklin was able to get 'acquainted' with him. In any event the invitation itself was a coup. The long audience with the Earl of Dartmouth, complete with plaudits for William, is also worth noting, as is the work of both Postmasters General, Franklin's bosses at the Post Office, in bringing it about. But the key contact here was Grey Cooper himself. Cooper was not a run-of-the-mill place seeker. He was a top lawyer with a highly successful practice and it had taken a good deal of persuasion, a strong financial inducement and a plum Parliamentary seat for him to join, in October 1765, a ministry that he had recently successfully defended in print.[44] As for Cooper being 'an old acquaintance', we certainly know that he had been in touch with Franklin since at least 1762, when there was a note from him asking Franklin whether two ladies might join him in attending an armonica recital.[45] Three months after Franklin's letter to William his confidence in Cooper would prove to have been extremely well placed.

∽

News of opposition from the Assemblies had been reaching the government in London over the summer and there had been some details of mob action. In October a more complete picture began to emerge from the succession of reports arriving from America. Governor Bernard of Massachusetts reported that mob violence had persuaded Andrew Oliver, the Stamp Act Distributor, to resign, but not before Oliver's house and that of Thomas Hutchinson, Bernard's Lieutenant Governor and the colony's Chief Justice, had been destroyed. A letter from the military Commander-in-Chief in America, General Gage, gave a full round-up of events, including the house destruction in Massachusetts and that in Maryland and Rhode Island. He reported a concerted and successful plan to frighten the Stamp officers into resigning.[46] Yet in spite of that, and strangely in view of his own evidence, Gage wrote on 12 October that he thought the resistance would subside once the Act was introduced on 1 November.[47] The ministry decided to wait and see. Franklin did not. He argued for the suspension of the Act. With energy and good contacts, Franklin was by far the most active of the agents in London over the succeeding weeks. When Gage's confidence proved completely misplaced, Franklin's words carried even greater weight.

Rioters in New York followed their threat against the Stamp Distributor with active destruction of the property of senior government officials. There were continued breakdowns in public order in Boston.

All this was worrying enough. What was worse was that the merchants of New York and those of Philadelphia refused to import British goods. As a consequence their British counterparts in the City of London and the ports, fearing for their livelihoods in a time of economic downturn, started lobbying very hard for repeal. There was also a more general fear that the loss of the American markets for an extended period would create riots by discarded workers in the manufacturing towns and bring a return to the more fashionable streets of London of the aggrieved weavers of Spitalfields, who had attacked the coach of the Duke of Bedford and trapped him in his house over four days the previous May.[48]

Franklin continued to be proactive during this period. With gusto he joined the propaganda war against Grenville and those who counselled coercion. Writing as 'Pacificus', Franklin sneeringly dismissed the previous Prime Minister as 'that great economist' in a manner reminiscent of Penn's contempt for Franklin himself as 'the electrician'.[49] Of course, in the modern meaning of the word, it was Franklin who was far more of an economist. He saw the benefits to trade and commerce of having greater liquidity through the use of paper currency and understood how tax receipts would increase over time by stimulating trade in the short term. In addition, both his commercial and scientific backgrounds led him naturally to see the importance of encouraging industrial research and development.

Though for tactical reasons he had used mercantilist arguments in his *The Interest of Great Britain Considered*, he recognized the inflexibility of the British mercantilist trading system, which might have made sense when developed a century before when the population of the American colonies had been tiny in comparison to Britain.[50] But he believed that the economic treatment of the colonies as basically an exporter of primary products in exchange for manufactures from Britain was now unnecessarily restrictive. In his view the Navigation Acts, with their stipulation that all American trade – including that with foreign ports – had to be carried in British ships, were completely out of date. His firm belief remained, as had been the case immediately after the Albany Conference a dozen years earlier, that Americans should be allowed to manufacture; after all, as he had written then, 'what imports it to the general state, whether a merchant, a smith, or a hatter, grow rich in *Old* or *New* England?'[51] because, after all, they were part of one country.

Franklin was going to have the opportunity to argue the case with Grenville in person, because in January 1766 the Rockingham government decided that they had to bow to the mounting pressure, but in a way that saved face in Parliament. A committee was set up to investigate the matter, but this was no hole-in-the-corner affair, because the committee consisted of the whole House of Commons. Evidence was to be taken over three days from interested parties including merchants and manufacturers.[52]

Franklin was the major witness on the third day, 13 February. He was nothing short of superb. This might seem surprising from someone who had no great gift for oratory, but the format of question and answer suited him down to the ground. He was also brilliantly prepared. The easiest questions, unsurprisingly, came from Grey Cooper MP. Franklin also had some sympathetic ones from merchant MPs. Bur more than half were from supporters of the Act and he faced a great deal of hostile questioning from Robert Nugent (whom he was soon to get to know far better as Lord Clare) and from George Grenville himself.[53]

Strahan was delighted at his friend's performance. As he wrote to Hall: 'To this very Examination, more than to anything else, you are indebted to the *speedy* and *total* Repeal of this odious Law. The Marquess of Rockingham told a Friend of mine a few Days after, That he never knew Truth make so great a Progress in so very short a Time.'[54]

Franklin's various roles made him an extremely important witness for the government. As Deputy Postmaster General for North America he was not only a Crown appointee but someone who had travelled widely there. He was both a well-known American and, as a colonial agent, an official representative. He was able to articulate the best case for the government, helped no doubt by collusion with Grey Cooper at least and possibly with others.

A sufficient number of MPs were convinced by his testimony that the colonies 'will acquiesce in the authority {of the legislature}' and would naturally return to obedience if the Stamp Act were repealed, unless the alternative of coercion were chosen in which case, he said, the British troops 'will not find a rebellion; they may indeed make one.'[55]

A majority of MPs also followed his arguments that the American objection was to 'internal' taxes rather than what might be considered 'external' ones on imports, and that 'resolutions of right would give them very little concern, if they are never attempted to be carried into practice'. On that latter point, the use of a Declaratory Act, he could state with confidence that 'The Colonies will probably consider themselves in the same situation, in that respect, with Ireland; they know you claim the same right with regard to Ireland, but you never exercise it.'[56] It was a command performance. He had highlighted how the circle might be squared.

The Stamp Act was repealed and the Declaratory Act, asserting Parliament's right to legislate for the colonies, was introduced at the end of February. Not everyone believed that the Declaratory Act was a sensible solution, with William Pitt, for one, voting against it.

Nor, it should be noted, was the Quartering Act removed from the Statute Book.

When news reached Philadelphia, David Hall helped ensure that Franklin got due credit. The agent for Pennsylvania was hailed as a hero and it certainly enhanced his reputation in the rest of the colonies.[57] Franklin had repaired a difficult situation for the government, but also for himself, and emerged to great acclaim.

⁓

Their actions over America were not enough to keep the Rockingham administration in office, because they failed to address their principal concern, which was to maintain the confidence of both King and Parliament at home. Rockingham's relationship with the King was better than Grenville's had been – it could hardly have been worse – but it was far from ideal. His overall command of Parliament was shaky and he himself was an abysmal Parliamentary performer. All it took was for the Duke of Grafton to resign as Secretary of State on 14 May to ensure that the government tottered. As Grafton himself put it, the government 'wanted strength, which one man only could supply'.[58] That man was William Pitt, the big beast of British politics. He was ready to return to government, but only as Prime Minister. The King was keen to install him, in order, finally, to secure political stability.

Franklin could see that he would be required to try to gain influence with new ministers. As he wrote to the Pennsylvania Assembly Committee of Correspondence on 10 June, his best course would be to go on his planned summer trip of six to eight weeks, which he declared 'necessary to my health' and which he had been unable to undertake the previous year. This was particularly sensible as both ministers and officials had decided, just as he reported, to 'lie awhile upon their Oars' until the business season returned and the new ministry had established itself.[59]

Franklin's timing on this was almost exact. Once the King was sure that Pitt was willing to return, a small difficulty was conflated into a large one as a pretext for Rockingham's removal on 30 July 1766.[60]

11

1766–1770

Pivotal Years

In the sixth year of King George's reign and with Pitt as the new head of government, it appeared that political stability had finally returned to the country. Pitt's brilliant management of the Seven Years' War was not forgotten. As Edmund Burke, Rockingham's secretary, had noted about Pitt the previous year, 'He has it in his power to come into the service of his country, upon any plan of politics he may choose to dictate.'[1] In the spring of 1766, Pitt had shown himself ready to take charge with a series of dominant performances in the Commons. Strahan, by no means a wholly admiring observer, commented that Pitt treated the whole house 'like a Parcel of Schoolboys' because of his 'truly superior Talents'.[2] 'Mr Pitt, it is agreed on all sides, is the only man that can at present extricate us from our present and more immediate difficulties',[3] was Strahan's conclusion. Having brought success in the war Pitt would now, so it was anticipated, bring coherence to the management of Britain's new empire.

The ministry did not begin well when the great man changed his identity. Pitt's image as the 'Great Commoner' had been dented after his resignation in 1761 by his gaining a peerage for his wife in her own right, and a large pension for himself. It was now badly damaged by his elevation to the Lords as the Earl of Chatham. Franklin had gained access to Chatham's three predecessors as Prime Minister, but he could not make any connection with Chatham – but then virtually no one could. Chatham carelessly left the management of the Commons in other hands, but he was blessed with George III's absolute support. There was every sign that this would be an active administration, but then, as early as October, Chatham disappeared to Bath and stayed there a month. He made two speeches in the Lords in the new Parliamentary session, but he was back in Bath in December and it began to become clear that what was first thought to be just a physical ailment was in fact a severe mental incapacity. Chatham was mired in depression. Each minister in the government would have to make his own way.

∽

Chatham's absence had no immediate effect on Franklin and it is fair to say that he had better links to senior members of the ministry than ever before. Grey Cooper continued as Secretary to the Treasury; and the Earl of Shelburne, the Secretary of State with overall responsibility for American affairs, was one of three 'Friends' towards America that Franklin mentioned by name, along with Chatham and Camden (the new Lord Chancellor), in his report to the Assembly.[4] But Galloway was worried. He wrote to Franklin that William Allen had been making much of the fact that Shelburne's Countess was Granville's daughter and thus Thomas Penn's niece by marriage. Franklin was able to reassure him that Shelburne was of the 'Opinion Mr Penn ought to part with the Government voluntarily, and said he had often told him so; but however that might be, he said that the Relation between them could and should have no Influence with him'. In that same letter Franklin wrote that 'nothing in my Power shall be wanting to push the Matter vigorously to a Conclusion, if possible this Winter'.[5] He was confident because he and Shelburne had a rapport. Shelburne had opposed the Stamp Act and was supportive of another of Franklin's interests: the creation of a new colony along the Ohio River. This was a supreme case of Franklin's sense of public duty being mixed with a quest for private profit. Franklin was not alone in this approach, far from it; he was true to the spirit of the age, including in his desire for American lands, with leading British ministers and potential ministers involved in schemes.[6]

The new colony had an additional importance to Franklin in that it could provide a reserve position in case his ambitions to unseat

Thomas Penn were thwarted. It was not part of the 'chess game' with Penn, but a completely different 'match' to be played simultaneously.

Franklin had long advocated organized settlement as part of his plan for combining the vast lands of America, the richness of its resources and the potential of a healthier and fast-breeding population for the benefit of the British empire. He also wanted to enjoy its benefits personally. In 1764 he joined the rush for lands in Nova Scotia as part of a collective scheme and in early 1766 bought 2,000 acres on his own account, which the Board of Trade granted in June 1767. But Franklin had also long been interested in plans for settlement on the productive soil of the Ohio River Valley. It was a scheme promoted by a fellow Philadelphian, Samuel Wharton, who with the partners in his firm was looking urgently to recoup recent losses because of Pontiac's Rebellion, as reflected in their later description as 'Suffering Traders'. However, there was one immediate and massive impediment to the scheme: the lands lay on the far side of the Appalachians and thus beyond the border for settlement decreed by the Royal Proclamation of 1763, which Shelburne himself had supported and John Pownall made a matter of urgency after the uprising.[7] Shelburne did not see the border as necessarily an insuperable problem and was happy to discuss matters with Franklin over dinner, which he did on numerous occasions over the next two years. Franklin's tantalizing letter from John Pringle of 1763 mentioning Shelburne would indicate that he and the Irish Earl had established a rapport before Franklin's 1762 return to America and at a time when Shelburne was a protégé of the Earl of Bute. They certainly shared a scientific curiosity – literally so when they were sent mammoth fossils together in one package by George Croghan, the Deputy Superintendent of Indian Affairs.[8]

Croghan and, even more importantly, the Superintendent, Sir William Johnson, were in charge of the negotiations with Indian tribes over frontier lands. In 1766 Croghan and Johnson were brought into the Ohio scheme, joining others including Governor William Franklin who had in mind the creation of a specific new colony.[9] All those involved would gain from the settlement scheme, but it could be argued, so would Britain and its American colonies, as it would be a means of helping to reduce the debt.

Franklin sprang very quickly into action, telling William on 12 September that he was about to see Shelburne 'recommending your plan for a colony'. But he also sounded a note of caution about a change in the Presidency of the Board of Trade: 'We have, however, suffered a loss in Lord Dartmouth, who I know was inclined to a grant there in favour of the soldiery, and Lord Hillsborough is said to be terribly afraid of dispeopling Ireland.'[10] Franklin would come to know the accuracy of that description of Hillsborough. Mass emigration from Ulster was threatening the plantation system on which the wealth of Hillsborough and that of his neighbouring great landowners was based. If land companies had an interest in colonization over the American border, Hillsborough had an interest in the near-superhuman task of preventing it. How, one might ask, had he been able to gain his position at the Board of Trade? A simple answer is that he was keen to have it when others were not. In spite of the efforts of Lord Halifax over a decade and of Shelburne in just a few months which he spent infuriating his Grenville government colleagues, it was an administrative department, not a policy-making one. Hillsborough both wanted the job and had done it before. He had taken over from Shelburne in September 1763 and been exceptionally assiduous at attending meetings.[11] He had left office with his friend Grenville; a year later he was back. He might not make policy, but he could block and delay and advise Shelburne's fellow members of the Cabinet. The effect can be seen in Franklin's less hopeful letter to his son of 27 September, which began positively enough with 'His Lordship had read your plan for establishing a colony there, recommended by Sir William Johnson, and said it appeared to him a reasonable scheme', yet was followed by 'but he found it did not quadrate with the sentiments of people here'. Shelburne advised caution, even after Hillsborough left the Board of Trade after just a few months to take up the considerably lighter duties of being Franklin's nominal boss as one of the two Postmasters General. Hillsborough was biding his time, waiting for the political position to clear.

⁂

The Prime Minister failed to return to Westminster in January 1767, at the end of the Christmas recess, and there was no coherent direction of the Commons. The Rockingham, Grenville and Bedford factions recognized weakness and launched a co-ordinated attack. They led the opposition in a humiliating rejection of the government's Land Tax proposals presented by Charles Townshend, the Chancellor of the Exchequer, and moved a Parliamentary amendment that reduced the tax from four shillings in the pound to three.[12] For the Rockinghams and Grenvilleites it was the type of cynical move that gave credence to the 1764 observation of the visiting George Croghan that 'The people here spend their time in nothing but abusing one another and striving who shall be in power with a view to serve themselves and their friends, and neglect the public.'[13] Townshend was criticized for an inert performance and it would have been normal for the government to resign, but this one did not.

Chatham did recover sufficiently to see the King on 12 March, but it was the final time as the Prime Minister of an administration that would last, at least formally, for another eighteen months. Chatham's early debilitation created a vacuum, something that political life, like nature, abhors. Those ministers with prime portfolios and strong personalities ran their own departments and also sought to give direction to the whole. Those who gained pre-eminence were the Duke of Grafton and the Earl of Shelburne, both Chatham protégés, and Charles Townshend who, following a prodigiously advantageous marriage a decade before, had become a law unto himself. But this was by no means a stable and co-operative triumvirate. The temporary dominance of one of them in 1767, with his ability to pass a crucial piece of legislation through the Commons, was to upset the relationship between Parliament and the colonies in a way that was never, in spite of the efforts of Franklin and many others, to be remedied.

Aaron Burr might have been speaking for aspiring eighteenth-century British politicians as well as himself when he wrote that the purpose of politics is 'fun, honour and profit', although for Charles Townshend, as for Burr, the pursuit of 'honour' did not seem of uppermost concern. Nor were honours, at least not for himself, but rather for a wife for whom, though she was the daughter of one duke, the mother of another and the widow of an earl, he successfully lobbied to have her made a baroness in her own right. Profit was another matter, in spite of the vast wealth of his wife. Townshend did exceptionally well from covert speculation in East India Company stock, via surrogates, at the very time he was the principal minister considering future regulation of the company and notably going against Chatham's stated policy in the recommendations he made.[14] From his approach to politics in general and to the House of Commons in particular, Townshend's principal objective seemed to be to have fun. Early in 1767, Chatham had serious second thoughts about Townshend's suitability to be the Chancellor of the Exchequer or to have any role in his government. Townshend had already denounced his own Prime Minister's distinction between internal and external taxes for America as 'perfect nonsense'[15] and Chatham sought to replace him with the far more reliable Lord North. Yet when North declined, Chatham, in his weakened state, let things lie. Townshend was further emboldened. As Grafton, Chatham's nominal deputy, later remarked, no one had the authority to rein him in.[16]

On 8 May Townshend presented a completely different figure to the one defeated in the Commons over the Land Tax. He electrified the House with what instantly became famous as 'the Champagne Speech'. How drunk he genuinely was and how 'off the cuff' his speech matters far less than his command of the Commons with an hour-long performance containing, in Horace Walpole's words, 'torrents of wit, ridicule, vanity, lies and beautiful language'.[17] As to content, Townshend criticized the Crown's frequent change of ministries and called for the 'restitution of the first post in administration to the House of Commons', with the clear implication that the old ministry was defunct and he should lead a new one.[18] Yet even that was of far less importance than his extraordinary theatrical bravura performance, and at its conclusion the House was 'in a roar of rapture'. However, Walpole also provided a shrewd judgement: 'Nobody but he could have made that speech; but nobody but he would have made [it], if they could. It was at once a proof that his abilities were superior to those of all men, and his judgement below that of any man. It showed him capable of being, and unfit to be, First Minister.'[19]

In reality 'First Minister' was what Townshend was: able to use Commons support to push forward his own policies regardless of the views of his Cabinet colleagues. In no case was this more true than in policy relating to America. As Namier and Brooke explain it:

> The key posts in Chatham's Cabinet were held by men who professed friendship for America and who were opposed to taxation of the colonies by the British Parliament. Chatham himself, Lord Chancellor Camden, and Shelburne, who was primarily responsible for the administration of the colonies, had all voted against the Declaratory Act; while Grafton, head of the Treasury, and Conway, Minister in the House of Commons, had taken the lead in the repeal of the Stamp Act.[20]

Just five days after the 'Champagne Speech', Townshend introduced the duties on glass, paint, paper and tea that bear his name.[21]

But even worse, Townshend made clear that these taxes would be used to pay the governors of royal colonies. At a time when cost-cutting was imperative these duties were aimed at funding an additional expenditure that the colonists were adamant they should cover themselves. Franklin knew from the experience with the Proprietors of Pennsylvania what that would mean: he who paid (or bribed) the piper called the tune. This was an overtly political act. Townshend never expected the duties to produce anything like the £500,000 that he had rigorously hunted down and claimed from other departments.[22] That sum had covered the gap created by the drop in the Land Tax. His half a million in savings was also an amount greater than the estimated £400,000 per annum continuing cost of maintaining the army in America.[23] The duties were more than just a bone to throw to the backbenchers and a way of wrong-footing Townshend's political opponents, such as the Rockinghams who offered little opposition, having decided, for political expediency, that these were 'external' taxes. They were popular and passed with little opposition.[24] They were Townshend's single-minded demonstration that it was possible to make the American colonists contribute to the British government's costs.

From statements he had made earlier in the year, it is clear that Townshend fully understood the implications of his proposals: they were completely in line with observations he had made as a Junior Minister at the Board of Trade under Halifax in 1754, when he had opposed the Albany Plan, believing that any intercolonial collaboration could only be achieved through an Act of the Westminster Parliament and, like Halifax, that the colonies had taken on powers through 'salutary neglect'.[25]

As the editors of the Franklin Papers explain, there was a fundamental difference in interpretation on the two sides of the Atlantic as to the relative importance of a governor's instructions, a colony's Charter and established law.[26] No potential Prime Minister attempted to square this particular circle until Chatham did so with his plan in 1775.

Franklin considered the point in the final short section of his *Autobiography*, written in the last few months of his life. Recalling his conversation with Earl Granville in 1757 and the fact that he had maintained, correctly, that Parliament had not passed the 1744 Bill to give the Crown additional powers, he added: 'It seemed that they had refused that Point of Sovereignty to the King, only that they might reserve it for themselves.'

Whether Townshend acted primarily for reasons of political tactics or due to long-held principle is of far less importance than that his duties were seen by many American colonists as the practical implementation of the Declaratory Act.

Less than three months later, on 4 September, Townshend was dead, carried off by a sudden 'putrid fever' at the early age of forty-two. The consequences of the duties that bore his name would long live on.

✧

Franklin had downplayed the importance of the Declaratory Act at the time and had written that it was 'merely to save Appearances' for the Rockingham government; and 'I think we may rest secure notwithstanding such Act, that no future Ministry will ever attempt to tax us, any more than they venture to tax Ireland.'[27] Yet in little over a year a new administration had done so.

Fortunately for Franklin the position on the proposed frontier company was looking better. In August he had dined *à trois* with both Secretaries of State, Shelburne and Henry Seymour Conway. He again raised the land scheme, as approved by Sir William Johnson, and as he reported to William, 'the Secretaries appeared finally to be fully convinced, and there remained no obstacle but the Board of Trade', now under the remit of Franklin's Stamp Act interrogator Robert Nugent, Viscount Clare.[28] On 25 November Franklin wrote that he had again dined privately with Shelburne, who reported that he had himself written a discussion paper for the King in Council supporting the new settlements, which they seemed to approve. Shelburne also said that, since the Board of Trade had not yet responded, Franklin should 'go to Lord Clare as from him, and urge the business there', which he did the next morning and found a more sympathetic ear than he expected.

Shelburne had also amused Franklin at the dinner with a particular anecdote. He had shown his paper to the Dean of Gloucester, the virulently anti-American Josiah Tucker, 'who very sagaciously remarked that he was sure that paper was drawn up by Dr Franklin, he saw him in every paragraph; adding that Dr Franklin wanted to remove the seat of government to America; that, says he, is his constant plan'. That was certainly one way of interpreting Franklin's plans for America, as part of a great British Empire. As for Franklin's reaction to the accusation, he was most certainly not put out – he regarded it as a 'pleasant circumstance'.[29]

cৄ০

The government had needed to be remodelled after Townshend's sudden death. His exact replacement as Chancellor of the Exchequer was straightforward: this time Lord North accepted the position. Of Chatham's two young lieutenants, the thirty-year-old Earl of Shelburne and the thirty-one-year-old Duke of Grafton, it was the slightly older man in the traditional prime-ministerial post of First

Lord of the Treasury to whom the Cabinet looked for a lead in place of the permanently absent Chatham.

When Franklin wrote to William on 25 November, the new session of Parliament was only in its second day. Although the Townshend duties were being fiercely opposed in America and the proposal for royal government over Pennsylvania had still not been accepted, Franklin had not given up hope of improvement in either case and he was now more optimistic about the Ohio Valley. Considering the crises of the previous fifteen months, the position could have been much worse and it was with that thought that he wrote to William: 'The present ministry seem now likely to continue through this session of parliament; and perhaps if the new parliament should not differ greatly in complexion from this, they may be fixed for a number of years which I earnestly wish as we have no chance for a better.'[30]

But then he did not know what the Duke of Grafton was planning.

⁂

In December 1767 the Duke of Bedford's brother-in-law, Earl Gower, and the fellow Bedfordite Viscount Weymouth joined the Cabinet. The following January Lord Hillsborough left one part of Franklin's life as Postmaster General and entered another in the newly created office of Secretary of State for the Colonies and, as such, absorbed that part of Shelburne's responsibilities. Franklin wrote to William: 'I am told there has been a talk of getting me appointed under secretary to Lord Hillsborough; but with little likelihood as it is a settled point here that I am too much of an American.'[31] Though he did welcome the possibility that Hillsborough, with greater support among his colleagues than the now isolated Shelburne, would finally make Pennsylvania a royal province. On 20 February he wrote with relish that he imagined Thomas Penn had 'anxiety and uneasiness ... painted on his brow'[32] about the prospect.

But once again the action of one American colony together with the counter-reaction of a British minister provoked uproar along the entire Atlantic seaboard. In February 1768 the Massachusetts House of Representatives sent a circular letter to the other continental colonies, which sought collective agreement that taxes should only be imposed by the Assemblies themselves. This was reported to Hillsborough by the colony's Governor, Sir Francis Bernard, and in April Hillsborough sent his own circular letter to all the colonial governors ordering them to instruct their Assemblies to ignore the Massachusetts initiative and, should they refuse to do so, to prorogue or dissolve them immediately.[33] It was an action as badly timed as it was heavy-handed. Eight colonies had already agreed to support Massachusetts before the letter arrived and the remaining four did so afterwards. By the end of the year the support was unanimous.

The representatives of Massachusetts, the colony of Franklin's birth, refused to retract their letter and in July Governor Bernard prorogued the House. They had already backed their action in March by blocking British imports and by June Hillsborough had ordered General Gage to send troops to Boston. So began a slow but remorseless dance of insistence creating ever greater resistance stretching all the way to 1775.

Events in Boston had a remarkable impact on Pennsylvania, the colony of Franklin's home. Hillsborough's action strengthened those of Franklin's and Galloway's opponents, who argued that royal government might be worse than Proprietary rule. Unaware of the impact of Hillsborough's letter to the governors and, most probably, of the letter itself, Franklin was still hopeful that the Secretary of State would make Pennsylvania a royal province. On 2 July he was writing to Galloway that Hillsborough's 'inclinations are rather favourable towards us (so far as he thinks consistent with what he supposes the unquestionable rights of Britain)', and he was more concerned about the influence of the Bedfordites and most particularly feared that 'they would sooner or later draw in their friend Mr Grenville in after them' to replace Shelburne as Secretary of State.[34]

⁂

One Bedfordite, the Earl of Sandwich, Hillsborough's successor at the Post Office, was presenting a more immediate problem. On 2 July 1768, Ben had written to William that Sandwich was seeking to remove him from the Deputy Postmastership, with his long absence from America being used as the pretext. The source of this intelligence was Grey Cooper, Secretary to the Treasury, whom Ben happily described as 'my fast friend'.³⁵

Cooper was doing his best to give Franklin access to the Duke of Grafton, his own overlord at the Treasury. Cooper scheduled meetings and then rescheduled them. In truth the Duke had much to occupy his attention. Forced through Chatham's incapacity to take his own decisions, Grafton's leadership in the Lords made him responsible for giving the government direction, or at least for holding it together. There was popular unrest, provoked by the return of John Wilkes. And on a personal level, Grafton's bitterly estranged but not yet divorced Duchess was about to give birth to a child by another peer, the Earl of Upper Ossory, and the Duke had just sought and gained custody of the third of their three children. As for Grafton's own irregular liaison with Nancy Parsons, a tailor's daughter and courtesan, that was, as yet, just the subject of gossip.³⁶

When Cooper did finally manage to get Franklin in front of Grafton, the American representative was greeted very politely, but was told by the Minister that urgent business called him away and he was asked whether they could rearrange a time for the following Tuesday – a meeting that Grafton was then unable to make. These were not deliberate snubs and Franklin did not treat them as such. For Grafton it was a question of the pressure of priorities and in any case, as Franklin reported to his son, Cooper was able to give the assurance that 'if I {Franklin} chose to reside in England, my merit was such in his {Grafton's} opinion, as to entitle me to something better here'.³⁷ These sentiments were echoed by Lord North, Grafton's Chancellor of the Exchequer. Cooper took Franklin to see him in Grafton's absence and North 'said very obligingly, after talking of some American affairs, "I am told by Mr Cooper that you are not unwilling to stay with us, I hope we shall find some way of making it worth your while."' At this Franklin thanked his lordship and replied, 'I should stay with pleasure if I could any ways be useful to government.' After which, and the exchange of further cordialities, Cooper took Franklin by carriage to his country house at nearby Richmond, there to dine and stay the night.³⁸

Franklin opens his heart to his son in his July report, as is made clear by the phrase 'you see by the nature of this whole letter that it is to yourself only'. He tells William something that he could not conceivably have told Deborah: that his decision to remain in London or return to Philadelphia would ultimately not be due to any consideration he had for his wife. Instead it would depend upon events:

> A turn of a die may make a great difference in our affairs. We may be either promoted, or discarded; one or the other seems likely soon to be the case, but it is hard to divine which. I am myself grown so old as to feel much less than formerly the spur of ambition, and if it were not for the flattering expectation that by being fixed here I might more effectually serve my country, I should certainly determine for retirement, without a moment's hesitation.[39]

However, if it was 'promotion', he would be happy as, 'having lived long in England, and contracted a friendship and affection for many persons here, it could not but be agreeable to me to remain among them some time longer, if not for the rest of my life'.

He rightly trusted Grey Cooper, recommended by John Pringle as 'the honestest man of a courtier that he ever knew', and he also thought that for a worthwhile role he could 'cordially attach himself' to the Duke of Grafton, from 'sincere respect for his great abilities and amiable qualities'. This was an understandable tactical move for Franklin anyway, with Shelburne fractious and isolated in Cabinet and stripped of all influence over America. In June Hillsborough completed his takeover of American affairs when the Board of Trade was added to his remit. Franklin wrote that he had dined with the displaced Lord Clare just two days before the latter's dismissal, that they had had 'a good deal of conversation on our affairs' and that Clare 'seemed to interest himself with all the attention that could be supposed in a minister who expected to continue in the management of them'.[40] However, Clare may have had some inkling because, Ben told William, 'at parting, after we had drank a bottle and a half of claret each' Clare had hugged and kissed him, 'protesting he never in his life met with a man he was so much in love with'. For those who can imagine the scene, Ben's following sentence of 'This I write for your amusement' would seem somewhat unnecessary.[41]

⁊

During a long meeting with Hillsborough in August, Franklin finally received a decision on Pennsylvania's future colonial status. He had begun the day with the clear expectation that the petition for royal government would be granted; he ended it by concluding that he could 'move the Matter no farther during the Administration of a Minister that appears to have a stronger Partiality for Mr Penn than any of his Predecessors'.[42]

Franklin sought to soften the blow to Galloway with the words, 'a party is growing in our favour' that seeks to 'arraign the Conduct of Lord Hillsborough, and render him odious', and thus he thought it wise to 'stay ... a little longer here, till I see what Turn American Affairs are like to take'. For once his words were totally inadequate. Thomas Penn's Proprietary rule had survived. Hillsborough, who was to continue in his role under three prime ministers from 1768 to 1772, was to prove an inflexible opponent of change. By the time Hillsborough was forced from office – with the final straw being his unreasonable opposition to another of Franklin's concerns – the British authorities had long dropped all interest in changing Penn's Proprietary governance. Franklin, Galloway and their supporters had lost: the implicit and then explicit aim of Franklin's missions to England had failed. It is reasonable to conclude, like James Hutson, that the shock of Franklin's report of his August 1768 meeting with Hillsborough seriously affected Galloway's health.[43] Galloway did, though with one leave of absence, retain the Speakership of the Assembly right up to 1775, just as Franklin continued to act for it in London, with his 'staying a little longer' lasting the best part of seven years. But the closeness between the two men had gone, particularly on Galloway's side. They had previously both regularly written long letters, each describing the other as 'dear friend' and signing 'most affectionately'. Galloway's letters were now sporadic, short, clipped and formal.

As for Franklin, there would be no way that he would want to return to Philadelphia in his former role as a mere member of the Assembly of Pennsylvania still under the Proprietary grip of Thomas Penn. That would have been a humiliating step downwards in a life and career that had for such a long time moved ever upwards.

He still of course retained his position as agent for Pennsylvania's Assembly in London and, since April, had taken on a similar role for Georgia. He continued as Deputy Postmaster for America. He was also seeing other opportunities on both sides of the Atlantic that would mix his own advance with public advantage. One could potentially bring him an important role in a British administration and a permanent life in London. The other would give him power with wealth back in America, not in Pennsylvania but in a completely new province in the Ohio Valley.

Franklin's future in the autumn of 1768 was uncertain. The privileged position he had enjoyed since his role in the repeal of the Stamp Act was at an end. He was concerned about Hillsborough, and even more that George Grenville would take advantage of the continuing instability to bargain his way back into government and precipitate 'a breach' between Britain and America.[44] That particular nightmare scenario for Franklin did not occur, because Chatham at last clarified his position by resigning in October 1768. Shelburne joined him in opposition. Grafton was finally confirmed as Prime Minister.

Franklin's hopes in Grafton, for both himself and America, were to be disappointed.

Grafton faced an escalation of the problems in the American colonies. Resistance to the Townshend duties had continued and deepened after Boston's introduction of a formal non-importation agreement on 1 August 1768 (commencing on 1 January 1769), followed by ports across the colonies, including New York (which introduced the restrictions even more speedily) and Philadelphia (from 1 April 1769).[45]

In October 1768, General Gage's 4,000 troops, following Hillsborough's instructions, arrived at Boston. However, as Bernard Bailyn
argues, 'the feared and hated regiments were in fact ineffective, indeed
worse than useless: they were too powerful and too numerous to be
politically safe to use as a constabulary in controlling street riots ...
yet their presence was provocative'.[46]

Within months of Franklin seeing the end of his ambition for royal
rather than Proprietary government, events were justifying those who
had long argued against it. Yet Franklin for a long time had had a
foreboding that he did not even share with his son, but instead with
one of the greatest of his friends in Scotland, Lord Kames. The letter
showed Franklin's ability to envisage different scenarios, to anticipate
the worst while planning for the best. It was written as early as 1767
after the Assembly of New York had refused to comply with the
Quartering Act, and at around the time of Townshend's humiliation over the Land Tax.[47] Franklin included the following: 'Sure I am
that, if Force is used, great Mischief will ensue, the Affections of the
People of America to this Country will be alienated, your Commerce
will be diminished, and a total Separation of Interests be the final
Consequence.'[48] He continued with great feeling, and his fear in the
long term was not so much for America as for Britain:

> I have lived so great a Part of my Life in Britain, and have formed
> so many Friendships in it, that I love it and wish its Prosperity, and
> therefore wish to see that Union on which alone I think it can be
> secured and established. As to America, the Advantages of such an
> Union to her are not so apparent. She may suffer at present under the
> arbitrary Power of this Country; she may suffer for a while in a Sep-
> aration from it; but these are temporary Evils that she will outgrow.
> Scotland and Ireland are differently circumstanced. Confined by the
> Sea, they can scarcely increase in Numbers, Wealth and Strength so as
> to overbalance England. But America, an immense Territory, favoured
> by Nature with all Advantages of Climate, Soil, great navigable Rivers
> and Lakes, &c. must become a great Country, populous and mighty;
> and will in a less time than is generally conceived be able to shake off
> any Shackles that may be imposed on her, and perhaps place them

on the Imposers. In the mean time, every Act of Oppression will sour their Tempers, lessen greatly if not annihilate the Profits of your Commerce with them, and hasten their final Revolt: For the Seeds of Liberty are universally sown there, and nothing can eradicate them.[49]

He bemoaned the fact that 'Every Man in England seems to consider himself as a Piece of a Sovereign over America; seems to jostle himself into the Throne with the King, and talks of OUR Subjects in the Colonies.' He complained that it had long been understood that 'suits arising in the colonies and disputes between them' were subject to the King in Council and not to Parliament. In the same way 'internal' taxes were the preserve of the Assemblies, while reserving to Parliament all 'external' taxes required for the regulation of trade.

Showing the haphazard nature of the postal service, Kames never received the letter in 1767. Franklin sent it to him again on 21 February 1769, adding, 'Things daily wear a worse Aspect, and tend more and more to a Breach and final Separation.'[50] The cry at the time of the Stamp Act was 'No taxation without representation' and calls were then made for American representation in Parliament, but by 1769 the latter was not seriously considered, certainly not by Franklin. The most important point was for the colonies to be left to run their own internal affairs under the 'King in Council' and not have their sovereignty given to the 'King in Parliament' at Westminster and see themselves sacrificed as Britain sought to bring greater coherence to the rule of its empire. But one side was citing rights and the other claiming responsibilities. Friction between them created reaction and counter-reaction. As these increased and reinforced each other, the arguments of the two sides would become louder and Franklin was not alone in his apprehension. Edmund Burke, also writing in 1769, believed that 'The Americans have made a discovery, or think they have made one, that we mean to oppress them: we have made a discovery, or think we have made one, that they intend to rise in rebellion against us ... we know not how to advance; they know not how to retreat ... Some party must give way.'[51]

Something was needed to alter this dynamic. By 1769 Franklin saw it as lying in a change of government. The hopes that Franklin had held at the beginning of the Chatham administration were now long disappointed. Prime Minister Grafton definitely had ability but his fifteen-month ministry was a failure. The Duke was distracted by his messy personal affairs, including the scandal around the Duchess and his own defiance of social convention in publicly parading Nancy Parsons as his consort. That last element at least disappeared when Grafton divorced in March 1769, dropped Nancy and started courting the Duke of Bedford's niece, marrying her at Woburn in late June. By that time his premiership, which had much to occupy him politically, would only have another seven months to run.

Much of Grafton's period of office as acting and then official Prime Minister was spent in dealing with the issues created by John Wilkes and the consequent threat to social order. Wilkes affected the ministry's treatment of American affairs both directly and indirectly. In terms of government focus, America was relegated to secondary consideration, much to Franklin's growing consternation; and the challenge of Wilkes and the lawless Wilkesite mobs created a defensive mindset of much wider relevance. The Wilkes phenomenon strengthened the resolve of those in Parliament and Cabinet who favoured a resolute response to anyone they regarded as presenting a challenge to their authority, something Wilkes did continually by standing for election for Middlesex though Parliament continuously debarred him. Wilkes was backed by the courts and might thus claim that the shout of 'Wilkes and Liberty' was justified, but he was not in practice the true friend of America he claimed to be. Franklin certainly was not fooled. In April 1768 he was describing Wilkes as 'an outlaw ... of bad personal character', telling William that 'the scenes have been horrible. London was illuminated two nights running at the command of the mob for the success of Wilkes', and that those householders who refused to light their candles 'had all their windows put out'.[52] In May he wrote to Galloway that 'All respect to law and government seems to be lost among the common people, who are moreover continually enflamed by seditious scribblers to trample on authority and everything that used to keep them in order.'[53]

Ironically, what he was seeing in London was what he had satirically advocated in 'Felons and Rattlesnakes', due to the effect of discharging soldiers on the streets at the end of the Seven Years' War, the consequences of which were still working their way through. In 1763 it was estimated that over 200,000 men or 3 per cent of the entire population were discharged.[54] In time of war many of the most destitute, desperate and indeed criminal within the lower ranks of society sought escape by joining the forces. There was a backwash with the advent of peace. Tens of thousands were dumped onto a labour market at a time of economic contraction, with violent criminal consequences. It has been estimated that the most serious capital offences, such as highway robbery and burglary, both went up by more than 50 per cent in time of peace.[55] Nowhere was more affected than London. These were men who had been ready to join the Spitalfields weavers in rioting against the Duke of Bedford. Now they were delighted to riot for Wilkes. The problem was that protests on the streets of London and those of Boston were becoming conflated. The Sons of Liberty in Boston were publishing messages of support for Wilkes, causing Franklin to write to William about American action with the caution that 'It hurts you here with sober sensible Men, when they see you so easily infected with the Madness of English Mobs.'[56] At around the same time he was writing with disgust in his personal notes that 'Here the Actions of one or two Mobs are ascribed to the whole People of America. If this is so then ascribe the Actions of Wilkes' Mob to the whole People of Britain.'[57]

∽

By 1769 Grafton was certainly not a Chathamite. Most of the Chathamites, marshalled by Shelburne, were in concerted opposition along with the followers of Rockingham and Grenville. Grafton had turned to the authoritarian Bedfordites for support in Parliament and, without being overtly cynical about what became an evidently long and happy marriage, his choice of Bedford's niece as the new Duchess of Grafton helped to consolidate the connection.

It was during this period of courtship, on 1 May 1769, that the fate of the Townshend taxes was decided by nine present and one absentee member of the Cabinet. Grafton showed himself sensitive to the current of feeling in America by recommending that the taxes should be repealed in their entirety during the new session of Parliament that autumn. In this he was supported by Lords Camden and Granby and by Henry Seymour Conway. The two Bedfordites, Gower and Weymouth, supported Hillsborough in the view that the tax on tea should remain. They felt that it was in principle less objectionable to the Americans than that on the other products, being merely a traded commodity rather than an English manufacture. However, they also considered that its retention would affirm the right, as set out in the Declaratory Act, for Parliament to tax the colonists. Besides which, it was the only one of what Grafton would later refer to as 'these trifling taxes' that brought in anything approaching significant revenue, around three-quarters of the entire Townshend tax take. North used it, following Townshend, to pay colonial salaries.

North supported its retention as did Secretary of State Rochford. Grafton had thus been outvoted five to four by his own Cabinet. He later maintained, with some justification, that had Sir Edward Hawke not been ill and thus absent, then those in favour of complete repeal would have carried the day. And as Professor P.D.G. Thomas rightly says of this: 'By such accidents is history made.'[58]

However, had Grafton given, at the time, the same weight to the measure's importance as he was to do in his much later *Memoirs*, then he would have focused his attention and better managed the matter. This is implicit in the prominence he gives in those *Memoirs* to some extraordinary actions of Lord Hillsborough. Grafton felt these to be sufficiently disturbing that he went to great trouble to research the relevant papers in order to reproduce them. For, as he tells his readers: 'Considering what important consequences this very decision led to; there is no minute part of it, on which you should not be informed.'[59] And he proved himself to be more attentive as an elderly historian than as a young Prime Minister, because these documents – a mid-June exchange of letters between Hillsborough and a furious Lord Chancellor Camden – support Grafton in a bitter accusation against the former.

Hillsborough, notwithstanding the fact that he had got his way on the vote, decided to disregard the Cabinet's agreed view on how the decision should be recorded and then communicated in a 'circular letter to all the Governors in America'. As was customary, Hillsborough, as the minister responsible, drafted a Cabinet minute for approval by his colleagues. On its presentation, suitable amendments were agreed by the majority. These, in Grafton's words, 'were too evidently displeasing to his lordship'.[60] And Hillsborough simply chose to ignore them in his speedily dispatched letter. Subsequently, in his replies to Camden, he put up a very thin case in arguing that the letter conformed to what the Cabinet had actually agreed.

What Hillsborough had done, and deliberately so, was to issue a powerful reassertion of the main principle of the Declaratory Act that 'no measure should be taken which can {in} any way derogate from the legislative authority of Great Britain over the colonies'. This was precisely what the Cabinet had asked to be removed from the written record. The letter to the governors, which the Cabinet had wished to be emollient towards the Americans, was instead aggressive. As Grafton himself concluded, 'This circular was calculated to do all mischief, when our real minute might have paved the way to some good.'[61]

It might seem, on the face of it, mysterious that Camden did not at that time force the issue with his Cabinet colleagues. However, he was by then in open disagreement with Grafton and the others in favouring a more lenient treatment of Wilkes. This had effectively made him a semidetached member of the Cabinet and he was, because of that, planning to realign with a reinvigorated Chatham.[62] Like Grafton, he had a lot on his mind and it took precedence over the letter to the governors, thus neatly illustrating its place in the general scheme of things during 1769.

Hillsborough was showing himself to be no friend of America. But he was the man with whom colonial governors such as William Franklin and colonial representatives including William's father now had to deal. For the elder Franklin, the ease of access provided by Lord Shelburne and the opportunity for thoughtful and private discussions over dinner had been replaced by something else entirely.

With that in mind, Franklin and his fellow shareholders in the Ohio scheme should have treated a surprisingly generous action of

Hillsborough's with the greatest suspicion. Shelburne's good offices, Clare's co-operation and the Privy Council's approval had given Sir William Johnson authority to negotiate with Indian tribes to enable the area for possible white settlement to be formally increased. With consummate negotiating skill and the ruthless sacrifice of the rights of weaker tribes in order to compensate the more powerful, Johnson had achieved this at a conference at Fort Stanwix, on the western border of the New York colony, the subsequent Treaty of Fort Stanwix being agreed in November 1768. This gained a vast amount of land for potential settlement because, in the words of Alan Taylor, though 'the new boundary extended only a modest distance beyond New York's settlements' it 'then bulged westward across Pennsylvania and then down the Ohio River as far as the mouth of the Tennessee River. This added the south-western quarter of Pennsylvania, all of present-day West Virginia and most of Kentucky to the colonial domain.'[63]

But formal permission for settlement was still required from the Privy Council, which also had to consider the claims of existing colonies such as Virginia, as well as those of petitioners seeking to create a new one. The Ohio scheme's chief promoter, Samuel Wharton, funded by William Franklin, travelled over from Philadelphia to London the following spring and found the Governor's father extremely helpful in providing contacts. Thomas Walpole, nephew of the great Prime Minister Sir Robert, not only joined the scheme but took a leading role, and as the numbers and prominence of its supporters grew so did its ambitions. The Grand Ohio Company was created and it applied for a grant for 2,400,000 acres.[64] It was when the petition, signed by Walpole, Wharton, Benjamin Franklin and Richard Jackson, was at length heard by the Board of Trade that Hillsborough made his helpful suggestion that the application be increased to 20 million acres with the words, 'ask for *enough to make a Province*'.[65] It was taken up. They played straight into Hillsborough's hands. Such a large acreage would necessitate the formal establishment of a new colony, with its attendant institutions. The Privy Council would need to refer back to the Board of Trade. The company soon realized their mistake and it was one they had time to ponder at length, as Hillsborough personally delayed matters over the next three years. As with Thomas Penn and the 'Heads of Complaint', Franklin had been treated as a fool. That was not something he was willing to forget.

12

Home Comforts and Discomforts

Franklin's relationship with Polly had not been quite the same following his return from America. The letters between them continued, but now they were more practical and, in her case especially, tended to be short. The science education had definitely come to an end. All this was completely understandable. In 1757 she was a young, enthusiastic girl of eighteen, eager to learn about the world. By the time of a despondent letter from her to Franklin of 26 October 1768, she was a spinster of nearly thirty, fretting that her care for her ageing and increasingly fractious aunt would be at the sacrifice of her own health and happiness.

Such a confession to Franklin was a sign that they were still close; and perhaps it was to cheer her up that he sent her details of the new phonetic form of English that he was creating as a kind of shorthand. With his 'alphabet', he sent a letter to explain style and a translation. He flattered her by asking for her advice and saying that he thought she could help him to complete the task.[1] There was something of the younger Polly when she used the alphabet in writing back and, with total honesty, concluded with 'In sart yi biliiv ui myst let pipil spel an in cheer old ue', or rather 'In short I believe we must let people spell on in their old way.'[2]

Then, on 31 August of the following year, a meeting at the seaside town of Margate lifted her gloom completely. The next day she wrote to Franklin:

I met with a very sensible Physician yesterday, who prescribes Abstinence for the Cure of Consumption. He must be clever because he thinks as *we* do. I would not have you or my Mother surprised, if I should run off with this young man; to be sure it would be an imprudent Step at the discreet Age of Thirty but there is no saying what one should do if solicited by a Man of an insinuating Address and good Person, though he may be too young for one, and not yet established in his Profession. He engaged me so deeply in Conversation and I was so much pleased with him, that I thought it necessary to give you Warning, though I assure you he has made no Proposal.

How I rattle![3]

She was re-enlivened. The phrase 'He must be clever because he thinks as *we* do' was to prove correct in both parts. The object of her excitement, Dr William Hewson, was engaged in ground-breaking research on the lymphatic system. Later that year, in November, he was to read two papers on the subject at the Royal Society: these would in time win him the Copley Medal for 1769. By March 1770 he had been elected to the Royal Society, with his partner William Hunter proposing him and Sir John Pringle (a commender of his work for some years)[4] and one Dr Benjamin Franklin supporting the nomination.[5]

Polly was extremely eager to have Franklin's opinion. She was not worried about Hewson being good enough for her, but rather whether she was good enough for him, particularly as her bequest from her aunt was far from certain. Franklin told her that his concern for her happiness was equal to any father's and reassured her that she should not worry about her aunt's fortune. She should consider herself to be sufficient incentive in itself: 'I am sure that were I in his Situation in every respect, knowing you so well as I do, and esteeming you so highly, I should think you a Fortune sufficient for me without a Shilling. Having thus more explicitly than before given my Opinion, I leave the rest to your sound Judgement, of which no one has a greater Share.'[6]

On 10 July 1770 Hewson married Polly. He was established in his profession and he was obviously not too young, being – like Polly herself – born in 1739, though his birthday was near the end of the year. The newlyweds set up house together on the other side of Covent

Garden, in Holborn.[7] They were a short distance from Craven Street and were there in late September: Mrs Stevenson, taking English Sally Franklin with her, left to see a friend in Rochester and asked the Hewsons to look after the household and, with it, Dr Franklin.

Franklin marked that occasion by reporting on it. He produced a newspaper called *The Cravenstreet Gazette*, dated 22 to 26 September.[8] It was a work of satire, but of the gentlest kind. Written by Franklin for his own entertainment and that of his household, it gives a day-by-day account of the mishaps in Mrs Stevenson's absence. It is a piece of fun, but of historical interest for giving a glimpse of Franklin's domestic routine in London. It shows a man at ease in his home environment – so much so that it confirms that Craven Street was more than just a 'home from home'.

The holidaying Mrs Stevenson was given the persona of 'Queen Margaret' and the Hewsons were dubbed First Minister and, more importantly, First Ministress. The ministry's initial misfortune, as reported by the *Gazette*, was Franklin's inability to locate the key to the drawers thought to contain his laced dress shirts, something trivial in itself but important in that it prevented him from going to St James's Palace to join the annual commemoration of George III's Coronation. This, with the King's and Queen's birthdays, was one of the great court events of the year. The shirts were found, too late, all, as comically reported, to the distress of 'the *great* Person (so called from his enormous Size)' aka 'Dr Fatsides', that is to say Franklin himself. But no matter, as Craven Street had its own court report in the *Gazette*.

Though of course the 'new Ministry', like many another, started with good intentions, it was frustrated by practicalities. For instance, meeting over afternoon tea, it agreed to fix a new lock on the street door or to have another key made for the old one, so as to save the whole house from being disturbed by the returning maid. This was sensible of them, because security was an important consideration when theft from insecure houses was the commonest of crimes. As the French visitor Henri Misson had noted almost a century before, it was the breaking and entering of houses that was the capital offence and not the thefts themselves.[9] Thus when a thief named William Harrison was found guilty of stealing a silver candlestick from a house in Craven Street in December 1769, he was transported rather than hanged, because he had tricked his way into the house rather than by forcing an entry.[10] However, having convened, the divided 'Cabinet Council' could not agree which action to take over the lock, so the matter was shelved.

They did decide that there should be a 'Reformation of Manners, and a more strict Observation of the Lord's Day' and thus no cooking on Sundays: a cold shoulder of mutton and an apple pie would be fine for dinner. These were just good intentions, as the ministerial couple failed to stir themselves to go to church; and 'it seems the *great* Person's broad-built-bulk lay so long abed, that Breakfast was not over until it was too late to dress {for church}. At least this is the Excuse.' However the 'Clause of *cold Dinner*' was still enforced.

The next day 'the *great* Person' dined out with his Monday Club at the George & Vulture and was disappointed in its offering of 'cold Round of boiled Beef ... he rather dislikes Beef', believing that beef was a poor substitute for venison and even preferring mutton. Besides which, too much beef produced an allergic reaction. The day got no better that evening, as there was 'high Play at the Groom Porter's {Hewson again} at Cravenstreet House'[11] and 'the Great Person' lost money, presumably at cards. The *Gazette*, somewhat acidly, 'supposed the Ministers, as is usually supposed of all Ministers, shared the Emoluments among them'.

On the Tuesday, in a letter to the editor under the soubriquet 'INDIGNATION',[12] Franklin complains that he was offered the 'bare Blade-bone' of Saturday's mutton, apparently after the house cat had eaten almost the last of it the day before. This is countered by Polly, aka 'the First Ministress', under a pseudonym:

It is, Sir, a piece of Justice you owe our righteous Administration to undeceive the Public on this [Occasion] by assuring them [of] the Fact that there was provided, and actually smoking on the Table under his Royal Nose at the same Instant, as fine a Piece of Ribs of Beef, roasted, as ever Knife was put into, with Potatoes, Horseradish, pickled Walnuts etc. Which Beef his Highness might have eaten of, if so he had pleased to do; and which he forbore to do, merely from

a whimsical Opinion (with Respect be it spoken) that Beef doth
not with him perspire well, but makes his Back itch to his no small
Vexation, now that he hath lost the little Chinese Ivory Hand [at]
the End of a Stick, commonly called a *Scratchback*, presented to him
by her Majesty. This is the Truth and if your boasted Impartiality is
real, you will not hesitate a Moment to insert this Letter in your very
next Paper. I am though a little angry with you at present. Yours as
you behave – {signed} A HATER OF SCANDAL.

It had been another bad day for 'the *great* Person'. He had narrowly
missed being scalded with hot water when Polly knocked against a
table during afternoon tea.

As editor, Franklin had previously reported the absence of 'Queen
Margaret' at the local market, presumably Hungerford Market, which
was a few dozen yards from the back door: 'We hear that the Lady
Chamberlain of the Household {Polly again} went to Market this
Morning by her own self, gave the Butcher whatever he asked for the
Mutton and had no Dispute with the Potato Woman – to their great
Amazement – at the Change of Times!' Again as editor, Franklin
had complained: 'We hear that, from the Time of her Majesty's leav-
ing Craven Street House to this Day, no Care is taken to file the
Newspapers; but they lie about in every Room, every Window and
on every Chair, just where the Doctor lays them when he has read
them. It is impossible Government can long go on in such Hands.'

There was a final flurry of complaint with the following report:
'Stocks: Biscuit very low; Buckwheat and Indian meal, both sour;
Tea, lowering daily in the Canister.' However, the ministry asserted its
authority in the end, with Wednesday's editorial postscript telling us:
'Those in the Secret of Affairs do not scruple to assert soundly that our
present First Ministress is very notable, having this day been at Market,
bought excellent Mutton Chops and Apples four a penny, made a fine
Apple Pie with her own Hands and mended two pairs of Breeches.'

Meanwhile Deborah Franklin kept up the house in Philadelphia
in readiness for the day of her husband's return. When Ben Franklin
had been in business in Philadelphia, Deborah had looked after the
shop literally. Now she was continuing to do so figuratively.

∽

For all the delights of Craven Street, Franklin was far from house-bound, as he wrote to William: 'my company {being} so much desired that I seldom dine at home in winter'.[13]

He was particularly proud of one occasion when he was invited to St James's Palace to dine with a king in October 1768. That King, Christian VII of Denmark, married to Caroline Matilda, George III's sister, was visiting London. Franklin was sitting one place away from him. Between them was the Royal Society President, the Earl of Morton, who stepped into the role of French-English translator. Franklin was so pleased with the occasion that he sent William a rough sketch of the table placings. On the other side of the King, to his right, was Admiral George Rodney.[14]

∽

It is no wonder that the lean athlete of his younger days had filled out to become 'Dr Fatsides'. Franklin was forced to ignore his own 1742 advice as 'Poor Richard' to 'Keep out of the Sight of Feasts and Banquets as much as may be; for 'tis more difficult to refrain good Cheer, when it's present, than from the Desire of it when it is away'.[15] The result was that, though in 1762 he was telling his sister Jane about a 'Touch of the Gout', by 1765 he was writing to a friend about a 'Visitation . . . that confined me near a Fortnight'.[16]

As for knowledge at the time, gout was generally seen to be an unavoidable consequence of good living and, if hereditary, good breeding. Indeed Lord Chesterfield, when waiting to hear whether he had rheumatism or gout, opined that 'I wish it were a declared gout, which is the distemper of a gentleman; whereas the rheumatism is the distemper of a hackney-coachman or [sedan] chairman'.[17] Horace Walpole believed that gout forestalled other diseases and treatments, writing that 'the gout certainly carries off other complaints . . . and in my opinion a disorder that requires no physician, is preferable to any that does',[18] and 'all that claret and port are very kind to you, when they prefer the shape of lameness to that of apoplexies, or dropsies, or fevers, or pleurisies'.[19] In this he was echoing the contemporary view.[20]

It was certainly known that claret, port and Franklin's favourite madeira were culprits – but what gentleman would want to be without them? As long before as 1683 Thomas Sydenham, renowned as the 'English Hippocrates', had argued that 'the gout generally attacks those aged persons who have spent the most part of their lives in ease, voluptuousness, high living, and too free a use of wine and other spirituous liquors'.[21] Sydenham could not offer a cure, but advised exercise and distillations of herbs into bitters. He also suggested various lighter diets that needed to be strictly followed. One such was based on drinking milk 'without adding anything to it, except perhaps a piece of bread once a day'. However, this was a life sentence because Sydenham then admitted that for those 'quitting it, and returning to the ordinary way of living of healthy persons, though they used the mildest and slenderest diet, the *gout* immediately returned with more violence than ever'.[22] Bread dipped in milk was known as milksop. This was very much a case of once a milksop, always a milksop. Far better to trust that one would be lucky and avoid gout and, if not, to put up with its intermittent horrific visitations. No one would want to exclude themselves from the food and drink of the social round and thus from Society itself. However, as for its supposed benefits in keeping worse ailments at bay, Franklin was decidedly equivocal. As he wrote: 'I may possibly be, as they tell me, greatly *obliged* to the Gout; but "The *Condition* of this *Obligation* is *such*" that I cannot heartily say, *Thank-ye*.'[23]

Franklin's favourite venison, together with other game, shellfish and oily fish such as anchovies and herring, are all today listed as among the foods best avoided by gout sufferers.[24] They were all highly prized in the eighteenth century and liberally enjoyed by the well-to-do, game all the more so because the enclosure of great landed estates made venison and even hare more difficult to obtain. But it was also a question of quantity as well as perceived quality of food.

As Defoe had described in 1726, at the time of Franklin's first stay in London, good food was plentiful for those with money to spend. And, just as the population of London had surged during the following decades, so had the supply of food to feed it. The Agricultural Revolution's improvements in husbandry, including the introduction of winter fodder, extended the period when fresh meat was available. By the same token, preserving meat was less necessary and preserved meat less popular, with the exception of pork and ham[25] – though Franklin liked his bacon and ham to have crossed the Atlantic, together with dried venison and, surprisingly, smoked beef.

It was because of the vast numbers of animals driven into London – cattle, pigs and sheep, together with geese and turkeys in their specially made boots – that the 'New Road', following much of the northern border of today's Congestion Charge Zone, was built in 1756/7.[26] It was at least 40 feet wide in order to cope. In theory this allowed Oxford Street to continue in its process of gentrification, but there were still some drovers who, eager to avoid the charges of the new toll road, infuriated the new residents by taking the shortcut down to Smithfield.[27] It has been estimated that by the mid-century 80,000 cattle alone were driven there annually.[28]

By Defoe's time there were fourteen established markets for selling meat that also sold fish, other foodstuffs and a variety of goods.[29] These included Westminster, St James's and Hungerford, with the latter, helpfully for Mrs Stevenson, being a general market.[30] Covent Garden was not far for her, or her maid, if she wanted a larger selection of herbs, fruit and vegetables. Fresh milk was available from the dairy herd in St James's Park; and bread and baked goods could either be made at home or bought from a local bakehouse.[31] Mrs Stevenson did not need to rely on the chance street vendors who sold door-to-door and whose dubious hygiene and suspect goods were heavily satirized at the time by the likes of Smollett in his novel *The Expedition of Humphry Clinker*, published in 1771.[32] Nor indeed, with Westminster market nearby, did Margaretta Acworth, whose household reference gives us a better indication than the eighteenth century's commercial cookery books of what the well-to-do, as opposed to the staggeringly rich, actually ate. As it illustrates, the two courses of dinner with guests would each have at least two or three dishes. The first would include soup, which would be eaten first and then replaced with a fish dish.[33] The first course was one of mainly savoury dishes – though the English medieval tradition of pies and puddings that mixed sweet and savoury continued – and the second, perhaps with lighter meat dishes and with fish and shellfish, would also include a greater number of sweeter assortments.[34] The dishes were sampled tapas- or meze-style, with the guests encouraged by their hostess to take or leave whatever they wanted. In addition there might be a dessert, 'a feast for the eyes as well as the palate, with fruits, jellies, marmalades and other sweetmeats attractively set out in a variety of little dishes and in pyramids on raised dishes'.[35] After which the ladies would retire for coffee or tea and the men would move on to more serious drinking.

The principle of the two courses with a selection of dishes held good whether one was catering for a small dinner party, a large one or a full-scale banquet – the main difference being that the greater the household and the more special the occasion, the more numerous the dishes from which to choose. The same was true for dessert, which had moved on from the original French *desservir* (to clear the table) to being a major reason to stay there.

As to the main constituent of dinner, meat, if Mrs Acworth's household was typical of the well-to-do, then beef, mutton and chickens aplenty were eaten, as was veal.[36] Traditionally more popular on the Continent than in England,[37] veal's increasing popularity was a sign, together with the greater use of cream, of the success of the French influence so decried by Hannah Glasse and many others but integrated into their books. Mrs Glasse could not and did not ignore fashion, but rather in her own way helped to create it; for example she used East Indian spices 'to make a curry the Indian way', the first known curry recipe in an English cookbook.[38]

Fresh fish and shellfish were readily available to Londoners; much rarer was a new luxury favourite – turtle. Franklin would certainly have enjoyed these in Philadelphia fresh from the Delaware River, and Captain Nathaniel Falconer, one of his packet-boat friends, is known to have brought him one from the West Indies in 1765.[39]

London was surrounded by market gardens. To the west they stretched from Kensington to Chiswick and then beyond to Twickenham.[40] Seasonal non-salad vegetables tended just to be boiled, smothered in flour and butter and, increasingly as the century progressed – as with meat dishes – served with cream.[41] They might also be enjoyed out of season in pickled form, a definite preference to the scraggy offerings of winter, which could soon blacken in London markets with, in Franklin's words, 'the Air full of floating Sea Coal Soot'.[42] Fresh herbs were lavishly used, as were spices – with mace, nutmeg, cloves and caraway being particularly popular.

Franklin liked his apples baked, but this was out of preference, rather than the traditional fear of eating raw fruit. It was now understood that it was the filth on the skin or the filthy water in which the fruit was washed that caused problems, rather than the flesh of the fruit itself. Like some vegetables, fruit was made into chutneys for the long periods when it would be out of season, or it was preserved in syrup.

For those wishing to finish the meal with something savoury, there would be cheese. Pehr Kalm, the Swedish friend of Collinson and then Franklin, wrote of his stay in London that 'Cheese nearly always concludes the meal. Commonly, there is set on the table, whole, a large and strong cheese, and each person cuts what he likes from it.'[43] The eighteenth century's better transportation enabled a great variety of regional cheeses to be offered. William Franklin had a liking for Cheshire,[44] but for Ben none would have surpassed his favourite. That was the one which Renaissance popes had sent to kings as a princely reward for their loyalty: Parmesan.[45] Cheese was a foodstuff Franklin sent home to Deborah. In April 1766 he sent her 'a Box with three fine cheeses' and wrote, rather touchingly, that 'Perhaps a Bit of them may be left when I come home.'[46] In which case it is likely that at least one was a Parmesan, because, as he later jokingly wrote to John Bartram, 'I confess that if I could find in any Italian Travels a Receipt {i.e. recipe} for making Parmesan Cheese, it would give me more Satisfaction than a Transcript of any Inscription from any old Stone whatever.'[47] Of course, practical man that he was, he tried to make a Parmesan-style cheese, or rather get his friends to do so. In spite of having one of them observe the cheese-making process in Italy and himself sending recipes and samples to others so 'that you may be acquainted with it, and know when you have hit it', the quest continued. As late as 1786 his grandnephew Jonathan Williams was writing from Boston to tell him that he had distributed the recipe for making Parmesan cheese to capable farmers.[48]

If a large London or country dinner was the precursor for an evening's entertainment, the company might reassemble for music or cards. There would be tea and coffee for the gentlemen and, if anyone was peckish, cakes and bread and butter. Finally, if anyone wanted it, there was supper. That would be simple, more of a snack than a meal: perhaps cold meat and cheese on toast (Welsh Rarebit or Rabbit), toasted cheese placed on toast (Scotch Rabbit), or wine-soaked toast topped with cheese and then baked (English Rabbit)[49] – Hannah Glasse offers simple recipes for all three. The alcohol would continue to flow. Franklin, more interested in conversation than intoxication, was more abstemious than some, but even during the Seven Years' War, 'no questions asked', French claret and brandy might be available as well as the more patriotic port and madeira. Cider punch and, of course, beer were popular longer drinks, though from the mid-century the latter could be produced at 'vinous strengths' at the breweries attached to great aristocratic houses.[50]

There would be no difficulty in piling on the pounds, as attested in 1770 by *The Cravenstreet Gazette*. However, at least in theory, Franklin had various means of keeping in trim.

13

1770–c.1771

Seeking Balance

By 1770 Franklin was becoming frustrated and angry at Britain's treatment of her American colonies as one giant farm and forest of raw materials to feed the mother country's manufactures. He fell upon a 1766 anti-colonial pamphlet by Dean Tucker of Gloucester that described premiums given to the colonies 'as bounties' and angrily scribbled in the margins: 'What you call Bounties given by Parliament and the Society {of Arts} are nothing more than Inducements offered us ... to quit a Business profitable to ourselves and engage in one that shall be profitable to you; this is the true Spirit of all your Bounties.'[1] The man who had been delighted to chair the Society of Arts Committee of Colonies and Trade, who had been so optimistic when testifying to the Commons for the repeal of the Stamp Act, now took a very different tone.

His views were in sympathy with government critics in Philadelphia such as Charles Thomson, who at the request of the Committee of Merchants in Philadelphia sent Franklin a copy of their letter to their London counterparts. It asked the London merchants to use their influence with the government and in Parliament to address American grievances. In his covering letter of 26 November Thomson anticipated that 'Parliament will no doubt at their meeting take under consideration the affairs of America', and to that end he was keen that Franklin 'should be fully acquainted with the temper and disposition of the Colonies' so that he could best act on their behalf.[2] In a clear and succinct summary that showed why Thomson was to become Secretary to the First Continental Congress in 1774,[3] he added his own powerful and distinct encapsulation of what many in the colonies now saw as a deliberately draconian policy to destroy the legislative authority as well as the taxation powers of the colonial Assemblies. A policy, moreover, that employed aggressive customs officers backed by the fierce justice of British Admiralty courts, together with an army 'left in America after the late war, under pretence of securing and defending it, {which} is now publicly declared to be for the purpose of enforcing obedience to the authority of Parliament'.[4]

Active man that he was, Franklin circulated the letter. As he replied to Thomson in March 1770: 'Your very judicious letter of 26 November being communicated by me to some Member of Parliament, was handed out among them ... It had due Weight with several, and was of considerable Use. You will see that I printed it at length in the *London Chronicle* with the Merchants' Letter.'[5] Thomson's letter was published under a pseudonym, as was Franklin's reply. The contents of the latter were circulated widely in Philadelphia and then published in newspapers, first in Philadelphia and then Boston. The identity of their author became well known on both sides of the Atlantic, where the reaction was markedly different. In Philadelphia he was described by the merchants as 'a Gentleman of undoubted Veracity in *London*, in whom we have the greatest Confidence and Reliance',[6] but in the hostile London press he was scorned as 'Dr Doubleface' and 'the Judas of Craven Street'.[7]

Franklin stated that British manufacturers deprived of their American markets would 'soon begin a Clamour that much Pains has hitherto been used to stifle', and ended the letter with a rallying cry for the non-importation campaign, believing that 'if we do not now persist in this Measure till it has had its full Effect, it can never again be used on any future Occasion with the least prospect of Success, and that if we do persist another year, we shall never afterwards have occasion to use it'. He was, though, wrong in his estimation of the influence of the British manufacturers. The ministry failed to back down.

Non-importation did collapse, with the colonies withdrawing action one by one; New York's merchants stopped in July 1770,

Philadelphia's in September and, last of all, Boston's in October. However, there seems little doubt that Franklin's letter did extend the boycott and it certainly burnished his credentials with some, though not all, of the growing number of radicals across the Atlantic.

In London many considered Franklin's sentiments to be, at the very least, completely unacceptable from a man whose Post Office position was a government one – particularly as he had attacked the government directly and the Bedford faction in the most ferocious terms:

> Though both the Duke of Grafton and Lord North were and are in my Opinion rather inclined to satisfy us, yet the Bedford Party are so violent against us, and so prevalent in the {Privy} Council, that more moderate Measures could not take Place. This Party never speak of us but with evident Malice; Rebels and Traitors are the best Names they can afford us, and I believe they only wish for a colourable Pretence and Occasion of ordering the Soldiers to make a Massacre among us.

Yet what was taken badly in London was well received by Franklin's supporters in Philadelphia. These included his loyal leather-apron men, his 'White Oaks and mechanics' craftsmen supporters, who had kept wavering merchants true to the cause of non-importation. They had become radicalized and supported existing activists such as Thomson. Galloway was alarmed. In September 1770 he wrote to Franklin that he knew that General Gage had written to the ministry in London about Franklin's letter, and warned him with the words, 'This has truly given me much Concern and uneasiness as I fear the Consequences not only on your private Account but on that of the Public.' He also attempted to steer Franklin away from Thomson with: 'Pray be cautious in future what you write to that Man, who is void of Principle or Virtue.'[8] That was something that Franklin was not inclined to do.

A near-complete extract of Franklin's letter to Thomson was sent to Boston, and its sentiments went down so well that a majority in the Massachusetts House of Representatives supported Franklin's appointment as their agent in London. Thomas Cushing, the

Speaker of the House, would be Franklin's main contact for the next four and a half years, but he also reported to their four-man Committee of Correspondence, which in late 1770 included, as well as Cushing, John Hancock and John and Samuel Adams. The last of these, though, was one of a radical minority led by himself and James Otis that did not completely trust Franklin and supported the Virginian Arthur Lee, who, as 'Junius Americanus', had written a string of virulent anti-government articles in the London press. In the ensuing compromise Lee was chosen as an 'alternate' or deputy to cover for Franklin's absence or death. It was not a happy arrangement, as Lee possessed, in the memorable words of one historian, 'his own psychopathology' and nursed a bitter hatred of Franklin.[9] Dr Franklin should have known Dr Lee long enough to have gauged his personality, having proposed him as a Fellow of the Royal Society in 1766 and 'signed a Bond for him for his Contributions and paid his Admission fee in December 1767',[10] but he would learn that such generosity did not necessarily bring lasting gratitude.

Franklin was now the agent in London for four colonies: Pennsylvania, Georgia, New Jersey (which he had taken up in 1769)[11] – and Massachusetts. This gave him a considerably increased workload of routine business, though he had capable assistance from his great-nephew Jonathan Williams, who was brought over from Boston as a twenty-year-old in 1770 to continue his education and to work for his great-uncle as his financial clerk.[12] But it is a fair question to ask why at the age of sixty-four Franklin took so much on. In particular, why did he take on the problems of Massachusetts? Especially after an event in March that heightened passions. It was one that Franklin had predicted as the likely consequence of British troops occupying Boston: on 5 March, five among a group of unarmed American civilian protesters were shot and killed by panicked British soldiers in what has become known as the Boston Massacre.

One explanation for Franklin's multi-agenting is that he did so for financial reasons: the eighteen-year partnership agreement with David Hall had come to term in 1766 and he certainly needed to make up the shortfall of around £500 in order to continue his agreeable lifestyle.[13] Had he gained an Under-Secretaryship with the British government he might have earned an annual fee income of £500, as David Hume did in a year from January 1767 working for Henry Seymour Conway at the Northern Department.[14] Such an opportunity was not going to present itself in 1770 without a change of government. Franklin also had to consider that his Post Office salary was vulnerable: it was only the support of one of the Postmasters, Francis Dashwood, Lord Le Despencer, that had kept him in post following his non-importation appeal and protected the £300 a year that came with it, not to mention the free postage and the use of the fast packet ships for transporting goods across the Atlantic quickly and securely.[15] The income from the new agencies promised to more than make up the difference, though payment could be slow at best.[16]

One can also conclude that he not only enjoyed his lifestyle in London, but relished the challenge of influencing events there. It is hard to disagree with Jerry Weinberger's straightforward judgement about Franklin, particularly when applied to this part of his life, that 'He was moved to politics, in my view, not by pride or anger and certainly not by any sense of moral obligation, but rather because he liked it, as much as he liked chess, and ... Franklin did what Franklin liked.'[17]

‰

On 16 January 1771, Franklin visited Lord Hillsborough. Like his encounter with Granville in 1757, this was a noteworthy event which Franklin committed to paper. In the absence of an account from Hillsborough, some historians have accepted Franklin's version verbatim; but a little bit of context, not least that provided by the editors of the Franklin Papers, shows that the episode was somewhat more complex.[18] There is something in the preamble and in the identity of the person to whom Franklin sent the following report that puts another complexion on the matter entirely:

At the earnest Instance and Request of Mr Strahan. I went this Morning to wait on Lord Hillsborough. The Porter at first denied his Lordship, on which I left my Name and drove off. But before the

Coach got out of the Square, the Coachman heard a Call, turned and went back to the Door, when the Porter came and said, His Lordship will see you, Sir. I was shown into the Levée Room, where I found Governor Bernard, who I understand attends there constantly. Several other Gentlemen were there attending, with whom I sat down a few Minutes. When Secretary Pownall came out to us, and said his Lordship desired I would come in.

I was pleased with this ready Admission, and Preference (having sometimes waited 3 or 4 Hours for my Turn) and, being pleased, I could more easily put on the open cheerful Countenance that my Friends {i.e. Strahan}[19] advised me to wear. His Lordship came towards me, and said "I was dressing in order to go to Court; but hearing that you were at the Door, who are a Man of Business, I determined to see you immediately." I thanked his Lordship and said that my Business at present was not much, it was only to pay my Respects to his Lordship and to acquaint him with my Appointment by the House of Representatives of the Province of Massachusetts Bay to be their Agent here, in which Station if I could be of any Service – I was going on to say, to the Public – I should be very happy; but his Lordship whose Countenance changed at my naming that Province cut me short by saying, with something between a Smile and a Sneer.

LH   I must set you right there, Mr Franklin, you are not Agent.

BF   Why; my Lord?

LH   You are not appointed.

BF   I do not understand your Lordship. I have the Appointment in my Pocket.

LH   You are mistaken. I have later and better Advices. I have a Letter from Governor Hutchinson. He would not give his Assent to the Bill.

BF   There was no Bill, my Lord; it is a Vote of the House.

LH   There was a Bill presented to the Governor, for the Purpose of appointing you, and another, one Dr Lee, I think he is called, to which the Governor refused his Assent.

BF   I cannot understand this, my Lord. I think There must be some

Mistake in it. Is your Lordship quite sure that you have such a Letter?

LH   I will convince you of it directly. [Rings the Bell]. Mr Pownall will come in and satisfy you.[20]

A servant fetched John Pownall, who said that the letter from Governor Hutchinson did not mention the matter and had refused consent to something else entirely. But to Hillsborough that was not the point: an agent with a permanent position needed to be jointly appointed by the assembly and the Governor. This was something that Franklin contested, saying, 'I cannot conceive, my Lord, why the Consent of the Governor should be thought necessary to the Appointment of an Agent.' This, as Franklin described it, brought 'a mixed Look of Anger and Contempt' from Hillsborough and the words, 'I shall not enter into a Dispute with you, Sir, upon this Subject.'

But the dispute did go on. It ended when Hillsborough handed back the credentials and Franklin left with the words: 'I beg your Lordship's Pardon for taking up so much of your time. It is I believe of no great Importance whether the Appointment is acknowledged or not, for I have not the least Conception that an Agent can at present be of any Use to any of the Colonies. I shall therefore give your Lordship no farther Trouble.' For an agent to use such language to a Secretary of State and peer of the realm was no less than shocking. It did not go unnoticed. Franklin told Samuel Cooper in Boston: 'I have since heard that his Lordship took great Offence at some of my last Words, which he calls extremely rude and abusive. He assured a Friend of mine, they were equivalent to telling him to his Face that the Colonies could expect neither Favour nor Justice during his Administration. I find he did not mistake me.'[21]

That was the point. As Franklin continued: 'It is true, as you have heard, that some of my Letters to America have been echoed back hither ... Great Umbrage was taken, but chiefly by Lord H', and added: 'One Encouragement I have, the Knowledge that he is not a Whit better liked by his Colleagues in the Ministry than he is by me, that he cannot probably continue where he is much longer, and that he can scarce be succeeded by anybody who will not like me the better for his having been at Variance with me.'

Franklin was creating the effect that he wanted. He was credentializing himself and showing his tactics to an audience far more important than Hillsborough – one composed of those radical leaders in Boston who doubted his sincerity. He certainly needed to watch his back, as Arthur Lee was still describing Franklin in a June 1771 letter to Sam Adams as 'not the dupe but the instrument of Lord Hillsborough's treachery'.[22]

The identity of the recipient of Franklin's report is important. Samuel Cooper was a politically active Boston clergyman whom Franklin had known for over twenty years. They shared scientific interests and he was one of those for whom Franklin procured an academic honour from a cash-strapped Scottish university – in Cooper's case an honorary divinity degree from Edinburgh.[23] Like James Bowdoin, a Boston merchant and scientific enthusiast, Cooper was both a long-standing friend of Franklin's and within the inner circle of the Adams–Otis–Hancock group.[24] Cooper was a man whom Franklin trusted and a safe conduit for circulating his report. A small detail in the preamble is also important, that of 'At the earnest Instance and Request of Mr Strahan. I went this Morning to wait on Lord Hillsborough.' This would point to the fact that Strahan, now a government-supporting MP and the King's Official Printer, had acted as an intermediary, quite possibly at Franklin's own request. To have used Strahan for such a purpose and then to have betrayed him through his behaviour was not impossible for Franklin, who could show an extraordinarily ruthless streak when it suited him.

Whatever might have been the supposed purpose of the meeting it could not have been solely to enable Franklin to present his credentials. That was something to be done with Under-Secretary Pownall and was beneath the remit of the Secretary of State, as Hillsborough pointed out to Franklin and which the latter already knew from his other agencies. As to whether a colony's governor needed to be involved in the appointment of a permanent agent for a royal colony, Hillsborough was technically right. It had traditionally been a joint appointment, but had recently fallen into abeyance and was something that he was determined to reverse. Franklin would have known that also. There can be no doubt that he set up the confrontation deliberately. He was not interested in credentializing himself with the minister but instead with suspicious radicals in the American colonies.

His actions certainly had an immediate effect. Hillsborough refused to have anything further to do with him. There were other consequences, not least for Governor William Franklin.

By June 1771 William was writing confidentially to Strahan about Lord Hillsborough's conduct:

> The truth of the matter is that Lord H has really no cause of quarrel with me, but having been disappointed in his late attempts to injure my father he is now endeavouring to hurt him through me. For which purpose he catches at every the minutest trifle, and even blames me for things that he ought to approve, he has no reason (other than the natural connection between us) to imagine that I entertain the same political opinion with my father with regard to the disputes between Britain & America.[25]

It was certainly ironic that when Hillsborough complained that Governor Franklin was sending letters to Hillsborough via his father, the Governor was able to point to the fact that Dr Franklin was his own appointee as well as the New Jersey Assembly's.

William's way of coping with Hillsborough's hostility was to attempt 'to steer my little bark quietly through all the storms of political contest'.[26] He did, however, act decisively in cutting off all contact with Samuel Wharton, whose fear that Dr Franklin's unpopularity in government circles would damn the Grand Ohio project had led him to seek to distance himself by adding to scurrilous rumour rather than refuting it. Wharton was right to worry, because, as Strahan in April had written to William about Ben and the potential colony, 'Your Father could not stir in this Business as he is not only on bad Terms with Lord Hillsborough, but with the *Ministry in general*.'[27]

The head of the ministry had changed in early 1770, but the policy had not.

In July 1769 a seemingly rejuvenated Earl of Chatham had caused a sensation by presenting himself at one of the King's thrice-weekly levées at St James's Palace. He received a twenty-minute private audience with the King, but not before snubbing Prime Minister Grafton with 'cold politeness'.[28] Over the succeeding months he ruthlessly undermined his former lieutenant and during January 1770 Camden and Granby, Chathamites both, resigned. Grafton, with a dwindling Parliamentary majority, ensured that a hesitant Lord North accepted the King's conditional offer to take over, and then formally resigned on 30 January. On the face of it, North might have been expected to have an even looser grip on power than his predecessor, because he was a politician without a personal following. For though he was the nephew of the Earl of Halifax and had first entered the lowest ranks of government in 1759 under the Duke of Newcastle, to whom he was more distantly related, it was his administrative talents rather than his political connections that had made him an extremely valued colleague throughout the 1760s in all governments except, tellingly, that of Rockingham, Newcastle's political heir.[29] By 1770 he could not be classified as an 'old Corps Whig', or a Tory, but as someone who stood outside party or faction. That, if looked at in terms of the operation of politics in the 1760s, would appear to have made him exceptionally vulnerable to opposition attack, and, unsurprisingly, he was not expected to survive long. Yet he would remain Prime Minister for the rest of Franklin's time in England. In 1770, after nearly a decade of turbulence, Britain at last gained a Cabinet that was secure in power.

A new form of equilibrium had been reached. North was admired for his application to business, particularly in financial matters where, like Pitt the Younger later in the century, he skilfully ran the nation's finances while leaving his own in chaos.[30] As the heir to a peerage he could sit in the Commons rather than the Lords and thus, unlike King George's three previous First Ministers, was able to manage Commons business personally. That he did very well, being a clear spokesman for the government with a command of detail, ready wit and winning personal style. Lord North was given a fair hearing by

the bulk of the independent Members. Crucially, he had the confidence of the King. George admired North's qualities as a minister,
a man and, increasingly, a good friend. In terms of the emotional
quality of this relationship, there was a similarity with that of George
and Bute, except this time it was George who, though by nine years
the younger man, was to be the dominant partner. Acting for the
King at the beginning of the reign, Bute had sought, through the
'King's Friends', to gain support in Parliament for a government free,
as he saw it, from corrupt factional managers. Now, after all the
upheavals of the 1760s, stability had been secured because the King
had gone one better than capturing Parliament: he had captured
the Prime Minister. North was dependent on the King. And not
just financially so, although George did clear North's debts. George
had him in emotional thrall. On many occasions, due to the strain
of a job that included acting as First Minister, Chancellor of the
Exchequer and government spokesman in the Commons across all
departments, North tried to resign. But George would not let him.
Instead, he bolstered him up and appealed to his loyalty. North then,
with backbone stiffened, returned to the fray.

That is not to say that the King dictated policy: he most certainly
did not. In the words of P. D. G. Thomas, 'the old idea of Whig
mythology that George III had ambitions of autocratic monarchy
is complete nonsense'.[31] The King would appoint prime ministers,
have a say in further Cabinet appointments; but once those were
made he did not decide what they did. He would make his views
known to the Prime Minister and to other individual ministers, but,
as observed by Lord Hillsborough from his own direct experience,
the King would 'conform to his Ministers, though he will argue with
them, and very sensibly; but if they adhere to their own opinion,
he will say "Well. Do you choose it should be so? Then let it be."'[32]
Crucially, the King did not sit in Cabinet because, as Thomas concludes, 'It was the cabinet, albeit often influenced by royal opinions,
that made decisions on policy.'[33]

Stability at the top of the administration was reflected within the
Cabinet. Though there were departures over the succeeding five years
– such as Weymouth resigning in 1770 in protest during a Falklands

crisis with Spain, and Hillsborough being forced out in 1772 – these were far fewer than during any comparative length of time in the 1760s. This was partly due to the fact that North took a very collegiate approach as regards policy: concentrating on his own wide responsibilities, he gave his Cabinet colleagues free rein. With Lords Gower, Suffolk and Sandwich in place, men who were endemically or increasingly anti-American by inclination were potentially in a position to block conciliation.

It was part of Benjamin Franklin's responsibilities to monitor what was happening in Parliament and he did so faithfully. Before the end of the second month of the North ministry, he was writing in his March letter to Charles Thomson that 'The Rockingham and Shelburne People, with Lord Chatham's Friends, are disposed to favour us if they were again in Power,' yet adding, 'which at present they are not like to be.'

Even with a revived Chatham, the opposition looked unlikely to break the ministry's grip on the Commons. Franklin cited the belief at Westminster of 'the idle Notion of the Dignity and Sovereignty of Parliament, which they are so fond of, and imagine will be endangered by any farther {sic} Concessions'. This he thought 'prevailed I know with many to vote with the Ministry' and, in truth, he was worried that even the more pro-American elements would also 'be for keeping up the Claim of parliamentary Sovereignty, but without exercising it in any Mode of Taxation'.

The American colonists did not even have the benefit of a grouping of thirty to forty MPs like the British-based West Indian interests, who, under the leadership of William Beckford, could be relied upon to vote en bloc when necessary and who were better able to act in concert with the City of London, where Beckford was Lord Mayor in 1762 and again in 1769.[34] The West Indian grandees had certainly been able to protect their sugar interests.

ॐ

Yet even though all these factors had locked the existing policy in place, Franklin had not given up hope of a change, not even after his 'interview' with Hillsborough in January 1771. The British empire with Britain at its hub, was the world's greatest power; its American colonies offered an almost unimaginable bounty of potential resources; for the one to reject the other would be unnatural, like a parent rejecting a child. One positive episode, such as the removal of Hillsborough, might alter the course of events; that, at least, might also enable the application for the Grand Ohio grant to proceed. As it happened, the Grand Ohio grant would be the cause and not the effect.

Throughout his life, Franklin valued fresh air and exercise. In his time in London, he took full advantage each summer of the long Parliamentary recess to get out of the city to clear his lungs. After staying in Hampshire with Jonathan Shipley, the Bishop of St Asaph, and his family in 1771, Franklin wrote, 'I now breathe with Reluctance the Smoke of London, when I think of the sweet Air of Twyford', and what is particularly remarkable, regarding smoke, is the date of the letter, which is the summer's day of 24 June.[35] The next year, in a missive to Thomas Cushing, Franklin wrote that 'My Constitution, and too great Confinement to Business during the Winter, seem to require the Air and Exercise of a long Journey once a Year, which I have now practiced {sic} for more than 20 Years past.'[36]

He certainly knew how, in theory, he should balance diet and exercise, writing that 'The Quantities of Food and Exercise are relative things; those who move much, may, and indeed ought to eat more; those who use little Exercise should eat little. In general Mankind, since the improvement of Cookery, eat{s} about twice as much as Nature requires.'[37]

The great empiricist was able to give advice to Catherine Shipley, daughter of his friend Bishop Shipley, based on his own experience: 'Suppers are not bad if we have not dined, but restless Nights naturally follow hearty Suppers after full Dinners', though he did jokingly end the letter by saying that the best thing for pleasant dreams is 'A GOOD CONSCIENCE'.[38]

He was more earnest when writing to William in 1772, after the

New Jersey Governor had suffered ill health in his forties. Franklin Sr stressed the importance of raising the heart rate:

> In considering the different kinds of exercise, I have thought that the *quantum* of each is to be judged of, not by time or by distance, but by the degree of warmth it produces in the body. Thus when I observe if I am cold when I get into a carriage in a morning, I may ride all day without being warmed by it; that if on horseback my feet are cold, I may ride some hours before they become warm; but if I am ever so cold on foot, I cannot walk an hour briskly without glowing from head to foot by the quickened circulation.

He even estimated the difference, thinking that it was better exercise to walk one mile than ride five. He also saw the benefit of step exercises, believing that 'there is more {value} in walking *one* mile up and down stairs, than in *five* on a level floor. The two latter exercises may be had within doors, when the weather discourages going abroad; and the last may be had when one is pinched for time, as containing a great quantity of exercise in a handful of minutes.'

Franklin measured the effect of using dumbbells and concluded that 'the dumb bell is another exercise of the latter compendious kind; by the use of it, I have in forty swings quickened my pulse from 60 to 100 beats in a minute, counted by a second watch. And I suppose the warmth greatly increases with quickness of pulse.'[39]

He had long known the value of raising the heart rate before eating: 'Use now and then a little Exercise a quarter of an Hour before Meals, as to swing a Weight, or swing your Arms about with a small Weight in each Hand; to leap, or the like, for that stirs the Muscles of the Breast.'[40] He was also consistent – at least in theory – in noting the value of a sensible diet and cardiorespiratory exercise for mind as well as body. As 'Poor Richard' he had written in 1742: 'Eat and drink such an exact Quantity as the Constitution of thy Body allows of, in reference to the Services of the Mind.'[41] In 1772 he advised Deborah to 'Eat light Foods, such as Fowls, Mutton, &c. and but little Beef or Bacon, avoid strong Tea, and use what Exercise you can; by these Means, you will preserve your Health better, and be less Subject to Lowness of Spirits.'[42] This was good general advice, though it did not address an underlying change that Franklin seemed unable to comprehend or even acknowledge.

However, towards the end of his stay in London, Franklin was beginning to suffer the consequences of ignoring 'Poor Richard's' good sense on diet and lifestyle. This was very much a case of 'do as I say, not as I do'. In 1773 Franklin first noticed a 'Scab or Scurf on my Head, about the Bigness of a Shilling'. His friend Sir John Pringle was able to treat it, but also, as Franklin relates, 'advised my abstaining from salted Meats and Cheese, which Advice I did not much follow, often forgetting it'.[43] Franklin did notice that his skin condition, thought to be psoriasis, improved when a gout attack forced him to reduce his consumption of rich foods and wine. That would make sense as it is now thought that the two conditions are linked and the result of a build-up of uric acid that may have owed something to Franklin's genes, increasing age and inactivity, and long-term lead poisoning through its use in pipes and even in the production process of his beloved madeira wine.[44] However, Franklin was philosophical about the gout and the later additional agony caused by kidney stones. He had suffered from the underlying condition for nearly three decades by the time he died and in his eighties was still writing: 'People who live long, who will drink of the cup of life to the very bottom, must expect to meet with some of the usual dregs, and when I reflect on the number of terrible maladies human nature is subject to, I think myself favoured in having to my share only the stone and the gout.'[45]

However, though he accepted the received wisdom on gout, he rejected the general attitude towards ventilation. In that he was way ahead of his time. The commonly held view was that cold 'fresh Air' should be kept out of rooms. To Franklin this 'has been a great Mistake... a number of Persons crowded into a small Room thus spoil the Air in a few Minutes, and even render it mortal, as in the Black Hole at Calcutta'.[46] He believed that fresh air, even if cold, should not only be allowed into a room but also onto a person and thus took what he called air baths. He described why in a letter of 1768:

...the cold bath has long been in vogue here as a tonic; but the shock of the cold water has always appeared to me, generally speaking, as too violent; and I have found it much more agreeable to my constitution to bathe in another element, I mean cold air. With this view I rise early almost every morning, and sit in my chamber, without any clothes whatever, half an hour or an hour, according to the season, either reading or writing. This practice is not in the least painful, but on the contrary agreeable; and if I return to bed afterwards, before I dress myself, as sometimes happens, I make a supplement to my night's rest of one or two hours of the most pleasing sleep that can be imagined.[47]

His belief in fresh air led him to challenge a commonly held nostrum, which he expressed in a 1773 letter to Thomas Percival, a Fellow of the Royal Society, friend of David Hume and pioneer in the field of public health: 'From many Years' Observations on myself and others, I am persuaded we are on a wrong Scent in supposing Moist, or cold Air, the Causes of that Disorder we call a Cold. Some unknown Quality in the Air may perhaps sometimes produce Colds, as in the *Influenza*; but generally I apprehend they are the Effects of too full living in proportion to our Exercise.'[48]

Through directing his powers of observation and empirical analysis Franklin was on the right track with his 'unknown Quality in the Air'. Pretty impressive, as the causes of the common cold were still being hotly disputed in the pages of the *British Medical Journal* well into the twentieth century.[49] In this case Franklin had the advantage of long conversations with his great friend Joseph Priestley, whose brilliant and extensive paper on 'Observations on different kinds of air' had just won him the Copley Medal the previous year. At the end of his letter to Percival, Franklin wrote: 'excuse, if you can, my intruding into your province'. He regarded the much younger man as a distinguished colleague, a member of a fraternity that he greatly respected – that of natural philosophers.

14

Movements

Franklin certainly made the most of his summer holidays. In 1761 he travelled with William and Richard Jackson to the university cities and mercantile centres of Holland and Flanders. In 1766 he spent two months with the newly made baronet Sir John Pringle, travelling to and through Germany. In 1767 the two of them left London for six weeks at the end of August,[1] principally to enjoy Paris and Versailles, where they were presented to Louis XV who was both gracious and courteous, though Franklin reassured Polly in his report that 'No Frenchman shall go beyond me in thinking my own King and Queen the very best in the World and the most amiable.' The journey had begun with Franklin in a foul temper and 'engaged in perpetual Disputes with the Innkeepers, Hostlers and Postillions' all the way through Kent, but his mood had lifted by the time he reached Paris and he reflected that 'Travelling is one Way of lengthening Life, at least in Appearance. It is but a Fortnight since we left London; but the Variety of Scenes we have gone through makes it seem equal to Six Months living in one Place.'[2] The trip had been a success and he and Pringle returned to France in 1769.

In 1771 Franklin, true to his belief in the benefit of a change of air, made a number of journeys. So extensive were these that they were not so much a series of holidays but more like a travelling sabbatical. On 18 May he left London with his friends John Canton and the Dutch physician and scientist Jan Ingenhousz, together with his great-nephew Jonathan Williams. This was no less than a tour of the industrial North and Midlands, mixed with visits to the vast country mansions of Whig grandees, including the Marquess of Rockingham's Wentworth Woodhouse, with over 300 rooms, and the Duke of Devonshire's Chatsworth. It was a chance to see extraordinary natural features, such as the vast cavern in Derbyshire then called the Devil's Arse and now known by the more modest name of the Peak Cavern; but there were also man-made marvels to take in, such as the Bridgewater Canal and a variety of hugely impressive industrial enterprises that manufactured silver plate in Sheffield, tin plate in Rotherham, pottery and silk at Derby and 'good ale' at Burton on Trent. The journey took in new industrializing towns such as Manchester and Leeds, where they visited Joseph Priestley, and there were overnight stays with John Whitehurst in Derby and Erasmus Darwin in Lichfield. Then onto Matthew Boulton's vast ironworks at Soho in Birmingham, which employed 700, and, finally, the road home, arriving in London a mere fortnight after they left.[3]

Perhaps it is understandable after such a concentrated itinerary that his next journey, just a few weeks later, was the much shorter one to Twyford to stay with the Shipleys. There Franklin remained, but hardly in order to relax, as he sat down and wrote a little over 25,000 words of his autobiography, in two visits during June and August.[4] At the end of August he was away again on a three-month trip, first to Ireland with Richard Jackson and then to Scotland.

The latter gave Franklin the chance to stay five days with his great friend Henry Home, Lord Kames, at Blair Drummond near Stirling. He also spent two days at the Carron Iron Works near Falkirk and two or three in Glasgow. For the rest of his Scottish month he was in Edinburgh, where he arrived 'Through Storms and Floods' and 'lodged miserably at an Inn' for the first night.[5] But relief was at hand, because the deist David Hume played the Good Samaritan. Hume was a great friend of both Strahan and Pringle and he and Franklin had got to know each other during Hume's thirty-month stay in London between 1767 and 1769. He now had an elegant house in the New Town and invited Franklin to live there for the rest of his time in the city, where he entertained him 'with the greatest Kindness and Hospitality'.[6] Franklin was much more forthcoming in comparison to his 1759 visit there with William. He felt able to speak freely – where he might have been more guarded in London – and he was with people he knew, liked and trusted. As he wrote to William, he once more met the cream of the Scottish Enlightenment, men such as William Robertson, Principal of Edinburgh University and pre-eminent historian, together with his colleague the distinguished philosopher Adam Ferguson. Franklin wrote a sad note to Sir Alexander Dick after his return to London, regretting, ''Tis an uncomfortable Thing, the Parting with Friends one hardly expects ever again to see.'[7] Probably the more so because his trip to Scotland had been a great success, shown by the light-hearted, almost puckish letter he received from David Hume afterwards.[8] His spirits were raised when he stopped off at Preston on the journey south, as what had promised to be a difficult meeting went very well indeed.

☙

The sojourn in Scotland, in spite of the appalling weather on his arrival, had been rather more relaxing than the time in Ireland. Franklin had been shocked by some of the conditions he had seen there. As he commented in a letter to Cushing:

> Ireland is itself a fine Country, and Dublin a magnificent City; but the Appearances of general extreme Poverty among the lower People are amazing: They live in wretched Hovels of Mud and Straw, are clothed in Rags, and subsist chiefly on Potatoes. Our New England Farmers of the poorest Sort, in regard to the Enjoyment of all the Comforts of Life, are Princes when compared to them. Such is the effect of the Discouragements of Industry, the Non-Residence not only of Pensioners but of many original Landlords who lease their Lands in Gross to Undertakers that rack the Tenants, and fleece them Skin and all.

In Dublin Franklin attended Parliament and also, as he wrote to Galloway, 'had a good deal of Conversation with the Patriots', whom he found to be 'all on the American side of the Question'.[9] He even went so far as to relay to Cushing 'that our growing Weight might in time be thrown into their Scale, and, by joining our Interest with theirs, might be obtained for them as well as for us a more equitable Treatment from this Nation', i.e. Britain.[10] That was the sort of comment, should Hillsborough have discovered it, that would have confirmed him in his recent abuse of Franklin to Strahan as a 'factious turbulent Fellow, always in Mischief'.[11] It was a remark that was no doubt intended to get back to Franklin, as was that of 'Republican, Enemy to the King's Service', which was a slander and completely untrue.[12]

Hillsborough, though, was not absent from Ireland. He was in Dublin at the same time as Jackson and Franklin. Moving in the same circles, they encountered each other at Dublin Castle, where they all dined as guests of the Lord Lieutenant, Marquess Townshend.[13] The occasion went well: Hillsborough was absolutely charming. He insisted that they come to stay with him and his family at Hillsborough Castle near Belfast. This was an invitation that Jackson, as Counsel to the Board of Trade,[14] felt himself obliged to accept. We have to gauge Franklin's chosen course of action from letters he sent to three regular correspondents, with different descriptions for each. That to Galloway is simple: there was mention of Ireland, but deliberately none of Hillsborough. That to William hints at a desire to avoid confrontation, saying that Franklin had planned to go to Armagh and meet up with Jackson, post-Lord Hillsborough, in Belfast, but that there was no connecting coach – all of which sounds vaguely possible. That to Cushing, written more immediately, has a different tone, explaining that Hillsborough 'pressed us so politely that it was not easy to refuse without apparent Rudeness, as we must pass through his Town of Hillsborough and by his Door; and as it might afford an Opportunity of saying something on American Affairs, I concluded to comply with his Invitation'.[15] Once there, Hillsborough was the most solicitous of hosts. As Franklin described it, 'we were detained by a thousand Civilities from Tuesday to Sunday' and 'his Attentions to me in every Circumstance of Accommodation and Entertainment were very particular'. The peer even put his own cloak around Franklin's shoulders to protect him from the cold when he went out. Actually Hillsborough knew that was something that would be necessary as he had asked his eighteen-year-old heir,[16] Lord

Kilwarlin, to drive Franklin forty miles around the countryside at breakneck speed in his phaeton, the carriage equivalent of today's top-of-the-range high-performance two-seater sports car, so that the American could have a look at the Irish equivalent of the highlights of his English tour earlier in the year – manufacturing plants and grand houses.

When it came to conversation, Hillsborough was beguilingly moderate, representing himself as 'a good Irishman, censuring the English Government for its Narrowness with Regard to Ireland', and saying that Britain was wrong to restrain American manufactures.[17] As Franklin wrote to his son, 'Does not all this seem extraordinary to you?'[18] To cap it all, when Franklin left, Hillsborough told him he would not just like to see him in London but often. So, in the New Year, when everyone had returned to London, Franklin tried to do so.

Franklin succinctly tells the story:

> When I had been a little while returned to London I waited on him to thank him for his civilities in Ireland, and to discourse with him on a Georgia affair. The porter told me he was not at home. I left my card, went another time, and received the same answer, though I knew he was at home, a friend of mine being with him. After intermissions of a week each, I made two more visits, and received the same answer. The last time was on a levée day, when a number of carriages were at his door. My coachman, driving up, alighted and was opening the coach door when the porter, seeing me, came out and surlily chid the coachman for opening the door before he had enquired whether my lord was at home; and then turning to me, said, 'My Lord is not at home.' I have never since been nigh him, and we have only abused one another at a distance.[19]

It is difficult to explain Hillsborough's behaviour in Ireland. Perhaps he had urgent business with Jackson and was, for that reason, polite to Franklin and more than happy to use Kilwarlin to ship him out for the day. But one can also interpret Hillsborough's conduct in terms of the aristocratic social conventions of the day: whereby, face to face, one hid one's true feelings under a guise of good manners, only to reveal them later in a public forum such as Parliament or more directly through one's actions. Whatever Hillsborough's reasons, the two episodes back-to-back merely served to increase Franklin's loathing. He now said of Hillsborough, 'I know him to be as double and deceitful as any man I ever met with.'[20] This was quite something, considering Franklin's long dealings with Thomas Penn and the Reverend William Smith.

Then in August 1772 Hillsborough left the Cabinet. Franklin tried to claim it was partly his doing, writing to William that 'The K{ing} too was tired of him, and of his administration, which had weakened the affection and respect of the Colonies for a Royal Government, with which (I may say it to you) I used proper means from time to time that his M{ajesty} should have due information and convincing proofs. More of this when I see you.'[21] In fact it was not Franklin himself but the new colony plan that was the cause of Hillsborough's demise.

What was still officially named the Grand Ohio Company was now generally called the Walpole Company, as Thomas Walpole had provided Samuel Wharton with his excellent connections and brought a number of the great and the good on board. So along with those with close connections to Franklin in London – such as Richard Jackson, John Sargent, William Strahan, Grey Cooper, Anthony Todd (with others from the Post Office) and Thomas Pownall – were the Lord Chamberlain and royal confidant the Earl of Hertford, the Chathamite Lord Camden, George Grenville's brother Earl Temple and, fatally for Hillsborough, his Cabinet colleagues Earls Rochford and Gower.[22] Rochford in particular was furious at the delay. The matter came to a head in the summer of 1772. In May the Board of Trade, under Hillsborough's direction, finally rejected the grant; in June the company petitioned the Committee on Plantations of the Privy Council. In July Rochford, supported by Gower and Suffolk, via that committee, upheld the petition – humiliating Hillsborough and forcing his resignation the following month. Hillsborough was replaced by Lord Dartmouth, Lord North's stepbrother, whom

Franklin had known and liked when he had been at the Board of Trade under Rockingham. Suddenly Franklin had hopes not only for the future colony but that the entire Anglo-American situation would be transformed.

He was in an altogether buoyant mood, telling William that, perhaps best of all, 'The K{ing} too has lately been heard to speak of me with great regard.'[23] Franklin was looking forward to reporting once more to the new Secretary of State in the autumn. In the meantime his expertise was needed in the scientific area that had established his fame.

✍

In 1769 the Dean and Chapter of St Paul's Cathedral had approached the Royal Society for advice on protecting the Cathedral from a lightning strike.[24] The Society appointed a five-man committee of their finest experts. Benjamin Franklin, John Canton, William Watson, Edward Delaval (the inspiration for the armonica) and Benjamin Wilson (Franklin's portraitist) were all Copley Medal winners. As might be expected, the thorough report of the committee was accepted. In the summer of 1772, a Royal Society committee was again formed in order to consider measures to protect the powder magazines at Purfleet. Franklin, Wilson and Watson were joined by Henry Cavendish, another Copley winner, and by John Robertson, a former Master of the Royal Naval Academy and the equivalent then of today's Executive Director of the Royal Society.[25]

Bearing in mind the consequences of not protecting powder magazines, the matter in hand was extremely important. There had been proof of this just three years before: the electrical charge from a lightning strike on a church tower in Brescia, Italy, that ran down into the vaults and ignited the hundred or so tons of pounds of gunpowder stored there. Three thousand people were killed and a sixth of the city was destroyed.[26]

In 1769 there had been areas of difference, but in 1772 the consultation of the Royal Society committee did not run at all smoothly. A furious row broke out between Wilson and Franklin, who was backed by the rest of the committee. The question at issue was whether the lightning conductors should end in the Franklin-approved points or in Wilson's proposed round knobs. This was not an argument about decoration but science. Wilson's contention was not that Franklin's rods were ineffective but the opposite. He believed that the points were too efficient in that they drew electrical charges onto rods that would not be capable of neutralizing the charge. Therefore they would increase the danger of explosion rather than negate it. Franklin's counter was that drawing as much as possible of the charge to the point was beneficial and that a properly earthed conductor could cope with any possible electrical discharge – besides which it had worked.[27] Wilson believed his argument had added force because earlier that year lightning had indeed struck one of the iron conductors at St Paul's with such force that it had grown red-hot and there had been some minor damage to the Cathedral. He believed that the point design was responsible, whereas the others believed it was the use of iron – in future the points would be of copper.[28] Wilson refused to back down, in fact he issued a dissenting report and accused his fellow committee members, whose recommendations were accepted, of negligence.[29] The Majority Committee report accused Wilson of wilful misrepresentation.[30] Franklin may now have been viewed with increasing suspicion by members of the governing coalition, but his scientific credentials were regarded as impeccable. All would change in 1777 when the Board House at Purfleet was struck by lightning: then the question of points or knobs and Franklin's science would become highly political. That, though, was still for the future.

❦

In October 1772 Franklin left 7 Craven Street. Mrs Stevenson 'accommodated her son-in-law' with number 7 and moved across the road, taking her long-term tenant with her. William Hewson's partnership with William Hunter had soured the previous year, with the senior partner accusing the junior, with little seeming foundation, of neglecting his work for his home life.[31] Franklin, who also knew Hunter, had agreed to act as a mediator.

Dr Hewson was certainly able to use the space at number 7 for conducting his anatomical experiments. Hewson's reputation was such that he had no difficulty attracting large numbers to the lectures he gave. The success of these may have meant that his requirement for dead bodies for demonstration purposes might have outstripped legal supply: certainly a very large quantity of human bones was found during renovation work at Craven Street prior to its reopening as Benjamin Franklin House in 2006.[32]

Franklin had complained to Deborah that the actual move had been a troublesome affair, but in reality he was not much bothered by it as he escaped the worst by spending a fortnight with Lord Le Despencer at West Wycombe.[33] Besides which, it had the benefit of bringing Polly back to Craven Street, along with her first-born son who was Franklin's godson and then nearly eighteen months old. By the following February Franklin was putty in the hands of the little boy, who would shortly call him 'Papa Doctor'; and after rhapsodizing about him in a letter to Deborah Franklin he realized that he needed to balance matters by ending the letter, 'It makes me long to be at home to play with Ben', his daughter Sally's child and a grandson he had never seen.[34]

⁊

Sally had married Richard Bache in Philadelphia in 1767. Franklin had opposed the marriage. Bache had confessed to financial difficulties in a letter of 21 May to his prospective father-in-law and William had also written to Ben to say that Bache had a 'Load of Debt greatly more than he is worth, and that if Sally marries him they must both be entirely dependent on you for Subsistence'.[35] But William must have realized that Sally, abetted by her mother, was not going to be put off, because at the end of his note he wrote 'Burn this', which Ben, with a tendency to carelessness in matters of letters and secrecy, plainly failed to do. Deborah's quiet support for Sally must be assumed, because in a series of letters that summer she signally failed to mention Sally and Bache, leading an exasperated Ben to write in August, 'In your last Letters you say nothing concerning Mr Bache.' In fact all she said in a mid-October letter of reply, just an aside in a long letter of family information and domestic detail, was that Sally and Bache were 'disappointed', which was a reference to Franklin's opposition to the match. But they went ahead anyway and were married at the end of October.

Bache wrote to Franklin after the marriage and continued to do so. He at last received a reply dated 13 August 1768 and was told, 'you should not wonder that I did not answer your Letters. I could say nothing agreeable.' However, there was an olive branch, as Bache had sensibly sent his accounts to his father-in-law and these seemed to promise sunnier times ahead for his business. Hence Franklin continued with 'Time has made me easier. I hope too, that the Accounts you give me of your better Prospects are well founded, and that by an industrious Application to Business you may retrieve your Losses.'[36] Even so, with Franklin choosing to ignore a *fait accompli* he did not like, there was no rapprochement. But then, in 1771, Bache came over to England. He arrived at Craven Street in the autumn to find Franklin on his travels in Ireland and Scotland, but he obviously made an extremely favourable impression on Mrs Stevenson and Polly, who in turn wrote highly positive comments in letters to Franklin. These helped to soften him up. They met at Bache's parents' house at Preston at the end of October and everything changed, as Bache explained in a letter after his return, with Franklin, to London. This, tellingly, was written to his mother-in-law and told her that Franklin had received him 'with open arms'.[37] The editors of the Franklin Papers rightly describe the Preston meeting as 'a momentous occasion'.[38] A trust was forged and in the middle of the following February, following Bache's return to America, Franklin granted him power of attorney, jointly with Deborah, to collect his debts there.

At around the same time, Franklin wrote to Sally suggesting that she take over the management of the household she and Bache shared with Deborah. It is instructive of his changing attitude to both women.

In January 1757, in writing to his friend Strahan, Franklin had described Sally, then a girl of thirteen years and four months, as 'indeed a very good Girl, affectionate, dutiful and industrious, has one of the best Hearts, and though not a Wit, is for one of her Years by no means deficient in Understanding'.[39] That is hardly the outstanding endorsement of a pushy parent, particularly as the two fathers had for years floated the idea of a match between Sally and William Strahan Jr. In 1760, when Sally was sixteen and a half and young William around three years older, Strahan Sr raised the subject again, this time in all seriousness.[40] The two men sat down and discussed the match, which would have been a good one for Sally. As Franklin well knew, a successful printer/publisher could be extremely wealthy and Strahan – already the publisher of Johnson's *Dictionary* and who would go on to do the same for Gibbon's *Decline and Fall of the Roman Empire* and Adam Smith's *Wealth of Nations* – was one of the most successful of the century.[41] But the decision was left to Deborah, who said 'no', and Franklin did not argue. Bearing in mind his ambition for himself and for William this would seem strange, but it was consistent with his not taking Sally with him to London in 1764. There was not the excuse of Sally being under age, as she was then a mature woman of twenty-one;[42] and Franklin was not shy about bringing relatives into the house at Craven Street. For instance, his great-nephews Jonathan and Josiah Williams would both arrive from Boston in 1770, which enabled the latter, himself a talented blind musician, to be tutored by John Stanley.[43] Then of course there was young Temple, William's son, regularly home for the school holidays. Perhaps, when it came to Sally, Franklin thought his daughter less suited to be a Society lady in London than a household manager in Philadelphia. The latter was what he suggested in January 1772.[44]

But there was another reason for his suggestion. It was contained in that January letter to Sally: ''Till my Return you need be at no Expense for Rent, &c. as you are all welcome to continue with your Mother, and indeed it seems to be your Duty to attend her as she grows infirm.'[45] This was a recognition, on one level at least, that his wife's health was failing. In June 1769 he had written to Deborah, 'I rejoice to hear you so soon got over your late Indisposition.'[46] But that rather underplayed what had happened. Deborah had suffered a stroke. One can identify this in the letter that Thomas Bond, Franklin's old friend and co-founder of the Pennsylvania Hospital, sent that same month: 'Your good Mrs Franklin was affected in the Winter with a partial Palsy in the Tongue, and a sudden Loss of Memory, which alarmed us much, but she soon recovered from them, though her constitution in general appears impaired. These are bad Symptoms in advanced Life and Augur Danger of further Injury on the nervous System.'[47]

Franklin was able to gain a second opinion on the basis of this information from no less an authority than Sir John Pringle, physician to the Queen. He sent it to his wife. Deborah thanked them, but said she was now fine really and that she had just collapsed through the stress of looking after sick and dying relations, low spirits and, of course, learning that her husband was going to stay away so much longer.[48] She was refusing to accept that anything had changed and so was her husband. In a letter of 1 May 1771 he upbraided Deborah for poor book-keeping and financial management. He had some justification for concern, because she had through unauthorized borrowing exceeded a covert limit he had placed on her monthly expenditure; but surely there was none for the way he lashed out by writing, 'I know you were not very attentive to Money-matters in your best Days, and I apprehend that your Memory is too much impaired for the Management of unlimited Sums, without Danger of injuring the future Fortune of your Daughter and Grandson.'[49] Putting his own somewhat sketchy financial management to one side, the mention of young Ben in this context was not only unfair but extremely unkind, because doting on the boy she called the 'the Kingbird' had become the major focus of her life. One cannot escape the feeling that Franklin felt that through her failing health Deborah was somehow failing him. She was more than a domestic partner to him: she was a business partner, the guardian of his interests in Philadelphia.

In terms of simple business practicalities he could recognize the change, which helps to explain why Richard Bache was given power of attorney so quickly after his belated acceptance by Franklin. In more fundamental terms Franklin did not want to address what had happened to his wife. Out of duty, he continued to write, but his letters lacked the continuing spark of those to his youngest sibling Jane Mecom.[50] Deborah's letters show a narrowing world, one where her response to his enquiry about visitors was 'very few people come to see us'[51] – this at a time when he was taking on ever greater responsibilities in London for the American colonies. When she told him of lapses of memory or of physical infirmities he ignored them, played them down or told her of his own invigoration after a holiday.[52]

He was not the only party to the deception: his children and son-in-law left him in the dark about Deborah's decline. Letter after letter from them either ignored her health entirely or described her as 'well'. Whether this was done mainly to protect him or because they believed he would soon be home is unclear. He may have been partially deceived by letters such as that from Sally as late as 30 October 1773, which told him that her mother, having given way for just a few months, was now back running the household.[53] But it seems that he wanted to be deceived; the clues were all there in the diminishing world addressed in the letters from his wife. The last surviving letter of those she wrote to him, dated a day before Sally's, complained, bitterly, that she had not heard from him or of him for some time. She apologized that she had no general news as she no longer went out. There is a last bit of business, about the pet grey squirrel – then a great rarity in England – which she had sent at his request. Otherwise the focus is entirely on her grandchildren, whom she calls 'the Best in the world', before saying that Sally would write because she could not write any more.[54]

Though he was to receive further letters from her in 1773 they have not survived. There were to be none in 1774.

⁊

The squirrel was a replacement for one Franklin had given to Georgiana Shipley, the eighteen-year-old daughter of his great friend Jonathan, the Bishop of St Asaph. Happy as he was to have created a second family for himself in London, he was also delighted to have found a young protégée to take on the role that the matronly Mrs Hewson had long left behind. Polly herself had suggested that her friend Dolly Blunt could fill the vacancy she had created, but the good-natured Dolly was not clever or lively enough. Georgiana was not the intellectual equal of Polly, but she was vibrant and fun. Franklin could tease her and she him. As for the fate of Mungo, that first squirrel, it was a time for tears, as it had escaped and been killed by a dog. When he heard of Mungo's death, Franklin immediately penned a touching twenty-two-line elegy in dramatic form. He was a busy man, but not one so busy as to neglect this duty.

When Ben had written to William in August 1772 that he seldom dined at home in winter, he added that he 'could spend the whole summer in the country houses of inviting friends' should he so wish.[55] The Shipleys were to the fore in this. Jonathan Shipley was the brother of William, who was the founder of the Society of Arts. He and Franklin moved in the same intellectual and political circles. The Shipleys provided the peace and tranquillity of a country retreat that enabled Franklin to start his autobiography.

Another frequent host was Francis Dashwood, Lord Le Despencer. Le Despencer was Franklin's boss at the Post Office and Franklin was grateful for his support against enemies who wanted him sacked over the letter to Philadelphia supporting American non-importation.[56] That did not mean that Franklin was expected to be on his best behaviour at the estate at West Wycombe. Nor indeed, in spite of Le Despencer's past reputation, should he be prepared to throw all caution to the wind and be on his worst.

Le Despencer was a disreputable friend of real note and reputation. As the youthful Sir Francis Dashwood, he had been infamous for extreme irreligious and anti-Roman Catholic activities, including, so it is said, hiding himself in the dark recesses of the Sistine Chapel before the penitential ceremonies during Holy Week so that he could emerge from the gloom and give severe assistance with the aid of an English horsewhip.[57] There were wild tales of the activities of Dashwood and his 'Medmenham Monks' as late as the early 1760s, with even John Wilkes professing himself shocked at witnessing scenes of sexual depravity. However, as Wilkes was at the time involved in what was a highly entertaining campaign of smear and counter-smear with his former friends Lords Sandwich and Le Despencer, his account must remain suspect.[58] Equally improbable are strange tales involving a baboon, satanic rites and orgies, which evolved and gained credence through the efforts of Wilkes and the poet Charles Churchill, and the popularity of salacious novels.[59]

As regards Franklin's own reputation, that of his great friend has wrongly been allowed to besmirch it. Whatever had gone before, by the time Franklin got to know him well in the early 1770s[60] Le Despencer was a man in his sixties and had understandably slowed down a bit. The limit of his and Franklin's supposedly salacious activities was the intellectual exercise of abridging the Book of Common Prayer, with a view to removing all digression and repetition. As they said in their Preface, they succeeded in 'shortening the service near one half'[61] without altering 'a word in the remaining Text; not even to substitute who for which in the Lord's Prayer, and elsewhere, although it would be more correct'.[62] They did so, as they also said in the Preface, to assist 'many pious and devout Persons, whose age or infirmities will not suffer them to remain for hours in a cold church'.[63] For them both, this was both intellectually stimulating and fun. They obviously enjoyed each other's company, as was shown by Franklin's long stays in 1772, 1773 and 1774 and by this assessment: 'I am in this House as much at my Ease as if it was my own, and the Gardens are a Paradise. But a pleasanter Thing is the kind Countenance, the facetious {witty} and very Intelligent Conversation of mine Host, who having been for many Years engaged in public Affairs, seen all Parts of Europe, and kept the best Company in the World, is himself the best existing.'[64] One can also see why Dashwood would have liked Franklin, who, as John Adams conceded, 'had wit at will'.[65]

∽

At the end of October 1772, Franklin visited Lord Dartmouth at the first opportunity following the latter's return from his estate at Sandwell. Dartmouth began by saying that he was sorry that he had been away earlier in the summer when Franklin had visited nearby Birmingham (en route to Preston and the Baches), as he would have liked to see him. The exchange of compliments continued and both Dartmouth and Under-Secretary Pownall took the opportunity to remark on William's excellence as a governor. Ben was more than happy to pass that on, but he included the cautionary note that 'time will show' whether matters in general would go more smoothly and he was extremely wary of the continuing influence of Pownall and his long-time colleague William Knox.[66]

A few days later Franklin returned and he and Dartmouth

discussed some meaningful business. Cushing had sent him a Massachusetts House of Representatives petition to the King to be given to the Secretary of State, which requested that the salary of the Governor once more, as before the Townshend Acts, be paid by them and not the British government. Its motive was clear: it was to curb what they regarded as the unrestrained independence of the unpopular Governor Thomas Hutchinson. Dartmouth counselled patience, believing that the petition was sure to be rejected and that its presentation would merely inflame matters. It was at one with his general approach of hoping that everything would be settled by the removal of the Townshend duties – except for tea – and a lack of precipitate action by either side. Franklin, having just restored relations with the Colonial Office, did not want to lose them immediately; on the other hand he had been given clear instructions by Cushing on behalf of the Massachusetts House. He decided to take Dartmouth's counsel, for in one sense Franklin was also waiting on events, in his case for a shock that would provoke a more general change of attitude within Britain. As he had written to Lord Kames in 1767, Franklin had no doubt about the long-term prosperity of America – he even pondered, in a later letter to a French philosopher, about the possibilities of reincarnation, such was his 'very ardent desire to see and observe the state of America a hundred years hence.'[67] He was not so concerned about saving America for Britain but instead was more worried about saving Britain for British America. In 1763, back in Philadelphia, he had missed London, as he had written to Polly:

Of all the enviable Things England has, I envy it most its People. Why should that petty Island, which compared to America is but like a stepping Stone in a Brook, scarce enough of it above Water to keep one's Shoes dry; why, I say, should that little Island enjoy in almost every Neighbourhood more sensible, virtuous and elegant Minds than we can collect in ranging 100 Leagues of our vast Forests. But, 'tis said, the Arts delight to travel Westward. You have effectually defended us in this glorious War, and in time you will improve us.[68]

A decade later he was expecting that a war with France or Spain would improve Britain. In such an event Britain would need the colonies and make concessions, or so Franklin thought and communicated to Noble Wimberly Jones in Georgia in 1770[69] – and would do so more urgently to the Massachusetts House in 1773.[70] It was an understandable prediction, because there might have been war on several occasions: such as in 1768 after France annexed Corsica and, most dangerously, with Spain and France in 1770/1 over the Falklands, which Secretary of State Lord Weymouth and Under-Secretary Robert Wood seemed keen to precipitate in order to bring Chatham back to the helm and which Rochford, with skill, was able to allay.[71] The Grafton and North governments shared Franklin's belief in the possibility of war against the Bourbon powers – to the extent that it was a major preoccupation. Yet the effect, in the shorter term, was that the resulting diplomatic activity and supporting military and naval preparations combined with other pressing concerns – including the rising strength of Russia, the finances of the East India Company, fears about Ireland and the ongoing sore of Wilkesite agitation – in continually taking political and administrative focus away from the American colonies.[72]

However, perhaps it is not surprising that in 1772 Franklin delighted in telling William that 'several of the foreign ambassadors have assiduously cultivated my acquaintance, treating me as one of their *corps*' – though he suspected that they did so in the hope that 'Britain's alarming power will be diminished by the defection of her Colonies'.[73] It would be wrong, though, to suspect him of treasonous intent. Far from it: in December he made a dramatic move designed to save the relationship between Britain and America, not to sunder it.

15

Drawn to the Cockpit

On 2 December 1772 Franklin wrote Thomas Cushing a letter in two parts. In the first he described in very great detail how he had presented the petition to Lord Dartmouth at their first business meeting the month before and that, after much discussion and pressing of the case, he had respected Dartmouth's wish to delay it. Franklin pointed out that the new Secretary of State had been a great supporter of the repeal of the Stamp Act, that he seemed 'still to have good Dispositions towards us' and, in any case, Franklin felt it would be better to encapsulate all their grievances in one petition. If Franklin had in mind the fate of the flimsy 'Heads of Complaint' he had presented to the Penns, this line of reasoning is completely explicable. But it would also be quite understandable if he had harboured grave misgivings about his failure to obey the instructions from the Massachusetts House, particularly as there were some there who doubted him, fuelled by the malice of his 'alternate', Arthur Lee.

That provides some context for the letter's second part and its accompanying enclosures. Yet the import of his words should not be overshadowed: 'On this Occasion I think it fit to acquaint you that there has lately fallen into my Hands Part of a Correspondence, that I have reason to believe laid the Foundation of most if not all our present Grievances.'[1]

The enclosures were letters written by the men who were now Governor and Lieutenant Governor of Massachusetts, Thomas Hutchinson and his wife's brother-in-law Andrew Oliver. They were addressed to Thomas Whately, architect of the Stamp Act and

George Grenville's Parliamentary manager until Grenville's death in 1770.[2] Both Hutchinson (then Lieutenant Governor and Chief Justice) and Oliver (the Massachusetts Stamp Distributor) had their houses burned down during the protests against the Stamp Act, but hostility against Hutchinson went back further, to 1760, when the then Governor, Sir Francis Bernard, had made him Chief Justice. The legalistic John Adams had been appalled by the appointment, because Lieutenant Governor Hutchinson was not a lawyer; but that was nothing to the outrage of James Otis Sr, who had expected the role and who consequently became, with his son, a bitter enemy and opponent.

Hutchinson had known Franklin for a long time, all the way back to the Albany Conference of 1754, when they and Thomas Pownall had proposed their plan of Union for British America. They had exchanged letters in 1765, at a time when Hutchinson was writing widely to people in London in the hope that he might find assistance in his bid for compensation for the loss of his house. But he and Franklin were not personally close. Franklin certainly had no compunction in serving up Hutchinson and Oliver as sacrifices, but he did so for what he regarded as a crucial purpose, to 'lay the Blame where it ought to lay, and by that means promote a Reconciliation.'[3] He believed that when men such as Cushing saw the letters they would conclude that the two officials had sought to introduce and profit from 'creating Enmities between the different Countries of which the Empire consists'[4] and had fed false information to London to achieve their aims. That would, so his logic went, exculpate the authorities in London.

There were certainly some striking phrases in the controversial letters, none more so than in one written in January 1769 by Hutchinson: 'There must be an abridgment of what are called English liberties. I relieve myself by considering that in a remove from the state of nature to the most perfect state of government there must be a great restraint of natural liberty. I doubt whether it is possible to project a system of government in which a colony 3000 miles distant from the parent state shall enjoy all the liberty of the parent state.'[5] This was damning. Though as William Pencak points out, if this statement is put in the context of a much longer document it is just possible to interpret it as seeking to constrain not liberty itself but the claims of the patriots.[6] Unfortunately for Hutchinson, he was someone who could be easily quoted out of context.

There was certainly a whiff of conspiracy in Hutchinson's letter of 20 October 1769, with the words 'I must beg the favour of you to keep secret everything I write, until we are in a more settled state; for the party here, either by their agent, or by some of their emissaries in London, have sent them every report or rumour of the contents of letters wrote from hence.'[7] Hutchinson, as he would discover, was not quite right with the 'everything', but had good reason for his caution, as revelations in 'the contents of letters' had brought the departure of Governor Bernard earlier that year. This was the tactic that in December 1772 Franklin was trying to repeat, though ostensibly he wanted those revelations to be made to a select few in the Massachusetts House of Representatives.

In his letter to Cushing, he wrote, 'I am not at liberty to tell through what Channel I received it; and I have engaged that it shall not be printed, nor any Copies taken of the whole or any part of it; but I am allowed and desired to let it be seen by some Men of Worth in the Province for their Satisfaction only.' He even stated who those 'Men of Worth' might be: the other members of the Committee of Correspondence, some named individuals such as Samuel Cooper but also 'a few such other Gentlemen as you may think it fit'.[8] If, bearing in mind his past experience with the 'low jockey' letter about Thomas Penn, Franklin believed that the offending letters could be so restricted, then he was being hopelessly naïve. What is more likely, however, is that he weighed whether full publication would be at least better than not using them at all and he had decided to risk the former.

The Hutchinson letters proved to be particularly explosive, because their publication interacted with two other initiatives in 1773, one from the British government and one from Hutchinson himself.

In reading Bernard Bailyn's *The Ordeal of Thomas Hutchinson*, it is easy to have some sympathy for its subject. He was working as Governor with little support from London and with a diminishing number of friends in an exceptionally hostile atmosphere. By the standards of the time he was honest and was working himself into a state of physical and nervous exhaustion for what he was convinced was the welfare of America as part of Great Britain.[9] He had handled the army in Boston with some sensitivity and had, with sympathetic management, prevented a full-blown collapse of public order after the Boston Massacre. What he had not been able to do was to calm the political situation in the town and in January 1773 he took action that made it significantly worse. With a Massachusetts General Court, of Council and House of Representatives, that was united in hostility, and with town meetings – principally that of Boston itself – taking politics to the streets, he sought to warn the Council and House with the words, 'no line can be drawn between the supreme authority of Parliament and the total independence of the colonies.'[10] The House made it clear which of these two choices it preferred, with 'there is more reason to dread the consequences of absolute uncontrolled supreme power, whether of a nation or a monarch, than those of a total independence.'[11]

Hutchinson received no support from an infuriated Dartmouth, who wrote to Cushing in a private capacity in an attempt to calm things down. This only succeeded in undercutting Hutchinson further and made matters worse. Then Franklin's package with the letters arrived.

By July 1773 Franklin was writing of Dartmouth that 'He is truly a good Man, and wishes sincerely a good Understanding with the Colonies, but does not seem to have Strength equal to his Wishes.'[12] Dartmouth in his private letter to Cushing had pleaded for the House to disavow their answer to Hutchinson;[13] but Cushing, in his equally private response, replied that it was something that could be neither rescinded nor revoked.[14] Franklin and Dartmouth offered suggestions to each other at a meeting on 5 May, but really there was no way round it.

On 2 June, with the fact of the Hutchinson letters known and tales of their content becoming so exaggerated that even Oliver supported their publication, Cushing made them public at the House and two weeks later they were printed. On 23 June, the House voted by eighty votes to eleven to send a petition to the King for the removal of Hutchinson and Oliver. It was dispatched immediately to Franklin.

Already travelling across the Atlantic in the opposite direction was a letter from Franklin to Cushing dated 4 June about the Tea Act. It was primarily an attempt by the British government to deal with another imperial problem: the poor finances of the East India Company. It sought to resolve them by enabling the company to send the tea direct to America, rather than via Britain, and by removing all the related British duties. Tea would henceforth be far cheaper than before the imposition of the Townshend duty and would undercut the smuggled, untaxed Dutch tea. However, as a point of principle the Townshend duty remained. In his letter Franklin correctly anticipated the likely reception in Boston:

> It was thought at the Beginning of the Session, that the American Duty on Tea would be taken off. But now the Scheme is, to take off as much Duty here as will make Tea cheaper in America than Foreigners can supply us; and continue the Duty there to keep up the Exercise of the Right. They have no Idea that any People can act from any Principle but that of Interest; and they believe that 3d. in a Pound of Tea, of which one does not drink perhaps 10lb in a Year, is sufficient to overcome all the Patriotism of an American!

It was a point of principle that was taken up with particular vigour by merchants like John Hancock who combined their legitimate business with smuggling. It only remained to see what might happen when the clippers carrying the East Indian tea arrived at the American ports.

∽

The petition arrived with Franklin in August and this time he presented it to Dartmouth immediately. Dartmouth would present it himself in the autumn, after he returned from his estate.

That summer Franklin was particularly delighted to note that among the numerous invitations to stay he received one for West Wycombe and another for Twyford on the very same day. As he wrote to William: 'If I were disposed to be idle I could pass my time agreeably enough; for at all their Houses everyone seems desirous

Benjamin Franklin as a gentleman in London. The bust on his desk is of Sir Isaac Newton.

Duke of Grafton

Lord North

Bute's successors as George III's Prime Minister, up to 1775, were Grenville, Rockingham, Chatham, Grafton and North. Franklin was to have some form of contact with all of them.

In early 1775 George III 'was not a tyrant, but perfectly capable of being a pedant'.

'Honest Whig' friends of Franklin

John Canton

Richard Price

Joseph Priestley

Price and Priestley had close ties with Franklin and the Earl of Shelburne – Price as Shelburne's spiritual adviser and Priestley as his Secretary.

'The Death of the Earl of Chatham'

A Key for Mr. Copley's Plate of the
DEATH OF THE LATE EARL OF CHATHAM.

The title of the group portrait is colloquial because Chatham's death came a month after his collapse in the Lords.

The mocking reaction of the Rockingham group showed the division of the opposition and disgusted observers.

9 Alexander Wedderburn   10 Edward Thurlow
11 Lord George Germain   12 Lord North
18 Dr Jonathan Shipley   23 Earl Gower
24 Earl of Sandwich   26 Earl of Dartmouth
32 Lord Camden   39 William Pitt the Younger
46 Earl of Chatham   47 Earl of Shelburne
48 Earl Temple   51 Duke of Richmond
52 Marquess of Rockingham   55 Earl of Bessborough

Earl of Sandwich branded Franklin 'an enemy' to Britain.

Josiah Quincy came to Britain on a secret mission from Boston.

In later life – Shelburne (far right) with his trusted political lieutenants, Dunning and Barré

Franklin in France, successfully projecting a very different image to the London portrait.

The personification of 'Poor Richard', or rather 'Bonhomme Richard'.

Caleb Whitefoord, Franklin's Craven Street neighbour and wine merchant, was just one of Franklin's friends who was part of the British peace delegation in Paris.

David Hartley, Franklin's fellow scientist and, in 1783, the British plenipotentiary. Seen here with the Treaty of Paris at his side.

of contenting me. Wycombe too is quite a Paradise, and Twyford another – with more Saints in it'.[15]

He had already spent some time with Le Despencer in July as they had stayed together at the Queen's College, Oxford, to see Lord North installed as Chancellor of the University. Franklin did not exchange any words with the Prime Minister but he did with Lord Hillsborough, whom he met by chance. The two men were polite, almost friendly to each other, which was a sublime show of eighteenth-century hypocrisy. That very morning Anthony Todd of the Post Office had told Franklin how much Hillsborough resented his loss of office, and for that he blamed the colony project in general and Franklin in particular. This was matched on Franklin's side by his report of the encounter and his assessment of Hillsborough as being completely duplicitous, not to mention 'the most insincere, and the most wrong-headed ... of all the Men I ever met'.[16]

From Oxford, Le Despencer and Franklin travelled to West Wycombe, as did, when all the ceremonials were completed, Lord North and his family. This was obviously a surprise for both North and Franklin, and an unpleasant one. History does not relate whether Dashwood had arranged this for a serious purpose or as one of his jokes, but it undoubtedly had a comic side. There certainly were not any summit talks to settle the American dispute. Unfortunately we only have Franklin's somewhat archly told side of the story about Lord North and the occasion:

Displeased with something he said relating to America, I have never been at his Levées,[17] since the first. Perhaps he has taken that amiss ... He seemed studiously [to avoid] speaking to me. I ought to be ashamed to say that on such [occasions] I feel myself to be as proud as any body. His Lady indeed was more [gracious. She came,] and sat down by me on the same Sofa, and condescended to enter into a Conversation with me agreeably enough, as if to make me some Amends. Their Son and Daughter were with them. They stayed all Night, so that we dined, supped, and breakfasted together, without exchanging three Sentences.[18]

All one can say is 'Well done, Lady North!'

North had been happy enough to chat with Franklin five years before in lieu of Grafton, the then Prime Minister. Perhaps the reason for his coolness was because North saw Franklin as an open political opponent, as a man mixing with the opposition not just in America but in Britain. As an example of this, Franklin had certainly spent time at Loakes Manor, just a couple of miles away from West Wycombe.

Loakes Manor, renamed Wycombe Abbey in the next century and now a famous school, was then the second estate of the Earl of Shelburne. In 1772 Franklin had spent six days there in 'rather good company', as recounted by the Abbé Morellet, a friend of both Franklin and Shelburne. Their host was Thomas Fitzmaurice (Shelburne's brother) and the other guests were Colonel Isaac Barré (Shelburne's chief lieutenant in the House of Commons), Dr Hawkesworth (writer and playwright as well as Polly Hewson's friend) and David Garrick (the greatest actor of the age). Morellet describes Franklin's demonstration of a favourite party trick, when he seemed to calm the 'wind ruffled' waters on a brook with a wave of his cane that released the oil secretly stored within it.[19] Such an entertainment is perfectly in keeping with the note in the Franklin Papers describing Fitzmaurice and Franklin as part of 'a circle of friends who combined jolly companionship with philosophical interests and experimentation',[20] not to mention their liking for a competitive game of cribbage. But Franklin also had other intimates who were exceptionally important to the Earl of Shelburne. Chief among them were Richard Price and Joseph Priestley. Price became Shelburne's spiritual adviser after the Earl was devastated by the death of his wife in 1771. Priestley in 1773, on Price's recommendation, joined Shelburne in a role that he himself described as 'nominally that of *librarian*, but I had little employment as such ... In fact I was with him as a friend.'[21]

Price and Priestley were two of the people closest to Franklin during his final decade in London. He supported their nomination to become Fellows of the Royal Society, in 1765 and 1766 respectively. Moreover, they were both active Honest Whigs, helping, with others like their fellow dissenter and author Andrew Kippis, the merchant and Jamaican estate owner Samuel Vaughan and the lawyer John 'Honest Jack' Lee, to fill the void in the Club left by the early death of John Canton in 1772.[22] Price and Priestley were important intellectual figures as well as both caring and sensitive nonconformist church ministers. They were extremely supportive of American rights and of Franklin personally, though they regretted his views on religion, with Priestley later writing: 'It is much to be lamented, that a man of Dr Franklin's general good character, and great influence, should have been an unbeliever in Christianity'[23] – this from a man who, in the early 1770s, saw Franklin nearly every day that they were both in London.[24]

Franklin's interest in religion was more of an intellectual exercise and if one applied a label to him it would probably be that of 'deist'. Like his friend Le Despencer, Franklin enjoyed a good sermon. He had done since being left spellbound, though unconverted, by the brilliance of the great nonconformist preacher George Whitefield in Philadelphia more than thirty years before.[25]

Franklin was staying with Le Despencer at West Wycombe once again in the early autumn of 1773, when Paul Whitehead, a noted wit and another of Dashwood's frequent guests, ran one morning into the breakfast parlour with a copy of the *Public Advertiser*, newly delivered from London. The chatter stopped abruptly when he announced 'Here's news for ye! *Here's the king of Prussia, claiming a right to this kingdom!*' All stared, including Franklin, as Whitehead began to read the piece. Then, stopping after a few paragraphs, Whitehead looked Franklin full in the face and declared '*I'll be hanged if this is not some of your American jokes upon us.*' As Ben continued in his letter to William, 'The reading went on, and ended with abundance of laughing, and a general verdict that it was a fair hit: and the piece was cut out of the paper and preserved in my lord's collection.'[26] But this article, 'An Edict by the King of Prussia',[27] and its Swiftian September companion piece entitled 'Rules by Which a Great Empire May Be Reduced to a Small One',[28] were a sign of Franklin's frustration that the removal of Hillsborough had not settled the Anglo-colonial dispute.

Franklin had hoped to create some British understanding of the American position through heavy satire, but what was holding the public's attention in the press was another matter entirely; it was the growing ferocity of open letters between John Temple and William Whately about the Hutchinson affair. No one in London, besides the 'Gentleman of Character and Distinction' (as Franklin described the provider of the correspondence), knew who had obtained them or who had sent them to Boston. Cushing had, in that respect, honoured Franklin's request for secrecy. Whately and Temple were the two prime suspects; Whately because his brother had died that spring and he was his executor; Temple because he was a cousin of George Grenville (Thomas Whately's former political leader), who might have been loaned or given the letters. Temple could have obtained them after Grenville's death in 1770 or even from Thomas Whately's papers, because William Whately had, at some point in 1772, allowed Temple unsupervised access to them. Furthermore Temple had a motive to want to destroy Hutchinson, as the Governor had engineered his dismissal from a lucrative post in Massachusetts.

The mutual claim, counter-claim and insult finally reached the point where a challenge was offered and accepted. Neither of them had any natural talent for duelling. They fired their pistols at each other and both missed. Then as James Srodes memorably describes it, they 'flailed with swords, sliding about the muddy field in the twilight. Whately was felled and cut a number of times before onlookers rescued them both. Newspaper ridicule and public laughter prompted Whately to talk of another challenge' as the two men now argued about who had been guilty of turning the 'trial by combat' into a farce.[29]

Franklin was away with the Shipleys in Twyford and unaware of the first duel until it had happened.[30] A more cynical man might have let a rematch go ahead. Instead, on Christmas Day 1773, he sent a short letter to the *London Chronicle*. His key sentence was: 'I alone am the person who obtained and transmitted to Boston the letters in question. Mr W. could not communicate them, because they were never in his possession; and, for the same reason, they could not be taken from him by Mr T. Franklin did not reveal the name of the 'Gentleman of Character and Distinction' and his identity is still not certain, though Bernard Bailyn points his finger very firmly at Thomas Pownall, a predecessor to Hutchinson as Governor of Massachusetts, at odds with him and hoping to be his successor.[31]

Although he admitted responsibility, Franklin was totally unapologetic. He dismissed the idea that these were *'private letters between friends'* but described them as 'written by public officers to persons in public station, on public affairs, and intended to procure public measures' designed 'to incense the Mother Country against her Colonies, and, by the steps recommended, to widen the breach, which they effected'.[32] As such it had been his duty to send them to the Massachusetts House.

The letter was widely reprinted and, suffice it to say, the English press did not agree with Franklin's reasoning. But the Hutchinson letters were just one of four different elements that would fuse together at the Cockpit offices of the Privy Council, when Alexander Wedderburn, the government's Solicitor General, would subject Franklin to what can only be described as an hour-long verbal assault.

⸎

Dartmouth had at last submitted to the King the petition from the Massachusetts House of Representatives for the removal of Governor Hutchinson and Lieutenant Governor Oliver and it was referred to the Privy Council Committee for Plantation Affairs. The date for the hearing was set for 11 January. It was only on the 8th that Franklin was called to appear and just the day before the hearing that he learned that Hutchinson's solicitor, Israel Mauduit, had asked to be represented by Counsel. Because Franklin and the solicitor acting for the House of Representatives felt that the House would be at a disadvantage unless they called in their own barristers, they asked for a postponement, which was granted. The hearing was now set for 29 January. This was a fateful delay, because to the existing controversial elements – the House's petition to remove the government's own appointees and then the matter of the letters – was added a third:

on 20 January London received the news of the Boston Tea Party. Over a hundred individuals, white men bizarrely and haphazardly disguised as Mohawk Indians, had unloaded 340 chests of tea from three ships into Boston harbour. Their open defiance of the British government's Tea Act caused a sensation.[33] It is not definitely known whether men such as John Hancock and Samuel Adams participated in the event, but the colony's elected representatives were held to blame. The mood in London was one of outrage. As a result, what could have been a short, sparsely attended meeting at the Cockpit, with the Massachusetts petition quickly heard and instantly thrown out, had been transformed into a lengthy inquisition. There had been twelve Privy Counsellors at the preliminary hearing, but there were thirty-five present on the 29th.[34] Franklin had a friend there in Le Despencer, but there were many who were far from friendly, including Hillsborough. The large contingent were not there from a sense of duty but because they expected a piece of theatre. Even the Archbishop of Canterbury and Bishop of London turned up, but it was not to offer Franklin spiritual consolation.

The Privy Council were far from alone: the public area was packed. It was not so much a cockpit as a bear pit, or perhaps better described by Franklin himself as an arena for 'bull baiting'. In this he was the 'bull' and the 'baiter' in chief was the Counsel for Hutchinson, Alexander Wedderburn, the government's Solicitor General. Wedderburn was considered to be 'stiff and pompous' in private conversation, but reckoned to be a brilliant public orator on the right occasion.[35] Wedderburn himself was the fourth of the four elements that created the storm that burst over Franklin's head.

Wedderburn, unusually for Franklin, was a Scot who did not take to him. Though Wedderburn had in fact long cast off his overt Scottishness, because the first thing he did on moving from the Scottish to the English Bar in 1757 was to have elocution lessons to anglicize his accent.[36] He did, however, retain his Scottish connections and had been close to Bute, who helped him establish himself as a King's Counsel. After Bute's resignation and the ties linking the 'King's Friends' dissolved, Wedderburn made a nuisance of himself by being an extremely effective opposition speaker. So effective, indeed, that

North brought the ambitious and careerist Wedderburn into his government.

Wedderburn had other targets that day: his legal opponents were not just acting for the opposition, they were *of* the opposition. Leading for the petition was John Dunning who was Shelburne's closest legal adviser, indeed as close to Shelburne as Lord Camden was to the Earl of Chatham; he was supported by 'Honest Jack' Lee, who was the legal adviser to the Rockingham group. Their position was straightforward: Hutchinson and Oliver had lost the confidence of the Massachusetts House and should be replaced. Their speeches were barely audible, with Dunning particularly hampered because he was suffering from bronchitis and unable to rise above the hubbub which the President of the Council, Earl Gower, did nothing to abate. When it came to Wedderburn's turn, Gower – one of the leading Bedfordites, whom Franklin had so abused in his 1770 letter to Charles Thomson – let him have free rein in his attack on Franklin.

Wedderburn mocked Franklin as not even a proper agent, accused him of acting for 'the most malignant of purposes' and described him as someone who 'has forfeited all the respect of societies and of men.'[37]

One observer in the audience was Edward Bancroft, a friend of both Priestley and Franklin who would, ostensibly, work for Franklin in France. Another was Joseph Priestley himself. Bancroft described Franklin's expression: 'The muscles of his face had been previously composed, so as to afford a placid tranquil expression of countenance, and he did not suffer the slightest alteration of it to appear during the continuance of the speech in which he was so harshly and improperly treated.'[38]

Priestley was not the sort of man who would be able to push his way through a sea of people. Fortunately for him, he ran into Edmund Burke in the street, who most definitely was. Priestley gives an unsparing account, not even being gentle about his great friend, fellow Yorkshireman and Honest Whig, John Lee:

> When we got to the ante-room, we found it quite filled with persons as desirous of getting admission as ourselves. Seeing this, I said, we should never get through the crowd. [Burke] said, 'Give me your arm';

and, locking it fast in his, he soon made his way to the door of the Privy Council. I then said, 'Mr Burke you are an excellent leader'; he replied, 'I wish other persons thought so too.'

After waiting a short time, the door of the Privy Council opened, and we entered the first; when Mr Burke took his stand behind the first chair next to the President, and I behind that the next to his. When the business was opened, it was sufficiently evident, from the speech of Mr Wedderburn, who was Counsel for the Governor, that the real object of the court was to insult Dr Franklin. All this time he stood in a corner of the room, not far from me, without the least apparent emotion.

Mr Dunning, who was the leading Counsel on the part of the Colony, was so hoarse that he could hardly make himself heard; and Mr Lee, who was the second, spoke but feebly in reply; so that Mr Wedderburn had a complete triumph. At the sallies of his sarcastic wit, all the members of the Council, the President himself (Lord Gower) not excepted, frequently laughed outright. No person belonging to the Council behaved with decent gravity, except Lord North, who coming late, took his stand behind the chair opposite to me.

When the business was over, Dr Franklin in going out, took me by the hand in a manner that indicated some feeling. I soon followed him, and going through the ante-room, saw Mr Wedderburn there surrounded with a circle of his friends and admirers. Being known to him, he stepped forward as if to speak to me; but I turned aside and made what haste I could out of the place.

The petition was of course recommended for dismissal and the report in the Privy Council Register categorizes it as 'founded on resolutions formed on false and erroneous allegations' and 'groundless, vexatious and scandalous and calculated only for the seditious purpose of keeping up a spirit of clamour and discontent'.[39]

Priestley saw Franklin the following day: 'The next morning I breakfasted with the Doctor, when he said, "He had never before been so sensible of the power of a good conscience; for that if he had not considered the thing for which he had been so much insulted, as one of the best actions of his life, and what he should certainly do again in the same circumstances, he could not have supported it."'[40] Franklin had put on a brave face, but he had suffered the same fate in London as Hutchinson had received in Boston: he had been branded as an agent provocateur. Almost eight years after his triumph over the Stamp Act repeal he had been humiliated.

Unsurprisingly, Priestley commented, 'Dr Franklin, notwithstanding he did not show it at the time, was much impressed by the Business of the Privy Council.' Franklin did well remember that day, even recalling what he was wearing. He gave an account of the atmosphere in a letter to Cushing:

> Not one of their lordships checked and recalled the orator to the business before them, but on the contrary (a very few excepted) they seemed to enjoy highly the entertainment, and frequently burst out in loud applauses. This part of his speech was thought so good, that they have since printed it in order to defame me everywhere, and particularly to destroy my reputation on your side the water, but the grosser parts of the abuse are omitted, appearing, I suppose in their own eyes, too foul to be seen on paper.[41]

He echoed that in a letter to Galloway with 'they seem to have been ashamed of it when in black and white, and have omitted much of it, so that compared to the Verbal Speech, the printed one is perfectly decent'.[42]

Franklin took revenge when he was offered the opportunity, but it would be completely wrong to think that Franklin was alienated from the entire British political class. Eighteenth-century politics was a rough house of verbal insult even if, in the confines of the Privy Council, it did not take on the physical violence of a Wilkesite mob.

Strangely, the Cockpit actually clarified Franklin's political position as a clear representative of colonial interests. The opposition consulted him openly, whereas the government would later do so unofficially and through third parties.

16

The Last Year in London

Two days after the Cockpit Franklin was dismissed from his position as Deputy Postmaster for America. As he was now persona non grata, he resigned his Massachusetts agency, but continued to work for the House unofficially, with Arthur Lee taking his official place.

There was much work to be done. Franklin wrote to the House's Correspondence Committee on 2 February 1774, suggesting that reparation be made to the East India Company: 'I cannot but wish and hope that before any compulsive Measures are thought of here, our General Court will have shown a Disposition to repair the Damage and make Compensation to the Company.'[1] He later approached the government and offered to cover the loss himself in the hope of later recovering it from the colony. That could have ruined him, but, perhaps fortunately, the offer was refused.[2]

Even the friends of America supported a degree of correction after the Tea Party, with Shelburne's lieutenant, Isaac Barré, offering a 'hearty affirmative' to the enforced closure of Boston's port, believing 'Boston ought to be punished' and reparation made.[3] They stopped there, but the British administration did not, because the Boston Port Act was just one of four Coercive Acts, otherwise known in America as the Intolerable Acts, passed between March and May. The Massachusetts Government Act sought to clamp down on town meetings and declared the Governor's Council a body to be appointed by the Privy Council in London. The Administration of Justice Act transferred all possible court action against British officials, from riot suppression or revenue collection, to England. Finally, a new

Quartering Act thrust British troops into Boston houses with the words, 'when available barracks were too far from the scene where troops were required'. This last brought predictable results, with the more sober citizens of Boston and the less disciplined British soldiery proving an unhappy combination, as Franklin's sister Jane Mecom reported from Boston: 'One can walk but a little way in the street without hearing there Profane language', being the least of it. There were fights: 'the towns being so full of Profligate soldiers and many such officers there is hardly four and twenty hours Passes without some fray amongst them'; and assaults on shopkeepers over drink.[4]

Arthur Lee organized petitions to the King and both Houses of Parliament in March and May 1774, before departing to the Continent, including France and Rome, until December.[5] These were signed by Franklin and other prominent Americans in London, but with as little effect as Franklin's appeals to popular opinion through a stream of pseudonymous newspaper articles. They were though a way of letting off steam, as was a mutually sarcastic and poisonous exchange of letters with Dean Josiah Tucker.

Franklin hardly hid himself away from his usual activities after 29 January 1774. Just two weeks later he was at a house specially adapted by David Hartley (later that year a Rockinghamite MP) and used for demonstrations of a new fireproofing system. Franklin was not there alone; he attended with, among others, Price, Priestley, the freethinking Bishop of Carlisle, the Unitarian minister Theophilus Lindsey and various lords, whom sadly the sources do not name.[6] Le Despencer may have been unable to come to Franklin's aid at the Cockpit or this time to protect his Post Office job, but he was most certainly not going to desert his great friend. For instance, they continued going to church together in their quest for a decent service and attended Lindsey's opening of the Essex House Chapel in April.[7] Needless to say, Franklin was again staying at West Wycombe during August.

Franklin continued his correspondence with scientists and in going to his clubs. He even had a new one, which he had co-founded, 'over a Neck of Veal and Potatoes, at the Old Slaughter Coffee House', early the previous year.[8] This club, which was called the Thirteen (as that was its maximum number of members) or the Wednesday Club, met fortnightly, sometimes at Craven Street. Its purpose was to study deistic philosophy and Franklin's co-founders were Thomas Bentley (Josiah Wedgwood's business partner), Major Richard Dawson from the Purfleet Arsenal and David Williams, a former dissenting minister whom Franklin dubbed 'The Priest of Nature'. Williams and Franklin worked together on a universal liturgy, which was a more serious work than his Prayer Book with Le Despencer.[9]

Franklin attended the Royal Society Club, still as a guest, thirteen times between February 1774 and January 1775.[10] It was at Sir John Pringle's in the spring that he overheard Colonel Clarke, an ADC of the King, suggest the best way to treat American males and solve the crisis. As Franklin recalled, Clarke proposed 'that, with a Thousand British grenadiers, he would undertake to go from one end of America to the other, and geld all the Males, partly by force and partly by a little Coaxing'.[11] This idea formed the basis for Franklin's 'On Humbling our Rebellious Vassals'. Printed in the *Public Advertiser* of 21 May, Franklin took on the guise of 'An Independent Freeholder of Old Sarum', itself a joke as it was the rottenest of rotten boroughs, with two Members of Parliament and absolutely no resident electors.[12] In the article he described in great detail how Clarke's plan could be executed and pointed to all sorts of supplementary benefits: imports could be cut – there would be no need for operatic castrati from Italy; exports would be boosted – with eunuchs for the Ottoman Empire; there would be no rebellious subjects in America in fifty years' time; and finally, 'It would effectually put a Stop to the Emigrations from this Country now grown so very fashionable.' The article is one of Franklin's funniest satires, but it was one with a bitter edge. He was not just worried about those around the King, but about the King himself. In July 1773 Franklin had confided in William a belief that 'Between you and I, the late Measures have been, I suspect, very much the King's own, and he has in some Cases a great Share of what his Friends call *Firmness*.' He was wrong in that, because the King did not make measures, but the nature of Franklin's combination of hopeful and fearful thinking came in the next phrase, which was: 'Yet, by some Painstaking and proper Management, the wrong Impressions he has received may be removed, which is perhaps the only Chance America has for obtaining *soon* the Redress she aims at. This entirely to yourself.'[13] He had seen the King as a last court of appeal, but a year later he must have heard of George III's strong approval of the Coercive Acts and his brushing aside the first of Lee's petitions and his patently ignoring the second.[14]

Franklin was not much occupied by the Colonial Office. On 21 April John Pownall wrote to him asking whether he had the authority to act as agent for the Pennsylvania Assembly, receiving in reply Franklin's copy of a note to that effect from Philadelphia dated 15 October 1773. Pownall wrote again, just a few days later, to say that though laws in Pennsylvania were under discussion he had 'not received any directions from their Lordships to require Dr Franklin's Attendance', though Franklin was invited the following month.[15]

Franklin certainly did not approach John Pownall or Dartmouth about the affairs of the Walpole Company, now called the Vandalia Company.[16] After the defeat of Hillsborough, Samuel Wharton had been slow to move things forward because, with the grant likely to succeed, he sought to make more money from an increasing number of shareholders at a higher price. Belatedly the application had gone to the Law Officers, who further delayed matters, because Attorney General Thurlow had specifically demanded Franklin's removal from the company.[17] Thus, on 7 January 1774, Franklin had given Walpole his resignation from the list of shareholders, though he ensured that he kept the shares.

Franklin was being kept busy by William Whately, who had filed a Chancery suit against him, also on 7 January. This had the ostensible aim of having the original Hutchinson and Oliver letters returned, but the more specific ambition of bringing Franklin to court and under oath, so he could be forced to reveal how he had obtained them. Two days after the Cockpit, Thomas Life, Franklin's solicitor for the case, engaged Dunning and Lee, to be joined in short time by Richard Jackson and Charles Sayer. After many meetings with Franklin and his barristers, Life drew up his answer on Franklin's behalf at the end of April. The case and the cost continued and cast a darkening shadow over Franklin in the months ahead. Whately would not give it up and Franklin believed that Whately was being used as a proxy by the government.[18]

During the first few months of a year of extreme challenge, the sixty-eight-year-old Franklin had the reassurance of his settled home in Craven Street. That is, until 18 April, when William Hewson's knife slipped while dissecting a corpse and he cut himself. Hewson died of septicaemia on 1 May and Franklin displayed his anguish in a letter written to Deborah four days later: 'He was an excellent young Man, ingenious, industrious, useful, and beloved by all that knew him. She {Polly} is left with two young Children, and a third soon expected. He was just established in a profitable growing Business, with the best Prospects of bringing up his young Family advantageously. They were a happy Couple! All their Schemes of Life are now overthrown!'[19]

∽

At the end of August, when delegates from twelve of the thirteen colonies were preparing to attend the First Continental Congress at Philadelphia, Franklin received his invitation to meet the Earl of Chatham.[20] He was flattered to be consulted by the Great Man but was forthright in his opinions, which did, however, chime with Chatham's. Franklin was sufficiently buoyed by the meeting to write to Thomas Cushing that he had 'reason to think a strong Push will be made at the very Beginning of the Session to have all the late Acts reversed, and a solemn Assurance given America that no future Attempts shall be made to tax us without our Consent'. He knew that this could not come from what he called the 'present mad Administration', but had hopes of a 'Union of the Friends of Liberty, in both Houses' at Westminster and that the 'Unanimity and Firmness {of Congress} will have great Weight here, and probably unhorse the present wild Riders'.[21] Congress certainly played their part in that respect as the other colonies offered their support to Massachusetts with a petition to the King for the redress of their grievances.[22]

∽

Franklin continued to receive enquiries from his fellow scientists and letters asking for assistance in practical matters or for references for themselves or supplicants. The Franklin Papers contain a particularly interesting example of a reference he gave, directed to his son-in-law, Richard Bache. It was for someone who had a recommendation from the mathematician and Royal Society Fellow George Lewis Scott.[23]

Dear Son   London, 30 September, 1774

The bearer, Mr Thomas Paine, is very well recommended to me, as an ingenious, worthy young man. He goes to Pennsylvania with a view of settling there. I request you to give him your best advice and countenance, as he is quite a stranger there. If you can put him in a way of obtaining employment as a clerk, or assistant tutor in a school, or assistant surveyor (of all which I think him very capable), so that he may procure a subsistence at least, till he can make acquaintance and obtain a knowledge of the country, you will do well, and much oblige your affectionate father. My love to Sally and the boys.

B. Franklin[24]

As it happened, the thirty-seven-year-old Paine became an essayist.

⁓

Earlier that month Franklin had written another letter to be carried home, this time one to his wife:

London, Sept. 10. 1774

It is now nine long Months since I received a Line from my dear Debby. I have supposed it owing to your continual Expectation of my Return; I have feared that some Indisposition had rendered you unable to write; I have imagined anything rather than admit a Supposition that your kind Attention towards me was abated. And yet when so many other old Friends have dropped a Line to me now and then at a Venture, taking the Chance of its finding me here or not as it might happen, why might I not have expected the same Comfort from you, who used to be so diligent and faithful a Correspondent, as to omit scarce any Opportunity?

This will serve to acquaint you that I continue well, Thanks to God. It would be a great Pleasure to me to hear that you are so. My Love to our Children; and believe me ever Your affectionate Husband, B. Franklin

He never heard from his 'dear Debby' again, but then there is no sign that he sent her any further letters. There is no indication that the Baches and William ever gave Franklin an indication of her true condition. Yet, because he did not ask them, perhaps they concluded that he did not want to know.

On Wednesday, 17 December, Bache wrote a letter telling Franklin that Deborah had suffered a major stroke, one that deprived her of speech, the previous Sunday.[25] We do not know whether he received it, but he certainly did the ones that were sent on Wednesday the 24th, from both Bache and William, that told him that she had died three days before on Sunday the 21st. For the first time, with a note of anger, William tells his father of Deborah's condition. Referring to the stroke she had suffered a full five years before, he wrote that 'Her Death was no more than might be reasonably expected after the paralytic Stroke she received some Time ago, which greatly affected her Memory and Understanding.' He then continued, 'She told me ... that she never expected to see you unless you returned this Winter, for that she was sure she should not live till next Summer. I heartily wish you had happened to have come over in the Fall, as I think her Disappointment in that respect preyed a good deal on her Spirits.'[26] In short, she had finally lost hope of ever seeing her husband again, and given up.

As the editors of the Franklin Papers note, it is strange that now should be the moment for William to divulge these details. But, having done so, he went on to tell of his worries about his father's health and safety and that he could not understand the delay in returning home to his family. He bluntly stated his reasons:

> If there was any Prospect of your being able to bring the People in Power to your Way of Thinking, or of those of your Way of Thinking's being brought into Power, I should not think so much of your Stay. But as you have had by this Time pretty strong Proofs that neither can be reasonably expected and that you are looked upon with an evil Eye in that Country, and are in no small Danger of being brought into Trouble for your political Conduct, you had certainly better return, while you are able to bear the Fatigues of the Voyage.

William sugared the pill by saying that his father would be returning 'to a Country where the People revere you, and are inclined to pay a Deference to your Opinions.'

Though that might not necessarily have meant William himself. William, for so long close to his father and supportive of him,[27] had obviously been stung by Ben's comments in recent letters such as 'you, who are a thorough Courtier, see every thing with Government Eyes,'[28] so also added 'However mad you may think the Measures of the Ministry are, yet I trust you have Candour enough to acknowledge that we are no ways behind hand with them in Ins[tances] of Madness on this Side the Water.' Thus though he continued tactfully with 'However, it [is] a disagreeable Subject, and I'll drop it,'[29] it is clear that he was questioning his father's judgement, telling him that he was fighting a lost cause, and trying to protect him from himself. William would have his answer in a letter of nearly 20,000 words.

There is no record of Franklin having an emotional reaction to his wife's death or of any later remorse.[30] He would have received the news in London towards the end of February 1775, and he took ship the next month, together with Temple, William's son, with whom he was now very close. But when William wrote the letter, Ben still had some hopes of a political solution.

∽

On 17 November another potential peacemaker arrived in London. General Gage had written to Lord Dartmouth about 'a person whose name is kept secret' who was shortly to sail to London, remarking 'there is something mysterious concerning the Object of his Voyage'.[31] That someone was thirty-year-old Josiah Quincy Jr from Boston. He doubled in being both the son of a friend of Franklin's in Boston and a radical member of Samuel Adams's inner circle.[32]

He took tea with Franklin that first day, describing him in his journal as 'warm in our cause and confident of our ultimate success'.[33] The next day Quincy spent two hours with Lord North, who was happy to give him as much time as he wanted, even seeming reluctant to let him leave. One thing became clear as they discussed the Boston port closure, and it was that North believed that unless the government had reasserted its authority over the colonies it would have been voted down in Parliament. He insisted that the port closure was 'the most lenient measure that was proposed'.[34]

A few days later Quincy spent three hours with Thomas Pownall, who was very keen to stoke ill-feeling against Hutchinson.[35] Then, on the following Thursday, he spent an hour and a half with Dartmouth, who was as courteous as his stepbrother Lord North. With both of them, Quincy placed the blame for the problems in Massachusetts squarely on Hutchinson. But the latter was in England and speaking up for himself and the ministers made it clear that it was he they believed, with Under-Secretaries John Pownall and William Knox later telling Hutchinson himself that North had described Quincy to them after his departure as 'a bad, insidious man, designing to be artful without abilities to conceal his design'.[36]

Unsurprisingly, Quincy spent the vast majority of his time with the opponents of government policy. David Hartley, now a Rockingham-ite MP, was extremely keen to meet him and did so on a number of occasions during December 1774. Through Richard Price, Quincy met Shelburne. He spent two hours with him on 12 December, saw him again on the 30th, after seeing Priestley, and then, after a brief stop in Bath where he met Colonel Barré and the duellist John Temple, returned to Shelburne's vastly impressive estate at Bowood to spend a couple of days. He disappointed Shelburne in not staying longer.

But the person to whom Quincy was closest during his three and a half months' stay was Franklin. Theirs was a mutual admiration. Quincy wrote to his father, 'Your friend Dr Franklin is a *truly* great and good man.'[37] Franklin, calling Quincy 'amiable and valuable', reflected his regret that the younger man had been weakened by tuberculosis, by writing 'I am much pleased with Mr Quincy. 'Tis a thousand Pities his strength of Body is not equal to his Strength of Mind.'[38] Franklin and Price took Quincy along to the Royal Society and then the Club of Honest Whigs on the evening after he had met Dartmouth. The following month Franklin invited him to his new Wednesday Club, where the group debated the morality of capital punishment. Quincy was frequently at Craven Street having tea, they very often dined *à deux* or with others, and Franklin took him to stay with his 'Honest Whig' merchant friend Samuel Vaughan out in the countryside at his estate at Wanstead. Franklin and Quincy's closeness was noticed by Hillsborough, who remarked in the House of Lords just a fortnight after Quincy's arrival that he believed 'that there were then *men* walking in the streets of London, who ought to be in Newgate or at Tyburn': that they should either be imprisoned or hanged. When challenged by the Duke of Richmond, Hillsborough made it absolutely clear that he meant Franklin and his young friend Josiah Quincy.[39] And Hillsborough was not a lone voice; it is likely that Franklin knew that at least one Cabinet member, the Earl of Suffolk, was pressing for his arrest.[40] There was also the continuing threat that William Whately would succeed in bringing him in front of a court.

❧

But Franklin was also involved in negotiations. His position as someone thought to be aligned with the Boston radicals made him seem a possible medium for negotiations. As Jonathan Dull describes it, 'members of the British government who were concerned about the deteriorating situation turned to him as a potential peacemaker. They believed he had power to negotiate on behalf of the colonies; Franklin did not, but he was willing to make suggestions.'[41] The go-betweens were Franklin's old friend Dr Fothergill and fellow Quaker David

Barclay, who later brought in Lord Hyde, a Privy Counsellor whom Franklin respected. Hyde was a more senior intermediary with the members of the government entering these secret negotiations, who were either North or Dartmouth – who was Fothergill's patient – or probably both. Franklin threw himself into action, and within a week he provided seventeen 'hints' for his friends for possible negotiation; but in spite of days spent drawing up proposals neither side could make a move from their fixed positions.

Another channel of communication was opened when a carrot was dangled effectively in front of Franklin. This was not a government job, which Franklin certainly had no interest in now. It was a game of chess. His opponent, and a worthy one, was the Hon. Caroline Howe. He agreed to a rematch a few days later, when the subject of politics was raised. He was, though, surprised to be introduced to her brother, Rear Admiral Viscount Richard Howe, at a further game on Christmas Day. This prompted many further meetings with Lord Howe, including a joining of the two channels when he met both Hyde and Howe. In February 1775 there was even talk of a breakthrough with Howe going to America, along with Franklin, as a Peace Commissioner. That initiative, however, fizzled out.

The problem was that neither side would nor could blink first. The American demand that the British government must renounce its rights to tax the colonies and to legislate for them was not acceptable to North, let alone to his colleagues Gower, Sandwich and Suffolk. Nor did Franklin expect it to be. He believed that if the colonies raised the stakes in what was becoming a full-scale trade war, through introducing a complete ban on British imports, their manufacturers and merchants would force a change of policy by bringing down the government.[42]

The game of chess on Christmas Day was obviously a diversion in an incredibly busy schedule. So busy that he was not able to get to Twyford for Christmas in spite of Georgiana Shipley trying to tempt him with 'Books, Chess and Electricity'.[43] It even took a whole week from his receipt of the colonial Congress's petition for him to have the time to travel to Hayes in Kent to discuss it with Chatham, who heartily approved it.

There would be further meetings with Chatham and with his close colleague Lord Camden before Franklin arrived at the House of Lords lobby on 20 January 1775. Josiah Quincy was also an observer that day and was completely star-struck by Chatham's performance. Quincy had seen David Garrick on stage and had described him as 'not without his faults as an Orator'.[44] In contrast he described Chatham's speech as 'a blaze of genius,'[45] and this in reaction to what was the mere warm-up for the main speech on 1 February. Sadly, Quincy was not able to see that, as his tuberculosis had worsened. On 26 January he moved to Islington for better air, where he was treated by Dr Fothergill. Just the night before he had dined with the Earl of Shelburne at his house in Berkeley Square with a small but cohesive group that included Drs Franklin, Price and Priestley and Counsellors Dunning and John Lee, all to discuss the 'papers from America' to be considered by Parliament. [46]

Chatham did not discuss the proposal for his plan in its final version with Franklin or, at any stage, with Rockingham, in spite of the efforts of the Duke of Richmond to co-ordinate the government's opponents. In any case Chatham, although going further than the Rockinghams with their rigid adherence to the Declaratory Act, still maintained the supremacy of Parliament, even if only as it concerned the whole empire. He maintained the right to use a standing army in America, but not for the purposes of coercion and, with that in mind, all the existing coercive acts were to be dropped, once Congress, which would be recognized, agreed to Chatham's proposed solution. It would be for local Assemblies to tax their own populations and for Congress to agree a perpetual revenue for the King. It was a platform for negotiation, recognizing the colonies as a collective unit, as had the Albany Plan that Franklin, Hutchinson and Pownall had proposed way back in 1754.[47] Perhaps if Chatham had remained the vital William Pitt of the Seven Years' War and had presented this proposal to the House of Commons in 1767, then his prestige as the victor of the Seven Years' War and the force of his personality might have carried the measure through Parliament. But by 1775 it was too late for both the man and the measure.[48] It was defeated by an overwhelming majority and Chatham could take small comfort from the fact that it was by a factor of two to one rather than the customary three to one.[49]

Franklin has been accused of failing as a colonial representative and blamed for having exacerbated an already deteriorating situation through his release of the Hutchinson letters. But though the latter point cannot be contradicted, it was marginal to the outcome. By March 1775 Franklin was finally relegated to the role of infuriated observer, as the ministerial side in Parliament 'asserted that we were all Knaves, and wanted only by this Dispute to avoid paying our Debts'.[50] He summed up the reaction in the House of Lords to Chatham's initiative: 'Lord Chatham's Bill, though on so important a Subject, and offered by so great a Character, and supported by such able and learned Speakers as Camden etc., was treated with as much Contempt as they could have shown to a Ballad offered by a drunken Porter.'[51]

✍

Even then he had not given up hope and had an important standard-bearer in Quincy. The Bostonian had been ill for much of February and been cheered by his many visits from Franklin, Priestley and Price, David Hartley, Arthur Lee and Lee's brother William, together with a great number of others whom Quincy could accurately describe as 'my friends – who are many and affectionate'.[52] All the time he was under the care of the diligent and kind Dr Fothergill, who advised him not to hazard the effects of a long sea voyage but to get well in the countryside and recover properly in the spring. That he could not do. He needed to return to Boston to relay the state of affairs in London, with Franklin writing in a letter to Quincy's father: 'your son's return at this time, when writing is so inconvenient, may be of singular service'. By the end of his stay he and Franklin were in complete accord. Three days before Quincy sailed he and Franklin talked:

I opened the discourse by telling him of the opinions of Dr Price, Dr Priestley, William Lee, Arthur Lee and others on those subjects. The

Doctor utterly dissented from them all: he entered largely into the subject, and spoke the most substantial good sense and solid wisdom for near an hour. I wish I might with propriety enter his discourse: it would do lasting honour to his sagacity, judgement, morality and benevolence. I was charmed. I renounced my own opinion. I became a convert to his. I feel a kind of enthusiasm which leads me to believe that it was something almost supernatural which induced this discourse and prompted the Doctor to speak so fully and divinely upon the subject. This interview may be a means of preventing much calamity and producing much good to Boston and the M. Bay, and in the end to all America.[53]

Sadly, we do not know what 'singular service' Quincy would have provided or what message he would have taken from Franklin or anyone else. He became ill again and, without the tender care of Dr Fothergill, his condition worsened as his ship lay becalmed off the North American coast. His journal was finished in another hand, that of a sailor, because Quincy was too weak to write. All that he would disclose was that 'fifteen or twenty most staunch friends to America, many of them the most learned and respectable characters in the kingdom', had wanted him to go immediately to Boston and pass on a personal message. He agreed that 'It appeared of high importance that the sentiments of such persons should be known in America', that it 'might have been of great advantage to both countries' but that 'to commit their sentiments to writing was neither practicable nor prudent at this time'. It was not a message he could entrust with anybody else and it died with him, just hours before the ship reached port at Gloucester, Massachusetts.

One cannot know for certain what Quincy's message would have been, but from the position Franklin took when he reached America and from Quincy's other observations we can come to a firm conclusion. Franklin believed passionately in the potential of what might be termed a Greater Britain, with the British Isles and America working together. He had long believed that they could economically dominate the world long into the future. He also calculated that the colonies already had the ability to bring a change of policy by cutting off the supply of American raw materials and boycotting British goods. Quincy met Franklin a day before he sailed, and Franklin told him that 'he had the best intelligence that the manufacturers were bitterly feeling and loudly complaining of the loss of the American trade' and advised: 'Let your adherence be to the non-importation and non-exportation agreement, a year from next September, or to the next sessions of Parliament, and the day is won.'[54] Franklin believed that Congress must stand firm but also that Massachusetts should 'By no means take any step of great consequence (unless on a sudden emergency) without advice of the Continental Congress' because if it came to war, 'only New England could hold for ages against this country' and then only for seven years.

Intriguingly, at that meeting Franklin also told Quincy that he was an 'intimate of the Spanish and French ambassadors', describing the latter as 'a great shrewd man'. As early as July 1775, Franklin would write to Margaret Stevenson from Philadelphia and advise her to invest in land, rather than stocks, as he believed that 'some European power' would be drawn into the war he believed Britain had begun.[55]

On 16 March, four days before Franklin left London, he drafted a memorandum that he intended to send to Lord Dartmouth. He showed it to Thomas Walpole who, Franklin reported, 'looked at it and at me several Times alternately, as if he apprehended me a little out of my Senses',[56] but who agreed to check it with his neighbour, Lord Camden. After consulting Camden, Walpole wrote Franklin a note, but was so keen to restrain him that he also met him personally the next day to give the same message, that his 'Memorial' 'might be attended with dangerous consequences to your person, and contribute to exasperate the Nation'.[57] It was wise advice because Franklin's anger had got the better of him. 'Franklin furioso' had taken over. He had boiled at the contempt for his colonial fellow countrymen that he had heard in the House of Lords and at the derision of the Earl of Sandwich in particular. Sandwich had dismissed the Bostonians as 'a set of poor dastardly fellows' and, in a manner reminiscent of Colonel Clarke, had said that 1,000 British regulars 'would be able to drive 100,000 such Poltroons into the Sea.'[58] This was not the expression of a foolish ADC, but that of an important minister of the Crown. In response Franklin had, on behalf of the Massachusetts Bay colony, written Dartmouth what could only be construed as a threatening letter.

Franklin was no longer of any potential political use in London. The warrant for his arrest was served when he was at sea. It was in fact related to the Whately case, but had he stayed, the initiative would have been taken by the government itself.

On board the *Pennsylvania* packet on course for Philadelphia, Franklin followed the pattern of his voyage from London almost fifty years before. This time he had young Temple to help him in his scientific observation, taking water samples in an attempt to understand the workings of the Gulf Stream.[59] As he had done five decades earlier with his 'Plan of Conduct', Franklin also used the Atlantic crossing to consider his recent past and to contemplate the future. This time he was considering not just himself, but British America.

Aftermath – 'A Little Revenge'

The *Pennsylvania* packet docked at Philadelphia on 5 May. Though his 'Journal of Negotiations in London' was addressed to his son, Franklin did not see William for several weeks. When they did meet, at Galloway's estate at Trevose, it soon became clear that Ben was not only on the opposing side to Galloway but also to his own son, who would choose to become a leading loyalist. It would be William who would end his days in London. Temple had to choose between his father and the grandfather he knew far better: he chose his grandfather.[1]

The Second Continental Congress began just five days after Franklin's arrival. Had Josiah Quincy lived he would have smoothed Franklin's path, but many of the much older man's new young colleagues did not know what to make of their famous fellow countryman. Franklin adopted his normal demeanour on meeting groups containing people he did not know: he listened much and said little. Some Congressmen even suspected that Franklin, with a long residence in London and a Royal Governor as a son, was a secret supporter of the British government. It took time for them to realize that, on the contrary, he was a dedicated foe.

Franklin was certainly writing to politicians in Britain, but to government opponents and old friends such as Jonathan Shipley and Joseph Priestley and to the Rockinghamites David Hartley and Edmund Burke, with whom he was now more in tune than he had been in London. He also composed a letter addressed to Strahan dated 5 July. It was written following the British bombardment of the Atlantic coast and incineration of property – including some of Franklin's own[2] – and after the loss of life at the Battle of Bunker Hill. Franklin addressed Strahan as one of the MPs who were of the 'Majority which has doomed my Country to Destruction ... begun to burn our Towns, and murder our People', and denounced him as an enemy. It was written but not sent. He probably thought better of it, as he did on another occasion in 1780.[3] In his cordial letter to Strahan of three months later he asked to be remembered to Grey Cooper and Sir John Pringle.[4]

The Briton who was the subject of Franklin's lasting fury, as the dispute became a war, was King George III. John Adams in later life recalled Franklin's 'habitual acrimony'[5] towards the King: 'He often, and indeed always, appeared to me to have personal animosity and very severe resentment against the King. In all his conversations, and in all his writings, when he could naturally, and sometimes when he could not, he mentioned the King with great asperity.'[6]

This was not just a case of Franklin elevating the target for his vitriol, as his priorities advanced from issuing complaints to the Proprietors of Pennsylvania to protecting the rights of colonial Americans. As with Thomas Penn and Lord Hillsborough, this was enmity with a personal edge. The King had let him down. As Franklin had said at his London meeting with Lord Granville in 1757, he was certain that the King (or the government on his behalf) could not legally revoke the chartered rights of the colonial Assemblies. More than that, he believed that the monarch was the ultimate protector of the Assemblies against the prerogative claims of the Westminster Parliament – and he still believed it in 1773 when he had described King George as 'perhaps the only Chance America has for obtaining *soon* the Redress she aims at'. Yet when Congress sought to use the King as a final 'court of appeal' to settle their grievances through their Olive Branch Petition in the summer of 1775, George III avoided hearing it until North had issued in the King's name 'A Proclamation for Supressing Sedition and Rebellion' that declared the colonies to be in 'open and avowed rebellion'. As Andrew O'Shaughnessy explains, George III 'had good constitutional reasons for his action since the petition essentially invited him to act against Parliament'.[7] This he not only had no desire to do, but felt he had no right to do either. George III was not a tyrant, but he was most emphatically a pedant.

Franklin, who had invested such hopes in the young King and his mentor Lord Bute, had already lost faith in the power of petitions,[8] but was particularly scathing about the way it was treated.[9] The 'Proclamation for Supressing Sedition and Rebellion' was merely further confirmation of what Franklin already knew, that Britain's 'mangling ministers' had rejected the opportunity to create a vast and Great British empire including the new colony of Vandalia and the lands beyond. He and not they had understood the continent's potential, which was why he desperately wanted to add Canada to the United States.

Albeit unwittingly, Franklin provided the instrument for revenge against the King. By a strange explosive conjunction of events, akin to the news of the Boston Tea Party arriving just before Franklin's appearance at the Cockpit, the report of George III's reaction to the Olive Branch Petition reached the Continental Congress at Philadelphia on the very day that Thomas Paine's *Common Sense* was published.[10] As Thomas Jefferson later attested, it was so well written that people believed that 'Thomas Paine' was a pseudonym for Benjamin Franklin.[11] *Common Sense* caused a sensation, referring 'to the Royal Brute of Britain', rejecting the monarchy and clearly articulating the case for independence.[12] It was an intellectual foundation stone for all that followed.

There was a strong political reason for Franklin's animus against George III. Rather less expectedly, there was also, from 1777, a scientific one, because Franklin the politician and Franklin the scientist had, in the mind of George III, become one.

On 15 May 1777, lightning struck the Board House at the Ordnance depot at Purfleet. The Board of Ordnance asked the Royal Society to investigate. In actual fact the damage was comparably light. The lightning had travelled into an unattached metal cramp* holding a parapet together, then through stone and brick, before finding lead guttering and then travelling to earth. The fault was with the cramp,

---

* Used to secure stonework.

not with the conductor's skyward point. However, that was not the judgement of Benjamin Wilson. Nor was it the King's, to whom Wilson, as artist rather than scientist, had an important connection. George III put the blame full square on Franklin. Franklin, supposedly the pre-eminent expert in such matters, had overshadowed Wilson on the two committees designed to protect first St Paul's and then Purfleet from lightning strikes, yet, in very short order, these had both been struck. Franklin was now an avowed enemy of Britain. To the King the answer seemed obvious: this was misadventure.

Wilson was keen to use the opportunity to prove his theory and the King more than happy to give him the finance to do so. Thus a large model and an 'artificial cloud' were created,[13] so that Wilson could seem to win the argument. This he did to his own satisfaction and that of the King, who, certain that even 'the apple-women in the street' would be convinced, commanded that the pointed lightning conductors at Buckingham House be replaced.[14] The King, so it is said, also ordered Franklin's friend, Sir John Pringle, as President of the Royal Society, to validate Wilson's theory to the detriment of Franklin's. Pringle, however, refused and allegedly told him that his powers as President did not extend to changing the laws of nature. Whether caused by royal intimidation, or through declining health, Pringle resigned the Presidency and also his position as Physician to the King, after three decades of service to the Royal Family.[15]

Wilson's experimental method was soon proved to be flawed and Franklin's vindicated. It is Franklin's reaction to George III's involvement in the dispute which is the most interesting. In October 1777 he described 'the King's changing his pointed Conductors for blunt ones' as 'a Matter of small Importance to me'. But then he could not resist adding, 'If I had a Wish about it, it would be that he had rejected them altogether as ineffectual. For it is only since he thought himself and Family safe from the Thunder of Heaven that he dared to use his own Thunder in destroying his innocent Subjects.'[16] George III and Franklin were in strange agreement: Franklin the politician and Franklin the scientist were as one.[17]

By the very narrow definition of his specific instructions, Franklin failed in both his missions to London: the Pennsylvania Assembly was not able to tax the Proprietors on an equitable and permanent basis; nor was it able to oust them and establish Pennsylvania as a royal colony. But such a judgement is harsh, for though he was keen enough to try, Franklin was not empowered to succeed. That is equally true of his attempts to sustain the relationship between Britain and its colonies. He failed; but it was not for want of trying. He himself rather touchingly summed up his efforts in his letter of 20 July 1776 to Lord Howe, sixteen days after the Declaration of Independence. Howe had just arrived in America, not as a peace broker but as the British military Commander-in-Chief:

> Long did I endeavour with unfeigned and unwearied Zeal, to preserve from breaking that fine and noble China Vase the British Empire: for I knew that, being once broken, the separate Parts could not retain even their Share of the Strength or Value that existed in the Whole, and that a perfect Re-Union of those Parts could scarce even be hoped for. Your Lordship may possibly remember the Tears of Joy that wet my Cheek when, at your good Sister's in London, you once gave me Expectations that a Reconciliation might soon take place. I had the Misfortune to find those Expectations disappointed, and to be treated as the Cause of the Mischief I was labouring to prevent. My Consolation under that groundless and malevolent Treatment was that I retained the Friendship of many Wise and Good Men in that Country, and among the rest some Share in the Regard of Lord Howe.[18]

In the decade before 1775, the major problem in reconciling the conflicting claims of the British Parliament and the colonial Assemblies was political instability within Britain itself. Chatham, potentially the major political figure, had the vision but not the personal strength at the optimum time to settle the American question. The focus of factional leaders in Parliament was on the battle for political control. Certainly the different groups had differing ideological positions and George Croghan exaggerated when, in 1764, frustrated at the slowness of government decision-making, he categorized leading politicians and their factions as men in pursuit of power for purely personal advantage.[19] That said, even those factions sympathetic to America, led by Chatham and Rockingham, could not bring themselves to collaborate effectively in opposition, such was their mutual loathing. Perhaps this is best summed up by Samuel Vaughan's son Benjamin, who wrote to Franklin in 1778 about the physical collapse of Chatham in the House of Lords that led to his death a month later: 'I believe I never told you what had made me warm against the Rockinghams. It was first four or five of the chiefs getting in a circle and laughing, the day Lord Chatham fell which these eyes beheld.'[20]

Franklin had predicted that a major shock would bring down the government. He believed that a complete breakdown of trade between the two countries would convince a sufficient number of independent MPs to vote with the opposition and put them in power. It was not enough: the government did not fall until after the disaster of Yorktown. Franklin's expectation that the uproar of British merchants and manufacturers would pressurize the government into concessions was forlorn. It had not happened during the non-importation crisis of 1769, when Franklin had described the merchants as moving slowly and the manufacturing towns refusing to move at all; and it failed to materialize in 1774/5 for the same reasons. Perhaps, if the campaign had been as long and sustained as he had proposed to Quincy, there might have been some effect, but it is unlikely. British merchants and manufacturers would not attain major Parliamentary power until well into the next century.

In late 1774 William predicted that his father would not be 'able to bring the People in Power to your Way of Thinking' or be instrumental in 'those of your Way of Thinking's being brought into Power'.[21] British political stability had finally been gained from 1770 through the competence of Lord North and the support of his King; the increasingly repressive policies of North's government were locked in place by members of his Cabinet and the support of MPs and Lords happy to remain uninformed about the potential of a Great British North America.

Franklin's great friend Dr Fothergill, who had worked so hard to find a peaceful solution in 1775, later summed up the ignorance and indifference of those 'backbenchers':

> ...those who supported the measures of Government against that country were almost total strangers to America, to the country, and to its inhabitants... The knowledge of America was confined to the Merchants and Traders chiefly. It was a country talked of; but no people save those immediately interested in its produce, knew anything about it. From the debates upon the STAMP ACT, some little information arose, but this was forgotten in a few years.[22]

♾

Seventeen months after Franklin had arrived from Europe he crossed the Atlantic again, accompanied by a sixteen-year-old Temple and another grandson, six-year-old Benjamin Bache. On 21 December 1776 they arrived in Paris. It was cold and Franklin was wearing a beaver hat to protect his balding head. He had long been revered for his scientific reputation by France's aristocratic intellectuals and, by luck or design, he had created exactly the image that the French aristocracy wanted, that of the frontiersman savant. The image, complete with his printer's fur collar, was that of 'Bonhomme Richard'. Franklin took the salons of Paris and Versailles by storm. His long silences were taken as deep thought and that made his every word the more valued.[23]

Franklin memorabilia proliferated even to the extent that began to annoy young Louis XVI, who commissioned his own piece of Frankliniana for a swooning courtier – a chamber pot with Franklin's face on the bottom of its inner surface.[24] As in London, Franklin was cultivating an image. This was one he acted out to the full, because he had a very serious purpose: to bring France into the war against Britain and to keep her there. In 1778 when the first was achieved, he wore a particular velvet coat to the treaty signing; when asked why, he said: 'To give it a little revenge. I wore this Coat on the day Wedderburn abused me at Whitehall.'[25] As to the second, he built an extraordinarily strong relationship with, for America, the most important man in the kingdom, the Foreign Minister, the Comte de

Vergennes, who provided the financial and military support that was crucial to the final outcome on the battlefield.

John Adams, whom Franklin found to be a difficult colleague in France – though one of the least dysfunctional of a group that in the first years included Arthur Lee – worried that Franklin would be given too much credit by posterity. Adams later wrote plaintively: 'The essence of the whole will be *that Dr Franklin's electric rod smote the earth and out sprang General Washington. Then Franklin electrified him, and thence forward those two conducted all the Policy, Negotiations, Legislations, and War.*'[26] Such a monopoly of fame is as ridiculous as Adams intended it to be. However, Washington and Franklin, in their different ways, were both essential for winning the war.[27]

Letters between Franklin and his friends and contacts in Britain had been maintained in 1775 and early 1776. He had heard from Polly that she had secured the bulk of her aunt's estate after a legal battle. As well as keeping in touch with Strahan, he corresponded with close friends such as Jonathan Shipley and Joseph Priestley, who felt able to send him the good wishes of Shelburne and Barré as late as February 1776. However, as the conflict between Britain and the colonies escalated into full-scale war the correspondence dwindled away as, from the British side, it was forbidden by law. Even the long position papers from David Hartley dried up after he believed they were no longer getting through; and some of Margaret Stevenson's missives did not surface until years later.[28] After Franklin arrived in Paris he received letters from, among others, Polly, Thomas Walpole and David Hartley – who also made a short visit cum peace parley. Intriguingly, Franklin surmised that Hartley arrived not at Rockingham's suggestion, but Shelburne's.

Once France entered the war, communication again became difficult. Letters between Hartley and Franklin were generally more official and about the exchange of prisoners. Georgiana Shipley, though, seemed to delight in ignoring the strictures, not only those of the authorities but ones from her own father, and she wrote a number of letters addressed to Franklin, in a very thin alias, as 'M. Francois'. She gave him family news together with snippets about Priestley and Price, who were great friends of the Shipleys as well as Franklin.

There were other better-disguised and more secret communications. It seems almost certain that Shelburne and Franklin were in secret contact during the war. This conclusion is based on more than the logic that Franklin would seek to covertly liaise with the man he had hoped would return to power earlier in the decade. It does not even relate to the fact that Shelburne, who could be awkward and waspish with his ministerial colleagues, had obviously got on well with Franklin both during his time in office and later in opposition; and with whom, in return, Franklin had enjoyed a closer and more promising relationship than with any other government minister. Nor is it due to the extraordinary number of people who linked them: for instance, Shelburne's brother Thomas Fitzmaurice, Price, Priestley, Jonathan Shipley (described as 'for many years [Shelburne's] close friend among the bishops'),[29] Benjamin Vaughan, and both the Abbé Morellet and Madame Helvétius, whom Shelburne had known since his trip to France in 1771. Nor, indeed, is it because of someone who often goes unnoticed, a Frenchman named Lewis Fevre, who worked as a clerk for Franklin in London from the spring of 1772 right up to March 1775 and then went to work for Shelburne as a 'confidential servant' for the next twenty years.[30]

It stems from a specific accusation by a Colonel William Fullarton on 20 March 1780. It was one that began in the Commons and continued by letter. The charge was that Shelburne had been 'in direct correspondence with the enemies of England',[31] and it was an accusation that Viscount Stormont sought to echo in the Lords the following month, when he spoke of 'treasonable correspondence.'[32]

It was clear that the principal of these 'enemies' was Franklin,[33] because Fullarton had been Secretary to the British Embassy in Paris between 1775 and 1778 and Stormont the Ambassador. Fullarton may have supported his accusation with the words, 'I heard it surmised by all Paris,'[34] but only because he and Stormont could not possibly have betrayed their real and extremely valuable source. In fact they had been the recipients of a vast number of documents from Dr Edward Bancroft, Franklin's close aide and the undetected British spy in the American camp.*[35] Employing a method still successfully used by the Secret Intelligence Service two centuries later, Bancroft repeatedly delivered quantities of documents to a hole in a tree, this one being on the south side of the Tuileries. The volume and quality of information was exceptional. So was the speed of its delivery, with its swiftness bringing great embarrassment to the British on the occasion that their protest to Vergennes about the contents of a highly secret memorandum from the American Commissioners arrived in advance of the document in question.[36]

Such was the seriousness of Fullarton's accusation that Shelburne issued a challenge. The resulting duel did not go as Shelburne planned as he received a flesh wound in the groin, after which, much to his annoyance, the seconds prevented any further firing. And so, although the mutterings were to continue, honour was deemed to have been satisfied, on this occasion at least.[37]

Official communication with Franklin was naturally restored when, on the North government's resignation, Shelburne returned as Secretary of State in the spring of 1782. Many compliments and happy remembrances of times past were exchanged at the renewal of their acquaintance. Shelburne and his Chathamite faction were at last in uneasy government coalition with the Rockinghams. The Marquess of Rockingham was Prime Minister and Charles James Fox, his leader in the Commons, was the other Secretary of State and nominally in charge of the peace negotiations. Fox's envoy, Thomas Grenville, was completely outmanoeuvred, because Richard Oswald, Shelburne's man, had been in place in Paris for three weeks and established as the channel of communication to Franklin before Grenville even arrived. Rockingham died in July and Shelburne, as the new Prime Minister, made Oswald's the sole negotiating mission. Franklin was to provide a final service to Britain.

The British were now tactically astute. Not only had the trust between Britain and her colonies broken down, but specifically that between Britain and Franklin. Shelburne and his advisers helped to re-establish it through the individuals whom they sent to Paris.

* He was not definitively unmasked until 1889.

Oswald had been recommended by Shelburne's close confidant, Benjamin Vaughan. Oswald was chosen as someone that Vaughan was sure Franklin would like: a Scottish merchant with a calm temperament and the same age as Franklin, a businessman who had spent many years in America and, finally, someone more interested in the future of Anglo-American trade than systems of government. This was a clever choice, and another one was extremely subtle: because, instead of opting for Richard Jackson, who was now not only a 'walking index' but a government minister,[38] they sent Caleb Whitefoord, Franklin's former Craven Street neighbour, friend and wine merchant, as a surprise visitor to Paris the day before Franklin's first meeting with Oswald. He smoothed the path and then acted as Secretary to the British mission for the duration.[39] Finally, Benjamin Vaughan himself, a devoted former school pupil of Priestley and the son of Franklin's fellow 'Honest Whig' Samuel Vaughan, also arrived after Shelburne became Prime Minister. All this was important because it was Franklin, rather than his fellow Peace Commissioners, John Jay who arrived in the summer and John Adams in October, who was the more pro-French in attitude. The importance of sending the friendly British faces to Franklin was that they started the talks and kept them going. In November the negotiations moved forward at speed with a final contribution from Henry Laurens, a fourth Commissioner and Vaughan's brother-in-law, before a Provisional Treaty was agreed on the final day of the month. It was for a separate provisional peace with Britain. Shelburne had hoped for some sort of political union with at least some of the States, but the far greater British priority was to secure Canada and the sugar-rich islands of the Caribbean. For that Britain agreed to sanction American independence. It was for Franklin to tell a shocked Vergennes what the Americans had done and to ask for, and amazingly receive, a fresh money grant to keep them going until the final peace was signed. Though Vergennes did declare that France had been 'poorly repaid for what we have done for the Unites States of America and for securing them their existence'.[40] Franklin's final, if reluctant, service to Britain had been to sell out the French.

As in 1763, the compromises required by the peace treaty brought howls of protest in Parliament, marshalled by the extraordinary new opposition led by Fox and North. It was enough to bring down Shelburne's government after a life of under a year. The formal Treaty of Paris, little different from the provisional version, was finally signed in September 1783. The major signatory for the new British government was David Hartley.

∝

The French as a whole did not blame Franklin. He became his new nation's first Ambassador to France and continued to be lauded. For instance, in 1783 Maximilien Robespierre, then a provincial lawyer, wrote the great scientist what is best described as a fan letter. Robespierre and Jean-Paul Marat were opposing advocates in a case to decide whether lightning conductors should be allowed in the province of Artois, and Robespierre sent Franklin the printed version of his successful oration. In his accompanying letter he described Franklin as someone 'whose least merit is to be the most illustrious and wisest man in the universe'.[41] In the same spirit, the French Assembly wore mourning for three days when he died in 1790; whereas, in contrast, though the US House of Representatives voted to wear mourning for a month, the proposal was defeated without compromise by the Senate.[42]

In 1785 Franklin and his two grandsons left for America. Stopping briefly at Southampton, he was delighted that the Shipleys and Benjamin Vaughan had travelled down to see him. Less so to meet his son William, who had suffered ill treatment as a loyalist and whom Ben had done nothing to help. It was a short business meeting, where William, having little choice, sold his New Jersey lands to Temple for a pittance and in return accepted the largely worthless stake in Nova Scotia. Ben and William Franklin never saw each other again.

Franklin would have liked to spend some time in England, but he realized that might be difficult. As he wrote to Polly in January 1783, soon after the Provisional Treaty, he thought that as far as England was concerned it would be best 'not to come too soon, lest it should seem braving & insulting'. His letter was a reply to one he had just received with the news that Polly's mother had died. Franklin wrote that 'The Departure of my dearest Friend, which I learn from your last Letter, greatly affects me. To meet with her once more in this Life, was one of the principal Motives of my proposing to visit England again before my Return to America.'[43] He had greatly missed Mrs Stevenson in France, particularly as a landlady turned household manager, telling her in 1779, 'I have nothing to complain of but a little too much Business, & the Want of that Order and Economy in my Family that reigned in it when under your prudent Direction.'[44]

Margaret Stevenson's death was another to follow those of Fothergill, Pringle, Kames and Le Despencer. Franklin sought to cheer himself by issuing an invitation to Polly. He wrote: 'Spring is coming on, when Travelling will be delightful. Can you not, when your Children are all at School, make a little Party, and take a Trip hither? I have now a large House delightfully situated, in which I could accommodate you & two or three Friends; and I am but half an Hours Drive from Paris.'[45] She did not come then, but she did, and with her family, for the whole of the following winter.[46] In 1786 Polly and family moved to Philadelphia and she would be at Franklin's bedside along with Sally, Franklin's actual daughter, when he died in 1790.

Franklin's home was Philadelphia and could not be Vandalia. Wharton's dawdling in the bid to squeeze out more sales had been crucial. The Law Officers, Thurlow and Wedderburn, had finally produced a Draft of the Charter on May Day 1775, but there could be no further progress until the troubles with America were over. By then it was too late, because under America's new political settlement the State of Virginia blocked the grant of an area to their west broadly equivalent to modern West Virginia. Returning to Philadelphia in 1785, Franklin received a hero's welcome and took on the role of first citizen in a Pennsylvania now purged of the Penns, though the former Proprietors had received some, albeit small, compensation for their lands.[47]

∞

Shelburne had made a good peace with Franklin and his fellow Americans in Paris. The commerce between Britain and America not only quickly recovered but its volume was soon far greater than pre-war levels, with the value of British exports to North America in 1797–8 more than double that of 1772–3.[48] Franklin's dream of a great British and American trading empire was still alive, albeit now it would be between two separate nations. Although even then, as Andrew O'Shaughnessy has noted, 'British influence remained so pervasive that Thomas Jefferson and the Republican Party feared that the United States might become a client state of Britain.'[49] Franklin had previously and secretly revealed a different vision. Even after the War of Independence, he still retained a small part of his dream of a British American confederation. It was, however, the American-centred one that Dean Josiah Tucker had suspected.

In 1784 Franklin half-jokingly mentioned the idea in a letter to his old friend Strahan, and it was expressed with the heavy caveat of 'You will say my *Advice* smells of *Madeira*. You are right. This foolish Letter is mere Chit-chat *between ourselves*, over the *second* Bottle.' Franklin instructed Strahan to keep the rumination to himself and two named close friends – at last he was acknowledging the dangers of careless correspondence. His idea was this: 'You have still one Resource left, and that not a bad one since it may re-unite the Empire. We have some Remains of Affection for you, and shall always be ready to receive and take care of you in case of Distress. So, if you have not Sense and Virtue enough left to govern yourselves, even dissolve your present old crazy Constitution, *and send Members to Congress*.'[50]

SELECTED LIST OF PLACES TO VISIT
AND RELATED ORGANIZATIONS

Details are relevant at the time of writing. Readers are advised to consult the relevant websites.

In London and Britain

Benjamin Franklin House at 36 Craven Street, just off London's Strand and close to Trafalgar Square, is a heritage 'gem'. It was Franklin's home in London between 1757–1762 and again between 1764–1775. Furthermore, it is his only surviving home in Britain or America still in existence. First opened to the public in January 2006, to celebrate the 300th anniversary of Franklin's birth, it is a dynamic museum and educational facility. Its exceptional charm lies in its dramatic reconstruction of Franklin's life in London in the context of the house in which he lived. www.benjaminfranklinhouse.org. The House's website also includes a 'Franklin Trail', with information about Dr Franklin's connections with historic sites and institutions both within London and further afield in Britain and Ireland. http://www.benjaminfranklinhouse.org/site/sections/about_franklin/trail.htm

Some of the 'Franklin Trails' current featured sites are:

Soho House, the Georgian home of Franklin's industrialist friend, Matthew Boulton, and regular meeting place of the Lunar Society. http://www.birmingham museums.org.uk/soho/visit

West Wycombe, the Palladian home of Franklin's notorious friend, Francis Dashwood, Lord Le Despencer. It was here that Franklin had his 'silent' encounter with Lord North. It is a National Trust property open in the summer months. http://www.nationaltrust.org.uk/west-wycombe-park-village-and-hill/visitor-information/

Hillsborough Castle is where Franklin stayed with Wills Hill, Lord Hillsborough in 1771 and when he 'was offered a thousand civilities' by a man who became an inveterate enemy. Though it is now the official royal residence in Northern Ireland, it is open to the public. http://www.hrp.org.uk/HillsboroughCastle/history-and-stories

London Historians was launched in 2010 as a club for Londoners who'd like to learn more about their city's history. It organizes visits, talks, walks, social events and discounts to selected historical attractions and exhibitions. It is well linked to local history groups around the capital. It has a rapidly expanding membership and tens of thousands of followers on social media. www.london historians.org

The William Shipley Group is an independent body dedicated to extending knowledge about the history of the Royal Society for the encouragement of Arts, Manufactures and Commerce (RSA). Benjamin Franklin was an active early member and then Committee Chairman. http://williamshipleygroup. btck.co.uk/

In Philadelphia

The Independence National Historical Park, part of the National Park Service, covers almost 54 acres in Philadelphia's Old City, and includes Independence Hall (a Unesco World Heritage Site), the Liberty Bell, Congress Hall, Franklin Court, and other historic buildings associated with the founding of the United States. http://www.nps.gov/inde/learn/news/index.htm

Independence Hall: Built between 1732 and the 1750s to be the Pennsylvania State House, the building originally housed all three branches of Pennsylvania's colonial government. Its Assembly Room was where the Second Continental Congress and, later, the Constitutional Convention met – and where The Declaration of Independence and US Constitution were signed by Franklin. http://www.nps.gov/inde/learn/historyculture/places-independencehall.htm

Franklin Court contains Robert Venturi's steel 'ghost structure' outlining the spot where Franklin's house stood and features the Benjamin Franklin Museum, a new museum that explores Franklin's life and character through artifacts, animations, and hands-on interactives. The Franklin Court complex also includes a working reproduction of an 18th century printing office, an architectural / archaeological exhibit, and an operating post office. http://www.nps.gov/inde/planyourvisit/benjaminfranklinmuseum.htm

The Historical Society of Pennsylvania is one of the oldest historical institutions in the United States and covers 350 years of American history. It is home to some 600,000 printed items and more than 21 million manuscript and graphic items. As well as containing a great number of documents relating to Benjamin and William Franklin, it houses the Penn family papers. http://hsp.org/

The American Philosophical Society is the oldest learned society in the United States, and was founded in 1743 by Benjamin Franklin for the purpose of 'promoting useful knowledge'. They have a total of over 4,000 books and documents relating to Benjamin Franklin, including the largest collection of Franklin's letters. http://www.amphilsoc.org/

The Library Company of Philadelphia is America's first successful public lending library and oldest cultural institution. It was founded in 1731 by Benjamin Franklin as a subscription library supported by its shareholders, as it is to this day. It houses over half a million rare books, manuscripts, pamphlets, broadsides, prints, and photographs relating to early American history. http://www.librarycompany.org/

The Franklin Institute was founded in 1824, in honour of Benjamin Franklin. In 1934, the Institute, with the help of the Poor Richard Club, built a science museum and planetarium as 'A Living Memorial' to Franklin, on Benjamin Franklin Parkway. Today, the Institute continues its dedication to public education and creating a passion for science by offering new and exciting access to science and technology. https://www.fi.edu/

University of Pennsylvania: Benjamin Franklin was the first president of the trustees of the Academy of Philadelphia that was later to become the University of Pennsylvania. The University has a welcome page for visitors, giving details of the museums, galleries and facilities open to the public. http://www.upenn.edu/highlights/visitors

Christ Church http://www.christchurchphila.org/Historic-Christ-Church/Church/Church-History-and-Those-Who-Attended/86/ was attended by members of the extended Franklin family and the Christ Church Burial Ground http://www.christchurchphila.org/Historic-Christ-Church/Burial-Ground/59/ is where they were interred.

BIBLIOGRAPHY

Pre-eminent Primary Sources for Benjamin Franklin

Leonard Woods Labaree, Ellen R. Cohn et al. 1960 onwards. *The Papers of Benjamin Franklin*. New Haven: Yale University Press. The essential resource for studying Benjamin Franklin now stands at forty-one published volumes of a projected forty-seven. The latest (published in 2014) takes Franklin's life up to 29 February 1784. The founding editor was Leonard Woods Labaree; the current editor is Ellen R. Cohn. Further information at http://franklinpapers.yale.edu.

   A digital version of the Franklin Papers, created and maintained by the Packard Humanities Institute, is available at http://franklinpapers.org. Fully searchable, though without the headnotes and footnotes of the published printed volumes, it is a useful companion to them.

Franklin, Benjamin. 2012. *Benjamin Franklin's Autobiography: An Authoritative Text, Contexts, Criticism*. Edited by Joyce E. Chaplin. A Norton Critical Edition. New York: W.W. Norton.

Other Primary Sources

Adams, Abigail. 1840. *Letters of Mrs Adams, the Wife of John Adams*. Edited by Charles Francis Adams. Boston: C.C. Little and J. Brown.

Adams, John. 1851. *The Works of John Adams, Second President of the United States*. Edited by Charles Francis Adams. Boston: Little, Brown.

Adams, John, Benjamin Rush and Julia Stockton Rush. 1892. *Old Family Letters*. Edited by Alexander Biddle. Philadelphia: Lipincott.

Almon, John. 1797. *Biographical, Literary, and Political Anecdotes, of Several of the Most Eminent Persons of the Present Age*. London: T.N. Longman and L.B. Seeley.

Banks, Joseph. 1963. *The Endeavour Journal of Joseph Banks, 1768–1771*. Edited by J.C. Beaglehole. Sydney: Angus & Robertson.

Boswell, James. 1956. *Boswell in Search of a Wife, 1766–1769*. Edited by Frank Brady and Frederick A. Pottle. New York: McGraw-Hill.

Burke, Edmund. 1922. *Letters of Edmund Burke: A Selection*. Edited by Harold Joseph Laski. World's Classics 237. London: Oxford University Press.

Chesterfield, Philip Dormer Stanhope. 1992. *Letters*. Edited by David Roberts. Oxford: Oxford University Press.

Cobbett, William. 1806. *The Parliamentary History of England from the Earliest Period to the Year 1803*. Edited by T.C. Hansard and J. Wright. London: printed by T.C. Hansard for Longman [et al.].

Defoe, Daniel. 1726. *The Political History of the Devil*. London: printed for T. Warner.

——. 1727. *The Complete English Tradesman: In Familiar Letters: Directing Him in All the Several Parts and Progressions of Trade*. London: printed for Charles Rivington.

——. 1962. *A Tour Through the Whole Island of Great Britain*. Everyman's Library. London; New York: Dent; Dutton.

Dickinson, John. 1764. *A Speech, Delivered in the House of Assembly of the Province of Pennsylvania, May 24th, 1764*. Philadelphia: printed and sold by William Bradford.

Fitzmaurice, Edmond George Petty. 1912. *Life of William Earl of Shelburne*. Vols I–II. London: Macmillan.

Fothergill, John. 1770. *Some Account of the Late Peter Collinson, Fellow of the Royal Society... in a Letter to a Friend*. London: private publication.

——. 1783. *The Works of John Fothergill*. Edited by John Coakley-Lettsom. London: printed for Charles Dilly.

——. 1971. *Chain of Friendship: Selected Letters of Dr John Fothergill of London, 1735–1780*. Edited by Betsy C. Corner and Christopher C. Booth. Cambridge, Mass.: Belknap Press of Harvard University Press.

Franklin, Benjamin. 1751. 'A Letter of Benjamin Franklin, Esq; to Mr. Peter Collinson, F.R.S. Concerning an Electrical Kite'. *Philosophical Transactions (1683–1775)* Vol. XLVII (January), pp. 565–7.

——. 1836–42. *The Works of Benjamin Franklin*. Edited by Jared Sparks. Boston: Hilliard, Gray and Company.

——. 1931. 'Account Book of Benjamin Franklin Kept by Him during His First Mission to England as Provincial Agent, 1757–1762'. Edited by George Simpson Eddy. *The Pennsylvania Magazine of History and Biography* Vol. LV (No. 2), pp. 97–133.

——. 1950. *Benjamin Franklin's Letters to the Press, 1758-1775*. Collected and edited by Verner W. Crane. Chapel Hill: University of North Carolina Press.

Franklin, William. 1911. 'Letters from William Franklin to William Strahan'. Edited by Charles Henry Hart. *The Pennsylvania Magazine of History and Biography* Vol. XXXV (No. 4), pp. 415–62.

Gage, Thomas. 1931. *The Correspondence of General Thomas Gage with the Secretaries of State, 1763–1775*. Compiled and edited by Clarence Edwin Carter. New Haven; London: Yale University Press; H. Milford, Oxford University Press.

Glasse, Hannah. 1774. *The Art of Cookery, Made Plain and Easy. By a Lady*. London: printed for W. Strahan et al.

Grafton, Augustus Henry FitzRoy. 1898. *Autobiography and Political Correspondence of Augustus Henry, Third Duke of Grafton, K.G.* Edited by William Reynell Anson. London: J. Murray.

Hayes, Kevin J. and Isabelle Bour (eds). 2011. *Franklin in His Own Time: A Biographical Chronicle of His Life, Drawn from Recollections, Interviews, and Memoirs by Family, Friends, and Associates.* Iowa City: University of Iowa Press.

Hewson, William. 1846. *The Works of William Hewson, F.R.S.* Edited by George Gulliver. London: printed for the Sydenham Society.

Johnson, Samuel. 1755. *A Dictionary of the English Language.* London: printed by W. Strahan.

Kalm, Pehr. 1892. *Kalm's Account of His Visit to England on His Way to America in 1748.* Translated by Joseph Lucas. London: Macmillan.

Kant, Immanuel. 1900. *Gesammelte Schriften.* Berlin: Georg Reimer.

Lichtenberg, Georg Christoph. 1938. *Lichtenberg's Visits to England: As Described in His Letters and Diaries.* Translated and annotated by Margaret Laura Mare and W.H. Quarrell. Oxford Studies in Modern Languages and Literature. Oxford: Clarendon Press.

Misson, Henri. 1719. *M. Misson's Memoirs and Observations in His Travels over England. With Some Account of Scotland and Ireland.* London: printed for D. Browne et al.

Morley, Henry. 1891. *The Spectator: Reproducing the Original Text.* London: George Routledge and Sons.

Northumberland, Elizabeth Seymour Percy. 1926. *The Diaries of a Duchess: Extracts from the Diaries of the First Duchess of Northumberland (1716–1776).* Edited by James Greig. London: Hodder and Stoughton.

'Old Bailey Online – The Proceedings of the Old Bailey, 1674–1913 – Central Criminal Court'. 2015. Accessed 7 July. http://www.oldbaileyonline.org/

Parliament. 1775. *The Parliamentary Register*: Vol. I, *House of Commons 1775.* London: printed for J. Almon.

——. 1775. *The Parliamentary Register*: Vol. II, *House of Lords 1775.* London: printed for J. Almon.

'Penn Family Papers, 1629–1834'. Collection 485. The Historical Society of Pennsylvania.

Petty-Fitzmaurice Family. 'The Bowood Papers'. Add MS 88906. Western Manuscripts. British Library.

Priestley, Joseph. 1809. *Memoirs of the Rev. Dr Joseph Priestley: To the Year 1795.* London: sold by Joseph Johnson.

Privy Council of England. 1908. *Acts of the Privy Council of England: Colonial Series.* Edited by William Lawson Grant, James Munro and Almeric William Fitzroy. Hereford: printed for HMSO by Anthony Brothers.

'Privy Council: Registers, George III'. 1540. Volumes, bundles and papers. PC 2. The National Archives, Kew.

Quincy, Josiah. 1825. *Memoir of the Life of Josiah Quincy, Jun. of Massachusetts*. Boston: Cummings, Hilliard.

Quincy Jr, Josiah. 1916. 'English Journal 1774–5'. *Proceedings of the Massachusetts Historical Society* Vol. L (October), pp. 433–98.

Ralph, James. 1728. *The Touch-Stone . . . By a Person of Some Taste and Some Quality*. London: printed and sold by the booksellers of London and Westminster.

Saussure, César de. 1902. *A Foreign View of England in the Reigns of George I & George II*. Edited and translated by Madame Van Muyden. London: J. Murray.

Stifler, James Madison. 1927. *'My Dear Girl': The Correspondence of Benjamin Franklin with Polly Stevenson, Georgiana and Catherine Shipley*. New York: George H. Doran.

Strahan, William and David Hall. 1886–8 and 1936–7. 'Correspondence between William Strahan and David Hall, 1763–1777. From the Originals in the Possession of the Historical Society of Pennsylvania'. *The Pennsylvania Magazine of History and Biography*. Philadelphia.

Sydenham, Thomas. 1788. *The Works of Thomas Sydenham, M.D.* Edited by George Wallis. London: G.G.J. and J. Robinson etc.

The Gentleman's Magazine (and Historical Chronicle). 1731–1907. London.

The Scots Magazine. 1790. Edinburgh: Sands, Brymer, Murray and Cochran.

Walpole, Horace. 1840. *Letters*. Edited by John Wright. London: R. Bentley.

——. 1848. *Letters Addressed to the Countess of Ossory, from the Year 1769 to 1797*. Edited by Robert Vernon Smith. London: R. Bentley.

Secondary Sources

Acworth, Margaretta. 1987. *Margaretta Acworth's Georgian Cookery Book*. Edited by Alice Prochaska and F.K. Prochaska. London: Pavilion.

Allan, D.G.C. 2000. '"Dear and Serviceable to Each Other": Benjamin Franklin and the Royal Society of Arts'. *Proceedings of the American Philosophical Society* Vol. CXLIV (No. 3), pp. 245–66.

Alvord, Clarence Walworth. 1959. *The Mississippi Valley in British Politics: A Study of the Trade, Land Speculation and Experiments in Imperialism Culminating in the American Revolution*. New York: Russell & Russell.

Anderson, Fred. 2001. *Crucible of War: The Seven Years' War and the Fate of Empire in British North America, 1754–1766*. London: Faber.

Ayling, Stanley. 1976. *The Elder Pitt, Earl of Chatham*. London: Collins.

Bailyn, Bernard. 1975. *The Ordeal of Thomas Hutchinson*. London: Allen Lane.

——. 1992. *The Ideological Origins of the American Revolution*. Cambridge, Mass.; London: Belknap Press of Harvard University Press.

——. 2003. *To Begin the World Anew: The Genius and Ambiguities of the American Founders*. New York: Knopf.

Barnett, Richard. 2012. 'Bitter Medicine: Gout and the Birth of the Cocktail'. *The Lancet* Vol. CCCLXXIX (Issue 9824), pp. 1384–5.

Black, Jeremy. 2001. *Eighteenth-Century Britain, 1688–1783*. Basingstoke: Palgrave.

——. 2006. *George III: America's Last King*. New Haven; London: Yale University Press.

——. 2011. *Debating Foreign Policy in Eighteenth-Century Britain*. Farnham: Ashgate.

Bloore, Stephen. 1930. 'Samuel Keimer'. *The Pennsylvania Magazine of History and Biography* Vol. LIV (No. 3), pp. 255–87.

Borman, Tracy. 2007. *Henrietta Howard: King's Mistress, Queen's Servant*. London: Jonathan Cape.

Boudreau, George W. 2011. 'The Philadelphia Years 1723–1757'. In *A Companion to Benjamin Franklin*, edited by David Waldstreicher. Blackwell Companions to American History. Oxford: Wiley-Blackwell.

——. 2012. *Independence: A Guide to Historic Philadelphia*. Yardley, Pa: Westholme.

Brands, H.W. 2002. *The First American: The Life and Times of Benjamin Franklin*. New York: Anchor Books.

Brears, Peter C.D. 2009. *Traditional Food in Shropshire*. Ludlow: Excellent Press.

Brett-James, Norman G. 1925. *The Life of Peter Collinson*. London: E.G. Dunstan & Co.

Brigham, Clarence Saunders. 1932. 'March Meeting. James Franklin and the Beginnings of Printing in Rhode Island'. *Proceedings of the Massachusetts Historical Society*, 3rd Series, Vol. LXV (October), pp. 535–44.

Brown, Peter Douglas. 1967. *The Chathamites*. London; Melbourne; New York: Macmillan; St Martin's Press.

Burnett, John. 1999. *Liquid Pleasures: A Social History of Drinks in Modern Britain*. London: Routledge.

Cantwell, Dick. 2012. 'Barley Wine'. In *The Oxford Companion to Beer*, edited by Garrett Oliver. New York: Oxford University Press.

Carp, Benjamin L. 2011. *Defiance of the Patriots: The Boston Tea Party & the Making of America*. New Haven; London: Yale University Press.

Chaplin, Joyce E. 2006. *The First Scientific American: Benjamin Franklin and the Pursuit of Genius*. New York: Basic Books.

Chin, T. and P.D. Welsby. 2004. 'Malaria in the UK: Past, Present and Future'. *Postgraduate Medical Journal*, March.

Christie, Ian. 1990. 'The Changing Nature of Parliamentary Politics 1742–1789'. In *British Politics and Society from Walpole to Pitt 1742–1789*, edited by Jeremy Black. Basingstoke: Macmillan.

Cochrane, James Aikman. 1964. *Dr Johnson's Printer: The Life of William Strahan*. London: Routledge & Kegan Paul.

Colley, Linda. 2003. *Britons: Forging the Nation, 1707–1837*. London: Pimlico.

Cookson, Brian. 2010. 'The Story of Old London Bridge'. *London Historians*, October.

Cowan, Brian. 2004. 'Mr Spectator and the Coffeehouse Public Sphere'. *Eighteenth-Century Studies* Vol. XXXVII (No. 3), pp. 345–66.

Cowell, Pattie. 2001. '"Much Depends Upon My Knowing": The Education of Polly Hewson'. In *Finding Colonial Americas: Essays Honoring J.A. Leo Lemay*, edited by Carla Mulford and David S. Shields. Newark, Del.; London: University of Delaware Press; Associated University Presses.

Crane, Verner W. 1954. *Benjamin Franklin and a Rising People*. The Library of American Biography. Boston: Little, Brown.

——. 1966. 'The Club of Honest Whigs: Friends of Science and Liberty'. *The William and Mary Quarterly*, 3rd Series, Vol. XXIII (No. 2), pp. 210–33.

Cummings, Hubertis Maurice. 1944. *Richard Peters, Provincial Secretary and Cleric, 1704–1776*. Pennsylvania Lives. Philadelphia: University of Pennsylvania Press.

Day, Ivan. 2000. *Eat, Drink, & Be Merry: The British at Table, 1600–2000*. London; Wappingers' Falls, NY: Philip Wilson Publishers.

Dobson, Mary J. 1997. *Contours of Death and Disease in Early Modern England*. Cambridge: Cambridge University Press.

Dull, Jonathan R. 2010. *Benjamin Franklin and the American Revolution*. Lincoln: University of Nebraska Press.

——. 2011. 'Franklin Furioso, 1775–1790'. In *A Companion to Benjamin Franklin*, edited by David Waldstreicher. Oxford: Wiley-Blackwell.

Eliot, Thomas D. 1924. 'The Relations between Adam Smith and Benjamin Franklin before 1776'. *Political Science Quarterly* Vol. XXXIX (No. 1), pp. 67–96.

Ellis, Markman. 2004. *The Coffee-House: A Cultural History*. London: Weidenfeld & Nicolson.

Finger, Stanley and Ian S. Hagemann. 2008. 'Benjamin Franklin's Risk Factors for Gout and Stones: From Genes and Diet to Possible Lead Poisoning'. *Proceedings of the American Philosophical Society* Vol. CLII (No. 2), pp. 189–206.

Flavell, Julie. 2010. *When London Was Capital of America*. New Haven; London: Yale University Press.

Frasca, Ralph. 2006. *Benjamin Franklin's Printing Network: Disseminating Virtue in Early America*. Columbia, Mo: University of Missouri Press.

——. 2006. 'The Emergence of the American Colonial Press'. *Pennsylvania Legacies* Vol. VI (No. 1), pp. 11–15.

Gallacher, Stuart A. 1949. 'Franklin's "Way to Wealth": A Florilegium of Proverbs and Wise Sayings'. *The Journal of English and Germanic Philology* Vol. XLVIII (No. 2), pp. 229–51.

Gardner-Medwin, David, Anne Hargreaves and Elizabeth Lazenby (eds). 1993. *Medicine in Northumbria: Essays on the History of Medicine in the North East of England*. Newcastle upon Tyne: Pybus Society for the History and Bibliography of Medicine.

Garraty, John A. and Mark C. Carnes, American Council of Learned Societies (eds). 1999. *American National Biography*. New York: Oxford University Press.

Geiter, Mary K. 2000. *William Penn*. Harlow: Longman.

George, M. Dorothy. 1996. *London Life in the Eighteenth Century*. London: Routledge/Thoemmes Press.

Gleason, J. Philip. 1961. 'A Scurrilous Colonial Election and Franklin's Reputation'. *The William and Mary Quarterly*, 3rd Series, Vol. XVIII (No. 1), p. 70.

Green, James N. and Peter Stallybrass. 2006. *Benjamin Franklin: Writer and Printer*. New Castle, Del: Oak Knoll Press.

Greene, Jack P. 2013. *Evaluating Empire and Confronting Colonialism in Eighteenth-Century Britain*. Cambridge: Cambridge University Press.

Greig, Hannah. 2013. *The Beau Monde: Fashionable Society in Georgian London*. Oxford: Oxford University Press.

Grimm, Dorothy F. 1956. 'Franklin's Scientific Institution'. *Pennsylvania History: A Journal of Mid-Atlantic Studies* Vol. XXIII (No. 4), pp. 437–62.

Guttridge, G.H. 1966. *English Whiggism and the American Revolution*. Berkeley, CA: University of California Press.

Hague, William. 2004. *William Pitt the Younger*. London: HarperCollins.

Hancock, David. 1995. *Citizens of the World: London Merchants and the Integration of the British Atlantic Community, 1735–1785*. Cambridge: Cambridge University Press.

Hanna, William S. 1964. *Benjamin Franklin and Pennsylvania Politics*. Stanford: Stanford University Press.

Hay, Douglas. 1982. 'War, Dearth and Theft in the Eighteenth Century: The Record of the English Courts'. *Past & Present* Vol. XCV, pp. 117–60.

Heilbron, J.L. 1979. *Electricity in the 17th and 18th Centuries: A Study of Early Modern Physics*. Berkeley; London: University of California Press.

——. 2007. 'Benjamin Franklin in Europe: Electrician, Academician, Politician'. *Notes and Records of the Royal Society of London* Vol. LXI (No. 3), pp. 353–73.

Home, R.W. 2009. 'Points or Knobs: Lightning Rods and the Basis of Decision Making in Late Eighteenth Century British Science'. *Transactions of the American Philosophical Society*, New Series Vol. XCIX (No. 5), pp. 97–120.

Huang, Nian-Sheng. 1994. *Benjamin Franklin in American Thought and Culture, 1790–1990*. Philadelphia: American Philosophical Society.

Humphreys, R.A. 1934. 'Lord Shelburne and the Proclamation of 1763'. *The English Historical Review* Vol. XLIX (No. 194), pp. 241–64.

Hutson, James H. 1969. 'Benjamin Franklin and William Smith: More Light on an

Old Philadelphia Quarrel'. *The Pennsylvania Magazine of History and Biography* Vol. XCIII (No. 1), pp. 109–13.

——. 1970. 'The Campaign to Make Pennsylvania a Royal Province, 1764–1770', Part I. *The Pennsylvania Magazine of History and Biography* Vol. XCIV (No. 4), pp. 427–63.

——. 1971. 'The Campaign to Make Pennsylvania a Royal Province, 1764–1770', Part II. *The Pennsylvania Magazine of History and Biography* Vol. XCV (No. 1), pp. 28–49.

——. 1972. *Pennsylvania Politics, 1746–1770: The Movement for Royal Government and Its Consequences*. Princeton: Princeton University Press.

Inglis, Lucy. 2013. *Georgian London: Into the Streets*. London: Viking.

Isaacson, Walter. 2004. *Benjamin Franklin: An American Life*. New York; London; Toronto: Simon & Schuster paperbacks.

Jarrett, Derek. 1973. *The Begetters of Revolution: England's Involvement with France, 1759–1789*. London: Longman.

Jenkins, Simon. 2003. *England's Thousand Best Houses*. London: Allen Lane.

Jennings, Francis. 1964. 'Thomas Penn's Loyalty Oath'. *The American Journal of Legal History* Vol. VIII (No. 4), pp. 303–13.

Johnson, Allen S. 1997. *A Prologue to Revolution: The Political Career of George Grenville (1712–1770)*. Lanham, Md: University Press of America.

Jones, R.V. 1977. 'Benjamin Franklin'. *Notes and Records of the Royal Society of London* Vol. XXXI (No. 2), pp. 201–25.

Kammen, Michael G. 1968. *A Rope of Sand: The Colonial Agents, British Politics, and the American Revolution*. Ithaca, NY: Cornell University Press.

Keane, John. 1995. *Tom Paine: A Political Life*. London: Bloomsbury.

Kenny, Robert W. 1940. 'James Ralph: An Eighteenth-Century Philadelphian in Grub Street'. *The Pennsylvania Magazine of History and Biography* Vol. LXIV (No. 2), pp. 218–42.

Ketcham, Ralph L. 1964. 'Benjamin Franklin and William Smith: New Light on an Old Philadelphia Quarrel'. *The Pennsylvania Magazine of History and Biography* Vol. LXXXVIII (No. 2), pp. 142–63.

Langford, Paul. 1991. *Public Life and the Propertied Englishman 1689–1798*. Oxford: Clarendon Press.

Lea, Elizabeth E. and William Woys Weaver. 2004. *A Quaker Woman's Cookbook: The Domestic Cookery of Elizabeth Ellicott Lea*. Mechanicsburg, Pa: Stackpole Books.

Lee, Richard Henry. 1829. *Life of Arthur Lee*. Boston: Wells and Lilly.

Lemay, J.A. Leo. 2006. *The Life of Benjamin Franklin*. 3 vols. Philadelphia: University of Pennsylvania Press.

Lepore, Jill. 2013. *Book of Ages: The Life and Opinions of Jane Franklin*. New York: Knopf.

Lewis, Janette Seaton. 1978. '"A Turn of Thinking": The Long Shadow of the *Spectator* on Franklin's "Autobiography".' *Early American Literature* Vol. XIII (No. 3), pp. 268–77.

Lopez, Claude-Anne. 1990. *Mon Cher Papa: Franklin and the Ladies of Paris*. New Haven; London: Yale University Press.

——. 2000. 'Three Women, Three Styles'. In *Benjamin Franklin and Women*, edited by Larry Edward Tise. University Park, Pa: Pennsylvania State University Press.

Lopez, Claude-Anne, and Eugenia W. Herbert. 1975. *The Private Franklin: The Man and His Family*. New York: Norton.

Lynch, Jack. 2003 'Wilkes, Liberty, and Number 45'. *Colonial Williamsburg Journal* http://www.history.org/Foundation/journal/summer03/wilkes.cfm.

MacArthur, W. 1951. 'A Brief Story of English Malaria'. *British Medical Bulletin* Vol. VIII, pp. 76–9.

McCusker, John J., and Russell R. Menard. 1985. *The Economy of British America, 1607–1789*. Chapel Hill: University of North Carolina Press.

Middlekauff, Robert. 1996. *Benjamin Franklin and His Enemies*. Berkeley; London: University of California Press.

Millburn, John R., and Henry C. King. 1988. *Wheelwright of the Heavens: The Life & Work of James Ferguson, FRS*. London: Vade-Mecum.

Miller, C.J. William. 1961. 'Franklin's "Poor Richard Almanacs": Their Printing and Publication'. *Studies in Bibliography* Vol. XIV (January), pp. 97–115.

Mitchell, B. R. 2011. *British Historical Statistics*. Cambridge: Cambridge University Press.

Morgan, Edmund S. 2002. *Benjamin Franklin*. New Haven; London: Yale University Press.

Morgan, Edmund S., and Helen M. Morgan. 1953. *The Stamp Act Crisis: Prologue to Revolution*. Chapel Hill: University of North Carolina Press.

Morgan, Kenneth. 2000. 'Business Networks in the British Export Trade to North America, 1750–1800'. In *The Early Modern Atlantic Economy*, edited by John J. McCusker and Kenneth Morgan. Cambridge: Cambridge University Press.

Mulford, Carla. 1999. 'Figuring Benjamin Franklin in American Cultural Memory'. *The New England Quarterly* Vol. LXXII (No. 3), pp. 415–43.

Namier, L.B., and John Brooke. 1964. *Charles Townshend*. London: Macmillan.

——. 1964. *The History of Parliament: The House of Commons 1754–1790*. London: HMSO for the History of Parliament Trust.

Newman, Simon P. 2012. 'Benjamin Franklin and the Leather-Apron Men: The Politics of Class in Eighteenth-Century Philadelphia'. In *Benjamin Franklin's Intellectual World*, edited by Paul E. Kerry and Matthew Scott Holland. Madison, NJ; Lanham, Md: Fairleigh Dickinson University Press; co-published with Rowman & Littlefield Pub. Group.

Nolan, James Bennett. 1938. *Benjamin Franklin in Scotland and Ireland, 1759 and*

1771. Philadelphia; London: University of Pennsylvania Press; H. Milford, Oxford University Press.

O'Shaughnessy, Andrew Jackson. 2000. *An Empire Divided: The American Revolution and the British Caribbean*. Philadelphia: University of Pennsylvania Press.

——. 2004. '"If Others Will Not Be Active, I Must Drive": George III and the American Revolution'. *Early American Studies* Vol. II (No. 1), pp. 1–47.

——. 2014. *The Men Who Lost America: British Command During the Revolutionary War and the Preservation of the Empire*. New Haven; London: Yale University Press; Oneworld.

Oxford Dictionary of National Biography http://www.oxforddnb.com/. Almost 60,000 British lives online.

Paston-Williams, Sara. 1993. *The Art of Dining: A History of Cooking & Eating*. London: National Trust.

Pearce, Edward. 2010. *Pitt the Elder: Man of War*. London: Bodley Head.

Pearl, Christopher. 2012. 'Franklin's Turn: Imperial Politics and the Coming of the American Revolution'. *The Pennsylvania Magazine of History and Biography* Vol. CXXXVI (No. 2), pp. 117–39.

Pencak, William. 1992. 'Politics and Ideology in *Poor Richard's Almanac*'. *The Pennsylvania Magazine of History and Biography* Vol. CXVI (No. 2), pp. 183–211.

Picard, Liza. 2000. *Dr Johnson's London: Life in London, 1740–1770*. London: Weidenfeld & Nicolson.

Pincus, Steve. 2012. 'Rethinking Mercantilism: Political Economy, the British Empire, and the Atlantic World in the Seventeenth and Eighteenth Centuries'. *The William and Mary Quarterly* Vol. LXIX (No. 1), pp. 3–34.

Porter, Roy. 2003. 'The Wonderful Extent and Variety of London'. In *London 1753*, edited by Sheila O'Connell. London: British Museum Press.

Potts, Louis W. 1981. *Arthur Lee: A Virtuous Revolutionary*. Baton Rouge: Louisiana State University Press.

Purvis, Thomas L. 1999. *Colonial America to 1763*. Almanacs of American Life. New York: Facts on File.

Quinlan, Maurice J. 1949. 'Dr Franklin Meets Dr Johnson'. *The Pennsylvania Magazine of History and Biography* Vol. LXXIII (No. 1), pp. 34–44.

Rakov, Vladimir A. and Martin A. Uman. 2003. *Lightning: Physics and Effects*. Cambridge: Cambridge University Press.

Reid, John Phillip. 1986. *Constitutional History of the American Revolution*. Madison: University of Wisconsin Press.

Rodger, N.A.M. 1993. *The Insatiable Earl: A Life of John Montagu, Fourth Earl of Sandwich, 1718–1792*. London: HarperCollins.

Rogers, Pat. 2004. *The Alexander Pope Encyclopaedia*. Westport, Conn.; London: Greenwood Press.

Ross, John F. 1940. 'The Character of Poor Richard: Its Source and Alteration'. *PMLA* Vol. LV (No. 3), pp. 785–94.

Sachse, Julius F. 1906. 'The Masonic Chronology of Benjamin Franklin'. *The Pennsylvania Magazine of History and Biography* Vol. XXX (No. 2), pp. 238–40.

Schaeper, Thomas J. 2011. *Edward Bancroft: Scientist, Author, Spy*. New Haven: Yale University Press.

Schiff, Stacy. 2006. *Benjamin Franklin and the Birth of America: Franklin's French Adventure 1776–85*. London: Bloomsbury.

Schlesinger, Arthur M. 1918. *The Colonial Merchants and the American Revolution, 1763–1776*. New York: Atheneum.

Schonland, B.F.J. 1956. 'Wilkins Lecture. Benjamin Franklin: Natural Philosopher'. *Proceedings of the Royal Society of London. Series A, Mathematical and Physical Sciences* Vol. CCXXXV (No. 1203), pp. 433–44.

Shipley, John B. 1956. 'Franklin Attends a Book Auction'. *The Pennsylvania Magazine of History and Biography* Vol. LXXX (No. 1), pp. 37–45.

Shirley, W. and James H. Hutson. 1969. 'Benjamin Franklin and Pennsylvania Politics, 1751–1755: A Reappraisal'. *The Pennsylvania Magazine of History and Biography* Vol. XCIII (No. 3), pp. 303–71.

Simmons, R.C. 2002. 'Colonial Patronage: Two Letters from William Franklin to the Earl of Bute, 1762'. *The William and Mary Quarterly*, 3rd Series, Vol. LIX (No. 1), pp. 123–34.

Skemp, Sheila L. 1990. *William Franklin: Son of a Patriot, Servant of a King*. New York; Oxford: Oxford University Press.

——. 2013. *The Making of a Patriot: Benjamin Franklin at the Cockpit*. New York: Oxford University Press.

Srodes, James. 2002. *Franklin: The Essential Founding Father*. Washington: Regnery Publishing.

Stumpf, Vernon O. 1970. 'Notes and Documents: Who Was Elizabeth Downes Franklin?' *The Pennsylvania Magazine of History and Biography* Vol. XCIV (No. 4), pp. 533–4.

Summerson, John and Howard Colvin. 2003. *Georgian London*. New Haven: published for the Paul Mellon Centre for Studies in British Art by Yale University Press.

Talbott, Page. 2005. 'Benjamin Franklin at Home'. In *Benjamin Franklin: In Search of a Better World*, edited by Page Talbott. New Haven: Yale University Press.

Taylor, Alan. 2006. *The Divided Ground: Indians, Settlers, and the Northern Borderland of the American Revolution*. New York: Knopf.

Thirsk, Joan. 2006. *Food in Early Modern England: Phases, Fads, Fashions 1500–1760*. London; New York: Hambledon Continuum.

Thomas, Peter David Garner. 1975. *British Politics and the Stamp Act Crisis: The*

First Phase of the American Revolution 1763–1767. Oxford; New York: Clarendon Press.

——. 1987. '"Thoughts on the British Constitution" by George III in 1760'. *Bulletin of the Institute of Historical Research* Vol. LX (No. 143), pp. 361–3.

——. 1991. *Tea Party to Independence: The Third Phase of the American Revolution, 1773–1776*. Oxford: Clarendon Press.

——. 2002. *George III: King and Politicians 1760–1770*. Manchester: Manchester University Press.

Thompson, F.M.L. (ed.). 1990. *The Cambridge Social History of Britain 1750–1950*. Cambridge: Cambridge University Press.

Tise, Larry E. (ed.). 2000. *Benjamin Franklin and Women*. University Park, Pa: Pennsylvania State University Press.

Treese, Lorett. 2002. *The Storm Gathering: The Penn Family and the American Revolution*. Mechanicsburg, Pa: Stackpole Books.

Tully, Alan. 2011. 'Benjamin Franklin and Pennsylvania Politics'. In *A Companion to Benjamin Franklin*, edited by David Waldstreicher. Oxford: Wiley-Blackwell.

Tyson, R.E. 2011. 'Population Patterns I, to 1770'. In *The Oxford Companion to Scottish History*, edited by Michael Lynch. Oxford Paperback Reference. New York: Oxford University Press.

Uglow, Jennifer S. 2003. *The Lunar Men: The Friends Who Made the Future, 1730–1810*. London: Faber.

Van Doren, Carl. 1939. *Benjamin Franklin*. London: Putnam.

Vickery, Amanda. 2010. *Behind Closed Doors: At Home in Georgian England*. New Haven: Yale University Press.

Warner, Jessica. 2003. *Craze: Gin and Debauchery in an Age of Reason*. London: Profile Books.

Warrell, David A. and Herbert M. Gilles (eds). 2002. *Essential Malariology*. 4th edn. London: Arnold.

Weinberger, Jerry. 2012. 'Benjamin Franklin Unmasked'. In *Benjamin Franklin's Intellectual World*, edited by Paul E. Kerry and Matthew S. Holland. Madison, NJ; Lanham, Md: Fairleigh Dickinson University Press; co-published with Rowman & Littlefield Publishing Group.

Weinreb, Ben and Christopher Hibbert (eds). 1987. *The London Encyclopaedia*. London: Papermac.

White, Jerry. 2012. *London in the Eighteenth Century: A Great and Monstrous Thing*. London: Bodley Head.

Wolf, Edwin (2nd). 1956. 'The Romance of James Logan's Books'. *The William and Mary Quarterly*, 3rd Series, Vol. XIII (No. 3), pp. 342–53.

——. 1974. *The Library of James Logan of Philadelphia, 1674–1751*. Philadelphia: Library Company.

Wolf, Edwin (2nd), and Marie Elena Korey. 1981. *Quarter of a Millennium: The*

Library Company of Philadelphia 1731–1981: A Selection of Books, Mss., Maps, Prints, Drawings and Paintings. Philadelphia: Library Company.

Wood, Gordon S. 2005. *The Americanization of Benjamin Franklin.* London: Penguin Books.

Wright, Esmond. 1986. *Franklin of Philadelphia.* Cambridge, Mass.: Belknap Press of Harvard University Press.

Wrigley, E.A. 2010. *Energy and the English Industrial Revolution.* Cambridge: Cambridge University Press.

Wroth, Lawrence C. 1942. 'Benjamin Franklin: The Printer at Work'. *Journal of the Franklin Institute* Vol. CCXXXIV (No. 2), pp. 105–32.

Zuckerman, Michael. 1993. 'Doing Good While Doing Well: Benevolence and Self-Interest in Franklin's Autobiography'. In *Reappraising Benjamin Franklin: A Bicentennial Perspective,* edited by J.A. Leo Lemay. Newark; London: University of Delaware Press; Associated University Presses.

NOTES

An attempt has been made to highlight those major archives, such as the American Philosophical Society, the Historical Society of Pennsylvania, Yale University and the Library of Congress, that house the original letters documented in *The Papers of Benjamin Franklin*. These are included within the following abbreviations used in the notes:

PBF   *The Papers of Benjamin Franklin*
APS   American Philosophical Society
BF   Benjamin Franklin
DF   Deborah Franklin
HSP   Historical Society of Pennsylvania
LC   Library of Congress
LCP   Library Company of Philadelphia
MHS   Massachusetts Historical Society
NYPL   New York Public Library
ODNB   *Oxford Dictionary of National Biography*
OED   *Oxford English Dictionary*
Penn   University of Pennsylvania Library
PMHB   *The Pennsylvania Magazine of History and Biography*
PML   The Morgan Library & Museum (formerly the Pierpont
       Morgan Library)
RSA   Royal Society of Arts
SRO   Scottish Record Office
WBF   *The Writings of Benjamin Franklin*
WF   William Franklin
WLCL   William L. Clements Library, University of Michigan

Though Polly Hewson (née Stevenson) is rightly described in the *PBF* document headings by her given name of Mary, here she is noted as Polly in order to match the main text. This is also the case with Sally Bache (née Franklin), here noted as Sally rather than Sarah.

⌒

SPELLING AND PUNCTUATION

1. BF to WF, 6 October 1773, *PBF* XX: 438. It is a shame that the original of the letter has been lost and that the editors of the *The Papers of Benjamin Franklin* were forced to reprint it faithfully from an early collection of 'Works' (see *PBF* XX: 436). One feels that Dr Franklin might have penned a considerable amount of capitalling and italicking in that paragraph.

PROLOGUE

1. *Parliamentary Register*, Vol. I, *House of Commons* (1775), p. 3.
2. *Lichtenberg's Visits to England*, trans. and annot. Margaret Laura Mare and W.H. Quarrell (1938), p. 84.
3. Horace Walpole, *Letters addressed to the Countess of Ossory*, ed. R. Vernon Smith, Vol. I (1848), p. 169.
4. Rockingham was one of the wealthiest peers in England; his Wentworth Woodhouse was the largest of the country palaces created by the eighteenth-century Whig aristocracy; see Simon Jenkins, *England's Thousand Best Houses* (2003), p. 920. Shelburne's previous performances in debate were worthy of this description, but that on 1 February was particularly so. See Walpole, *Letters addressed to the Countess of Ossory*, Vol. I, p. 169 and *ODNB* John Cannon, 'Petty, William, second earl of Shelburne and first Marquess of Lansdowne (1737–1805)', doi:10.1093/ref:odnb/22070.
5. BF to WF, 22 March 1775, *PBF* XXI: 547, LC.
6. Ibid., BF to WF, 22 March 1775, XXI: 546–7, LC.
7. See BF to Thomas Leech and Assembly Committee of Correspondence, 13 May 1758, *PBF* VIII: 67 note 9, Yale.
8. To BF from William Shipley, 1 September 1756, *PBF* VI: 500, APS and RSA.
9. Immanuel Kant, *Gesammelte Schriften* (1900), Vol. I, p. 472.
10. BF to WF, 22 March 1775, *PBF* XXI: 576, LC.
11. See Jeremy Black, *Eighteenth-Century Britain* (2001), p. 291.
12. BF to WF, 22 March 1775, *PBF* XXI: 581, LC.
13. Ibid., BF to WF, 22 March 1775, XXI: 582, LC.
14. Ibid.
15. Walpole, *Letters addressed to the Countess of Ossory*, Vol. I, p. 168.
16. *Parliamentary Register*, Vol. II, *House of Lords* (1775), pp. 29–30.
17. He was the eldest son of a living peer and thus sat in the Commons rather than the Lords.
18. *Parliamentary Register*, Vol. I, *House of Commons* (1775), p. 134.
19. BF to WF, 22 March 1775, *PBF* XXI: 598, LC.
20. Priestley, *Memoirs* (1809), p. 79.
21. A warrant for his arrest due to the action in Chancery brought by Thomas Whately was not served until 13 May – a week after Franklin had reached Philadelphia – but Lord Hillsborough and the Earl of Suffolk had sought government action *before* he left England.
22. BF to Priestley, 19 September 1772, *PBF* XIX: 299–300, LC.
23. BF to WF, 22 March 1775, *PBF* XXI: 548, LC.
24. Cobbett, *Parliamentary History of England*, Vol. XV (1813), p. 982.
25. BF to Wm. Shirley, 22 December 1754, *PBF* V: 450–51.

CHAPTER I: 1706–1724: LIFE BEFORE LONDON

1. Leo Lemay, *The Life of Benjamin Franklin*, Vol. I: *Journalist 1706–1730* (2006), pp. 25–7.

2. In 1752 Britain changed from the Julian to the Gregorian calendar and as part of the change the date moved forward eleven days. To avoid madness among historians and confusion among their readers, the former customarily give dates as they were lived.

3. Defoe, *Review of the State of the British Nation* 4, No. 126 (2 December 1707), p. 504. Cited by Steve Pincus, 'Rethinking Mercantilism: Political Economy, the British Empire, and the Atlantic World in the Seventeenth and Eighteenth Centuries', *Wm. & Mary Qtrly*, Vol. LXIX, No. 1 (January 2012), p. 33.

4. Pincus, ibid., p. 33, citing Defoe, *Review of the State of the British Nation* 4, No. 134 (20 December 1707), p. 536.

5. BF to Wm. Shirley, 22 December 1754, *PBF* V: 449–51.

6. Lemay, *Life of BF* I: 27.

7. Ibid., 31–2.

8. Leo Lemay's detective work (see Lemay, *Life of BF* I: 55–6) makes this seem most likely.

9. *Benjamin Franklin's Autobiography*, ed. Joyce E. Chaplin (2012) (hereafter *BF Autobiog.*), p. 21 and Lemay, *Life of BF* I: 69 and note 37 (p. 479) citing the *Catalogue of the Library Company of Philadelphia*, 1741.

10. *BF Autobiog.*, pp. 19–20.

11. Such as the Widows' Insurance proposal in 'Silence Dogood', No. 10, 13 August 1722, *PBF* I: 32–6.

12. Janette Seaton Lewis, '"A Turn of Thinking": The Long Shadow of the *Spectator* on Franklin's *Autobiography*', *Early American Literature*, Vol. XIII, No. 3 (Winter 1978/9), p. 269.

13. *Poor Richard Improved*, 1748, *PBF* III: 254.

14. Addison, *The Spectator (A New Edition)* (1891), ed. Henry Morley, Vol. I, No. 10, p. 42. See also Joyce Chaplin, *The First Scientific American: Benjamin Franklin and the Pursuit of Genius* (2006), p. 18.

15. See Lemay, *Life of BF* I: 149.

16. Ibid., 67.

17. *ODNB* Michael G. Hall, 'Mather, Cotton (1663–1728)', doi:10.1093/ref:odnb/18321.

18. Lemay, *Life of BF* I: 114.

19. Ibid., 188.

20. *BF Autobiog.*, p. 24.

21. Lemay, *Life of BF* I: 184–5.

22. *BF Autobiog.*, p. 33.

23. Ibid., p. 18.
24. Ibid., p. 18, Chaplin note 3; Lemay, *Life of BF* I: 333 (citing James Parton, *Life and Times of BF* [2 vols], Vol. I, p. 158, [1864]); Carl Van Doren believes that Mather was one of the inspirations for the Junto, see his *Benjamin Franklin* (1939), p. 73; and editors' Introduction to *Standing Queries for the Junto*, *PBF* I: 255–6, HSP.
25. BF to Samuel Mather, 7 July 1773, *PBF* XX: 287, LC.
26. Walter Isaacson, *Benjamin Franklin: An American Life* (2004), p. 29.
27. Lemay, *Life of BF* I: 108.
28. See 'Mr Spectator and the Coffeehouse Public Sphere', *Eighteenth-Century Studies*, Vol. XXXVII, No. 3 (Spring 2004), pp. 345–66, in which Brian Cowan argues persuasively that Addison and Steele sought to set codes for the public space of the coffee house to ensure that it was a forum for the exchange of ideas rather than for trivial tittle-tattle, especially p. 356 and Steele's naming of *The Tatler*.
29. BF to Benjamin Vaughan, 24 October 1788, *The Writings of Benjamin Franklin* (afterwards *WBF*), ed. Albert Henry Smyth, IX: 676, quoted by Chaplin in *BF Autobiog.*, p. 230.
30. *Poor Richard*, 1743, *PBF* II: 370.
31. Chaplin, Introduction to *BF Autobiog.*, xxi–xxii.
32. *BF Autobiog.*, p. 28.

CHAPTER 2: 1724–1726: A YOUNG MAN IN LONDON

1. Lemay, *Life of BF* I: 258.
2. *BF Autobiog.*, p. 41.
3. As per the subtitle of Jerry White's authoritative *London in the Eighteenth Century* (2012), taken from Defoe, *A Tour Through the Whole Island of Great Britain* (1724–6). See 1962 Dent Everyman edition Vol. I, p. 323.
4. *BF Autobiog.*, p. 42 top para.
5. Coincidentally also the son of a tallow chandler.
6. On widows' insurance, see *BF Autobiog.*, p. 18, Chaplin note 2.
7. Defoe, *The Complete English Tradesman* (1726), p. 386.
8. *BF Autobiog.*, p. 38.
9. Actually named after the Dukes of Brittany's house there pre-sixteenth century, *The London Encyclopaedia* (1987), ed. Ben Weinreb and Christopher Hibbert, p. 462.
10. *Shorter OED* (1973), p. 442.
11. White, *London in the Eighteenth Century*, p. 262.
12. James Ralph, *The Touch-Stone* (1728), p. 166.
13. Ibid., pp. 147–8.

14. White, *London in the Eighteenth Century*, pp. 302–13. Also *Lichtenberg's Visits to England*, trans. and annot. Mare and Quarrell, p. 28.

15. *BF Autobiog.*, pp. 42–3.

16. Ibid., p. 44.

17. Ibid., p. 50.

18. This is on the assumption that a pressman would earn around eighteen shillings (ninety pence in modern decimal currency) a week and a compositor a guinea (£1.05 pence) or slightly more. See White, *London in the Eighteenth Century*, p. 262 and p. 234.

19. With thanks to Professor Jerry White.

20. Dorothy George, *London Life in the Eighteenth Century* (1996), p. 289 and see White, *London in the Eighteenth Century*, pp. 332–3 for the close connection between the pub and the workplace.

21. *BF Autobiog.*, pp. 45–6.

22. Ibid., p. 46.

23. Ibid.

24. BF letter to Sloane, 2 June 1725, *PBF* I: 54, British Library.

25. *BF Autobiog.*, p. 44.

26. Ibid., p. 43.

27. Lemay, *Life of BF* I: 270.

28. *BF Autobiog.*, p 43.

29. See *BF Autobiog.*, p. 55 and Chaplin, *The First Scientific American*, p. 19. Bishop Berkeley believed that Locke's logic went even further towards atheism and produced his *A Treatise Concerning the Principles of Human Knowledge* to counter that.

30. Lemay, *Life of BF* I: 287.

31. *ODNB* M.M. Goldsmith, 'Mandeville, Bernard (bap. 1670, d. 1733)', doi:10.1093/ref:odnb/17926.

32. Ibid.

33. *BF Autobiog.*, p. 44.

34. Ibid., pp. 43–4.

35. BF 'Appeal for the Hospital', *PBF* IV: 147–54.

36. White, *London in the Eighteenth Century*, p. 4.

37. Defoe, *A Tour Through the Whole Island of Great Britain*, Vol. I, pp. 324–5.

38. Ibid, p. 349.

39. Ibid.

40. Ibid, p. 339.

41. Ibid, pp. 349–50.

42. Starting with his 'Journal of a Voyage, 1726', 22 July 1726, *PBF* I: 72–99.

43. Defoe, *A Tour Through the Whole Island of Great Britain* Vol. I, p. 325.

44. Henri Misson, *Memoirs and Observations* (1719), trans. Ozell, p. 177.

45. E.A. Wrigley, *Energy and the Industrial Revolution* (2010), pp. 62–3.
46. César de Saussure, *A Foreign View of England* (1902), ed. and trans. Madame Van Muyden, pp. 130–31.
47. White, *London in the Eighteenth Century*, p. 256.
48. Ibid., p. 262. A pound and five new pence (a pound and a shilling).
49. It was Duke Street then.
50. We don't know from where in Chelsea to where in Blackfriars. As an indicator the distance between the modern Blackfriars Bridge and the modern Chelsea Bridge is 2.73 miles http://www.visitthames.co.uk/dbimgs/Cruising Guide. pdf p. 31.
51. *BF Autobiog.*, pp. 48–9.
52. BF to O(liver) N(eave) (before 1769), *PBF* XV: 295–8.
53. *BF Autobiog.*, p. 49. The British and Pennsylvanian pound did not have the same value and there was no fixed rate of exchange between them. As the latter was the weaker currency, Thomas Penn contracted to have his quit rents paid to the value of the former.
54. *BF Autobiog.*, p. 50.
55. Chaplin, *The First Scientific American*, p. 34.
56. Ibid., pp. 30–31.
57. Franklin described this as an 'Erratum' and said that he had destroyed the copies (*BF Autobiog.*, p. 43 and Lemay, *Life of BF* I: 270). He was merely more cautious in later years about expressing these views and he did not destroy them at the time.
58. Chaplin, *The First Scientific American*, p. 18.
59. *The Alexander Pope Encyclopaedia* (2004), ed. Pat Rogers, p. 205. See Chaplin, *The First Scientific American*, p. 30.
60. *ODNB* Michael G. Hall, 'Mather, Cotton (1663–1728)', doi:10.1093/ref:odnb/ 18321.
61. Plan of Conduct, *PBF* I: 99–100.
62. *BF Autobiog.*, p. 50.

CHAPTER 3: 1726–C.1748: FOUNDATIONS

1. *BF Autobiog.*, p. 50, Chaplin note 1.
2. Lemay, *Life of BF* I: 376–7.
3. Sheila Skemp, *William Franklin* (1990), p. 4.
4. Lemay, *Life of BF* I: 265–7; *BF Autobiog.*, p. 50.
5. *BF Autobiog.*, p. 15.
6. Ibid., p. 54.
7. Stephen Bloore, 'Samuel Keimer', *PMHB*, HSP, Vol. LIV, No. 3 (1930), pp. 278–9.

8. *BF Autobiog.*, p. 59.

9. Bloore, 'Samuel Keimer', *PMHB*, HSP, Vol. LIV, No. 3, pp. 283–7.

10. Lemay, *Life of BF* I: 456.

11. Lawrence C. Wroth, 'Benjamin Franklin: The Printer at Work', *Journal of the Franklin Institute*, Vol. CCXXXIV, No. 2 (August 1942), p. 117.

12. For Deputy Postmaster at Philadelphia see *BF Autobiog.*, p. 97. Keith, as Governor, had tried to forge his own power base in the Assembly, one independent of both the Quaker leadership and, more to the point, the supporters of the Penn Proprietors who had appointed him. The Proprietors, fiercely hostile to anyone who challenged their authority, sacked him. He in turn sailed to London and appealed directly to the Crown. It was a dangerous gamble for a man without deep pockets. The Penns' influence was far greater and by 1734 Keith was imprisoned for debt in London's notorious Fleet, and with his political career destroyed. See *ODNB* W.A. Speck, 'Keith, Sir William, fourth baronet (*c.*1669–1749)', doi:10.1093/ref:odnb/68696; and *American National Biography* (1999), Vol. XII, pp. 465–6.

13. *BF Autobiog.*, p. 85.

14. *Poor Richard Improved*, 1758, *PBF* VII: 342.

15. Actually, in translation, an aphorism of Franklin's later friend Voltaire.

16. *BF Autobiog.*, p. 55.

17. Lemay, *Life of BF* I: 377.

18. *BF Autobiog.*, p. 95.

19. Clarence Saunders Brigham, 'James Franklin and the Beginnings of Printing in Rhode Island', *Proceedings of the Massachusetts Historical Society*, Vol. LXV (October 1932), p. 539.

20. Lemay, *The Life of Benjamin Franklin* Vol. II: *Printer and Publisher 1730–1747* (2006), pp. 172–3.

21. *Poor Richard*, 1739, *PBF* II: 218.

22. See C.J. William Miller, 'Franklin's "Poor Richard Almanacs": Their Printing and Publication', *Studies in Bibliography*, Vol. XIV (1961), p. 111.

23. John F. Ross, 'The Character of Poor Richard: Its Source and Alteration', *PMLA* Vol. LV, No. 3 (September 1940), pp. 785–6.

24. In the Preface to 1739 'Poor Richard' says: 'Besides the usual Things expected in an Almanac, I hope the professed Teachers of Mankind will excuse my scattering here and there some instructive Hints in Matters of Morality and Religion.' *PBF* II: 218.

25. Preface to *Poor Richard*, 1740, *PBF* II: 245–7.

26. See Chapter 1.

27. William Pencak, 'Politics and Ideology in *Poor Richard's Almanac*', *PMHB*, HSP, Vol. CXVI, No. 2 (April 1992), pp. 191–2.

28. Ross, 'The Character of Poor Richard', *PMLA* Vol. LV, No. 3, pp. 791–4 for the transition of 'Poor Richard'.

29. Lemay, *Life of BF* II: 212.

30. Ibid., II: 213.

31. Ralph Frasca, 'The Emergence of the American Colonial Press', *Pennsylvania Legacies*, Vol. VI, No. 1 (May 2006), p. 13.

32. Ibid.

33. Ralph Frasca, *Benjamin Franklin's Printing Network* (2006), p. 260 note 22.

34. Ibid., p. 92.

35. Frasca, 'The Emergence of the American Colonial Press', *Pennsylvania Legacies*, Vol. VI, No. 1, p. 13.

36. Frasca, *Benjamin Franklin's Printing Network*, p. 196.

37. Population figures in colonial America are difficult to estimate. Thomas L. Purvis's *Colonial America to 1763* (1999) gives Philadelphia figures of 5,000 for 1700; 6,500 for 1710; and next 8,000 for 1734 (Table 10.6 on p. 228). For comparison he gives for Boston (Table 10.2 p. 222) 1700 – 6,700; 1710 – 9,000; 1720 – 12,000; 1730 – 13,000. For New York (Table 10.4 p. 226) 1700 – 5,000; 1710 – 5,700; 1720 – 7,000; 1730 – 8,622. By 1760 Philadelphia = 23,750; New York = 18,000 and Boston = 15,361.

38. Michael Zuckerman, 'Doing Good While Doing Well: Benevolence and Self-Interest in Franklin's Autobiography', in *Reappraising Benjamin Franklin* (1993), ed. J.A. Leo Lemay, p. 443.

39. *BF Autobiog.*, p. 57, Chaplin note 9.

40. Ibid., p. 57.

41. Lemay, *Life of BF* I: 356.

42. George W. Boudreau, 'The Philadelphia Years 1723–1757', in *A Companion to Benjamin Franklin* (2011), ed. David Waldstreicher, p. 30.

43. Dorothy F. Grimm, 'Franklin's Scientific Institution', *Pennsylvania History*, Vol. XXIII, No. 4 (October 1956), pp. 441–4.

44. http://www.librarycompany.org/about/index.htm

45. Lemay, *Life of BF* II: 100.

46. Breintnall to Collinson, 7 November 1732, *PBF* I: 248–9, British Library, LCP.

47. BF to Michael Collinson, 8 February 1770, *PBF* XVII: 65–6, APS; and see also *PBF* III: 115–16 note 4.

48. Joseph Breintnall, Letter on behalf of the Directors of the Library Company to Joseph Hopkinson, 31 March 1732, in *Quarter of a Millennium: The Library Company of Philadelphia, 1731–1981* (1981), ed. Edwin Wolf 2nd and Marie Elena Korey, p. 4.

49. *The Library of James Logan*, ed. Edwin Wolf (1974), p. xviii.

50. Agreement between Louis Timothée and Directors of Library Company', 14 November 1732, *PBF* I: 250–52, NYPL; see *WBF* II: 245 note 1.

51. Letter of James Logan to Peter Collinson, 14 February 1750, footnote to *The Works of Benjamin Franklin*, ed. Jared Sparks, Vol. VI (1844), p. 100, Harvard, cited by *PBF* III: 458–9 note 3.

52. BF to James Logan, 20 January 1750, *PBF* III: 459.

53. Sparks, *The Works of BF*, Vol. VI, p. 100 footnote.

54. See Chapter 2, pp. 30–31.

55. George W. Boudreau, *Independence: A Guide to Historic Philadelphia* (2012), pp. 7–8.

56. Logan to Penn, 14 February 1750, Penn Letter Book, p. 28, HSP, quoted by Edwin Wolf, 'The Romance of James Logan's Books', *Wm. & Mary Qtrly*, Vol. XIII, No. 3 (July 1956), p. 350.

57. Ibid., p. 350 note 40.

58. http://www.archives.upenn.edu/histy/features/1700s/penn1700s.html

59. While, of course, one must acknowledge the impact on educational policy of religious differences between the colonies.

60. Alan Tully, 'Benjamin Franklin and Pennsylvania Politics', in *A Companion to Benjamin Franklin*, ed. David Waldstreicher, p. 113.

61. Though by that time Turnbull was neither still Chaplain to the Prince of Wales nor indeed alive, having according to the entry for him in the *ODNB* 'died from unknown causes in The Hague on 31 January 1748 while gathering information on the Jacobites for Lord Newcastle'. *ODNB* Paul Wood, 'Turnbull, George (1698–1748)', doi:10.1093/ref:odnb/40216.

62. http://www.archives.upenn.edu/primdocs/1749proposals.html#8b

63. Lemay, *The Life of Benjamin Franklin* Vol. III: *Soldier, Scientist and Politician 1748–1757* (2006), pp. xii and 208–9.

64. http://www.archives.upenn.edu/histy/features/1700s/penn1700s.html

65. http://www.amphilsoc.org/about

CHAPTER 4 C.1748–1757: CONDUCTOR

1. Royal Charter of 1681.

2. *ODNB* Mary K. Geiter, 'Penn, William (1644–1718)', doi:10.1093/ref:odnb/21857.

3. Boudreau, *Independence*, pp. 8–9.

4. Mary K. Geiter, *William Penn* (2000), p. 151.

5. *ODNB* Geiter, 'Penn, William (1644–1718)', doi:10.1093/ref:odnb/21857.

6. Boudreau, *Independence*, p. 12.

7. *ODNB* Charlotte Fell-Smith, 'Penn, Thomas (1702–1775)', doi:10.1093/ref:odnb/21855.

8. Boudreau, 'The Philadelphia Years 1723–1757', in *A Companion to Benjamin Franklin*, ed. Waldstreicher, p. 43.

9. Alan Tully, 'Benjamin Franklin and Pennsylvania Politics', ibid., p. 109.

10. Ibid., p. 110.

11. Ibid., pp. 110–11.

12. *Franklin in His Own Time* (2011), ed. Kevin J. Hayes and Isabelle Bour, extract from Memoir of Robert Aspland, p. 146.

13. Lemay, *Life of BF* III: xi.

14. Ibid., III: 57.

15. Hubertis Cummings, *Richard Peters, Provincial Secretary and Cleric 1704–1776* (1944), p. 133.

16. Ibid., pp. 134–6 cited by *PBF* III: 186 note 8.

17. Ibid., pp. 135–6.

18. *PBF* III: 186 note 9 citing Penn to Peters, 9 June 1748, Penn Letter Book, II: 232, HSP.

19. See Simon P. Newman, 'Benjamin Franklin and the Leather-Apron Men: The Politics of Class in Eighteenth-Century Philadelphia', in *Benjamin Franklin's Intellectual World* (2012), ed. Paul E. Kerry and Matthew Scott Holland, pp. 89–102.

20. Lemay, *Life of BF* III: 234.

21. Ibid., III: 171 and 337.

22. Fred Anderson, *Crucible of War* (2001), pp. 38–9 citing Francis Jennings, *Empire of Fortune* p. 82 note 28, which quotes Lords of Trade to Sir Danvers Osborne, 18 September 1753.

23. Anderson, *Crucible of War*, pp. 5–7.

24. Ibid., pp. 78–9.

25. Ibid., p. 80.

26. Including Lord Halifax and his junior minister Charles Townshend. Thomas Pownall, through his brother John (Halifax's Secretary at the Board of Trade), had access to Lord Halifax – but that did not mean that Halifax agreed with all of Thomas Pownall's recommendations.

27. See Chapter 1, pp. 11–12.

28. BF to Wm. Shirley, 22 December 1754, *PBF* V: 450–51.

29. Lemay, *Life of BF* III: xviii.

30. Ibid., III: 485–6. The Secretary of State was Sir Thomas Robinson, later 1st Baron Grantham (followers of *Downton Abbey* will be interested that there was a Lord Grantham, but it was a barony and not an earldom).

31. See Francis Jennings, 'Thomas Penn's Loyalty Oath', *American Journal of Legal History*, Vol. VIII, No. 4 (October 1964), pp. 303–13.

32. Lemay, *Life of BF* III: 170–72. Lemay also explains that in 1749–50 there had almost been a personal fallout when the Provincial Grand Master of North America had appointed Franklin as Grand Master of Pennsylvania and Allen had written to London and got the decision overturned in his favour. Franklin graciously accepted the position of Deputy instead.

33. *PBF* VII: 135 note 3 citing Peters to Penn, 14 February 1757, Peters Letterbook, HSP.

34. Lemay, *Life of BF* III: xviii.

35. *BF Autobiog.*, p. 142.

36. BF to Peter Collinson, 5 November 1756, *PBF* VII: 13, PML.

37. Lemay, *Life of BF* III: 523, citing Penn to Peters, 13 August 1756, Penn Papers, HSP.

38. Wm. Shirley and James H. Hutson, 'Benjamin Franklin and Pennsylvania Politics, 1751–1755: A Reappraisal', *PMHB*, HSP, Vol. XCIII, No. 3 (July 1969), p. 370.

39. Kant, *Gesammelte Schriften*, Vol. I, p. 472.

40. David Hume to BF, 10 May 1762, *PBF* X: 81–2, APS.

41. BF to WF, 22 March 1775, *PBF* XXI: 582, LC.

42. *The Works of John Adams*, ed. Charles Francis Adams, Vol. I (1856), p. 662.

43. *Scots Magazine*, Vol. LII (June 1790), p. 305. Reproduced in aftermatter of *BF Autobiog.*, ed. Chaplin, p. 276.

44. Carla Mulford, 'Figuring Benjamin Franklin in American Cultural Memory', *The New England Quarterly*, Vol. LXXII, No. 3 (September 1999), p. 430.

45. 'A Letter of Benjamin Franklin, Esq; to Mr Peter Collinson, F.R.S. Concerning an Electrical Kite', *Philosophical Transactions (1683–1775)*, Vol. XLVII (1751–2), pp. 565–7.

46. Fothergill, in *Some Account of the Late Peter Collinson* (1770), p. 4, credited him with 'promoting and preserving a most extensive correspondence with learned and ingenious Foreigners, in all countries, and on every useful subject'.

47. Ibid., p. 5.

48. BF to Collinson, 28 March 1747, *PBF* III: 118–19.

49. BF to Collinson, 4 February 1751, *PBF* IV: 113, Royal Society.

50. BF to Pringle, 21 December 1757, *PBF* VII: 298–300, Royal Society.

51. J. L. Heilbron, *Electricity in the 17th and 18th Centuries: A Study of Early Modern Physics* (1979), p. 318.

52. Ibid.

53. For a list of award winners see https://royalsociety.org/awards/copley-medal/

54. *ODNB* R.W. Home, 'Canton, John (bap. 1718, d. 1772)', doi:10.1093/ref:odnb/4576.

55. Chaplin, *The First Scientific American*, p. 134.

56. B.F.J. Schonland, 'Wilkins Lecture. Benjamin Franklin: Natural Philosopher', *Proceedings of the Royal Society of London*, Vol. CCXXXV, No. 1203 (12 June 1956), pp. 435–6. Chaplin, *The First Scientific American*, pp. 103–15.

57. Nian-Sheng Huang, *Benjamin Franklin in American Thought and Culture, 1790–1990* (APS, 1994), p. 241.

CHAPTER 5: 1757: RETURN TO LONDON

1. BF to Earl of Loudoun, *PBF* VII: 133 note 5.
2. *BF Autobiog.*, p. 151.
3. BF to Loudoun, 21 May 1757, *PBF* VII: 215, Huntington Library.
4. BF to DF, 27 May 1757, *PBF* VII: 218, APS.
5. Between the years 1688 and 1851 as per the National Maritime Museum, Falmouth. See http://www.nmmc.co.uk/online_exhibition/ole/template_home.php?ole_id=11
6. *BF Autobiog.*, p. 152, Chaplin note 3.
7. Ibid., p. 152.
8. BF to Strahan, 27 July 1756, *PBF* VI: 477, Yale.
9. At the time of writing in 2015.
10. See Chapter 3, p. 43.
11. 'Celia Single', *PBF* I: 241–2, HSP.
12. Stuart A. Gallacher, 'Franklin's "Way to Wealth": A Florilegium of Proverbs and Wise Sayings', *The Journal of English and Germanic Philology*, Vol. XLVIII, No. 2 (April 1949), p. 242.
13. *BF Autobiog.*, p. 92, Chaplin note 8.
14. *Poor Richard Improved*, 1758, *PBF* VII: 349.
15. BF to Strahan, 2 June 1750, *PBF* III: 479, HSP.
16. *BF Autobiog.*, p. 110.
17. *BF Autobiog.*, pp. 110–11.
18. Preface to *Poor Richard*, 1739, *PBF* II: 218. Rather brilliantly, Richard blamed the onerous initial contract agreed with the printer, aka one Benjamin Franklin.
19. BF to Collinson, 28 March 1747, *PBF* II: 118–19.
20. Defoe, *The Political History of the Devil* (1726), p. 269.
21. *Poor Richard*, 1743, *PBF* II: 370.
22. Letter from Joseph Priestley, in the *Monthly Magazine*, 1 February 1803, p. 1.
23. Now in the White House Art Collection, http://www.jfklibrary.org/Asset-Viewer/Archives/JFKWHP-1962-03-09-E.aspx
24. BF to Strahan, 19 October 1748, *PBF* III: 323, PML.
25. BF to Strahan, 6 December 1750, *PBF* IV: 77–8, APS.
26. http://scillypedia.co.uk/ShipwreckListing.htm
27. First built in 1680.
28. BF to DF, 17 July 1758, *PBF* VII: 243.
29. *BF Autobiog.*, p. 156.
30. Ibid., Chaplin note 3. Wilton House was and is the home of the Earls of Pembroke. It is fittingly described by Simon Jenkins in his *England's Thousand Best Houses*, p. 838, as 'one of the great houses of England'.

31. Norman G. Brett-James, *The Life of Peter Collinson* (1925), pp. 86–7.

32. BF to Strahan, 4 July 1744, *PBF* II: 410–11, Yale.

33. BF to Strahan, 26 April 1746, *PBF* III: 75, Penn.

34. BF to Strahan, 31 January 1757, *PBF* VII: 115–16, Huntington Library.

35. For the Johnson and Smith encounter see James Aikman Cochrane, *Dr John-son's Printer*, p. 163. Franklin did meet Smith when he travelled to Scotland in 1759, but there is no reliable record of any great contact between them; see Thomas D. Eliot, 'The Relations between Adam Smith and Benjamin Franklin before 1776', *Political Science Quarterly*, Vol. XXXIX, No. 1 (March 1924), pp. 67–96.

36. The meeting was that of 'The Associates of Dr Bray'; see Maurice J. Quinlan, 'Dr Franklin Meets Dr Johnson', *PMHB*, HSP, Vol. LXXIII, No. 1 (January 1949), pp. 34–44. For Franklin's views see *PBF* VII: 356. For details of King in Suffolk see BF to DF, 27 June 1760, *PBF* IX: 174–5, APS.

37. *BF Autobiog.*, p. 119.

38. Ian Christie, 'The Changing Nature of Parliamentary Politics 1742–1789', in *British Politics and Society from Walpole to Pitt 1742–1789*, ed. Jeremy Black (1990), p. 103.

39. *ODNB* John Cannon, 'Carteret, John, second Earl Granville (1690–1763)', doi:10.1093/ref:odnb/4804.

40. Ibid.

41. *BF Autobiog.*, p. 157.

42. BF to Isaac Norris, 19 March 1759, *PBF* VIII: 293, Yale.

43. *BF Autobiog.*, p. 157.

44. Ibid., Chaplin note 7.

45. BF to Isaac Norris, 19 March 1759, *PBF* VIII: 293, Yale.

46. From Benjamin Franklin to William Strahan, 21 March 1752, *PBF* IV: 281; BF to Strahan, 19 October 1748, *PBF* III: 323.

47. Michael G. Kammen, *A Rope of Sand* (1968), p. 4.

48. George Simpson Eddy, 'Account Book of Benjamin Franklin Kept by Him during His First Mission to England as Provincial Agent, 1757–1762', *PMHB*, HSP, Vol. LV, No. 2 (1931), p. 100.

49. BF to DF, January 1758, *PBF* VII: 369, APS.

50. A guinea being £1 and 1 shilling or £1.05 in new money – hence Franklin's carriage would have cost £12.60 – a small fortune in the 18th century. BF to DF, 19 February 1758, *PBF* VII: 380 note 1.

51. BF to DF, 19 February 1758, *PBF* VII: 380, APS.

52. Pattie Cowell, '"Much Depends Upon My Knowing": The Education of Polly Hewson', in *Finding Colonial Americas*, ed. Carla Mulford and David S. Shields (2001), p. 323.

53. Samuel Johnson, *A Dictionary of the English Language* (1755), Vol. I. Also see Jessica Warner, *Craze: Gin and Debauchery in an Age of Reason* (2003).

54. Brian Cookson, 'The Story of Old London Bridge', *London Historians* (October 2010), p. 1.

55. Hannah Greig, *The Beau Monde* (2013), pp. 4–8 and p. 262 note 18.

56. Ibid., p. 260 note 12 citing Paul Langford, *Public Life and the Propertied Englishman, 1789–1798* (1991), pp. 141–2.

57. Queens Mary II and Anne were more London-based.

58. Even Sir Robert Walpole was only able to survive the accession of George II (who hated his father and thus his father's ministers) because of the intercession of the new Queen, Caroline of Ansbach.

59. John Summerson and Howard Colvin (eds), *Georgian London* (2003), pp. 3–5, 22–4, 87–103.

60. E.A. Wrigley, *Energy and the Industrial Revolution*, p. 62.

61. Ibid.

62. F.M.L. Thompson (ed.), *The Cambridge Social History of Britain 1750–1950* (1990), Vol. II, p. 5.

CHAPTER 6: 1757–1758: A LONDON LIFE

1. The Proprietary was divided among William Penn's four sons by his second marriage. A fourth son, Dennis, had died before this time. Thomas Penn took on the Quarters of both John and Dennis as they did not have legitimate issue.

2. Robert Middlekauff, *Benjamin Franklin and His Enemies* (1996), p. 63.

3. *PBF* VII: 110–11, note 9, citing Peters to Penn, 31 January 1757, Peters Letterbook, HSP.

4. Ibid., VII: 110–11, note 9, citing Peters to Penn, 31 January 1757 and Penn to Peters, 14 May 1757, Penn Papers, HSP.

5. *BF Autobiog.*, p. 159.

6. James H. Hutson, *Pennsylvania Politics 1746–1770* (1972), pp. 42–3.

7. *Extracts from the Gazette*, 29 April 1731, *PBF* I: 215.

8. Hutson, *Pennsylvania Politics 1746–1770*, pp. 42–4.

9. Fothergill to Pemberton, 12 June 1758, HSP, in *Chain of Friendship: Selected Letters of Dr John Fothergill of London, 1735–1780* (1971), ed. Betsy C. Corner and Christopher C. Booth, p. 195.

10. BF to DF, 22 November 1757, *PBF* VII: 273, APS, in which he mentions 2 September letter (now lost).

11. D.G.C. Allan, '"Dear and Serviceable to Each Other": Benjamin Franklin and the Royal Society of Arts', *Proceedings of the American Philosophical Society*, Vol. CXLIV, No. 3 (September 2000), p. 249. Full title, 'Society instituted at London for the encouragement of Arts, Manufactures and Commerce'.

12. BF to DF, 22 November 1757, *PBF* VII: 273–4, APS.

13. Mary J. Dobson, *Contours of Death and Disease in Early Modern England* (1997), pp. 312–21. T. Chin, P.D. Welsby, 'Malaria in the UK: Past, Present and Future', *Postgraduate Medical Journal* (March 2004), http://pmj.bmj.com/content/80/949/663.full. W. MacArthur, 'A Brief Story of English Malaria', *British Medical Bulletin* (1951), Vol. VIII, pp. 76–9. Re London and Westminster, see 'Developing treatments', Museum of the Royal Pharmaceutical Society, p. 4, http://www.rpharms.com/museum-pdfs/c-malaria.pdf; David A. Warrell, 'Clinical features of malaria', in *Essential Malariology* (4th edn, 2002), ed. Warrell and Herbert M. Gilles, p. 192.

14. The editors of the *PBF* state that it was Hall who inserted it as a 'filler', *PBF* VII: 350 and 350 note 4. A Jill or Gill is just over two fluid ounces (Imperial).

15. Strahan to DF, 13 December 1757, *PBF* VII: 297.

16. 'William Franklin to the Printer of The Citizen', 16 September 1757, *PBF* VII: 258–63.

17. Fothergill to Pemberton, 12 June 1758, HSP, in *Chain of Friendship*, ed. Corner and Booth, p. 195.

18. WF to Elizabeth Graeme, 9 December 1757, *PBF* VII: 290–91, Harvard.

19. Skemp, *William Franklin*, pp. 36–7.

20. *ODNB* Boyd Stanley Schlenther, 'Franklin, William (1730/31–1813)', doi:10.1093/ref:odnb/62971.

21. Roy Porter, 'The Wonderful Extent and Variety of London', in *London 1753*, ed. Sheila O'Connell (2003), p. 9; and this is an estimate based on figures in *Colonial America to 1763*, ed. Thomas L. Purvis, p. 228. (It was a time of massive expansion of the Philadelphia population. Purvis gives 14,000 for 1750 and 23,750 for 1760.)

22. Greig, *The Beau Monde*, p. 94.

23. WF to Sally F, 10 October 1761, *PBF* IX: 365, APS.

24. See Skemp, *William Franklin*, pp. 36–7.

25. *PBF* VII: 110–11 note 9, Penn to Peters 14 May 1757, Penn Papers, HSP.

26. Verner W. Crane, 'The Club of Honest Whigs: Friends of Science and Liberty', *Wm. & Mary Qtrly*, Vol. XXIII, No. 2 (April 1966), p. 211.

27. R.V. Jones, 'Benjamin Franklin', *Notes and Records of the Royal Society of London*, Vol. XXXI, No. 2 (January 1977), p. 211.

28. He was the only Royal Society Fellow surnamed Wilson at the time.

29. Jones, 'Benjamin Franklin', *Notes and Records of the Royal Society of London*, Vol. XXXI, No. 2, p. 211.

30. 'A small fish allied to the salmon', *Shorter OED* (1973), p. 2028.

31. Codling is one of the oldest-established English apples that retains its shape when cooked, so ideal for pies and tarts.

32. Jones, 'Benjamin Franklin', *Notes and Records of the Royal Society of London*, Vol. XXXI, No. 2, p. 210.

33. Crane, 'The Club of Honest Whigs', *Wm. & Mary Qtrly*, p. 212.

34. Pringle to BF, [May?]1763, *PBF* X: 269, APS.

35. Crane, 'The Club of Honest Whigs', *Wm. & Mary Qtrly*, p. 213.

36. BF to Hugh Roberts, 26 February 1761, *PBF* IX: 280, HSP, cited by Verner Crane (above), p. 213.

37. Crane, 'The Club of Honest Whigs', *Wm. & Mary Qtrly*, pp. 210–13.

38. BF to John Ellicott, 13 April 1763, *PBF* X: 250, Royal London Hospital.

39. Anthony Merry to BF, 18 February 1780, *PBF* XXXI: 496, APS.

40. BF to Benjamin Vaughan, 26 July 1784, *WBF* IX: 241, LC.

41. Boswell, *Boswell In Search of a Wife, 1766–1769* (1956), ed. Frank Brady and Frederick A. Pottle, p. 300.

42. Crane, 'The Club of Honest Whigs', *Wm. & Mary Qtrly*, p. 223.

43. *Boswell In Search of a Wife, 1766–1769*, ed. Brady and Pottle, p. 292.

44. Sans Souci (literally, 'without care') being as Sanssouci the name of the Potsdam Palace of Frederick the Great, the Philosopher King.

45. *Boswell In Search of a Wife, 1766–1769*, ed. Brady and Pottle, p. 300.

46. BF to Priestley, 4 May 1772, *PBF* XIX: 126, APS.

47. For damper see BF to James Bowdoin, 2 December 1758, *PBF* VIII: 194–8. For Gulf Stream see BF to Anthony Todd, 29 October 1768, *PBF*: XV: 246–8, WLCL.

48. John R. Millburn, *Wheelwright of the Heavens: The Life and Work of James Ferguson* (1988), p. 193.

49. 'James Ferguson: Account of Franklin's Three-Wheel Clock', *PBF* VIII: 216–19.

50. BF to Giambatista Beccaria, 13 July 1762, *PBF* X: 127.

51. BF to Sir Alexander Dick, 11 December 1763, *PBF* X: 385, NYPL.

52. BF brought his blind great-nephew over from America so Stanley could teach him.

53. BF to Giambatista Beccaria, 13 July 1762, *PBF* X: 116–30. For Delaval see *PBF* X: 127. Pockrich has a number of different spellings (including Puckeridge, which Franklin used on p. 127). Pockrich had died in a fire in 1759 that had started in the room of his lodgings – see *PBF* X: 117 note 7.

54. http://www.benjaminfranklinhouse.org/site/sections/about_franklin/Issue%206%20Bifocal%20glasses.pdf and http://www.college-optometrists.org/en/college/museyeum/online_exhibitions/artgallery/bifocals.cfm

55. See *The Cravenstreet Gazette*, 22–6 September 1770, *PBF* XVII: 220–26, APS.

56. BF to DF, January 1758, *PBF* VII: 369, APS.

57. Sir Joseph Banks later introduced them successfully. See J.C. Loudon, *The Trees and Shrubs of Britain* (1838), Vol. II, Part 3, p. 1170.

58. Banks wrote in his Journal of 23 September 1769: 'We also today made a pie of the North American apples which Dr Fothergill gave me, which proved very good.' Though he added, 'if not quite equal to the apple pies which our friends in England are now eating, good enough to please us who have been so long deprived of the fruits of our native Country'. Obviously this was a question of taste. *The Endeavour Journal of Sir Joseph Banks, 1768–1771*, ed. J.C. Beaglehole (1963), Vol. I, p. 393.

59. BF to DF, 27 June 1760, *PBF* IX: 175, APS.

60. Page Talbott, 'Benjamin Franklin at Home', in *Benjamin Franklin: In Search of a Better World* (2005), ed. Talbott, p. 145.

61. £9 and 9 shillings or £9.45.

62. BF to DF, 19 February 1758, *PBF* VII: 381, APS. See Page Talbott (ed.), *Benjamin Franklin: In Search of a Better World*, pp. 137–8.

63. Pehr Kalm, *Kalm's Account of His Visit to England* (1892), trans. Joseph Lucas, p. 13.

64. Sara Paston-Williams, *The Art of Dining* (1993), pp. 203–4; Peter C.D. Brears, *Traditional Food in Shropshire* (2009), pp. 131–2; Hannah Glasse, *The Art of Cookery, Made Plain and Easy* (1774), p. 277.

65. Paston-Williams, *The Art of Dining*, p. 243.

66. DF to BF, 3 November 1765, *PBF* XII: 351, APS; BF to DF, 13 February 1768, *PBF* XV: 45, APS; and BF to DF, 28 January 1772, *PBF* XIX: 44, APS. See also William Woys Weaver, *A Quaker Woman's Cookbook: The Domestic Cookery of Elizabeth Ellicott Lea* (2004), pp. 320–21.

67. BF to DF, 28 January 1772, *PBF* XIX: 44, APS. It was at a time when he was trying and failing to obtain an audience with Lord Hillsborough.

68. See *The Cravenstreet Gazette*, 22–6 September 1770, *PBF* XVII: 220–6, APS.

69. Amanda Vickery, *Behind Closed Doors: At Home in Georgian England* (2010), p. 275.

70. Markman Ellis, *The Coffee-House* (2004), pp. 208–9; John Burnett, *Liquid Pleasures* (1999), p. 54.

71. *Kalm's Account of his Visit to England*, pp. 13–14.

72. Burnett, *Liquid Pleasures*, p. 55.

73. Thomas Penn letter of 12 January 1758, referring to the meeting as having happened 'today', dates it. *PBF* VII: 362 note 6, Thomas Penn to William Allen, 12 January 1758, HSP.

74. Whether it should be under Proprietary or Assembly control. See *PBF* VII: 361 note 2 and *PBF* VI: 451 note 5.

75. BF to Norris, 14 January 1758, *PBF* VII: 362, HSP.

76. Ibid., VII: 363–4 note 6, Thomas Penn to Richard Peters, 5 July 1758, HSP.

77. Ibid., VII: 360–61 note 8.

78. *Chain of Friendship*, p. 199 note 4.

79. *ODNB* W.A. Speck, 'Dunk, George Montagu, second earl of Halifax (1716–1771)', doi:10.1093/ref:odnb/8266.
80. BF to Joseph Galloway, 7 April 1759, *PBF* VIII: 313, Yale.
81. Fothergill to Pemberton, 12 June 1758, HSP, in *Chain of Friendship*, ed. Corner and Booth, p. 195.
82. Jonathan R. Dull, 'Franklin Furioso, 1775–1790', in *A Companion to Benjamin Franklin*, ed. Waldstreicher, pp. 78–9. See also Dull's *Benjamin Franklin and the American Revolution* (2010).
83. BF to Galloway, 7 April 1759, *PBF* VIII: 313, Yale.

CHAPTER 7: 1758 ONWARDS: BENJAMIN FRANKLIN'S
BRITISH FAMILY

1. BF to DF, 6 September 1758, *PBF* VIII: 134.
2. Ibid., VIII: 134.
3. Oxford followed suit by awarding him an honorary doctorate in 1762.
4. 'Epitaph of Josiah and Abiah Franklin', *PBF* VII: 230.
5. Josiah F to BF, 26 May 1739, *PBF* II: 229–30.
6. Quoted by Page Talbott in *Benjamin Franklin: In Search of a Better World*, p. 132.
7. Coll. Arm ms. G 12, p. 97, with thanks to Timothy Duke, Norroy and Ulster King of Arms.
8. The tankard is shown on p. 132 of *Benjamin Franklin: In Search of a Better World*, ed. Talbott, which was published to accompany the exhibition.
9. http://www.americanheraldry.org/pages/index.php?n=Notable.Declaration
10. BF to Jane Mecom, 17 July 1771, *PBF* XVIII: 185, APS.
11. See Introduction to 'Verses from Benjamin Franklin (the Elder)', 7 July 1710, *PBF* I: 4.
12. BF to Mary Fisher, 31 July 1758, *PBF* VIII: 118, HSP.
13. *BF Autobiog.*, p. 10. He refers to the notes of his own Uncle Benjamin, 'who had the same kind of Curiosity in collecting Family Anecdotes'. *A short account of the family of Thomas Franklin of Ecton in Northamptonshire, 21 July 1717* is in the Yale University Library.
14. Thomas Holme to BF, 9 January 1759, *PBF* VIII: 224 text, HSP, and note 8.
15. Ibid., VIII: 225 text, HSP, and note 6; and Anne Farrow to BF, 19 January 1759, *PBF* VIII: 239, HSP.
16. BF to Jane Mecom, 14 July 1759, *PBF* VIII: 414, APS.
17. £11.42 as expressed in today's decimal coinage.
18. Richard Quinton to BF, 4 January 1759, *PBF* VIII: 221–2 and note 2, HSP.
19. Hannah Walker to BF, 17 July 1769, *PBF* XVI: 179 note 8 ref. Payne to Margaret Stevenson, 10 August 1769, APS.

20. He died in 1691 in Banbury.

21. Thomas Franklin to BF, 28 January 1765, *PBF* XII: 28–9, APS.

22. Ibid., XII: 28 note 7.

23. BF to DF, 11 October 1766, *PBF* XIII: 446, APS.

24. Ibid., XIII: 446, APS.

25. BF to DF, 6 September 1758, *PBF* VIII: 146.

26. Julie Flavell, *When London Was Capital of America* (2010), p. 34 para 3.

27. For George II's relationship with Henrietta Howard see Tracy Borman's *Henrietta Howard: King's Mistress, Queen's Servant* (2007).

28. Abigail Adams, *Letters of Mrs Adams, the Wife of John Adams* (1840), ed. Charles Francis Adams, 2nd edn, Vol. II, pp. 55–6. See James Srodes, *Franklin: The Essential Founding Father* (2002), pp. 350–52.

29. Claude-Anne Lopez, *Mon Cher Papa: Franklin and the Ladies of Paris* (1990), pp. 260–62.

30. Talbott, *Benjamin Franklin: In Search of a Better World*, p. 131.

31. Including to this author in person.

32. Lemay, *Life of BF* III: xii–xiii and James N. Green and Peter Stallybrass, *Benjamin Franklin: Writer and Printer* (2006), p. 41.

33. Green and Stallybrass, *Benjamin Franklin Writer and Printer*, p. 40.

34. Talbott, *Benjamin Franklin: In Search of a Better World*, p. 131, quoting from *BF Autobiog.*, p. 66.

35. Talbott, *Benjamin Franklin: In Search of a Better World*, p. 137, quoting from BF to DF, 5 April 1757, *PBF* VII: 175, APS.

36. BF to DF, 14 January 1758, *PBF* VII: 359–60.

37. BF to DF, 17 July 1757, *PBF* VII: 243.

38. Talbott, *Benjamin Franklin: In Search of a Better World*, pp. 139–40, quoting from BF to DF, 19 February 1758, *PBF* VII: 383, APS.

39. Introduction to BF Memorandum for Mrs Stevenson (on or before 20 March 1775), *PBF* XXI: 539.

40. Srodes, *Franklin*, pp. 196–7.

41. As per his famous 'staircase' portrait in the Philadelphia Museum of Art.

42. Larry E. Tise in his Preface to *Benjamin Franklin and Women* (2000), p. x.

43. *ODNB* Karina Williamson, 'Hawkesworth, John (bap. 1720, d. 1773)', doi:10.1093/ref:odnb/12658.

44. James Bennett Nolan, *Benjamin Franklin in Scotland and Ireland* (1938), p. 63.

45. The editors of the *PBF* provide an itinerary in their Introduction to BF to DF, 29 August 1759, *PBF* VIII: 430–31. On his return trip to Scotland in 1771 Franklin stayed with Kames at Blair Drummond near Stirling.

46. BF to Kames, 3 January 1760, *PBF* IX: 9–10, SRO.

47. Birmingham did not gain city status until 1889.

48. BF to DF, 6 September 1758, *PBF* VIII: 144.

49. For Baskerville see BF to John Baskerville (1760), *PBF* IX: 257 note 3 and *ODNB* James Mosley, 'Baskerville, John (1706–1775)', doi:10.1093/ref:odnb/1624.

50. Even before his partnership with James Watt, Boulton was discussing steam engines with Benjamin Franklin and Erasmus Darwin; see *ODNB* Jennifer Tann, 'Boulton, Matthew (1728–1809)', doi:10.1093/ref:odnb/2983.

51. BF to Polly Stevenson (1759), *PBF* VIII: 455–6, LC.

52. BF to Polly Stevenson, 8 March 1762, *PBF* X: 64, Yale.

CHAPTER 8: 1758–1762: MOVES AND COUNTERMOVES

1. *PBF* VIII: 4 note 6.

2. *ODNB* Robert Lawson-Peebles, 'Smith, William (1727–1803)', doi:10.1093/ref:odnb/65048.

3. Documents on the Hearing of William Smith's Petition – III, 27 April 1758, *PBF* VIII: 46, HSP.

4. See Ralph L. Ketcham, 'Benjamin Franklin and William Smith: New Light on an Old Philadelphia Quarrel', *PMHB*, HSP, Vol. LXXXVIII, No. 2 (April 1964), particularly pp. 147–53.

5. BF to Galloway, 16 September 1758, *PBF* VIII: 150, Yale.

6. Paris to BF, 1–7 December 1758, *PBF* VIII: 193–4, HSP.

7. BF to Thomas and Richard Penn, *PBF* VIII: 187 note 1. See Penn Papers, HSP: Thomas Penn to Peters, 8 December; Penn to Benjamin Chew, 9 December; Penn to Wm. Allen, 9 December 1758.

8. Ketcham, 'Benjamin Franklin and William Smith: New Light on an Old Philadelphia Quarrel', *PMHB*, HSP, Vol. LXXXVIII, No. 2, pp. 156–8.

9. Hutson, *Pennsylvania Politics 1746–1770*, pp. 52–3.

10. Lemay, *Life of BF*, III: 175.

11. Ibid., III: 174.

12. *BF Autobiog.*, p. 114.

13. *ODNB* W.P. Courtney, 'Jackson, Richard (1721/2–1787)', doi:10.1093/ref:odnb/14546.

14. BF to Thomas Leech and Assembly Committee of Correspondence, 10 June 1758, *PBF* VIII: 88, Yale and APS.

15. BF to Strahan, 20 June 1752, *PBF* IV: 323, HSP.

16. Katherine French to BF (1765–1775), *PBF* XXI: 615, APS.

17. Editors' Introduction to 'The Morals of Chess', *PBF* XXIX: 751, APS.

18. Ibid., XXIX: 754–7, APS.

19. Ibid., XXIX: 753, APS.

20. Ibid., XXIX: 755, APS.

21. Editors' Introduction to Remarks on Thomas Penn's Estimate of the Province, 29 May 1759, *PBF* VIII: 361.

22. Ibid., VIII: 360–62.

23. In the *London Chronicle* of 26–9 May 1759.

24. BF to Norris, 9 June 1759, *PBF* VIII: 402, Yale.

25. Hutson, *Pennsylvania Politics, 1746–1770*, p. 51.

26. Ibid., p. 58 and *ODNB* Benjamin H. Newcomb, 'Denny, William (1709–1765)', doi:10.1093/ref:odnb/68536.

27. http://www.hrp.org.uk/BanquetingHouse/WhitehallPalaceandtheTudors

28. For instance, there was no great value to either side in winning a point about the 'exportation of bad staves' – incidentally one of the Assembly's points. For 'Prudential Algebra' see Prologue.

29. Editors' Introduction to Order in Council, 2 September 1760, *PBF* IX: 201–3. Though the final move came in early 1765 when Thomas Penn vetoed his nephew's 'victory' over a final point and supported the Assembly.

30. Ibid., IX: 203.

31. Franklin was present on 17 November 1760 (as Provincial Grand Master) and again in 1762 (as Grand Master of Pennsylvania). Julius F. Sachse, 'The Masonic Chronology of Benjamin Franklin', *PMHB*, HSP, Vol. XXX, No. 2 (1906), p. 239.

32. BF to WF, 22 March 1774, *PBF* XXI: 547 note 9.

33. Kammen, *Rope of Sand*, p. 70.

34. They also had different views on colonial management; ibid., p. 65.

35. BF to Isaac Norris, 9 June 1759, *PBF* VIII: 400, Yale.

36. Allan, '"Dear and Serviceable to Each Other": Benjamin Franklin and the Royal Society of Arts', *Proceedings of the APS*, Vol. CXLIV, No. 3, pp. 253–4.

37. Wilkes to BF, 23 December 1766, *PBF* XIII: 538, APS.

38. Allan, '"Dear and Serviceable to Each Other": Benjamin Franklin and the Royal Society of Arts', *Proceedings of the American Philosophical Society*, Vol. CXLIV, No. 3, p. 253 para 2.

39. See Chapter 6.

40. Observations Concerning the Increase of Mankind, 1751, *PBF* IV: 227–34. In particular see BF's point 24 on p. 234. In point 23 he made his remark against the settlement of 'Palatine Boors', p. 234.

41. *The Interest of Great Britain Considered* (17 April 1760), *PBF* IX: 77.

42. Christopher Pearl, 'Franklin's Turn: Imperial Politics and the Coming of the American Revolution', *PMHB*, HSP, Vol. CXXXVI, No. 2 (April 2012), p. 120; John J. McCusker and Russell R. Menard, *The Economy of British America, 1607–1789* (1985), gives a growth rate of 2,400 per cent between 1650 and 1770.

43. *PBF* editors' Introduction considers the nature of that assistance, *PBF* IX: 53–9.

44. 'Felons and Rattlesnakes', *PBF* IV: 131.

45. Ibid., IV: 132.

46. Ibid., IV: 133.

47. *BF Autobiog.*, pp. 152–4.

48. *The Gentleman's Magazine*, Vol. XXX (1760), pp. 486–7.

49. *The Diaries of a Duchess: Extracts from the Diaries of the First Duchess of Northumberland (1716–1776)*, ed. James Greig (1926), p. 79.

50. *The Works of John Adams*, ed. Adams, Vol. III (1851), p. 178.

51. Edmund S. Morgan, *Benjamin Franklin* (2002), pp. 124–6.

52. BF to Caleb Whitefoord, 9 December 1762, *PBF* X: 170–71 note 8.

53. William sent at least two of Lady Northumberland's cards to his sister Sally. See WF to Sarah Franklin, 10 October 1761, *PBF* IX: 365, APS.

54. WF to Sally F, 10 October 1761, *PBF* IX: 368, APS.

55. Jeremy Black, *George III: America's Last King* (2006), p. 109.

56. P.D.G. Thomas, *George III: King and Politicians 1760–1770* (2002), p. 3.

57. P.D.G. Thomas, '"Thoughts on the British Constitution" by George III in 1760', *Bulletin of the Institute of Historical Research*, Vol. LX, Issue 143 (October 1987), pp. 361–3.

58. Thomas, *George III: King and Politicians 1760–1770*, p. 3.

59. *BF Autobiog.*, p. 149.

60. Ibid., p. 40, Chaplin note 5.

61. *ODNB* James Falkner, 'Churchill, Sarah, Duchess of Marlborough (1660–1744)', doi:10.1093/ref:odnb/5405.

62. *ODNB* A.A. Hanham, 'Dodington, George Bubb, Baron Melcombe (1690/91–1762)', doi:10.1093/ref:odnb/7752.

63. Robert W. Kenny, 'James Ralph: An Eighteenth-Century Philadelphian in Grub Street', *PMHB*, HSP, Vol. LXIV, No. 2 (April 1940), p. 225.

64. Ibid, p. 228.

65. BF to DF 22 November 1757, *PBF* VII: 274, APS.

66. John B. Shipley, 'Franklin attends a Book Auction', *PMHB*, Vol. LXXX, No. 1 (January 1956), p. 45 citing British Museum Add.MS 35399, f. 275, Letter of 15 April 1762 of Thomas Birch to Lord Hardwicke.

67. *ODNB* Boyd Stanley Schlenther, 'Franklin, William (1730/31–1813)', doi:10.1093/ref:odnb/62971.

68. Skemp, *William Franklin*, pp. 38–9. The relationship had certainly been going on for some time. *PBF* X: 154–5 note 9 quotes Thomas Bridges (Richard Jackson's brother-in-law) writing to Jared Ingersoll, 'the Young Gentleman took unto him a Wife, I will not leave you to Guess who, for You cannot suppose it to be any other than his Old Flame in St James's Street', citing New Haven Col. Hist. Soc., Papers, IX (1918), p. 278.

69. Vernon O. Stumpf, 'Who was Elizabeth Downes Franklin?', *PMHB*, HSP, Vol. XCIV, No. 4 (1970), pp. 533–4.

70. Peter Collinson to BF, 21 October 1762, *PBF* X: 152, APS; and BF to Jane Mecom, 25 November 1762, *PBF*: X 154, APS.

71. Skemp, *William Franklin*, p. 40.

72. *PBF* X: 146–7 note 7.

73. *PBF* VII: 110–11 note 9, Penn to Peters, 14 May 1757, Penn Papers, HSP.

74. The whole event is explained in Ketcham, 'Benjamin Franklin and William Smith: New Light on an Old Philadelphia Quarrel', *PMHB*, HSP, Vol. LXXXVIII, No. 2 (April 1964), pp. 142–63; and in James H. Hutson, 'Benjamin Franklin and William Smith: More Light on an Old Philadelphia Quarrel', Vol. XCIII, No. 1 (January 1969), pp. 109–13.

75. Hutson ibid., p. 110.

76. *PBF* X: 146–7 note 7.

77. R.C. Simmons, 'Colonial Patronage: Two Letters from William Franklin to the Earl of Bute, 1762', *Wm. & Mary Qtrly*, Vol. LIX, No. 1 (January 2002), p. 131.

78. WF to Strahan, 25 April 1763, p. 424 and 14 October 1763, pp. 430–31 in 'Letters from Wm. Franklin to Wm. Strahan', ed. Charles Henry Hart, *PMHB*, Vol. XXXV, No. 4 (1911).

79. Duke of Northumberland's papers at Alnwick Castle, DNP: MS 121/10.

80. BF to Isaac Norris, 19 November 1760, *PBF* IX: 244–5, APS.

81. Actually £26,648 4 shillings and sixpence, BF to Isaac Norris, 19 November 1760, *PBF* IX: 245, APS.

82. BF to Trustees of the Loan Office, 13 February 1762, *PBF* X: 35–6, HSP and Yale.

83. Sargent Aufrere to BF, 15 January 1762, *PBF* X: 11, HSP.

84. William Smith: An Answer to Mr Franklin's Remarks, *PBF* XI: 498.

85. *PBF* IX: 313 note 1.

86. BF to Thomas Leech and Charles Norris, 14 January 1762, *PBF* X: 9, HSP.

87. See all *PBF* editors' notes to 'BF to Isaac Norris; Pennsylvania Assembly Committee of Accounts: Report, 9, 15 and 19 February 1763', *PBF* X: 193–7, HSP and APS.

88. Claude-Anne Lopez, 'Three Women, Three Styles', in *Benjamin Franklin and Women*, ed. Tise, p. 58.

89. BF to Polly Stevenson, 11 August 1762, *PBF* X: 142–3.

CHAPTER 9: 1762–1764: INTERMISSION

1. James Hamilton to Jared Ingersoll, 8 July 1762, *PBF* X: 113, MHS.

2. 'BF to Isaac Norris; Pennsylvania Assembly Committee of Accounts: Report

I, 9 February 1763', *PBF* X: 193–4, HSP and APS. And also see ibid., Reports II and III of 15 and 19 February 1763, pp. 194–7.

3. James E. Hutson, 'The Campaign to Make Pennsylvania a Royal Province, 1764–1770', Part I, *PMHB*, HSP, Vol. XCIV, No. 4 (October 1970), p. 449, citing Richard Peters's Diary, 1 November 1762, HSP.

4. 'BF To Isaac Norris; Pennsylvania Assembly Committee of Accounts: Reports I, II and III, 9, 15 and 19 February 1763', *PBF* X: 193–7, APS and HSP.

5. WF to Strahan, 25 April 1763, 'Letters from Wm. Franklin to Wm. Strahan', ed. Hart, *PMHB*, Vol. XXXV, No. 4, p. 424.

6. Ibid., p. 426.

7. *A Narrative of the Late Massacres*, 30 January 1764, *PBF* XI: 42–69.

8. Ibid., XI: 55.

9. Morgan, *Benjamin Franklin*, p. 131.

10. BF to Fothergill, 14 March 1764, *PBF* XI: 103, Yale.

11. Lorett Treese, *The Storm Gathering* (2002), pp. 47–8.

12. BF to Richard Jackson, 11 February 1764, *PBF* XI: 77, APS.

13. Hutson, 'The Campaign to Make Pennsylvania a Royal Province, 1764–1770', Part I, *PMHB*, HSP (October 1970), p. 450.

14. *ODNB* W.P. Courtney, 'Jackson, Richard (1721/2–1787)', doi:10.1093/ref:odnb/14546.

15. Hutson, 'The Campaign to Make Pennsylvania a Royal Province, 1764–1770', Part I, *PMHB*, HSP (October 1970), p. 443.

16. Ibid., pp. 439–40.

17. Ibid., pp. 453 and then 440.

18. Wm. Smith, Preface to John Dickinson, *A Speech, Delivered in the House of Assembly of the Province of Pennsylvania, May 24th, 1764* (1764), pp. iii–xv.

19. 'Preface to Joseph Galloway's Speech of 24 May', 11 August 1764, *PBF* XI: 297.

20. BF Papers – Papers from the Election Campaign (IV), 1764, *PBF* XI: 385.

21. J. Philip Gleason, 'A Scurrilous Colonial Election and Franklin's Reputation', *Wm. & Mary Qtrly*, Vol. XVIII, No. 1 (January 1961), p. 70.

22. Hutson, 'The Campaign to Make Pennsylvania a Royal Province, 1764–1770', Part I, *PMHB*, HSP (October 1970), p. 448.

23. Election Results in Philadelphia County, 1764, *PBF* XI: p. 394, APS.

24. 'John Dickinson and Others: Protest against the Appointment of Benjamin Franklin as Agent', 26 October 1764, *PBF* XI: 410–11.

25. 'Remarks on a Late Protest', 5 November 1764, *PBF* XI: 439, HSP.

26. William S. Hanna, *Benjamin Franklin and Pennsylvania Politics* (1964), p. 160 citing Penn Official Correspondence, HSP.

27. Esmond Wright, *Franklin of Philadelphia* (1986), p. 149.

28. For more on the White Oaks and their company see Simon P. Newman,

'Benjamin Franklin & the Leather Apron Men', in *Benjamin Franklin's Intellectual World*, ed. Kerry and Holland, pp. 96–7.

CHAPTER 10: 1764–1766: THE STAMP ACT

1. It is unclear whether he was a slave or an indentured servant. He is solely mentioned in the *PBF* in a 9 December 1764 letter of BF to DF, XI: 517, APS.
2. BF to Polly Stevenson, 12–16 December 1764, *PBF* XI: 521, APS.
3. Thomas Cumming to BF (1765–1774), *PBF* XII: 425, APS.
4. Johnson, *A Dictionary of the English Language*, Vol. II.
5. N.A.M. Rodger, *The Insatiable Earl: A Life of John Montagu, Fourth Earl of Sandwich, 1718–1792* (1993), p. 79.
6. Paston-Williams, *The Art of Dining*, pp. 244–5; and the 14th Earl of Morton to BF, 23 January (1761?), *PBF* IX: 272, APS.
7. Wm. and Margaret Strahan to BF (1765–75), *PBF* XII: 430, APS. The ladies were most probably Margaret and Polly Stevenson, p. 430 note 8.
8. Paston-Williams, *The Art of Dining*, p. 245.
9. *Kalm's Account of his Visit to England*, p. 15.
10. Glasse, *The Art of Cookery Made Plain and Easy*, pp. iv–v.
11. Ibid., p. 103.
12. BF to John Whitehurst, 27 June 1763, *PBF* X: 302, Yale.
13. Josiah Quincy, 'English Journal 1774–5', *Proceedings of the Massachusetts Historical Society*, Vol. L (October 1916–June 1917), p. 444.
14. Jack Lynch, 'Wilkes, Liberty, and Number 45', *Colonial Williamsburg Journal* (summer 2003), http://www.history.org/Foundation/journal/summer03/wilkes.cfm.
15. Strahan to BF, 18 August 1763, *PBF* X: 324–5, HSP.
16. BF to Strahan, 19 December 1763, *PBF* X: 407, PML.
17. *ODNB* Martyn J. Powell, 'Russell, John, fourth duke of Bedford (1710–1771)', doi:10.1093/ref:odnb/24320; and Hutson, 'The Campaign to Make Pennsylvania a Royal Province, 1764–1770', Part I, *PMHB*, HSP (October 1970), p. 450.
18. Pringle to BF (May) 1763, *PBF* X: 267 note 4, APS.
19. Ibid., X: 268, APS.
20. *Acts of the Privy Council of England (Colonial Series)*, Vol. IV (1911), p. 741 cited by Hutson, 'The Campaign to Make Pennsylvania a Royal Province, 1764–1770', Part II, *PMHB*, HSP, Vol. XCIV, No. 4 (January 1971), p. 30.
21. Ibid., quoting from Thomas Penn to John Penn, 30 November 1765.
22. BF to the Pennsylvania Assembly Committee of Correspondence, 12 April 1766, *PBF* XIII: 240, Rosenbach Foundation.
23. See P.D.G. Thomas, *British Politics and the Stamp Act Crisis* (1975), 'The Background to the Stamp Act', pp. 69–84, particularly p. 79.

24. *BF Autobiog.*, p. 54.
25. Morgan, *Benjamin Franklin*, p. 150.
26. Ibid.
27. BF to Joseph Galloway, 11 October 1766, *PBF* XIII: 449, WLCL.
28. Thomas, *British Politics and the Stamp Act Crisis*, p. 356.
29. For a list of colonies see Andrew O'Shaughnessy, *An Empire Divided* (2000), p. 251 note 1.
30. Allen S. Johnson, *A Prologue to Revolution: The Political Career of George Grenville* (1997), p. 187.
31. Ibid., p. 189.
32. Ibid., p. 190.
33. It had nearly doubled during the war and by the summer of 1763 stood at approximately £146 million; see Anderson, *Crucible of War*, p. 562.
34. Linda Colley, *Britons* (2003), p. 197.
35. *ODNB* J.V. Beckett, Peter D.G. Thomas, 'Grenville, George (1712–1770)', doi:10.1093/ref:odnb/11489.
36. Thomas, *British Politics and the Stamp Act Crisis*, p. 98.
37. BF to Charles Thomson, 11 July 1765, *PBF* XII: 207–8, LC.
38. Ibid., XII: 207, LC.
39. 'The Colonial Agents: Card to Christopher D'Oyly', 2 May 1765, *PBF* XII: 118–20.
40. Johnson, *A Prologue to Revolution*, p. 187.
41. DF to BF, 8 October 1765, *PBF* XII: 299–304, APS.
42. Hutson, 'The Campaign to Make Pennsylvania a Royal Province, 1764–1770', Part II, *PMHB*, HSP (January 1971), pp. 34–6.
43. BF to WF, 9 November 1765, *PBF* XII: 361–2, HSP.
44. *ODNB* W.P. Courtney, 'Cooper, Grey (*c.*1726–1801)', rev. Hallie Rubenhold, doi:10.1093/ref:odnb/6219.
45. From (Grey) Cooper to BF (1762), *PBF* X: 185, APS.
46. *The Correspondence of General Thomas Gage with the Secretaries of State, 1763–1775*, comp. and ed. Clarence Edwin Carter, Vol. I (1931), pp. 67–8.
47. Thomas, *British Politics and the Stamp Act Crisis*, pp. 141–2 and *The Correspondence of General Thomas Gage with the Secretaries of State, 1763–1775*, ed. Carter, Vol. I, pp. 69–70.
48. Strahan to David Hall, 7 April 1766, *Correspondence between William Strahan and David Hall 1763–7*, *PMHB*, HSP, Vol. X, No. 1 (April 1886), p. 98; *ODNB* Martyn J. Powell, 'Russell, John, fourth duke of Bedford (1710–1771)', doi:10.1093/ref:odnb/24320.
49. *Benjamin Franklin's Letters to the Press 1758–1775*, collected and ed. Verner W. Crane (1950), for Franklin's flurry of activity, especially p. 56 for 'economist'.
50. Thomas L. Purvis in *Colonial America to 1763* p. 13 gives a figure of 70,000

for the Anglo-Saxon population of the American colonies in 1660 when the population of England alone was over 5 million (5.130 million in B.R. Mitchell, *British Historical Statistics* [2011], p. 7). It is difficult to assess the population of Scotland before 1755, when it is thought to have been 1.265 million, thus a figure of around 1 million is very much an estimate. See R.E. Tyson, 'Population Patterns I, to 1770', in *The Oxford Companion to Scottish History* (2011), ed. Michael Lynch, pp. 487–9.

51. BF to Wm. Shirley, 22 December 1754, *PBF* V: 450–51.
52. Thomas, *British Politics and the Stamp Act Crisis*, pp. 217–25.
53. The editors of the *PBF* identify the questioners in their footnotes to 'Examination before the Committee of the Whole of the House of Commons', 13 February 1766, *PBF* XIII: 129–59.
54. Strahan to David Hall, 10 May 1766, *Correspondence, PMHB* (July 1886), HSP, p. 220.
55. 'Examination before the Committee of the Whole of the House of Commons', 13 February 1766, *PBF* XIII: 142. Answer to Question 121 (p. 148) and to Q. 83 (p. 142).
56. Ibid., Answer to Question 69, *PBF* XIII: 141. Interestingly, that was in response to a question by a member of the former ministry.
57. See editors' Introduction to 'Examination before the Committee of the Whole of the House of Commons', *PBF* XIII: 124–9.
58. Bishop of Carlisle to Grenville, 29 May 1766, Grenville Papers, 3.243, cited by *ODNB* Peter Durrant, 'FitzRoy, Augustus Henry, third duke of Grafton (1735–1811)', doi:10.1093/ref:odnb/9628.
59. BF to the Pennsylvania Assembly Committee of Correspondence, 10 June 1766, *PBF* XIII: 297–9.
60. *ODNB* S.M. Farrell, 'Wentworth, Charles Watson, second Marquess of Rockingham (1730–1782)', doi:10.1093/ref:odnb/28878.

CHAPTER 11: 1766–1770: PIVOTAL YEARS

1. *Letters of Edmund Burke*, ed. Harold Joseph Laski (1922), Burke to Henry Flood, 18 May 1765, cited by Edward Pearce in *Pitt the Elder* (2010), p. 303.
2. Strahan to David Hall, 10 May 1766, *Correspondence, PMHB* (July 1886), HSP, p. 222.
3. Ibid., p. 98.
4. Benjamin Franklin to the Speaker and Committee of Correspondence of the Pennsylvania Assembly, 22 August 1766, *PBF* XIII: 384, Yale.
5. BF to Galloway, 11 October 1766, *PBF* XIII: 448, WLCL; and Galloway to BF, 28 October 1766, *PBF* XIII: 478–9, APS.
6. Clarence Alvord in his footnote (no. 381) on p. 213 of *The Mississippi Valley in*

British Politics, Vol. I (1959), declares that 'The following names of Englishmen belonging to ministerial and allied circles have been noted among the speculators in American lands: Lord Eglington, Lord Dartmouth, Lord Holland, Lord Stirling, Lord Egmont, Lord Adam Gordon, Lord Temple, Charles Townshend, George Grenville, Thomas Pitt, Sir Jeffrey Amherst. This list could be greatly enlarged.'

7. R.A. Humphreys, 'Lord Shelburne and the Proclamation of 1763', *English Historical Review*, Vol. XLIX, No. 194 (April 1934), p. 249.

8. 'List of Fossils Sent by George Croghan to the Earl of Shelburne and Benjamin Franklin', 7 February 1767, *PBF* XIV: 28–9.

9. WF to BF, 30 April 1766, *PBF* XIII: 257, APS. See also Alvord, *The Mississippi Valley in British Politics*, Vol. I, p. 316 and pp. 320–21.

10. BF to WF, 12 September 1766, *PBF* XIII: 414.

11. *ODNB* Peter Marshall, 'Hill, Wills, first Marquess of Downshire (1718–1793)', doi:10.1093/ref:odnb/13317.

12. Thomas, *George III: King and Politicians 1760–1770*, pp. 162–3. Actually William Dowdeswell, the leader of the Rockinghamites in the Commons, introduced the amendment purely to pre-empt Grenville and seek to gain the credit for the Rockinghams. The reduction from 4 shillings to 3 meant a drop from 20 per cent to 15 per cent, there being 20 shillings in the pre-1970 £.

13. From a 10 March 1764 letter to Sir William Johnson. See Alvord, *The Mississippi Valley in British Politics*, Vol. I, p. 220.

14. *ODNB* Peter D.G. Thomas, 'Townshend, Charles (1725–1767)', doi:10.1093/ref:odnb/27619; and L.B. Namier and John Brooke, *Charles Townshend* (1964), pp. 172–3.

15. *ODNB* Marie Peters, 'Pitt, William, first earl of Chatham [Pitt the elder] (1708–1778)', doi:10.1093/ref:odnb/22337.

16. Autobiography of 3rd Duke of Grafton (1898), p. 127.

17. *The Letters of Horace Walpole*, ed. Paget Jackson Toynbee, Vol. VII, 1766–71 (1904), p. 105.

18. Thomas, *George III: King and Politicians 1760–1770*, p. 171.

19. *The Letters of Horace Walpole*, ed. Toynbee, Vol. VII, 1766–71, p. 106.

20. Namier and Brooke, *Charles Townshend*, pp. 172–3.

21. Popularly known as the 'Townshend Duties', actually called The Revenue Act, 7 George III, c. 46 (1767).

22. *ODNB* Peter D.G. Thomas, 'Townshend, Charles (1725–1767)', doi:10.1093/ref:odnb/27619.

23. Thomas, *George III: King and Politicians 1760–1770*, p. 162.

24. Thomas, *British Politics and the Stamp Act Crisis*, pp. 357–9 and Namier and Brooke, *Charles Townshend*, p. 179.

25. Namier and Brooke ibid., pp. 38–40 and p. 174. For 'salutary neglect' see

ODNB W.A. Speck, 'Dunk, George Montagu, second earl of Halifax (1716–1771)', doi:10.1093/ref:odnb/8266. See also Anderson, *Crucible of War*, p. 77.

26. Editors' Introduction to BF to James Bowdoin, 13 January 1772, *PBF* XIX: 8–10, MHS, HSP.

27. BF to Joseph Fox, 1 March 1766, *PBF* XIII: 186–7.

28. BF to WF, 28 August 1767, *PBF* XIV: 243.

29. BF to WF, 25 November 1767, *PBF* XIV: 325.

30. Ibid., XIV: 326.

31. BF to WF, 9 January 1768, *PBF* XV: 16.

32. BF to Thomas Livezey, 20 February 1768, *PBF* XV: 54.

33. Hutson, 'The Campaign to Make Pennsylvania a Royal Province, 1764–1770', Part II, *PMHB*, HSP (January 1971), p. 43.

34. BF to Galloway, 2 July 1768, *PBF* XV: 164 and see pp. 164–5 note 7 as to its likelihood.

35. BF to WF, 2 July 1768, *PBF* XV: 159–60.

36. *ODNB* Peter Durrant, 'FitzRoy, Augustus Henry, third duke of Grafton (1735–1811)', doi:10.1093/ref:odnb/9628.

37. BF to WF, 2 July 1768, *PBF* XV: 160.

38. Ibid., XV: 160–61.

39. Ibid., XV: 163–4.

40. BF to Galloway, 2 July 1768, *PBF* XV: 164.

41. BF to WF, 2 July 1768, *PBF* XV: 163.

42. BF to Galloway, 20 August 1768, *PBF* XV: 189, WLCL.

43. Hutson 'The Campaign to Make Pennsylvania a Royal Province, 1764–1770', Part II, *PMHB*, HSP (January 1971), p. 46 para 2.

44. BF to WF, 2 July 1768, *PBF* XV: 163.

45. Arthur M. Schlesinger, *The Colonial Merchants and the American Revolution, 1763–1776* (1918), pp. 120–29.

46. Bernard Bailyn, *The Ordeal of Thomas Hutchinson* (1975), p. 132.

47. As the editors of the *PBF* explain, XIV: 62–4, there is some ambiguity about the date (as being either 25 February or 11 April 1767) of BF's letter to Lord Kames. That said, they then make a highly persuasive case for the 25 February date, which this author accepts.

48. BF to Kames, 25 February 1767, *PBF* XIV: 67, SRO.

49. Ibid., XIV: 69–70, SRO.

50. BF to Kames, 21 February 1769, *PBF* XVI: 48, SRO.

51. Bernard Bailyn, *The Ideological Origins of the American Revolution* (1992), pp. 158–9.

52. BF to WF, 16 April 1768, *PBF* XV: 98–9.

53. BF to Galloway, 14 May 1768, *PBF* XV: 127.

54. Douglas Hay, 'War, Dearth and Theft in the Eighteenth Century', *Past & Present*, Vol. XCV (May 1982), p. 139.

55. Ibid., pp. 143–4.

56. BF to WF, 5 October 1768, *PBF* XV: 224, Cornell.

57. Marginalia in a pamphlet by Allan Ramsey, *PBF* XVI: 317.

58. Thomas, *George III: King and Politicians 1760–1770*, p. 206.

59. Autobiography of 3rd Duke of Grafton, p. 230.

60. Ibid.

61. Ibid., p. 233.

62. A 'semi-detached' member of the Cabinet was how John Biffen was categorized by Bernard Ingham in 1986.

63. Alan Taylor, *The Divided Ground* (2006), p. 44.

64. Editors' Introduction to 'The Formation of the Grand Ohio Company' (June 1769), *PBF* XVI: 163–4.

65. Editors' Introduction to 'Petition to the Treasury from Franklin and Others for a Grant of Land', 4 January 1770, *PBF* XVII: 8; and BF to WF, 14 July 1773, *PBF* XX: 310.

CHAPTER 12: HOME COMFORTS AND DISCOMFORTS

1. BF to Polly Stevenson, 20 July 1768, *PBF* XV: 173–8, APS.

2. Polly Stevenson to BF, 26 September 1768, *PBF* XV: 215–16, APS.

3. Polly Stevenson to BF, 1 September 1769, *PBF* XVI: 191.

4. *The Works of William Hewson, F.R.S.*, ed. George Gulliver (1846), p. xv.

5. Nicholas Wilford, 'The Life and Work of William Hewson, Haematologist and Immunologist', in *Medicine in Northumbria* (1993), ed. David Gardner-Medwin, Anne Hargreaves and Elizabeth Lazenby, p. 140; and editors' Introduction to 'Certificate of Nomination to the Royal Society', 17 May 1759, *PBF* VIII: 359 – Franklin supported Hewson's nomination for a Fellowship on 7 December 1769.

6. BF to Polly Stevenson, 31 May 1770, *PBF* XVII: 152–3, LC.

7. In Broad Street, which is nearly equivalent to the modern St Giles High Street that is just south-east of the junction of Tottenham Court Road and Charing Cross Road.

8. See *The Cravenstreet Gazette*, 22–6 September 1770, *PBF* XVII: 220–6, APS.

9. Misson, *Memoirs and Observations*, p. 27. See also White, *London in the Eighteenth Century*, p. 386 re the prevalence of non-forced-entry burglary.

10. The Proceedings of the Old Bailey, 1674–1913. http://www.oldbaileyonline.org Reference Number: t17700117-2.

11. The Groom was a royal office which arranged gambling for those attached to the court, to be abolished by George III in 1772 – see J. Crump, 'The perils of

play: Eighteenth-century ideas about gambling', pp. 8–9 http://www.histecon.
magd.cam.ac.uk/docs/crump_perils.pdf

12. British readers will recognize this as a forerunner of 'Disgusted of Tunbridge
     Wells'.

13. BF to WF, 19[–22] August 1772, *PBF* XIX: 259.

14. Victor of the Battle of the Saintes against the French in 1782.

15. *Poor Richard*, 1742, *PBF* II: 340.

16. BF to Jane Mecom, 11 November 1762, *PBF* X 153, APS; and BF to John Ross,
     8 June 1765, *PBF* XII: 172, HSP.

17. Lord Chesterfield to his son, 28 November 1765, *Lord Chesterfield's Letters*
     (1992), ed. David Roberts, pp. 340–41.

18. Walpole to the Rev. Cole, 25 April 1775, *Letters of Horace Walpole*, ed. John
     Wright (1840), Vol. IV, p. 132.

19. Walpole to George Montagu, 7 September 1763, ibid., Vol. III, p. 236.

20. Richard Barnett, 'Bitter Medicine: Gout and the Birth of the Cocktail', *The
     Lancet*, Vol. CCCLXXIX, Issue 9824 (14 April 2012), pp. 1384–5.

21. Thomas Sydenham, *Works*, Vol. II (1788), p. 181.

22. Ibid., pp. 223–4.

23. BF to John Ross, 8 June 1765, *PBF* XII: 172, HSP. 'The *Condition* of this
     Obligation is *such*' was a legal phrase, and with Ross being a lawyer, the editors
     of the *PBF* suggest that this was a joke between the two men. *PBF* XII: 172
     note 1.

24. http://www.ukgoutsociety.org/docs/goutsociety-allaboutgoutanddiet-0113.pdf

25. Paston-Williams, *The Art of Dining*, p. 204.

26. White, *London in the Eighteenth Century*, p. 68.

27. Liza Picard, *Dr Johnson's London* (2000), p. 16.

28. Paston-Williams, *The Art of Dining*, p. 204.

29. Defoe, *A Tour Through the Whole Island of Great Britain*, Vol. I, p. 343.

30. Lucy Inglis, *Georgian London: Into the Streets* (2013), p. 180.

31. *Margaretta Acworth's Georgian Cookery* Book (1987), Alice and Frank
     Prochaska (eds), p. 18.

32. E.g. 'It was but yesterday that I saw a dirty barrow-bunter in the street clean-
     ing her dusty fruit with her own spittle; and who knows that some fine lady
     of St James's parish might admit into her delicate mouth those very cherries'
     – Smollett, *The Expedition of Humphrey Clinker* (1825 edn), p. 133.

33. *Margaretta Acworth's Georgian Cookery Book*, p. 23.

34. See also Ivan Day, *Eat Drink, & Be Merry: The British at Table, 1600–2000*
     (2000), p. 50.

35. *Margaretta Acworth's Georgian Cookery Book*, p. 23.

36. Ibid., p. 22; Joan Thirsk, *Food in Early Modern England: Phases, Fads, Fashions
     1500–1760* (2006), p. 240.

37. Dorothy Hartley, *Food in England* (1999), p. 97.
38. Glasse, *The Art of Cookery Made Plain and Easy*; veal olives recipe on p. 37, and 'to make a curry the Indian way' pp. 101–12.
39. Nathaniel Falconer to BF, 5 April 1765, *PBF* XII: 100, APS.
40. *Margaretta Acworth's Georgian Cookery Book*, p. 11.
41. Paston-Williams, *The Art of Dining*, pp. 216–17.
42. BF to DF, 19 February 1758, *PBF* VII: 380, APS.
43. *Kalm's Account of His Visit to England*, p. 16.
44. He asked William Strahan to send him a whole Cheshire cheese in America. See WF to Strahan, 25 April 1763, 'Letters from Wm. Franklin to Wm. Strahan', ed. Hart, *PMHB*, HSP, Vol. XXXV, No. 4, pp. 426–7.
45. Henry VIII thus received 100 Parmesan cheeses from the Pope in 1511.
46. BF to DF, 6 April 1766, *PBF* XIII: 234, APS.
47. BF to John Bartram, 9 July 1769, *PBF* XVI: 172–3, Stanford.
48. Jonathan Williams Jnr to BF, 26 February 1786, the Williams, Jonathan mss., 1738–1869, Lilly Library, University of Indiana.
49. Paston-Williams, *The Art of Dining*, p. 217 and Glasse, *The Art of Cookery Made Plain and Easy*, p. 190.
50. Dick Cantwell, 'Barley Wine', in *The Oxford Companion to Beer* (2012), ed. Garrett Oliver, p. 93.

CHAPTER 13: 1770–C.1771: SEEKING BALANCE

1. BF marginalia in a pamphlet by Josiah Tucker, *PBF* XVII: 366, HSP.
2. Charles Thomson to BF, 26 November 1769, *PBF* XVI: 237.
3. And to continue in that role for the Second and Confederation Congresses right up to 1789. See *ODNB*, Boyd Stanley Schlenther, 'Thomson, Charles (1729–1824)', doi:10.1093/ref:odnb/61688.
4. Charles Thomson to BF, 26 November 1769, *PBF* XVI: 238.
5. BF to Charles Thomson, 18 March 1770, *PBF* XVII: 111, Union College.
6. Crane, *Benjamin Franklin's Letters to the Press 1758–1775*, p. 210.
7. Verner W. Crane, *Benjamin Franklin and a Rising People* (1954), p. 134.
8. Galloway to BF, 27 September 1770, *PBF* XVII: 229, APS.
9. Crane, *Benjamin Franklin's Letters to the Press 1758–1775*, p. 212.
10. Certificate of Nomination to the Royal Society, 17 May 1759, *PBF* VIII: 357 note 8.
11. Initially by the Assembly, but after Hillsborough's strictures in 1771 that the Governor should also be involved in the appointment, William was. See Skemp, *William Franklin*, p. 116.
12. Editors' Introduction to 'Journal, 1764–1776; Ledger, 1764–1776', 10 December 1764, *PBF* XI: 518, APS.

13. Van Doren, *Benjamin Franklin*, p. 356.

14. *ODNB* John Robertson, 'Hume, David (1711–1776)', doi:10.1093/ref:odnb/14141.

15. BF to Le Despencer, 26 July 1770, *PBF* XVII: 199–201, APS; and to Jane Mecom, 30 December 1770, *PBF* XVII: 314–15, APS.

16. Van Doren in *Benjamin Franklin*, p. 357 estimates that his Post Office and agency salaries came to £1,500. Georgia belatedly offered him a land grant in lieu of payment. This he never took up himself, but passed on to Temple. See Van Doren, *Benjamin Franklin*, p. 741 and p. 763.

17. Jerry Weinberger, 'Benjamin Franklin Unmasked', in *Benjamin Franklin's Intellectual World*, ed. Paul E. Kerry and Matthew S. Holland (2012), p. 21. See also his book *Benjamin Franklin Unmasked: On the Unity of His Moral, Religious and Political Thought* (2005).

18. Editors' Introduction to Franklin's 'Account of His Audience with Hillsborough', *PBF* XVIII: 9–12.

19. As the editors of the *PBF* attest, he replaced 'Mr Strahan' with 'Friends', *PBF* XVIII: 12 see note 3.

20. Franklin's 'Account of His Audience with Hillsborough', *PBF* XVIII: 12–16, APS.

21. BF to Samuel Cooper, 5 February 1771, *PBF* XVIII: 24–5, British Museum.

22. Richard Henry Lee, *Life of Arthur Lee*, Vol. I (1829), p. 216. Franklin might well have identified this himself after Speaker Cushing received an anonymous letter 'as from London', accusing Franklin of being a 'tool of L. H-h', which information Cushing passed on to Franklin's long-standing Boston friend Samuel Cooper, who wrote to him with words of reassurance.

23. *PBF* IV: 69–70 note 3.

24. 'Samuel Cooper', *American National Biography*, Vol. V, pp. 455–6.

25. See WF to Strahan, 18 June 1771, 'Letters from Wm. Franklin to Wm. Strahan', ed. Hart, *PMHB*, HSP, Vol. XXXV, No. 4, p. 448.

26. Ibid.

27. Strahan to WF, 3 April 1771, *PBF* XVIII: 65, APS.

28. Stanley Ayling, *The Elder Pitt, Earl of Chatham* (1976), p. 379.

29. *ODNB*, Peter D.G. Thomas, 'North, Frederick, second earl of Guilford [Lord North] (1732–1792)', doi:10.1093/ref:odnb/20304.

30. William Hague, *William Pitt the Younger* (2004), p. 580.

31. Thomas, *George III: King and Politicians 1760–1770*, p. 2.

32. Hutchinson Diaries and Letters Vol. 1, p. 378, quoted ibid., p. 4.

33. Thomas, *George III: King and Politician 1760–1770*, p. 4.

34. O'Shaughnessy, *An Empire Divided*, pp. 15–17.

35. BF to Jonathan Shipley, 24 June 1771, *PBF* XVIII: 137, Yale.

36. BF to Thomas Cushing, 13 January 1772, *PBF* XIX: 16, APS.

37. BF to Catherine Shipley, 2 May 1786, in James Madison Stifler, 'My Dear Girl': *The Correspondence of Benjamin Franklin with Polly Stevenson, Georgiana and Catherine Shipley* (1927), p. 272.

38. Ibid., pp. 272 and 277.

39. BF to WF, 19 August 1772, *PBF* XIX: 256–7, LC.

40. *Poor Richard*, 1742, *PBF* II: 340.

41. Ibid., II: 339.

42. BF to DF, 1 December 1772, *PBF* XIX: 395, APS.

43. 'Franklin's Journal of His Health', 4 October 1778 (–16 January 1780), *PBF* XXVII: 496, LC.

44. Stanley Finger and Ian S. Hagemann, 'Benjamin Franklin's Risk Factors for Gout and Stones: From Genes and Diet to Possible Lead Poisoning', *Proceedings of the American Philosophical Society*, Vol. CLII, No. 2 (June 2008), pp. 189 and 203.

45. BF to Le Veillard, 15 April 1787, *WBF* IX: 560–61 cited by Finger and Hagemann, pp. 205–6.

46. BF to Catherine Shipley, 2 May 1786. Stifler, 'My Dear Girl', pp. 272 and 273.

47. BF to Jacques Barbeu-Dubourg, 21 (28) July, 1768, *PBF* XV: 180–81.

48. BF to Thomas Percival, 15 Oct. 1773, *PBF* XX: 444–5, APS.

49. The *British Medical Journal*, Vol. 2, No. 4685 (21 October 1950), p. 952, Dr E. Wrigley Braithwaite stressing that 'cold and wet do not cause a common cold', but then, surprisingly, going on to say that 'the specific factor is psychological; the microbic secondary'.

CHAPTER 14: 1771–1772: MOVEMENTS

1. BF to DF, 28 August 1767, *PBF* XIV: 241, Yale.

2. BF to Polly Stevenson, 14 September 1767, *PBF* XIV: 250–55, LC.

3. 'Journal of Jonathan Williams, Jr, of His Tour with Franklin and Others through Northern England', 28 May 1771, *PBF* XVIII: 114–16, University of Indiana and Yale; and see Jennifer Uglow, *The Lunar Men* (2002), pp. 139–41.

4. Actually *c*.26,220 words. He got back on 13 August; see BF to Anna Mordaunt Shipley, 13 August 1771, *PBF* XVIII: 199, Yale.

5. BF to Strahan, 27 October 1771, *PBF* XVIII: 236, Princeton.

6. BF to WF, 30 January 1772, *PBF* XIX: 50, APS.

7. BF to Sir Alexander Dick, 11 January 1772, *PBF* XIX: 5, NYPL.

8. David Hume to BF, 7 February 1772, *PBF* XIX: 75–6, Harvard.

9. BF to Galloway, 6 February 1772, *PBF* XIX: 71, Yale.

10. BF to Cushing, 13 January 1772, *PBF* XIX: 21, APS.

11. BF to WF, 30 January 1772, *PBF* XIX: 47, APS.

12. Ibid., XIX: 47–8, APS.

13. Charles Townshend's elder brother.
14. L.B. Namier and John Brooke, *The House of Commons 1754–1790* (1964),Vol. II, pp. 669–72.
15. BF to Cushing, 13 January 1772, *PBF* XIX: 19, APS.
16. Charles Mosley (ed.), *Burke's Peerage, Baronetage and Knightage* (2003), Vol. I, p. 1177.
17. BF to WF, 30 January 1772, *PBF* XIX: 48, APS.
18. Ibid., XIX: 49, APS.
19. BF to WF, 19(–22) August 1772, *PBF* XIX: 257–8.
20. Ibid., XIX: 258.
21. BF to WF 17 August 1772, *PBF* XIX: 243.
22. Alvord, *The Mississippi Valley in British Politics*, Vol. II (1917), p. 98.
23. BF to WF, 19(–22) August 1772, *PBF* XIX: 259.
24. Serious damage had been caused to St Bride's in Fleet Street by a lightning strike in 1764.
25. See https://royalsociety.org/about-us/governance/executive-director/
26. Vladimir A. Rakov and Martin A. Uman, *Lightning: Physics and Effects* (2003), p. 2.
27. R.V. Jones, 'Benjamin Franklin', *Notes and Records of the Royal Society of London*, Vol. XXXI, No. 2, p. 215.
28. As at Purfleet. See R.W. Home, 'Points or Knobs: Lightning Rods and the Basis of Decision Making in Late Eighteenth Century British Science', *Transactions of the American Philosophical Society*, New Series, Vol. XCIX, No. 5 (2009), p. 102.
29. Ibid., p. 104.
30. Members of the Purfleet Committee to the Royal Society (after 10 December and before 17 December 1772), *PBF* XIX: 425–9, APS.
31. 'Memoir of Mr Hewson', p. 143 of 'Correspondence' in Thomas J. Pettigrew, *Memoirs of the Life and Writings of the Late John Coakley Lettsom*, Vol. I (1817), cited in *PBF*, 'Complaints of William Hunter against William Hewson' (July 1771), pp. 192–4 note 6.
32. The reopening marking the 300th anniversary of Franklin's birth.
33. BF to DF, 4 November 1772, *PBF* XIX: 365, APS, and 365 note 2.
34. BF to DF, 2 February 1773, *PBF* XX: 34, LC.
35. WF to BF, May 1767, *PBF* XIV: 174–5, APS.
36. BF to Bache, 13 August 1768, *PBF* XV: 186.
37. Bache to DF, 3 December 1771, *PBF* XVIII: 258, Yale.
38. Ibid., XVIII: 258 note 3.
39. BF to Strahan, 31 January 1757, *PBF* VII: 115, Huntington Library.
40. Claude-Anne Lopez and Eugenia W. Herbert, *The Private Franklin* (1975), pp. 76–7.

41. Ibid., p. 76.

42. Sally certainly was keen enough to want to sail to England with Bache in 1771. See Bache to DF, 3 December 1771, *PBF* XVIII: 257 note 2.

43. The brilliant blind organist and composer (see Chapter 6, p. 100).

44. Lopez and Herbert, *The Private Franklin*, p. 83.

45. BF to Sally Bache (née Franklin), 29 January 1772, *PBF* XIX: 46–7, APS.

46. BF to DF, 3 June 1769, *PBF* XVI: 144, APS.

47. Thomas Bond to BF, 9 June 1769, *PBF* XVI: 153, APS.

48. DF to BF, 20(–27) November 1769, *PBF* XVI: 230–32, APS.

49. BF to DF, 1 May 1771, *PBF* XVIII: 91, APS.

50. As brilliantly captured in Jill Lepore's *Book of Ages: The Life and Opinions of Jane Franklin* (2013). See BF's letter of 30 December 1770 for his use of her as a sounding board (*PBF* XVII: 313–16), APS. He ends it with the words, 'Let none of my Letters go out of your Hands.'

51. DF to BF, 13 December 1769, *PBF* XVI: 262–3, APS.

52. Lopez and Herbert, *The Private Franklin*, p. 170.

53. Sally Bache to BF, 30 October 1773, *PBF* XX: 453, APS.

54. DF to BF, 29 October 1773, *PBF* XX: 450, APS.

55. BF to WF, 19(–22) August 1772, *PBF* XIX: 259.

56. BF to Le Despencer, 26 July 1770, *PBF* XVII: 199–201, APS.

57. *ODNB* Patrick Woodland, 'Dashwood, Francis, eleventh Baron Le Despencer (1708–1781)', doi:10.1093/ref:odnb/7179.

58. Andrew O'Shaughnessy gives an account that is as entertaining as it is authoritative in his chapter on the Earl of Sandwich in *The Men Who Lost America*, pp. 320–21.

59. *ODNB* Patrick Woodland, 'Dashwood, Francis, eleventh Baron Le Despencer (1708–1781)', doi:10.1093/ref:odnb/7179; and *ODNB* James Sambrook, 'Franciscans (c.1750–c.1776)', www.oxforddnb.com/view/theme/71306

60. Van Doren, *Benjamin Franklin*, p. 437.

61. Franklin's 'Contributions to an Abridgement of the Book of Common Prayer, Before 5 August 1773', *PBF* XX: 347.

62. Ibid., XX: 351.

63. Ibid., XX: 346.

64. BF to WF, 3 August 1773, *PBF* XX: 340, LC.

65. *Works of John Adams*, Vol. I, p. 663.

66. BF to WF, 3(–4) November 1772, *PBF* XIX: 360–61, LC.

67. BF to Barbeu-Dubourg, post-15 April 1773, trans. Smyth, *WBF* VI: 43–4. This was after he believed, incorrectly, that some flies had been resuscitated by the sun's rays after apparently having been drowned in madeira; he speculated about himself and a few friends being placed in madeira and likewise

'resuscitated' after a century. Not surprisingly he concluded it was an idea well before its time.

68. BF to Polly Stevenson, 25 March 1763, *PBF* X: 232–3, Yale.
69. BF to Noble Wimberly Jones, 10 October 1770, *PBF* XVII: 243, Blumhaven Library and Art Gallery, Philadelphia.
70. BF to the Massachusetts House of Representatives, 7 July 1773, *PBF* XX: 281, LC.
71. *ODNB* Geoffrey W. Rice, 'Nassau van Zuylestein, William Henry van, fourth earl of Rochford (1717–1781)', doi:10.1093/ref:odnb/30312.
72. See Jeremy Black, *Debating Foreign Policy in Eighteenth-Century Britain* (2011).
73. BF to WF 19(–22) August 1772, *PBF* XIX: 259.

CHAPTER 15: 1772–1774: DRAWN TO THE COCKPIT

1. BF to Cushing, 2 December 1772, *PBF* XIX: 411, LC.
2. *ODNB* Rory T. Cornish, 'Whately, Thomas (1726–1772)', doi:10.1093/ref:odnb/29177.
3. BF to Galloway, 18 February 1774, *PBF* XXI: 109, WLCL and APS.
4. BF to Cushing, 2 December 1772, *PBF* XIX: 412–13, LC.
5. Appendix to Vol. XX (January to December 1773), 'The Hutchinson Letters', 20 January 1769, *PBF* XX: 550.
6. *ODNB* William Pencak, 'Hutchinson, Thomas (1711–1780)', doi:10.1093/ref:odnb/14289.
7. Hutchinson to Thomas Whately, 20 October 1769, *The Scots Magazine*, Vol. XXXV (August 1773), p. 412.
8. BF to Cushing, 2 December 1772, *PBF* XIX: 411–12, LC.
9. For an example see Bailyn, *The Ordeal of Thomas Hutchinson*, p. 168.
10. A. Bradford, *Speeches of the Governors of Massachusetts* (1818), pp. 339–40, cited by *ODNB* William Pencak, 'Hutchinson, Thomas (1711–1780)', doi:10.1093/ref:odnb/14289.
11. Bailyn, *The Ordeal of Thomas Hutchinson*, pp. 210–11.
12. BF to WF, 14 July 1773, *PBF* XX: 308, LC.
13. Morgan, *Benjamin Franklin*, p. 194.
14. Bailyn, *The Ordeal of Thomas Hutchinson*, p. 218 and Morgan, *Benjamin Franklin*, pp. 194–5.
15. BF to WF, 14 July 1773, *PBF* XX: 313, LC.
16. Ibid., XX: 310, LC.
17. As with those of King George, this was not like Louis XV's levées at the bedside but more of a morning attendance.
18. BF to WF, 14 July 1773, *PBF* XX: 307, LC.
19. Hayes and Bour (eds), *Franklin in His Own Time*, pp. 148–150.

20. Editors' note to Thomas Cumming to BF, 7 October 1763, *PBF* X: 348–9 note 4.

21. Priestley, *Memoirs*, p. 65 cited by Derek Jarrett, *The Begetters of Revolution* (1973), p. 132.

22. Crane, 'The Club of Honest Whigs', *Wm. & Mary Qtrly*, p. 221.

23. Priestley, *Memoirs*, pp. 79–80.

24. Ibid., p. 78.

25. *BF Autobiog.*, p. 101.

26. BF to WF, 6 October 1773, *PBF* XX: 438–9.

27. 'An Edict by the King of Prussia', 22 September 1773, *PBF* XX: 414–18.

28. 'Rules by Which a Great Empire May Be Reduced to a Small One', 11 September 1773, *PBF* XX: 391–9.

29. Srodes, *Franklin*, p. 246. See John Almon, *Biographical, literary and political anecdotes, of several of the most eminent persons of the present age*, Vol. III (1797), pp. 236–73.

30. Franklin's Public Statement about the Hutchinson Letters, 25 December 1773, *PBF* XX: 515 note 7.

31. Bailyn, *The Ordeal of Thomas Hutchinson*, pp. 235–6. Also see Quincy, 'English Journal', p. 444.

32. Franklin's Public Statement about the Hutchinson Letters, 25 December 1773, *PBF* XX: 515–16.

33. Benjamin L. Carp, *Defiance of the Patriots: The Boston Tea Party & the Making of America* (2011), pp. 129–30.

34. National Archives at Kew, Privy Council: Registers, George III, PC 2/117 Vol. 10 for 11 and 29 January 1775.

The Privy Counsellors in attendance on 11 January were: The Lord President (Earl Gower); the Earls of Suffolk, Sandwich, Rochford, Dartmouth; Lord George Germain, William Ellis, Sir Gilbert Elliot, George Rice, Lord Chief Justice Sir William de Grey, Sir Lawrence Dundas and Charles Jenkinson. The Privy Counsellors in attendance on 29 January were: The Archbishop of Canterbury (Frederick Cornwallis); The Lord President (Earl Gower); Duke of Queensbury; the Earls of Suffolk, Denbigh, Sandwich, Rochford, Marchmont, Dartmouth, Buckinghamshire, Hardwicke, Hillsborough; Lord George Germain; Viscount Townshend, Viscount Falmouth; Lord North; Bishop of London (Richard Terrick); Lord Le Despencer, Lord Cathcart, Lord Hyde, James Stuart Mackenzie, General Conway, Wellbore Ellis, Sir Gilbert Elliot, Hans Stanley, Richard Rigby, Sir John Eardley Wilmot, Thomas Townshend, George Onslow, George Rice, Lord Chief Justice Sir William de Grey, Sir Lawrence Dundas, Sir Jeffrey Amherst, Sir Thomas Parker and Charles Jenkinson.

35. *ODNB* Alexander Murdoch, 'Wedderburn, Alexander, first earl of Rosslyn (1733–1805)', doi:10.1093/ref:odnb/28954.

36. The Preliminary Hearing before the Privy Council Committee for Plantation Affairs etc., 11 January 1774, *PBF* XXI: 20 note 3.

37. The Final Hearing before the Privy Council Committee for Plantation Affairs etc., 29 January 1774, *PBF* XXI: 48.

38. Thomas J. Schaeper, *Edward Bancroft: Scientist, Author, Spy* (2011), p. 40, citing William Temple Franklin, *Memoirs of the Life and Writings of BF* (1818), I: 358–9.

39. National Archives, Privy Council: Registers, George III, PC 2/117 Vol. 10 for 29 January 1774.

40. *The Monthly Magazine*, No. 97 (1 February 1803), p. 2.

41. BF to Cushing, 15(–19) February 1774, *PBF* XXI: 92–3, MHS.

42. BF to Galloway, 18 February 1774, *PBF* XXI: 110, WLCL and APS.

CHAPTER 16: 1774–1775: THE LAST YEAR IN LONDON

1. BF to the Massachusetts House Committee of Correspondence, 2 February 1774, *PBF* XXI: 76.

2. BF to WF, 22 March 1775, *PBF* XXI: 554, LC; and BF to David Hartley, 2 February 1780, *PBF* XXXI: 437, LC.

3. H. W. Brands, *The First American: The Life and Times of Benjamin Franklin* (2002), p. 480.

4. Lepore, *Book of Ages*, pp. 165–6, citing Jane Mecom to BF 3(–21) November 1774, *PBF* XXI: 347, APS.

5. Louis W. Potts, *Arthur Lee: A Virtuous Revolutionary* (1981), p. 129.

6. See John Towill Rutt, Life and Correspondence of Joseph Priestley, Vol. I (1837), p. 227 footnote cited by Van Doren, *Benjamin Franklin*, p. 479.

7. Two Notes about the Opening of the Essex House Chapel (I), 17 April 1774, *PBF* XXI: 196.

8. Crane, 'The Club of Honest Whigs', *Wm. & Mary Qtrly*, pp. 222–3.

9. Ibid., p. 222.

10. Ibid., pp. 211–12 note 3.

11. BF to Strahan, 19 August 1784, *WBF* IX: 261 and see Crane, *Benjamin Franklin Letters to the Press 1758–1775*, p. 263 note 4.

12. Namier and Brooke, *The House of Commons 1754–1790*, Vol. I: 419. BF to Cushing, 13 January 1772, *PBF* XIX: 19, APS.

13. BF to WF, 14 July 1773, *PBF* XX: 308–9 LC.

14. Editors' Introductions to 'The Petition to the House of Lords against the Boston Port Bill', 26 March 1774, *PBF* XXI: 155; and to 'The Petition to the

House of Lords against the Massachusetts Government and Administration of Justice Bills', 11 May 1774, *PBF* XXI: 214.

15. John Pownall to BF, 26 April 1774, *PBF* XXI: 204 and 204 note 3.
16. This was in honour of Queen Charlotte who was said to be descended from Vandals, with Vandals obviously having better associations then than they do now.
17. 'Franklin's Ostensible Withdrawal from the Walpole Company: Two Letters', 24 January 1774, *PBF* XXI: 31–4 (I, LC) (II, NYPL).
18. William Whately's Chancery Suit: II and III, *PBF* XXI: 197–202, National Archives.
19. BF to DF, 5 May 1774, *PBF* XXI: 208–9, APS; and 209 note 9.
20. The one that did not attend was Georgia. Incidentally Franklin had ceased to be its agent in May, probably advisedly as they 'paid' late and in land rights.
21. BF to Thomas Cushing, 15 September 1774, *PBF* XXI: 306–8, National Archives.
22. Dated 26 October 1774. Dartmouth informed the American agents in London on 24 December that he had presented it to the King, who would lay it before the new Parliament in January. Peter D.G. Thomas, *Tea Party to Independence* (1991), p. 171.
23. Editors' Introduction to BF to Bache, 30 September 1774, *PBF* XXI: 325.
24. BF to Bache, 30 September 1774, *PBF* XXI: 325–6.
25. Bache to BF, 24 December 1774, *PBF* XXI: 401, APS.
26. WF to BF, 24 December 1774, *PBF* XXI: 403, APS.
27. William would not have been human if he had not resented a postscript to the letter from his father dated 19(–22) August 1772 (*PBF* XIX: 259–60) which gave belated and faint congratulations for an award, to be followed by the words, 'but you are again behind' as Ben goes into great detail about two prestigious awards he himself has won.
28. BF to WF, 7 September 1774, *PBF* XXI: 287, British Library and APS.
29. WF to BF, 24 December 1774, *PBF* XXI: 404, APS.
30. Lopez and Herbert, *The Private Franklin*, p. 172.
31. From General Gage to Lord Dartmouth, 25 September 1774, *The Correspondence of General Thomas Gage with the Secretaries of State, 1763–1775*, Vol. I, p. 375.
32. Hayes and Bour (eds), *Franklin in His Own Time*, p. 46.
33. Quincy, 'English Journal', p. 438.
34. Ibid., p. 440.
35. Bailyn, *The Ordeal of Thomas Hutchinson*, pp. 319–20.
36. Quincy, 'English Journal', p. 441 note 1.
37. *PBF* XXI: 513 note 6.

38. BF to James Bowdoin, *PBF* XXI: 507, MHS.
39. Josiah Quincy, *Memoir of the Life of Josiah Quincy, Jun.* (1825), p. 258.
40. *ODNB* Peter D.G. Thomas, 'Howard, Henry, twelfth earl of Suffolk and fifth earl of Berkshire (1739–1779)', doi:10.1093/ref:odnb/39576.
41. Dull, *Benjamin Franklin and the American Revolution*, p. 36.
42. Quincy, 'English Journal', p. 469.
43. Georgiana Shipley to BF with a Postscript from Her Father, 22 (December) 1774, *PBF* XXI: 396, APS.
44. Quincy, 'English Journal', p. 447.
45. Ibid., p. 461.
46. Ibid., pp. 465–6.
47. See John Phillip Reid, *Constitutional History of the American Revolution*, Vol. IV: *The Authority of Law* (1993), pp. 119–26.
48. See G.H. Guttridge, *English Whiggism and the American Revolution* (1966), p. 78.
49. Reid, *Constitutional History of the American Revolution*, Vol. IV: *The Authority of Law* (1993), pp. 122–4.
50. BF to WF, 22 March 1775, *PBF* XXI: 598, LC.
51. BF to Charles Thomson, 5 February 1775, *PBF* XXI: 478, LC.
52. Quincy, 'English Journal', p. 466.
53. Ibid., p. 468.
54. Ibid., p. 469.
55. BF to Margaret Stevenson, 17 July 1775, *PBF* XXII: 108, APS.
56. BF to WF, 22 March 1775, *PBF* XXI: 598, LC.
57. Thomas Walpole to BF, 16 March 1775, *PBF* XXI: 529, LC.
58. Editors' Introduction to 'A Proposed Memorial to Lord Dartmouth', 16 March 1775, *PBF* XXI: 526. See also their note 5 on the same page. This author has modernized spelling of 'paltroons' to 'poltroons'.
59. Brands, *The First American*, p. 493.

AFTERMATH: 'A LITTLE REVENGE'

1. Sheila Skemp, *The Making of a Patriot* (2013), pp. 139–41.
2. BF to Strahan, 5 July 1775, *PBF* XXII: 85, PML. See BF to John Sargent, 27 June 1775, *PBF* XXII: 72, APS and BF to Jonathan Shipley, *PBF* XXII: 95, Yale cited by Gordon Wood, *The Americanization of Benjamin Franklin* (2005), p. 54.
3. See *PBF* XXXI: 403–4 for two versions of another BF letter to Wm. Strahan (I: APS; II: PML). The first is angry and was not sent, whereas the calmer second version actually was.
4. BF to Strahan, 3 October 1775, *PBF* XXII: 218–19, National Archives.

5. *Works of John Adams*, Vol. III, p. 178.

6. Ibid. See also Andrew Jackson O'Shaughnessy '"If Others Will Not Be Active, I Must Drive": George III and the American Revolution', *Early American Studies*, Vol. II, No. 1 (Spring 2004), p. 1.

7. Andrew O'Shaughnessy, *The Men Who Lost America* (2013), p. 25.

8. Editorial note on the Olive Branch Petition, *PBF XXII*: 98–9.

9. In the short-lived peace conference with Lord Howe in 1776, Franklin said, according to the British Minutes, 'That America had considered the Prohibitory Act as the Answer to her Petition to the King; Forces had been sent out, and Towns destroyed.' 'Lord Howe's Conference with the Committee of Congress, 11 September 1776', *PBF XXII*: 603, NYPL.

10. *ODNB* Mark Philp, 'Paine, Thomas (1737–1809)', doi:10.1093/ref:odnb/21133.

11. John Keane, *Tom Paine: A Political Life* (1995), p. 114. See also Jefferson Papers – Thomas Jefferson to Francis Eppes – 19 January 1821.

12. O'Shaughnessy, *The Men Who Lost America*, p. 27 and *ODNB* 'Paine, Thomas (1737–1809)', doi:10.1093/ref:odnb/21133.

13. Heilbron, *Electricity in the 17th and 18th Centuries*, p. 381.

14. Ibid., p. 382.

15. *ODNB* J.S.G. Blair, 'Pringle, Sir John, first baronet (1707–1782)', doi:10.1093/ref:odnb/22805 and Van Doren, *Benjamin Franklin*, p. 429.

16. BF to Lebègue de Presle, 4 October 1777, *PBF XXV*: 26, Yale, cited by J. L. Heilbron, 'Benjamin Franklin in Europe', *Notes and Records of the Royal Society*, Vol. LXI, Issue 3 (2007), p. 366.

17. For a full account of the controversy see Home, 'Points or Knobs: Lightning Rods and the Basis of Decision Making in Late Eighteenth Century British Science'.

18. BF to Lord Howe, 20 July 1776, *PBF XXII*: 520–21, Huntington Library.

19. See Chapter 11, p. 175. Quotation from 10 March 1764 letter to Sir William Johnson see Alvord, *The Mississippi Valley in British Politics*, Vol. I, p. 220.

20. Benjamin Vaughan to BF, 6 September 1778, 6 September 1778, *PBF XXVII*: 374, APS.

21. WF to BF, 24 December 1774, *PBF XXI*: 403–4, APS.

22. Fothergill, from 'An English Freeholder's Address', *The Works of John Fothergill*, Vol. III (1784), ed. John Coakley-Lettsom, pp. 34–5. Also see Jack P. Greene, *Evaluating Empire and Confronting Colonialism in Eighteenth-Century Britain* (2013), p. vii.

23. Gordon Wood *The Americanization of Benjamin Franklin*, p. 181.

24. Ibid., p. 179.

25. Ibid., p. 191.

26. John Adams to Benjamin Rush, 4 April 1790, in Alexander Biddle (ed.), *Old Family Letters* (1892), Vol. I, p. 55.

27. Ellen Cohn, the Editor of the *Benjamin Franklin Papers*, has revolutionized the interpretation of Franklin's time in France by unearthing a vast wealth of correspondence from the records of the French ports, and showing that, at times when Franklin gave the appearance of doing very little, he was in fact extremely busy.

28. Margaret Stevenson to BF, 3 September 1776, *PBF* XXII: 586 note 8, APS.

29. Peter Douglas Brown, *The Chathamites* (1967), p. 39. When he had the opportunity, Shelburne nominated Shipley – unsuccessfully – to become Archbishop of Canterbury.

30. BF to Barbeu-Dubourg, 26 December 1772, *PBF* XIX: 438 note 7.

31. Cobbett, *Parliamentary History of England*, Vol. XXI (1814), pp. 293–6; and Colonel Fullarton's letter to Shelburne, British Library, Bowood Papers, Add. Ms. 88906, 10 ff. 108–93.

32. Cobbett, *Parliamentary History of England*, Vol. XXI, pp. 476–80.

33. See also Edmond George Petty Fitzmaurice, *Life of William Earl of Shelburne*, Vol. II (1912), pp. 52–3.

34. Colonel Fullarton's letter to Shelburne, British Library, Bowood Papers, Add. Ms. 88906, 10 ff. 108–193.

35. See Schaeper, *Edward Bancroft: Scientist, Author, Spy*, pp. 266–9.

36. Bernard Bailyn, *To Begin the World Anew: The Genius and Ambiguities of the American Founders* (2003), p. 66.

37. British Library, Bowood Papers, Add. Ms. 88906, 10 ff. 108–193; Fitzmaurice, *Life of Shelburne*, Vol. II, pp. 52–3; Cobbett, *Parliamentary History of England*, Vol. XXI, pp. 476–80.

38. 'Jackson, Richard (1721–87), of Weasenham, Norf.', in *The History of Parliament: The House of Commons 1754–1790* (1964), ed. L.B. Namier and John Brooke, Vol. II, pp. 669–72.

39. *ODNB* D.G.C. Allan, 'Whitefoord, Caleb (1734–1810)', doi:10.1093/ref:odnb/29282.

40. Stacy Schiff, *Benjamin Franklin and the Birth of America* (2006), p. 316.

41. Author's translation of M. de Robespierre to BF, 1 October 1783, *PBF* XLI: 62, Penn. See also Heilbron, 'Benjamin Franklin in Europe', *Notes and Records of the Royal Society*, Vol. LXI, Issue 3, p. 366.

42. *ODNB* J.A. Leo Lemay, 'Franklin, Benjamin (1706–1790)', doi:10.1093/ref:odnb/52466.

43. BF to Polly Hewson (née Stevenson), 27 January 1783, *PBF* XXXIX: 67, Yale and APS.

44. BF to Margaret Stevenson, 25 January 1779, *PBF* XXVIII: 423, LC.

45. BF to Mary Hewson, 27 January 1783, *PBF* XXXIX: 68, Yale, APS, LC.

46. Schiff, *Benjamin Franklin and the Birth of America*, pp. 376–7.

47. *ODNB* Charlotte Fell-Smith, 'Penn, Thomas (1702–1775)', doi:10.1093/ref:odnb/21855. They received compensation of £130,000 for their 24 million acres of land and the over £118,000 owed in rents.

48. Kenneth Morgan, 'Business Networks in the British Export Trade to North America, 1750–1800', in *The Early Modern Atlantic Economy*, ed. John J. McCusker and Kenneth Morgan (2000), p. 36.

49. O'Shaughnessy, *The Men Who Lost America*, p. 361. See also Gordon Wood, *Empire of Liberty* (2009).

50. BF to Strahan, 16 February 1784, *PBF* XLI: 573, Yale.

ACKNOWLEDGEMENTS

First of all, I must express my gratitude to the successive editorial teams of the, to date, forty-one volume *Papers of Benjamin Franklin* published by Yale University Press. I am also indebted to the numerous authors of previous books and articles on Dr Franklin. Two of that number have been particularly helpful to me, Jim Srodes in Washington and Joan Reid in London, with the latter giving me extended access to her large collection of books on Franklin as well hours of insight about a man of so many talents and ambitions. I am grateful to Lady Reid, her husband Sir Bob, and Márcia Balisciano for their personal kindness to me, and I am just one of a multitude who owe them a debt for their work in saving the Grade I Georgian Building at 36 Craven Street, and establishing it as the thriving Benjamin Franklin House museum and as a place of education about Franklin's life in London. As well as Director Márcia, I should like to thank her team at Benjamin Franklin House, notably Braena Sykes, Stephen Wilson, Mallory Horrill and, at the beginning of this project, Sally James.

My research in the United States was aided in 2014 by an International Fellowship at the Robert H. Smith International Center for Jefferson Studies, Monticello on the subject of 'Franklin and Jefferson in 1774 – Britons in Protest'. I am grateful to Leslie Greene Bowman, Andrew O'Shaughnessy and the Fellowship Committee for their Award and to Andrew and all at ICJS for making my stay at Kenwood such a productive and happy one. Other kind hosts in America were George Boudreau and Paul Alles in Philadelphia, Tim and Katie Tyler in Washington, and Jenny and Raymond Jones and Elizabeth Wall in Leesburg. As well as George Boudreau, the following in Philadelphia have been particularly helpful to me: Roy Goodman at the American Philosophical Society and, this year, Keith Thomson and the rest of his team there; Page Talbott at the Historical Society of Pennsylvania; John Alviti at the Franklin

Institute; Shaun Eyring and Doris Fanelli at the National Park Service; Jim Green at the Library Company; and Sherry Babbitt at the Philadelphia Museum of Art.

Back in the UK, people at a number of different institutions have readily and very promptly responded to my queries: Susan Bennett at the William Shipley Group for RSA History, Mike Rumsey at the Natural History Museum, Annie Pinder at the Parliamentary Archives and Mark Collins at the Parliamentary Estates Director-ate, Neil Handley at the College of Optometrists, and Christopher Hunwick at the Northumberland Estates. I have also benefited from the assistance of Keith Moore and his archival team at The Royal Society, and from the professional cooperation of the staff at the Manuscripts Room of the British Library, the Document Reading Room at the National Archives and, in particular, the Munby Rare Books Reading Room at the Cambridge University Library. With this book, as with my previous ones, I have also greatly benefitted from having instant access to the expert contributions in the *Oxford Dictionary of National Biography* which brings the lives of almost 60,000 Britons – including America's Founding Fathers such as Benjamin Franklin – to my desk top.

I have had scientific professorial help from Mark Warner, Peter Taylor and Alison Holmes, and historical from Jeremy Black, David Souden and Jerry White. Jerry gave me many a helpful suggestion and correction, following his detailed reading of the manuscript, as did Michael Hutchinson, Paul Petzold, and Benjamin Franklin House's Lady Reid and Márcia Balisciano. As ever, any factual errors that might trick their way into the finished book are my responsibil-ity alone.

Others who have provided insights, books and assistance are Barbara Scarcliffe, Andrea Tanner, Timothy Duke, Karen Hearn, Anne Morrison, Tom Holmes and Paul Duncanson.

The book owes its existence to my publisher Alan Samson and the sure guiding hand of my editor Lucinda McNeile. Others to whom I owe a debt at Weidenfeld/Orion are Jessica Purdue and Susan Howe, Simon Wright, Maggy Park, Claire Brett, Marissa Hussey and Kate Wright-Morris. Cathie Arrington has been a sympathetic and determined picture researcher and Linden Lawson has brought her expertise and calm to the copyediting.

I have an ideal publisher in North America for this book: Chris Rogers at Yale University Press. I am delighted to have the same publishing house as Franklin's own papers, and in Chris an enthusiastic and thoughtful supporter.

Finally, my immediate family have, as always, been not only extremely patient but provided active assistance through proof reading or photography, and in Arthur's case, both. I dedicate this book to them.

INDEX

NOTE: Writings by Benjamin Franklin (BF) appear directly under title; works by others under author's name. Page **numbers in bold** are optional primary references.